OTHER A T(
THE SCAREC

D0841104

205. *The A to Z of Australia* by James C. Docherty, 2010.
206. *The A to Z of Burma (Myanmar)* by Donald M. Seekins, 2010.
207. *The A to Z of the Gulf Arab States* by Malcolm C. Peck, 2010.
208. *The A to Z of India* by Surjit Mansingh, 2010.
209. *The A to Z of Iran* by John H. Lorentz, 2010.
210. *The A to Z of Israel* by Bernard Reich and David H. Goldberg, 2010.
211. *The A to Z of Laos* by Martin Stuart-Fox, 2010.
212. *The A to Z of Malaysia* by Ooi Keat Gin, 2010.
213. *The A to Z of Modern China (1800–1949)* by James Z. Gao, 2010.
214. *The A to Z of the Philippines* by Artemio R. Guillermo and May Kyi Win, 2010.
215. *The A to Z of Taiwan (Republic of China)* by John F. Copper, 2010.
216. *The A to Z of the People's Republic of China* by Lawrence R. Sullivan, 2010.
217. *The A to Z of Vietnam* by Bruce M. Lockhart and William J. Duiker, 2010.
218. *The A to Z of Bosnia and Herzegovina* by Ante Cuvalo, 2010.
219. *The A to Z of Modern Greece* by Dimitris Keridis, 2010.
220. *The A to Z of Austria* by Paula Sutter Fichtner, 2010.
221. *The A to Z of Belarus* by Vitali Silitski and Jan Zaprudnik, 2010.
222. *The A to Z of Belgium* by Robert Stallaerts, 2010.
223. *The A to Z of Bulgaria* by Raymond Detrez, 2010.
224. *The A to Z of Contemporary Germany* by Derek Lewis with Ulrike Zitzlsperger, 2010.
225. *The A to Z of the Contemporary United Kingdom* by Kenneth J. Panton and Keith A. Cowlard, 2010.
226. *The A to Z of Denmark* by Alastair H. Thomas, 2010.
227. *The A to Z of France* by Gino Raymond, 2010.
228. *The A to Z of Georgia* by Alexander Mikaberidze, 2010.
229. *The A to Z of Iceland* by Gudmundur Halfdanarson, 2010.
230. *The A to Z of Latvia* by Andrejs Plakans, 2010.
231. *The A to Z of Modern Italy* by Mark F. Gilbert and K. Robert Nilsson, 2010.
232. *The A to Z of Moldova* by Andrei Brezianu and Vlad Spânu, 2010.
233. *The A to Z of the Netherlands* by Joop W. Koopmans and Arend H. Huussen Jr., 2010.
234. *The A to Z of Norway* by Jan Sjåvik, 2010.
235. *The A to Z of the Republic of Macedonia* by Dimitar Bechev, 2010.
236. *The A to Z of Slovakia* by Stanislav J. Kirschbaum, 2010.
237. *The A to Z of Slovenia* by Leopoldina Plut-Pregelj and Carole Rogel, 2010.
238. *The A to Z of Spain* by Angel Smith, 2010.
239. *The A to Z of Sweden* by Irene Scobbie, 2010.
240. *The A to Z of Turkey* by Metin Heper and Nur Bilge Criss, 2010.
241. *The A to Z of Ukraine* by Zenon E. Kohut, Bohdan Y. Nebesio, and Myroslav Yurkevich, 2010.
242. *The A to Z of Mexico* by Marvin Alisky, 2010.
243. *The A to Z of U.S. Diplomacy from World War I through World War II* by Martin Folly and Niall Palmer, 2010.
244. *The A to Z of Spanish Cinema* by Alberto Mira, 2010.
245. *The A to Z of the Reformation and Counter-Reformation* by Michael Mullett, 2010.

The A to Z of Iceland

Guðmundur Hálfdanarson

The A to Z Guide Series, No. 229

THE SCARECROW PRESS, INC.
Lanham • Toronto • Plymouth, UK
2010

Published by Scarecrow Press, Inc.
A wholly owned subsidiary of
The Rowman & Littlefield Publishing Group, Inc.
4501 Forbes Boulevard, Suite 200, Lanham, Maryland 20706
http://www.scarecrowpress.com

Estover Road, Plymouth PL6 7PY, United Kingdom

British Library Cataloguing in Publication Information Available

Library of Congress Cataloging-in-Publication Data

The hardback version of this book was cataloged by the Library of Congress as
follows:

Guðmundur Hálfdanarson, 1956–
    Historical dictionary of Iceland / Guðmundur Hálfdanarson. — 2nd ed.
      p. cm. — (Historical dictionaries of Europe ; No. 66)
    Includes bibliographical references.
    1. Iceland—History—Dictionaries. I. Title.
    DL338.G82 2008
    949.12003—dc22   2008022467

ISBN 978-0-8108-7208-0 (pbk. : alk. paper)

☉™ The paper used in this publication meets the minimum requirements of
American National Standard for Information Sciences—Permanence of Paper
for Printed Library Materials, ANSI/NISO Z39.48-1992.
Printed in the United States of America

Contents

Editor's Foreword

Iceland bears only limited resemblance to its fellow European countries: its unique geographic features, physical remoteness, and sparse population set this relatively young nation apart. Yet, its political system, economic structure, and social concerns show only slight variations from those of the mainland countries. Iceland obviously has the greatest communality with Scandinavia, having been discovered and populated by Norwegians and then ruled by Danes. Its language, literature, and culture have also been shaped by this heritage. But it has often gone its own way, remaining steadfastly independent and strongly nationalistic in certain fields, especially foreign policy and defense of its economic base. As a result, while wholeheartedly European, it has only partaken selectively in the wider European integration. Thus, it remains a bit of an anomaly but in many ways an intriguing and successful one.

The purpose of this second edition of *Historical Dictionary of Iceland* is to inform outsiders—and even Icelanders—about this rather special country. This is first done through a chronology, which should be studied carefully, for without closer knowledge of its history, it is hard to make sense of the present. The introduction builds on this, fleshing out the historical skeleton and explaining how things have worked out as they have. The why is more difficult, but several hundred dictionary entries provide many of the explanations. They cover the most significant players, from old Norse times to the present day, including not only kings and presidents, prime ministers, and other politicians, but also leaders in many varied areas. Others describe basic institutions, climactic events, and essential economic, social, and cultural features. The bibliography is a good starting point for further research.

This edition is again written by Guðmundur Hálfdanarson, who was born, grew up, and studied in Iceland and elsewhere. He is a professor in the Department of History at the University of Iceland. His specialization is European social history, with a particular interest in nationalism, which fits in nicely with some of the underlying themes of this volume. But his views are unusually wide, as can be judged from some of the books he has written or edited that deal with nationalities, citizenship, and ethnicity and discrimination. Along with lecturing and writing, he has been since 2005 a cocoordinator of CLIOHRES.net, a European Union–funded research network of excellence. By now he has the knack of explaining Iceland to outsiders, and it would be hard to find anyone who does it better.

Jon Woronoff
Series Editor

Acknowledgments

A book like this is, by the nature of things, a collective effort, although I bear all responsibility for the final outcome. Thus, a number of colleagues and fellow historians assisted me in writing the first edition, and again I want to express my gratitude for their support. Professor Guðmundur Jónsson, wrote, for example, the first version of a number of entries on economic history, and Anna Agnarsdóttir, Gísli Gunnarsson, Gunnar Karlsson, Ingi Sigurðsson, Már Jónsson, and Þór Whitehead, all professors in the Department of History at the University of Iceland, read over entries in the first edition pertaining to their respective fields of expertise, giving informed and friendly advice and correcting my mistakes when necessary. My former students Ragnheiður Kristjánsdóttir, now a colleague, and Haraldur Dean Nelson assisted in the making of the original bibliography and on the collection of information for some of the most difficult entries. Various historical and biographical dictionaries have been an invaluable source of information, Einar Laxness's *Íslandssaga a–ö* (1995) and Páll E. Ólason's *Íslenzkar æviskrár* (1948–76) in particular. Helgi Skúli Kjartansson's excellent survey of the history of the 20th century (*Ísland á 20. öld*, 2002) made the revisions for the second edition much easier. The revolution in information technology in the last years has also facilitated the revisions, as most governmental institutions, political parties, nongovernmental organizations, newspapers, businesses, and so on now maintain websites with a wealth of useful information.

Note on the Icelandic Language

This dictionary uses the Icelandic alphabet consistently for all Icelandic words. The main deviations from the English alphabet are threefold:

1. A diacritical mark (´) over a vowel indicates a change in pronunciation. The vowel *a* is, for example, usually pronounced either as a short *a* in English (as in *act*) or as a long *a* (as in *father*), while the normal pronunciation of *á* is close to *ow* in *now* or *ou* in *mouse*.
2. Like Danish, Icelandic uses the diphthong symbol *æ*, but unlike Danish, it is pronounced similar to the English *i* in the words *ice* and *bite*. Like German and Swedish, Icelandic uses also the letter *ö*, which in Icelandic is pronounced as the English sound *i* in *fir* or *e* in *her*.
3. In addition, Icelandic uses one letter that is no longer found in any other Latin-based alphabets, that is, the letter *þ* (*Þ*), and another one that is only found in Faroese, that is, the letter *ð* (*Ð*). These two letters correspond to the two *th* sounds in English; *þ* is pronounced as the *th* in *thin* (unvoiced) and *ð* as *th* in the word *this* (voiced).

Following Icelandic custom, the letter *þ* is arranged after the letter *z* in the alphabetical order in this dictionary. To avoid confusion, the letters *æ* and *ö* are arranged as *ae* and *o* respectively in this dictionary (this is contrary to the normal Icelandic practice, where these two letters follow the *þ* to conclude the alphabet), and for the same reason the dictionary does neither distinguish between vowels with and without diacritical marks nor between *ð* and *d* when words are arranged in alphabetical order.

Finally, it should be noted that Icelandic retains the old Germanic custom of using patronymics, while family names are rare. This means that a child carries the first name of his or her father (or sometimes mother) in genitive as his or her last name, with the addition of *dóttir* (daughter) or *son* (son) depending on the gender of the child. Thus the daughter of Jón is Jónsdóttir, while his son would be Jónsson. In accordance with this system, first names — or the given names — are of much greater importance than surnames in Iceland, and people are, therefore, never called by their last names only. For this reason, Icelanders arrange persons by their first names in telephone directories, library catalogues, and other such directories that use alphabetical ordering. To avoid unnecessary confusion, however, this dictionary uses the English practice of listing people in alphabetical order by their last names.

Acronyms and Abbreviations

ABI	Agricultural Bank of Iceland (*Búnaðarbanki Íslands*)
ASÍ	*Alþýðusamband Íslands* (Icelandic Federation of Labor; *see also* IFL)
BP	British Petroleum
BSRB	*Bandalag starfsmanna ríkis og bæja* (Federation of State and Municipal Employees)
CBI	Central Bank of Iceland (*Seðlabanki Íslands*)
CIE	Confederation of Icelandic Employers (*Vinnuveitendasamband Ísland*; *see also* SA-CIE and VSÍ)
CP	Conservative Party (*Íhaldsflokkur*)
CPI	Communist Party of Iceland (*Kommúnistaflokkur Íslands*)
DV	*Dagblaðið Vísir* (Vísir Daily)
EEA	European Economic Area
EEC	European Economic Community
EFTA	European Free Trade Association
EU	European Union
FBI	Fisheries Bank of Iceland (*Útvegsbanki Íslands*)
FIYA	Federation of Icelandic Youth Associations (*Ungmennafélag Íslands*; *see also* UMFÍ)
GATT	General Agreement on Tariffs and Trade
GDP	Gross Domestic Product
GIA	Government Import Authority (*Landsverslun*)
GNP	Gross National Product
HÍ	*Háskóli Íslands* (University of Iceland; *see also* UoI)
HÍB	*Hið íslenska bókmenntafélag* (Icelandic Literary Society; *see also* ILS)
HRP	Home Rule Party (*Heimastjórnarflokkur*)
ICEX	Iceland Stock Exchange

IFL	Icelandic Federation of Labor (*Alþýðusamband Íslands*; see also ASÍ)
IHA	Icelandic Historical Association (*Sögufélag*)
ILS	Icelandic Literary Society (*Hið íslenska bókmenntafélag*; see also HÍB)
IMR	Infant Mortality Rate
INF	Intermediate Range Nuclear Forces
IP	Independence Party (*Sjálfstæðisflokkur*)
ÍSAL	*Íslenska álfélagið* (Icelandic Aluminum Company)
ISBS	Icelandic State Broadcasting Service (*Ríkisútvarpið*; see also RÚV)
ISC	Icelandic Steamship Company (*Eimskipafélag Íslands*)
ISK	The international currency code for the Icelandic *Króna*, the Icelandic monetary unit (*see also* Kr.)
ISWR	Icelandic Society for Women's Rights (*Kvenréttindafélag Íslands*)
IWC	International Whaling Commission
KHÍ	*Kennaraháskóli Íslands* (The Iceland University of Education)
Kr.	*Króna* (*see also* ISK)
Lbs	*Landsbókasafn Íslands-Háskólabókasafn* (National and University Library of Iceland)
LGM	Left-Green Movement (*Vinstrihreyfingin grænt framboð*; see also VG)
LP	Liberal Party (*Frjálslyndi flokkurinn*)
Mbl	*Morgunblaðið* (Morgunblaðið Daily)
MR	*Menntaskólinn í Reykjavík* (Secondary School in Reykjavík)
MRI	Marine Research Institute (*Hafrannsóknastofnunin*)
NAI	National Archives of Iceland (*Þjóðskjalasafn Íslands*; see also ÞÍ)
NATO	North Atlantic Treaty Organization
NBI	National Bank of Iceland (*Landsbanki Íslands*)
NMI	National Museum of Iceland (*Þjóðminjasafn Íslands*)
NPCI	National Power Company of Iceland (*Landsvirkjun*)
NPPI	National Preservation Party of Iceland (*Þjóðvarnarflokkur Íslands*)
OECD	Organization for European Cooperation and Development

OEEC	Organization for European Economic Cooperation
OMX	The Nordic Exchange
OR	*Orkuveita Reykjavíkur* (Reykjavík Power Authority; *see also* RPA)
PA	People's Alliance (*Alþýðubandalag*)
PP	Progressive Party (*Framsóknarflokkur*)
RDH	Reykjavík District Heating (*Hitaveita Reykjavíkur*)
RPA	Reykjavík Power Authority (*Orkuveita Reykjavíkur*; *see also* OR)
RÚV	*Ríkisútvarpið* (Icelandic State Broadcasting Service; *see also* ISBS)
SA-CIE	SA-Confederation of Icelandic Employers (*Samtök atvinnulífsins*; *see also* CIE and VSÍ)
SBI	Statistical Bureau of Iceland (*Hagstofa Íslands*)
SDA	Social Democratic Alliance (*Samfylkingin*)
SDP	Social Democratic Party (*Alþýðuflokkur*)
SDU	Social Democratic Union (*Bandalag jafnaðarmanna*)
SÍS	*Samband íslenskra samvinnufélaga* (Federation of Icelandic Cooperatives)
SUP	Socialist Unity Party (*Sameiningarflokkur alþýðu-Sósíalistaflokkurinn*)
ULL	Union of Liberals and Leftists (*Samtök frjálslyndra og vinstri manna*)
UMFÍ	*Ungmennafélag Íslands* (Federation of Icelandic Youth Associations; *see also* FIYA)
UN	United Nations
UNU	United Nations University
UoI	University of Iceland (*Háskóli Íslands*; *see also* HÍ)
US$	U.S. dollar
VG	*Vinstrihreyfingin grænt framboð* (Left-Green Movement; *see also* LGM)
VSÍ	*Vinnuveitendasamband Íslands* (Confederation of Icelandic Employers; *see also* CIE and SA-CIE)
WA	Women's Alliance (*Kvennalistinn*)
WTO	World Trade Organization
ÞÍ	*Þjóðskjalasafn Íslands* (National Archives of Iceland; *see also* NAI)

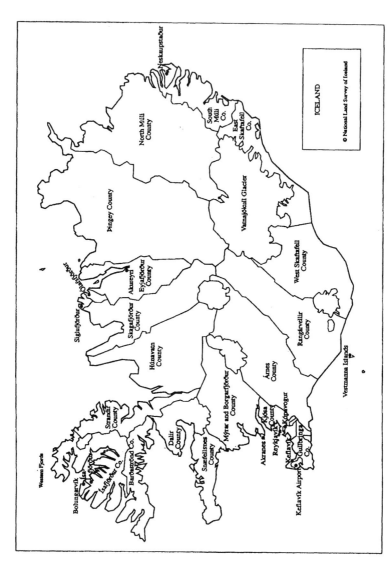

Map of Iceland

Chronology

The Settlement and Commonwealth Periods, ca. 870–1262

ca. 870–1100 Settlement of Iceland by Norway and the British Isles. The first permanent settler, Ingólfur Arnarson, is claimed to have come in 874.

ca. 930 A general assembly for the whole of Iceland, called Alþingi, convenes at Þingvellir for the first time. It meets in this place for a few weeks every year until 1798. This is conventionally seen as the beginning of the Commonwealth Period, lasting until 1262–64, when Iceland entered into the Norwegian monarchy.

999–1000 Leaders of Icelandic society peacefully accept, at Alþingi, to convert to Christianity to avoid civil war.

1056 Ísleifur Gissurarson is ordained as the first Catholic bishop in Iceland.

1096 Icelanders agree to pay tithe to the church.

1104 A major volcanic eruption in Mt. Hekla destroys the settlement in Þjórsár Valley in southern Iceland.

1106 Jón Ögmundsson is ordained as the first bishop of the Hólar Diocese. Iceland divides into two bishoprics: Skálholt, extending over the eastern, southern, and western quarters of the country, and Hólar, over northern Iceland.

ca. 1220–1262 The so-called Age of the Sturlungs, a very turbulent period of almost constant civil war between the leading families in Iceland. The period is named after the Sturlung family, one of the most powerful of these clans.

1241 **23 September:** Snorri Sturluson, the best known literary figure of medieval Iceland, is killed at his home, Reykholt, at the behest of the Norwegian king.

Iceland under Norwegian and Danish Kings, 1262–1872

1262–64 Icelandic chieftains accept to enter the Norwegian monarchy.

1271 A new legal code is adopted in Iceland called "Ironside" (*Járnsíða*). This law code moves Icelandic legal practices and administration closer to Norwegian norms.

1281 *Jónsbók* (John's Book), a new law book, is adopted in Iceland. It serves as one of the main foundations for the Icelandic legislation until the 19th century.

1380 The Norwegian and Danish monarchies unite under the Danish king, bringing Iceland under the authority of the Danish king.

1402 *Svarti dauði* (the Black Death), a plague epidemic, devastates Iceland.

1490 A new law is accepted at Alþingi in the form of a court ruling—commonly called the Pining ruling (*Píningsdómur*)—prohibiting foreign merchants to stay in Iceland over the winter and requiring cottagers to own livestock of the minimum value of three cows.

1494 Another plague epidemic strikes Iceland.

ca. 1410–1530s "The English Century." During this period, Iceland is, to a large degree, under the control of English fishermen, merchants, and adventurers. The Danish king tries to assert his authority in Iceland and manages to drive the English out during the first half of the 16th century.

1539 Gissur Einarsson, the first Lutheran bishop in Iceland, takes over the Skálholt diocese.

1540 An Icelandic translation of the New Testament is published in Denmark.

1550 **7 November:** Jón Arason, the Catholic bishop of the Hólar diocese, is executed. The Lutheran Reformation in Iceland is completed.

1564   30 June: *Stóridómur.* A statute is approved in Alþingi and ratified by the Danish king in 1565.

1584   *Guðbrandsbiblía*, the first complete Icelandic translation of the Bible and named after Bishop Guðbrandur Þorláksson, is printed at Hólar.

1602   20 April: A Danish trade monopoly is established in Iceland with a royal decree. The monopoly lasts until 1787 and is not fully abolished until 1855.

1627   June–July: Pirates from the Barbary Coast attack the eastern and southern coasts of Iceland in the so-called Raids of the Turks.

1662   26 July: Representatives of the Icelandic elite accept Danish absolutism at a meeting in Kópavogur.

1703   The first census is taken for the whole of Iceland, listing everyone by name, place of residence, age, family status, and occupation.

1707–9   A serious small pox epidemic hits Iceland; between 20 and 30 percent of the population is believed to have perished.

1751   The *Innréttingar*, a state-supported economic project, starts in Iceland. The centerpiece of the project is a small textile factory in Reykjavík.

1770   20 March: King Christian VII appoints a royal commission (*Landsnefnd*) to investigate the economic and social situation in Iceland.

1783–84   One of the largest volcanic eruptions in Icelandic history starts in the mountain Laki in southeastern Iceland on 8 June 1783; it lasts until February the following year.

1784–85   Around 20 percent of the Icelandic population dies of hunger and other causes during the so-called Famine of the Mist (*Móðuharðindi*) caused by the volcanic eruption in Laki.

1785   The Skálholt bishop's seat is moved to Reykjavík. **2 February:** The king appoints a new royal commission to investigate the economic situation in Iceland and to propose solutions to the serious crisis in the country.

1786   18 August: The Danish king publishes a royal charter for Reykjavík.

1787 **13 June:** The king issues a decree allowing all of his subjects to trade in Iceland. This is the first step in abolishing the hated monopoly trade in the country.

1795 Icelanders demand total freedom of trade in a public petition to the king called the Common Petition (*Almenna bænarskráin*).

1798 **20 July:** Alþingi meets for the last time at Þingvellir, as the assembly is moved to the emerging capital, Reykjavík.

1800 **6 June:** The king abolishes Alþingi. **11 July:** A new high court in Reykjavík takes over the responsibilities of Alþingi.

1801 The bishop's seat in Hólar is abolished. Iceland becomes one diocese under the bishop in Reykjavík.

1809 **25 June–22 August:** The so-called Icelandic Revolution; a Danish adventurer declares independence of Iceland, calling himself the protector of the country.

1811 **17 June:** Jón Sigurðsson, the future leader of the Icelandic nationalist movement, is born in northwestern Iceland.

1830 **12 January:** The last execution in Iceland, as the murderers Friðrik Sigurðsson and Agnes Magnúsdóttir are decapitated in Húnavatns County in northern Iceland.

1840 **20 May:** King Christian VIII asks a meeting of Icelandic royal officials to discuss the foundation of an elected assembly in Iceland, which is to be named Alþingi.

1843 **8 March:** The Danish king signs a law founding a new consultative assembly in Iceland called Alþingi. This may be seen as the first step toward democracy in Iceland because although the franchise is very limited, all but six of the representatives are popularly elected.

1845 **1 July:** Alþingi meets for the first time as a democratically elected assembly in Reykjavík.

1846 The Latin School at Bessastaðir is moved to Reykjavík.

1847 The College of Theology is founded in Reykjavík; this is the first institution of higher learning in Iceland and will later become one of the faculties of the University of Iceland.

1848 **5 November:** The first issue of *Þjóðólfur*, a semimonthly newspaper, is published in Reykjavík.

1851 **5 July:** An elected assembly meets in Reykjavík to discuss a new constitution for Iceland. It ends in an impasse on 9 August.

1855 **1 April:** The last vestiges of the Danish monopoly trade in Iceland are abolished as merchants from outside the Danish monarchy are allowed to trade freely in the country.

1871 **2 January:** King Christian IX ratifies the so-called Status Law (*Stöðulög*). The law, which had passed in the Danish parliament the year before, defines the status of Iceland in the monarchy and the amount of royal subsidies to be paid into the Icelandic budget.

The Governors' Period, 1873–1904

1873 Emigration to North America truly begins, as the first large groups of emigrants leave Iceland. **1 April:** Hilmar Finsen assumes the office of *Landshöfðingi*, or governor of Iceland, according to the Status Law of 1871. This begins the "Governors' Period" (*Landshöfðingjatími*) in Icelandic history.

1874 **5 January:** King Christian IX signs the first Icelandic constitution into law, thus ending Danish absolutism in Iceland. The Icelandic parliament is given limited legislative power in Iceland's domestic affairs, and basic civil liberties are secured. **5–8 August:** Icelanders celebrate the 1,000th anniversary of the Icelandic settlement at Þingvellir, with Christian IX attending. This is the first visit of a Danish king to Iceland.

1879 **7 December:** Jón Sigurðsson passes away in Copenhagen.

1881 Alþingi discusses a revision of the constitution for the first time, which will move the executive power into the country. The debates are not completed, but the constitutional revision remains the most important political issue in Iceland until the beginning of the 20th century.

1882 **12 May:** Farming widows are granted the right to vote in local elections in Iceland. This is the first step toward enfranchising women in Iceland.

1885 **27 August:** Alþingi passes the first bill to amend the constitution of 1874.

1886 **1 July:** The National Bank of Iceland (*Landsbanki Íslands*) opens its first office in Reykjavík. **29 September:** King Christian IX vetoes the constitutional revisions for Iceland.

1901 **24 July:** A new liberal government is formed in Denmark, opening the way for home rule in Iceland.

1902 The first motor put into an Icelandic fishing boat marks the first step toward increased mechanization of the Icelandic fisheries. **20 February:** The Federation of Icelandic Cooperative Societies is founded by representatives of three cooperatives in the northeast. The federation later becomes one of the largest companies in Iceland.

1903 **3 October:** King Christian IX ratifies a constitutional amendment granting Iceland a home rule government.

The Home Rule Period, 1904–1918

1904 **1 February:** Hannes Hafstein assumes his post as the first minister of the new Icelandic home rule. **7 June:** The Bank of Iceland (*Íslandsbanki*), a private bank in majority ownership of Danish investors, opens its first office in Reykjavík. **28 September:** The first Icelandic trawler company is founded in Hafnarfjörður.

1905 **6 March:** Coot, the first Icelandic trawler, comes to Hafnarfjörður. Industrial fisheries really begin in Iceland.

1906 **25 August:** A telegraph cable connecting Iceland with the rest of Europe is completed.

1907 **22 November:** King Frederic VII signs the first law stipulating compulsory and free schooling for most Icelandic children between the ages of 10 and 14. The same day he signs a law giving women equal political rights to men in the towns of Reykjavík and Hafnarfjörður.

1908 **24 January:** Four women are elected to the city council of Reykjavík from a women's ticket. **10 September:** Opponents of the

"Draft"—a bill that is to replace the Status Law from 1871—win a majority in Alþingi. The same day, a total ban on the sale of alcoholic beverages is accepted in a referendum.

1909 Björn Jónsson becomes the second minister of the Icelandic home rule as the opponents of the Draft defeat Hannes Hafstein in parliament. **30 July:** Women are granted the right to vote for and serve in all local councils in Iceland.

1911 **17 June:** The University of Iceland is founded in Reykjavík on the 100th anniversary of the birth of Jón Sigurðsson, the Icelandic national hero.

1913 **2 November:** The *Morgunblaðið* daily comes out for the first time.

1914 **17 January:** The Icelandic Steamship Company (*Eimskipafélag Íslands*) is founded in Reykjavík. **12 September:** Eric G. Cable comes to Iceland as British consul.

1915 **1 January:** The ban on alcohol comes into effect. **19 June:** A new constitution for Iceland grants women over 40 the right to vote in parliamentary elections.

1916 **12 March:** The Federation of Icelandic Labor and the Social Democratic Party is founded in Reykjavík. **22 June:** A new trade agreement between Great Britain and Iceland comes into effect. **16 December:** The Progressive Party is founded.

1917 **4 January:** Jón Magnússon becomes the first prime minister of Iceland as the number of ministers is increased from one to three.

Iceland: A Constitutional Monarchy, 1918–1944

1918 **1–18 July:** A committee of Icelandic and Danish parliamentary representatives meets in Reykjavík to discuss the relations between the two countries. The negotiations end with a proposal for a new Act of Union regulating Iceland's position in the monarchy. **1 December:** The Act of Union between Iceland and Denmark comes into effect. Iceland is declared a sovereign state in union with Denmark.

1920   16 February: The Icelandic Supreme Court meets for the first time. All three branches of government are, from that time, in Icelandic hands. **18 May:** Women are granted the same rights to vote as men.

1922   8 July: Ingibjörg H. Bjarnason is the first Icelandic woman to be elected to parliament.

1923   The Citizens' Party, a coalition of liberal and conservative parliamentary representatives, is formed as a counterbalance to the Social Democratic Party and the Progressive Party.

1924   24 February: The founding of the Conservative Party.

1928   Iceland becomes the first country in Europe to abolish capital punishment. The last execution in Iceland took place in 1830.

1929   25 May: The Independence Party is founded when the Conservative Party and the small Liberal Party merge.

1930   The National Hospital (*Landspítalinn*) opens in Reykjavík. The Reykjavík District Heating starts operations, using geothermal water to heat a few houses in the capital. **26–28 June:** Icelanders celebrate the 1,000th anniversary of Alþingi at Þingvellir. **29 November–3 December:** The founding of the Communist Party of Iceland. **21 December:** The Icelandic State Broadcasting Service begins radio transmissions in Reykjavík.

1932   9 November: *Gúttóslagurinn*, a violent scuffle between workers and police in Reykjavík.

1934   23 July: The Society of Icelandic Employers is founded by 82 employers in Reykjavík. The society is now called the SA-Confederation of Icelandic Employers and represents most employers on the private market. **29 July:** The formation of the so-called Government of the Laboring Classes, a red–green coalition government of the Progressive Party and the Social Democratic Party.

1936   1 April: Comprehensive welfare legislation comes into effect, establishing a modern welfare state in Iceland.

1938   24–27 October: The founding of the Socialist Unity Party of Iceland when a splinter group from the Social Democratic Party unites with the Communist Party of Iceland.

1940   **9 April:** Germany occupies Denmark, severing the ties between Iceland and Copenhagen. **10 May:** Iceland is occupied by British military forces, preventing German invasion of Iceland.

1941   **15 May:** Alþingi elects Sveinn Björnsson governor of Iceland, and he effectively replaces the Danish king as the head of the Icelandic state. **7 July:** U.S. military forces take over as the main defensive force in Iceland. **10 July:** Alþingi ratifies a defense treaty between the governments of Iceland and the United States.

The Republic of Iceland, 1944–

1944   **20–23 May:** The constitution of the Republic of Iceland is accepted by an overwhelming majority in a general referendum. **17 June:** The Republic of Iceland is founded with a public ceremony at Þingvellir; Alþingi elects Sveinn Björnsson as the first president of the republic. **21 October:** The so-called Modernization Government of the Independence Party, the Socialist Unity Party, and the Social Democratic Party of Iceland is formed under the leadership of Ólafur Thors, chairman of the Independence Party.

1946   **19 September:** The Keflavík Treaty between Iceland and the United States is passed. The Socialist Unity Party resigns from the Modernization Government to protest the treaty. **9 November:** Iceland enters the United Nations.

1948   **5 April:** The Law on the Scientific Conservation of the Icelandic Continental Shelf Fisheries is passed in Alþingi. All future expansions of the Icelandic fishing limits are based on this law.

1949   **30 March:** Iceland becomes a founding member of the North Atlantic Treaty Organization (NATO). Violent clashes between police and leftist demonstrators outside of the parliamentary building in Reykjavík.

1951   **5 May:** The governments of Iceland and the United States sign a defensive treaty whereby the United States assumes the responsibility of defending Iceland from foreign aggression. **8 May:** American military forces establish a base at Keflavík Airport.

1952   15 May: The Icelandic government extends the Icelandic fishing limits to four nautical miles. **29 June:** Ásgeir Ásgeirsson is elected the second president of the Republic of Iceland.

1953   14 February: Icelandic representatives take part in the opening of the first Nordic Council meeting in Copenhagen.

1955   28 October: The Icelandic writer Halldór Kiljan Laxness receives the Nobel Prize for literature in Stockholm.

1956   29 March: The majority in Alþingi demands the closing down of the NATO base in Keflavík. **4 April:** The People's Alliance is formed by the Socialist Unity Party and a splinter group from the Social Democratic Party. **24 July:** The first so-called Leftist Government is formed in Iceland. This is a coalition government of the Progressive Party, the Social Democratic Party, and the People's Alliance under the leadership of Hermann Jónasson, the chairman of the Progressive Party.

1958   1 September: The Icelandic fishing limits are extended to 12 nautical miles, starting a so-called cod war between Iceland and Britain.

1959   21 November: The so-called Reconstruction Government of the Independence Party and the Social Democratic Party is formed under the leadership of Ólafur Thors, chairman of the Independence Party.

1961   11 March: The British government accepts the extension of the Icelandic fishing limits to 12 nautical miles, ending the cod war between Iceland and Great Britain.

1963   14 November: A volcanic eruption begins under the ocean to the south of the Vestmanna Islands. A new island, Surtsey, is formed.

1965   1 July: The National Power Company of Iceland (*Landsvirkjun*) is established by the Icelandic state and the city of Reykjavík. The function of the company is to run the largest hydroelectric power stations in Iceland and to build a new station at Búrfell in the river Þjórsá, which opens the age of energy-intensive industries in Iceland.

1966   28 June: The Icelandic Aluminum Company (ÍSAL) is established as a subsidiary of the Swiss aluminum corporation Alusuisse.

1968   30 June: Dr. Kristján Eldjárn is elected the third president of the Republic of Iceland.

1970 **1 March:** Iceland joins the European Free Trade Association (EFTA). **2–3 May:** The Búrfell hydroelectric power station and the ISAL aluminum factory at Straumsvík are formally opened.

1971 **21 April:** The first Old Norse manuscripts are returned from Denmark and handed over to the Icelandic authorities in Reykjavík. **13 July:** The second so-called Leftist Government is formed as a coalition of the Progressive Party, the People's Alliance, and the Union of Leftists and Liberals. Ólafur Jóhannesson, chairman of the Progressive Party, serves as prime minister.

1972 **2 July–5 September:** The world championship in chess between the Russian world champion Boris Spassky and American challenger Bobby Fischer is held in an indoor sporting arena in Reykjavík. Fischer wins the title in this epic encounter, which has been dubbed the "Match of the Century," with 12.5 points in 21 games. **1 September:** The Icelandic fishing limits are extended to 50 nautical miles.

1973 **23 January:** A volcanic eruption begins in Heimaey, the largest island of the Vestmanna Islands' archipelago. All the 5,500 inhabitants have to be evacuated. **20 May:** A British squadron enters the Icelandic 50-mile fishing limits with the intention of protecting British trawlers fishing illegally—according to the Icelandic authorities—in the Icelandic fishing grounds. **31 May:** The presidents of the United States and France, Richard Nixon and Georges Pompidou, hold a summit in Reykjavík. **1 August:** Icelandair is formed through a merger of the two largest Icelandic airlines.

1974 **29 July:** Icelanders commemorate the 1,100th anniversary of the settlement of Iceland at Þingvellir.

1975 **15 October:** The Icelandic fishing limits are extended from 50 to 200 nautical miles. **24 October:** A one-day general strike of women in Iceland; 25,000 women demonstrate in Reykjavík's center, demanding gender equality.

1976 **19 February:** Iceland breaks its diplomatic ties with Britain to protest the British actions in the so-called cod war between the two nations. **1 June:** Britain and Iceland sign a treaty ending their fishing disputes.

1980 8 February: Gunnar Thoroddsen, deputy chairman of the Independence Party, forms a coalition government with the Progressive Party, the People's Alliance, and a splinter group from the Independence Party. **29 June:** Vigdís Finnbogadóttir is elected the fourth president of the Republic of Iceland.

1981 1 January: A new currency, the new Króna, replaces the old Króna.

1982 1 February: Organization for Women's Candidacy, or the Women's List, is founded in Reykjavík.

1983 The hyper inflation of the 1970s and 1980s reaches its highest point, as the consumer price index rises by 84 percent in 1983. **3 February:** Alþingi decides not to protest the whaling moratorium of the International Whaling Commission.

1986 18 August: Reykjavík celebrates its bicentennial as a chartered town. **11–12 October:** Soviet leader Mikhail Gorbachev and president of the United States Ronald Reagan hold a summit in Reykjavík. **9 November:** Members of the radical environmentalist group Sea Shepherd sink two whaling boats in Reykjavík harbor.

1990 2 February: Employers and trade unions sign the so-called National Compromise Agreement in the hope of ending the rampant inflation in Iceland.

1991 30 April: Davíð Oddsson, chairman of the Independence Party, forms his first government. This is a coalition government of the Independence Party and the Social Democratic Party.

1992 2 May: Iceland signs, with the other member countries of the EFTA, the European Economic Area (EEA) treaty with the European Union. **30 June:** Iceland resigns from the International Whaling Commission.

1993 12 January: The Icelandic parliament approves the EEA treaty.

1994 1 January: The EEA agreement comes into effect.

1995 23 April: Davíð Oddsson, the chairman of the Independence Party, forms his second coalition government, now with the Progressive Party.

1996 **29 June:** Ólafur Ragnar Grímsson is elected the fifth president of the Republic of Iceland.

1998 **26 November:** Sverrir Hermannsson, a former leading member of the Independence Party, forms the Liberal Party with a few of his supporters.

1999 **6 February:** The Left-Green Movement is formally founded.

2000 **5–6 May:** The founding congress of the Social Democratic Alliance. **17 and 21 June:** Two major earthquakes hit the southern part of Iceland.

2002 **8 April:** The Icelandic parliament passes a law permitting the National Power Company of Iceland to construct a 750 MW hydroelectric power station at Kárahnjúkar in the eastern part of the Icelandic highlands. **14 October:** Iceland reenters the International Whaling Commission.

2004 **2 June:** Ólafur Ragnar Grímsson vetoes a controversial law that is to regulate the ownership of media corporations in Iceland. **26 June:** Grímsson is reelected president of Iceland for his third term. **15 September:** Davíð Oddsson steps down as prime minister, while Halldór Ásgrímsson, chairman of the Progressive Party, forms a coalition government with the Independence Party.

2006 **15 June:** Ásgrímsson steps down as prime minister, and Geir H. Haarde, chairman of the Independence Party, forms a coalition government with the Progressive Party. **30 September:** The Icelandic authorities take over the military base in Keflavík as the last U.S. soldiers leave Iceland.

2007 **23 May:** Haarde forms a coalition government of the Independence Party and the Social Democratic Alliance. **9 June:** Alcoa formally opens a new aluminum factory at Reyðarfjörður in the eastern fjords of Iceland.

Introduction

Iceland is an island situated just to the south of the Polar Circle in the mid–North Atlantic Ocean. With a surface of 103,000 square kilometers (39,000 square miles), Iceland is similar in size to the state of Kentucky. It was formed around 20 million years ago through underwater volcanic eruptions at the place where the Midatlantic Ridge and a ridge extending from Scotland to Greenland cross. Compared to other parts of Europe, Iceland has a short geological history, and its formative process is still far from over. The eastern and western halves of the country are slowly drifting apart, with volcanic eruptions filling the fissures with fresh lava. Fire is not the only element that characterizes the Icelandic environment because, as the name of the country indicates, ice also is a dominant factor. There are four major glaciers in the country, including the largest glacier in Europe, Vatnajökull, which is around 8,300 square kilometers (3,200 square miles) in size.

A mountainous country, with three quarters of its surface area more than 200 meters (656 feet) above sea level, Iceland is sharply divided into an uninhabitable interior of rugged plateaus and mountains and coastal valleys and plains. Narrow fjords characterize the coastline in the eastern and northwestern parts of the country, with wider fjords and bays in the northern and western parts, while beaches of black volcanic sand dominate the landscape of the southern coast. Most of the Icelandic coastline, except for the southern part of the country, is endowed with natural harbors.

The Icelandic climate can best be described as temperate, at least in view of the northerly location of the country. Thus, summers in Iceland are cool, but the winters are relatively mild. From 1997 to 2006, the mean temperature in Reykjavík during the coldest month (February) was 0° C (32° F), while it was 11.4° C (52.5° F) on the average during the warmest summer month (July). The figures for northern Iceland are similar: -0.5° C (31° F) and 11.4° C (52.5° F), respectively, for the town of Akureyri. The weather in Iceland is rarely extremely cold and never very hot, as the Gulf Stream of the Atlantic Ocean evens out its climatic fluctuations. The average annual precipitation in Iceland ranges from around 1,700 millimeters (432 inches) in the south and southeastern coastal areas to just below 500 millimeters (127 inches) in the north. It is fairly evenly spread throughout the year, although the summer is usually the driest season.

The ecological system sets strict limits on the Icelandic plant life. Today, the country is almost totally void of trees and bushes, and large tracts, especially in the highlands, have become virtual deserts through incessant soil erosion. According to medieval sources, shrubs and birch trees covered the country at the time of the first settlement in the ninth century, but the fragile arboreal vegetation did not withstand prolonged human exploitation and slowly disappeared. In recent years, different government agencies have tried to reverse this trend without too much success.

While Iceland is the second largest inhabited island in Europe, Icelanders form one of the smallest independent nations in the world, with only 313,000 inhabitants in 2007. Around two thirds of the population live in the capital, Reykjavík, and its suburbs, while the rest are spread around the inhabitable area of the country. Until fairly recently, the Icelandic nation was unusually homogeneous, both in cultural and religious terms. Thus in 1981, around 98 percent of the nation had been born in Iceland, and 96 percent belonged to the Lutheran state church or other Lutheran religious sects. In 2007, these numbers were down to 89 percent and 86 percent, respectively, reflecting the rapidly growing multicultural nature of Icelandic society.

ENVIRONMENT AND NATURAL RESOURCES

The history of Iceland reflects its harsh ecological conditions in various ways. Although the country is not well suited for agriculture because the short summers render commercial grain growing almost impossible, animal husbandry remained the main occupation of its population for the first millennium of its history. Sheep and cattle were the most important domestic animals; the former raised for their milk, wool, and meat, and the latter primarily for their milk. Horses were used for transportation, but a total absence of roads made the use of wagons or other vehicles almost impossible in Iceland. Icelandic farming took the form of sedentary pastoralism, meaning that extensive mountain pastures were crucial for the feeding of the animals during the summer, while during the winter, farmers and peasants grazed their animals close to their farms and used hay from meadows as fodder for their livestock.

In congruence with these economic patterns, the rural population in Iceland was dispersed over the whole inhabitable area. Each farm needed a relatively large tract of land to be economically viable, a fact that made concentration into peasant villages impractical. Rather, the whole countryside was divided between separate farming households living on individual farms. The only common lands were the mountain pastures, which were usually separated from the inhabited lowland. For this reason, there were no hamlets or villages in Iceland to speak of until the end of the 19th and beginning of the 20th centuries, when the fisheries took over as Iceland's most important economic activity.

One of the paradoxes of Icelandic history is that until the late 19th century, most people regarded the natural resources that form the basis for the modern economy in Iceland as secondary to the use of land or saw them as nothing but a nuisance. Thus, fishing—although important for people in many parts of the country in the past—served as a subsidiary occupation to agriculture and was performed during the slack season in the rural areas. Moreover, rivers and hot springs, which are now the main sources of energy in Iceland, were of little use to Icelanders until they gained the technological prowess to exploit these resources during the early 20th century.

The Icelandic waters are ideal for the development of marine life because the country is situated where cold currents emanating from the Arctic Ocean and warm ocean currents originating in the South Atlantic meet. Primitive life forms, such as the so-called phytoplankton, or microscopic floating plants, are abundant in the top layers of the sea around Iceland, and they serve as sustenance for minuscule floating animals called zooplankton. The latter constitute the main source of nutrition for many types of fish and most fish larvae, in addition to the largest mammals in the sea, the baleen whales. At the bottom of the sea, species of invertebrates, such as mollusks, crustaceans, and polychaete worms, provide an ample source of nourishment for various types of bottom-feeding fish, including some of the most important species for the Icelandic fishing industry—species like cod and haddock.

During the late Middle Ages, foreign fishermen began to frequent Icelandic waters, but it was only during the 20th century that full use was made of the fishing grounds around the country. In that period, the Icelandic fishing industry developed rapidly, but increased mechanization and rapid technological development have led to a serious overexploitation of many stocks in the Icelandic waters. It is for this reason that the government has extended the Icelandic fishing limits in successive steps to the current 200 nautical miles, in part to have a better control over the amount of fish caught around the country and also to give the Icelandic fishing industry a monopoly over this natural resource.

For the Icelandic fisheries, cod has always been the most important species. It spawns outside the southwestern coast of Iceland in late winter, but for the rest of the year, it is spread around most of the island. Since the Second World War, the annual catch of Icelandic ships has fluctuated between around 200,000 and 460,000 metric tons, but based on the recommendation of marine biologists, the Icelandic government set the quotas for cod at 130,000 tons for the 2007–8 fishing season. For decades, herring was the other main stock caught by the Icelandic fishing fleet, but overexploitation and changes in the natural ecosystem led to a collapse in the Norwegian-Icelandic herring stock during the late 1960s. Because of rigorous preservationist policies, the stock is, however, beginning to return to Icelandic waters. To compensate for the decline in catches from traditional stocks, the Icelandic fleet has sought new species in recent years, such as capelin, and Icelandic fishermen have had to seek new fishing grounds outside the 200-mile fishing limits. Moreover, Icelandic shipowners have expanded their activities by investing in European and other international fishing companies.

The industrialization of the fisheries at the beginning of the 20th century led to revolutionary changes in the Icelandic economy and society. First, farming lost its dominant status in the economy, as it could not compete with the fisheries at a time of rapidly rising labor costs. Second, exodus from the countryside to the emerging towns and villages by the coast revolutionized the pattern of settlement in a few decades. Third, rapid increase in the Icelandic GDP pushed living standards in the country upward, transforming the nation in few decades from one of the poorest and most backward in Europe into one of the richest and most technologically advanced nations in the world.

These transformations in Iceland happened in part because the circumstances called for a radical change in the Icelandic economic system. During the late 19th century, rapid and persistent population growth put increasing pressure on the traditional occupations in Iceland, creating the need for new economic opportunities. Therefore, all attempts to preserve the traditional Icelandic social and economic system failed, and urbanization and industrialization relegated farming to a secondary position in society.

At the turn of the 21st century, Iceland stands again at crossroads regarding its use of natural resources. The traditional primary occupations, fisheries and farming, have both reached their limits of expansion, and Icelanders have been forced to look for new resources to sustain their high standards of living. Rich natural energy resources seem to provide the most promising opportunities in this respect; at the present, for example, Icelanders use less than one quarter of the exploitable hydroelectric and geothermal power that can be used to produce electricity in the country (10,000 GWh p.a. out of around 45,000–50,000 GWh p.a.). These sources will not be exploited without considerable environmental impact, however, as hydroelectric power plants need large reservoirs to even out seasonal flow in the rivers and drilling for hot water causes irreparable damage in ecologically sensitive areas. Increasing numbers of Icelanders have, therefore, protested what they see as a heedless destruction of Icelandic nature, turning the Icelandic energy policy into one of the most divisive issues in Icelandic politics.

HISTORY

The Settlement and the Commonwealth Period

According to historical sources, Iceland was first settled by people of Norse origin coming primarily from the western part of Norway through the British Isles. For this reason, the original settlers were a mixed group, as has been confirmed by the latest genetic research. According to recent studies, around 80 percent of the male settlers had their origins in Scandinavia, while the majority of the women were actually of British—including Irish—descent. Old Icelandic chronicles, such as the *Book of Settlement* and the *Book of Icelanders*, also mention that a few Irish Christian hermits (called *papar*) lived in Iceland at the arrival of the Norse settlers, but no conclusive archaeological evidence has confirmed these legends.

According to written sources, the Norse settlement of Iceland started around the year 870—with the year 874 accepted, through convention, as the exact date of the arrival of the first permanent settlers. The settlement of Iceland is seen as an integral part of general Viking expansion to the west, stretching as far as to Greenland and briefly reaching the coast of North America. The leading settlers were for the most part Norwegian chieftains, early Icelandic sources maintain, escaping the tyranny of the first king of unified Norway. Although this may have motivated some of the Icelandic settlers, population pressure and search for new economic opportunities are more plausible causes for the exodus to Iceland.

The settlers brought with them Scandinavian economic and social customs, and it was to Norway that Icelanders looked for a model for their legal system. Thus, around the year 930, Icelandic chieftains established a general assembly called Alþingi using Norwegian customs as the basis for their law codes and legal procedures. At Alþingi, which convened for two weeks every summer at a place called Þingvellir—meaning the assembly plains—in southwestern Iceland, laws were amended and courts held, making it the most important institution of the Icelandic legal and political system for centuries.

With the establishment of Alþingi, Icelanders developed both rudimentary legislative processes and a judiciary system for the whole country. They did not, however, create any centralized mechanism for enforcing the law. The most powerful men in the country were the chieftains (*goðar*), or the group of men who held the 36 to 39 chieftaincies (named *goðorð*) in Iceland. In Alþingi, the chieftains carried out what could be termed as legislative functions and named people into courts, but they had only limited executive authority.

This absence of a centralized state structure led to a gradual dissolution of the Icelandic system of authority. In the first centuries of its history, wealth and power were relatively equally distributed in Iceland, but during the last decades of the Commonwealth Period (930–1262), a few families seized control over most of the chieftaincies. After decades of open warfare in which the most powerful chieftains competed for hegemony in the country, Icelanders accepted the authority of the Norwegian king in the early 1260s in the hope that he would restore peace. Through a treaty with the king, which the Icelandic leaders approved in 1262–64, Iceland became a tributary province in the Norwegian monarchy. Thus, the country entered its long relations with the Scandinavian monarchical rule.

In spite of the violence, Icelandic cultural creativity reached its pinnacle during the 13th century. It was during this century that most of the family sagas were written, in addition to various other literary and historical works. We can trace the start of this literary production to the conversion to Christianity in Iceland, which happened at the start of the second millennium. The church introduced the technology of reading and writing to the Icelandic population, and although most of the Icelandic literature was secular in character, some of the Icelandic religious houses became centers of learning in late medieval Iceland. In the beginning, the written works were mostly of practical nature—beginning with the codification of the laws—but gradually they developed into more complex compositions. The family sagas, with their character development and artistic complexity, are Iceland's most important contribution to world culture, as they were unique at their time in Western literature.

Iceland under Norwegian and Danish Rule

During the 14th and 15th centuries, the cultural production that characterized the turbulent 13th century declined. For this reason, historical sources for the last period of the Middle Ages are relatively scarce. We know, however, that this was a difficult time in many respects. Two terrible plague epidemics devastated Iceland in the 15th century, and its ecological system gradually deteriorated as the climate got colder and overexploitation of the Icelandic vegetation lead to depletion of the natural birch woods and soil erosion. Political development in the late Middle Ages in Iceland followed general trends in the Nordic countries. Thus, when the kingdom of Norway entered a union with Denmark in 1380, Iceland effectively became a part of the Danish monarchy. In the mid-16th century, Icelanders converted to Lutheranism under pressure from the royal government. This enhanced the authority of the Danish king in Iceland because from now on, the church was a state institution under direct control of the king and his officials. Furthermore, the confiscation of the property of Icelandic monasteries made the king by far the single largest landowner in the country.

Increasing state integration marked the political and social development in Iceland from the late 16th to the late 18th centuries. From 1602, the king enforced a strict trade monopoly in his dependency, meaning that only Danish merchants whom he had granted special trading licenses had the right to trade in Iceland. This tied Iceland more firmly to the mother country, as Denmark dominated all of its economic and political relations with the external world. In 1662, when Icelanders acknowledged the absolute rule of the Danish monarch, the country became even more dependent upon the Danish state. From then on, all economic and political initiative in Iceland had to come from Copenhagen.

The introduction of absolutism did not lead to a sudden transformation of the Icelandic political and legal system, but in the long run, it caused significant changes in Icelandic administration and in the relations between the center and the periphery. In the last decades of the 17th century, Danish authorities reorganized the Icelandic administrative hierarchy and gave it more permanence and logical structure. As a result, Alþingi lost the last vestiges of its legislative power, evolving into a mere intermediary court between the Icelandic local courts and the supreme court in Copenhagen; this led to Alþingi's replacement in 1800 by the more effective and professional high court in Reykjavík.

The 18th century was one of the most difficult periods in the history of Iceland. At the beginning of the century, between a quarter and one third of the population died in a smallpox epidemic that struck the country in 1707–9; close to the century's end, around a quarter of the Icelandic population died in a famine that followed the tremendous Laki eruption of 1783–84. The late 18th century saw, however, the beginning of new trends in the government of Iceland. Inspired by the spirit of the European Enlightenment, Icelandic intellectuals and crown officials studied the plight of the country, writing exhortations with the aim of guiding the popular classes toward the road of progress. These men did not demand political autonomy for the Icelandic nation because to them, the Danish king was the most likely source of social and intellectual improvement in the country. In the following century, however, their effort inspired a new group of intellectuals who sought the regeneration of Icelandic society. Thus, romantic nationalism enchanted the generation of Icelandic students who came to Copenhagen in the late 1820s and early 1830s. Just as the Danish state was transformed into a nation-state, the Icelandic nationalists requested what they felt to be the natural rights of the Icelandic nation, that is, some form of sovereignty and independence from Denmark.

From the mid-19th until the early 20th century, the call for self-determination formed the basis for all political activity in Iceland. The first response to these requests was offered in 1843, when the king granted the country a separate consultative diet, carrying the name of the ancient assembly, Alþingi. In the summer of 1845, the newly elected Alþingi met for the first time in Reykjavík. For the next decades, it convened for a few weeks every second year, gathering representatives from all around the country. In the beginning, it had no legislative authority, consulting the king on Icelandic financial and legal matters. Alþingi became, however, a unifying symbol for the growing nationalist sentiment in Iceland and served as a platform for the emerging nationalist movement.

From the mid-19th until the early 20th century, Icelanders inched toward their ultimate goal: full independence from Denmark. During its first phase, the undisputed leader of this struggle was the philologist and archivist Jón Sigurðsson. He emerged as a political figure in the early 1840s, guiding Icelandic nationalism until his death in 1879. In 1874, Iceland received its first democratic constitution, abolishing absolutist rule. The constitution granted Alþingi a limited legislative power in Icelandic domestic affairs and secured fundamental democratic rights. The new constitution did not fulfill all the demands of the nationalists, however, as the minister of Iceland was a member of the Danish cabinet and resided in Copenhagen. The effective government of Iceland remained in the hands of the governor of Iceland (*landshöfðingi*), who was a royal official responsible only to the king,

Icelandic Home Rule and Sovereignty

In 1901, after decades of intense political struggle, a liberal government came to power in Copenhagen. The new ruling party was much more flexible in its Icelandic policies than its reactionary predecessors had been. Thus, in 1901, it accepted Icelandic demands for home rule, and the new regime was established for Iceland, with the transfer of the ministry of Iceland from Copenhagen to Reykjavík. This did not satisfy nationalist aspirations in Iceland, however, because the constitution of Iceland still treated the country as a Danish annex. At the end of the First World War, a committee of Icelandic and Danish parliamentary representatives solved this dilemma with a bilateral agreement between the two parliaments, which declared that Iceland was a sovereign state in union with Denmark. In the fall of 1918, a new Act of Union was passed in the Danish and Icelandic parliaments respectively, and it came formally into effect on 1 December of the same year. With the act, Iceland was effectively an independent monarchy, with the Danish king serving as its ceremonial head of state. Iceland continued to share foreign service with Denmark, but the Icelandic government set its own foreign policies.

These political changes took place at a time of rapid social and economic transformation in Iceland. During the first decades of the century, the Icelandic fishing industry mechanized rapidly, with motor boats and trawlers replacing rowboats and schooners. This economic modernization led to a total demographic reorganization of Icelandic society, as the towns around the coast grew very rapidly while the rural population decreased steadily. Moreover, increasing economic prosperity, growing proletarianization, and the end of the nationalist struggle called for new political alliances based on novel social realities. In just over a decade, from 1916 to 1930, a modern party system emerged in Iceland, with political organizations ranging from the Conservative Party on the right—changing its name to the Independence Party in 1929—to the Communist Party on the left. This was a sign of the general development of Icelandic society from being one of the poorest countries in Europe, totally dependent on economically backward agriculture, to becoming a modern, capitalist nation-state following the general trends in the social and economic development of the western world. With its own university founded in 1911, domestic banking institutions, and growing urban culture, Iceland—which had less than 100,000 inhabitants in 1918—was able to maintain its sovereignty and, in the end, to sever its ties with Denmark.

The Second World War had a great impact in Iceland, although the country was not a direct participant in the military conflicts. As an island in the Mid-Atlantic, Iceland became crucial for protecting communication and transportation between the United States and Europe during the turbulent years of the war. To secure the route to its American allies and to prevent German invasion in Iceland, the British army occupied Iceland in May 1940, a month after the Nazi forces had captured Denmark. The following year, after the government of Iceland had signed a defense treaty with the United States, the American armed forces took over military installations in Iceland. This freed the majority of the British soldiers stationed in Iceland for active combat on the European continent and in North Africa, and it moved Iceland decisively into the U.S. sphere of influence.

The Republic of Iceland

On 17 June 1944, the Icelandic republic was formally founded at Þingvellir, the place where the old Alþingi had met annually for almost nine centuries. Now, the country could become an independent member of the international community, a fact that was later confirmed with its entrance into international organizations, such as the United Nations and the North Atlantic Treaty Organization (NATO). When the cold war parted the world into two hostile camps, Iceland sided firmly with the United States and its western allies. Icelanders have always been hesitant, however, to sacrifice the sovereignty they gained through long nationalist strife. Thus, American military presence in Iceland after 1951 was the most divisive political question in the country for decades. Possible membership in the European Union (EU) has also faced strong opposition, although Iceland has participated fully in the economic and cultural cooperation with its neighbors through the European Free Trade Association (EFTA) and the European Economic Area (EEA) agreement, which came into effect on 1 January 1994.

Today, Iceland demonstrates most of the characteristics of a modern western society. It has maintained political stability through a democratic process that enjoys universal legitimacy. Rapid economic modernization has also secured its inhabitants one of the highest living standards in the world, and a comprehensive and highly developed health system has ensured them longevity and one of the lowest rates of infant mortality in the world. Icelanders face, however, formidable challenges in maintaining their status as an independent nation. First, the Icelandic economy is fairly fragile, as overexploitation threatens the fish stocks that remain among Iceland's principal economic resources. Second, the country is rich in unused energy resources because many of its rivers are still not harnessed and geothermal power is abundant. But using these resources will necessarily damage the pristine nature of the country, forcing the politicians and the Icelandic public to choose between environmental protection and industrial expansion. Finally, it remains to be seen if a country with just over 310,000 inhabitants will be able to manage its foreign relations in a complex and constantly changing world. With the new strategic concerns in the world, Iceland cannot rely on the attention it received from the United States through the cold war.

The Dictionary

– A –

ABSOLUTISM. Danish absolutism was formally instituted in 1660–61 when **King** Frederick III compelled the Danish aristocracy to renounce the last vestiges of the power they wielded in the selection of new kings. To secure the legitimacy of the new regime in Iceland, the Danish governor summoned the most influential leaders of the country to endorse the king's actions. At the meeting held at Kópavogur close to **Reykjavík** in late July 1662, the Icelandic representatives accepted the absolutist rule, albeit with certain reservations. This did not cause an immediate shift in the Icelandic administration, but gradually, the absolutist monarchy abrogated many of the local privileges that limited royal authority in Iceland. Thus, in the early 18th century, **Alþingi** became a mere court of law, serving as an appellate court between the local **county** courts and the supreme court in Copenhagen. Following these changes, the royal administration in Iceland was reorganized to make it more responsive to the government directives and directly dependent on the crown. As in other regions under the Danish monarchy, the country was made an *amt* (special administrative district), with a *stiftamtmaður* (governor) living in Copenhagen and an *amtmaður* (district governor) residing at **Bessastaðir** in Iceland.

During the late 18th century, the absolutist system took on its final form in Iceland. In 1770, the country was divided into two districts, each with one district governor, and a few years later (1787), the districts became three. Above them in the administrative hierarchy was a governor, serving also as district governor in one of the districts. From 1770, the governor lived in Iceland, but until then, the *stiftamtmaður* post had been little more than a ceremonial office for

Danish aristocrats. The absolutist system was in effect in Iceland until the early 1870s, or over two decades beyond its abolition in Denmark proper. The **constitution of 1874** granted Alþingi limited legislative power and the right to enact its own budget, thus ending the absolutist regime in Iceland. *See also* KÓPAVOGUR'S MEETING; LAWMAN.

ACT OF UNION. A legal act passed by the **Danish** and Icelandic parliaments in 1918 and accepted in a referendum in Iceland the same year. The act redefined the relationship between the two countries, granting the Icelandic nation full sovereignty. Hence, the Icelandic nationalist struggle was practically over.

A joint committee, formed by the Danish and Icelandic legislatures, wrote the act in the summer of 1918. The final negotiations took only a few weeks to complete, closing a long dispute between the two countries. The **constitution of 1874** and **home rule** in 1904 had gradually given Icelanders more autonomy in their internal affairs. These conciliatory arrangements did not meet Icelandic demands, however, because the Danish government did not acknowledge Iceland as a sovereign state. The Act of Union fulfilled the Icelandic desire for statehood, as its first article proclaimed Iceland and Denmark to be two free and sovereign states, united only by the same king. The act stipulated, however, that the Danish government would continue to manage Icelandic foreign affairs (*see* FOREIGN POLICY) at the behest of the Icelandic government and guard the Icelandic **fishing limits**, at least as long as Icelanders felt that they were incapable of taking care of these issues themselves.

The Act of Union had a profound impact on Icelandic politics and society. On the one hand, it gave the Icelandic nation almost total control over all three branches of its government. The foundation of the **Supreme Court of Iceland** in 1920 completed this development. On the other, with the end of the nationalist struggle, new issues and ideologies began to divide the nation into political factions. **Nationalism** remained a strong theme in Icelandic politics, but it was no longer the center of all political debates.

According to its 18th article, both the Danish and the Icelandic parliaments had the right to revoke the Act of Union at the end of

1943, provided that attempts to renegotiate the act were unsuccessful. As the German occupation of Denmark in 1940 blocked all communications with Copenhagen, the act had already become entirely ineffectual early in the war, and representatives of the two nations could not meet to renegotiate the act. Therefore, the Icelandic parliament decided unilaterally to terminate the union with Denmark in 1944 and to declare Iceland an independent republic. This policy received overwhelming support in a referendum held in 1944, and on 17 June of that year, the **Republic of Iceland** was founded at **Þingvellir.** *See also* THE DRAFT; WORLD WAR II.

ACTAVIS GROUP. The international pharmaceutical corporation Actavis Group traces its history back to the foundation of the Icelandic company Pharmaco in 1956. Originally, Pharmaco was a cooperative venture of a few Icelandic pharmacists, importing medicine from abroad. Pharmaco began the production of its own pharmaceuticals for the Icelandic market in 1960, and this operation was strengthened further with the foundation of its subsidiary, Delta, in 1982. Pharmaco began its international expansion in 1999–2000 with the acquisition of the Bulgarian pharmaceutical company Balkanpharma, and later it acquired similar businesses in Malta, Serbia, **Denmark,** Croatia, and India, among others. It is now one of the largest producers of generic drugs in Europe, employing over 11,000 people in approximately 40 countries. The corporate headquarters of Actavis are in Iceland, and currently it is one of the most valuable companies registered on the **Iceland Stock Exchange.**

AGE OF THE STURLUNGS. The last decades of the **Commonwealth Period,** or the time from 1200/20 to 1262, are traditionally named after one of the most prominent families in 13th-century Iceland, the Sturlung family. This was a turbulent period when various chieftains competed for political dominance in the country. Gradually, the old social system broke down as the lack of effective executive power rendered the rule of law almost impossible. In 1262–64, when the feuds had broken the power of the ruling families in Iceland and the general population had had its fill of the political upheaval, Icelanders agreed to enter into a contractual alliance with the **Norwegian** king. This marked the end of the Commonwealth Period.

The 13th century was not only a time of bloody feuds but also one of the most productive periods in Icelandic literary history. During the Age of the Sturlungs and the following decades, many of the most original family sagas were composed, along with historical works like the *Sturlunga Saga* compilation, which gives detailed accounts of the events and intrigues that characterized the period. Literary production did not end as abruptly as the political feuds, but by the end of the 13th century, it had lost most of its creative edge. *See also* LITERATURE; OLD COVENANT; SAGAS; STURLUSON, SNORRI (1178/9–1241); ÞÓRÐARSON, STURLA (1214–84).

AGRICULTURE. In general, Iceland is not particularly well suited for agriculture. The country's climate makes grain growing almost impossible, and its fragile vegetation and long winters limit the development of **animal husbandry**. In spite of these natural restrictions, during much of Iceland's history, agriculture was the most important sector of its **economy**.

Various historical sources and archaeological evidence confirm that grain—barley in particular—was cultivated in Iceland during the first centuries of its history, at least in areas most suitable for cultivation of crops. During the late Middle Ages, deteriorating climatic conditions and declining prices on world markets undermined grain production in Iceland, and it disappeared entirely in the 16th century. Since then, Icelandic agriculture has been based almost completely on animal husbandry, with sheep, cattle, and horses being the most important domestic animals. In large parts of the country, **fishing** also served as an invaluable source of income for farming households, as farmers and their servants often spent the slack seasons of the late winter in fishing stations by the coast.

From the time of the settlement until the late 19th century, around 90 percent of the working population was employed in agriculture. The natural habitat set its mark on the peasant economy, as farms were usually very small and spread over the inhabitable part of the country. Technological change was also very slow, as the organization of Icelandic agriculture was more or less the same at the end of the 19th century as it had been in the Middle Ages. With rapid **urbanization**, which started in the latter half of the 19th century, a domestic market for farming goods came into being at the same time as a transformation of the **labor market** increased the competition for labor in Iceland during the first decades of the 20th century. This transformed agricultural production in the last century; mechanization and technological progress have eliminated the farmers' need for hired hands, and farmers are increasingly at the mercy of fluctuating demand for the products.

The social and economic modernization of the 20th century has affected Icelandic agriculture in all aspects. In 2007, less than 4 percent of the active population was employed in agriculture, down from around one third in 1940. In the same period, dairy production had more than doubled, and production of meat had increased over 50 percent. This development was the result of a period of great expansion in Icelandic agriculture that lasted from the mid-20th century to the late 1970s. This was a time of generous state support to farmers, which was used to enlarge meadows and purchase modern farm equipment. In the long run, increased output created new problems for farmers, as it led to chronic overproduction of milk and mutton, traditionally their most important products. For this reason, farmers have had to reduce their production in recent years, especially because the state has scaled down the cumbersome system of farm subsidies set up during the **Great Depression**. The market for agricultural goods in Iceland is, however, still heavily protected, and the production is subsidized by the state. Unfortunately, state-sponsored programs, which were set up to diversify the farming production, were largely unsuccessful, while high production costs have thwarted most attempts to export farming goods. These economic difficulties, along with the declining political clout of the **farmers' associations**, make the future of Icelandic agriculture rather uncertain at the moment. *See also* LABOR BONDAGE; REGIONAL POLICY.

ÁGÚSTSSON, GUÐNI (1949–). Politician born in Árnes County on 9 April 1949 to a member of parliament for the **Progressive Party** (PP). Ágústsson studied at the Agricultural College at Hvanneyri, completing his exam in 1968. After that, he worked for years at the largest dairy in Iceland. In 1987, he was **elected** to **Alþingi** for the PP, where he has served since. He was minister of **agricultural** affairs in the coalition government of the **Independence Party** and the PP from 1999 to 2007. Ágústsson was elected vice chairman of the PP in 2001, and when **Jón Sigurðsson (1946–)** stepped down as chairman of the party in 2007, Ágústsson took his place. Ágústsson has remained very popular for most of his political career, although his political ideas and rhetoric are often seen as out of step with recent developments in Icelandic society. It remains to be seen, therefore, if he will be able to lead the PP toward political recovery.

AKUREYRI. This town, the largest township in Iceland outside the **Reykjavík** area, is often called the capital of northern Iceland. Because of Akureyri's central location, the royal administration chose it as one of the six certified marketplaces in Iceland in 1787. At that time, Akureyri was only a small hamlet of a few huts and one general store, but around the mid-19th century the town began to grow rapidly. As a result, in 1862, it was the first town in Iceland, after Reykjavík, to receive a town charter, providing it with an **elected** town council and a special town court. As the town grew in size, more services moved to Akureyri, and it became an administrative and cultural center for the surrounding **agricultural** region.

During the 20th century, the **population** of Akureyri grew more than tenfold, from 1,370 inhabitants in 1901 to around 17,000 in 2007. In this period, the town developed a strong industrial base while it continued to serve as a commercial center for the prosperous agricultural regions around it. Moreover, in 1928, the Akureyri high school was granted the right to offer university entrance exams, making the town an **educational** center for the northern and eastern parts of the country. This role was further enhanced in 1987, with the foundation of the University of Akureyri, a rapidly growing university college specializing in such fields as marine research, nursing, management, social sciences, and education.

ALMENNA BÆNARSKRÁIN. *See* THE GENERAL PETITION.

ALÞINGI. The parliament of Iceland, Alþingi is a central institution in Icelandic history and public life. It traces its name back to the beginning of the **Commonwealth Period**, although the modern, democratically **elected** Alþingi has little in common with its medieval namesake.

The old Alþingi met for the first time around the year 930 on Þingvellir (literally, "Assembly Plains"), which is about 40 kilometers (25 miles) northeast of **Reykjavík**. In the beginning, Alþingi was a public gathering, where people from all over the country met for two weeks during the early summer. The center of the assembly was Lögrétta, the law council, which was dominated by 39 chieftains (**goði**). Lögrétta formulated legal interpretations, but the chieftains nominated people to the *fimmtardómur* (high court) of the country and the four *fjórðungsdómar* (quarter courts) at Alþingi. The *lögsögumaður* (**law-speaker**) presided over Alþingi until 1271, when his title was changed to *lögmaður* (**lawman**).

With the union of Iceland and **Norway** in 1262–64, Alþingi gradually lost much of its prestige, although it remained a unifying symbol for the Icelandic ruling classes. From then on, it was the royal officials who controlled Alþingi, as the chieftaincies were abolished in the late 13th century. The role of this assembly was reduced further still after the introduction of **absolutism** in 1662. At this time, the vestiges of its limited legislative functions were totally abolished, and it became a mere appellate court. In 1798, Alþingi met for the last time at Þingvellir, after convening there every year for nearly nine centuries. After two sessions in the emerging capital, Reykjavík, the old Alþingi was abolished in 1800. A permanent *Landsyfirréttur* (**high court**) staffed with professionally trained judges appointed by the **king** replaced it the same year.

King Christian VIII founded the modern Alþingi in 1843 as a consultative assembly for Icelandic affairs. It had 20 elected representatives, one from each *sýsla* (**county**) in Iceland and one from the town of Reykjavík in addition to six members selected by the government in Copenhagen. The parliament was to meet every second year for four weeks in the summer to discuss bills introduced by the government and formulate collective petitions to the king. Resolutions passed in Alþingi had no binding authority, but the government usually took them into consideration when it proposed changes to the Icelandic legislation to the king. Alþingi met for the first time in this capacity in 1845.

The **constitution of 1874** granted Alþingi limited legislative power in domestic affairs and control over the Icelandic budget. This meant that no bill could become law in Iceland unless a majority in both houses of parliament approved it, but the king had the right to veto all bills passed in Alþingi—a prerogative he used frequently during the last decades of the 19th century. The constitution of 1874 divided Alþingi into 2 houses; 12 representatives sat in the upper house (until 1915, the king selected 6 of them, while the rest were popularly elected), and 24 democratically elected representatives sat in the lower house.

Since 1874, Alþingi has slowly become the most important institution of the Icelandic political system. Its primary functions pertain to its legislative authority, which it now shares with the **president** of the republic. Parliament also has strong influence on the executive branch because the government is responsible to Alþingi, and therefore, it has to have the support of the majority of the representatives in parliament. Moreover, Alþingi must approve the state budget, which gives it authority over all public spending in Iceland.

Today, regular sessions of Alþingi begin on 1 October every year and last until the following spring. It is composed of 63 members, and since 1990, it has met in 1 house. All bills presented to Alþingi are discussed in 1 of its 12 standing committees, and they require three readings in parliament before they are sent to the president for ratification. Alþingi holds its meetings in a parliamentary building, which was constructed in Reykjavík's center in 1880–81.

In the beginning, one representative was elected for each electoral district to a six-year term (shortened to four years in 1920). As demographic patterns began to change during the early 20th century, the electoral system tended to favor the rural areas at the expense of the emerging towns around the coast. After numerous attempts to correct the growing imbalance, the system was totally overhauled in 1959. With a constitutional amendment, the country was divided into eight constituencies in which 5 to 12 representatives were elected from party lists in each. This system was changed again in 1999, also as a response to a growing imbalance between the urbanized southwestern part of the country and the rest, reducing the number of constituencies to six, half of which are in Reykjavík and its suburbs. Each constituency sends 9 to 11 representatives to Alþingi, and following a system of proportional representation, each party receives a number of seats in accordance with its share of the popular vote. Since the 1930s, the Icelandic party structure has been relatively stable, with four major **political parties** receiving the lion's share of the votes in most parliamentary elections. *See also* CABINET; CONSTITUTION OF 1944; DENMARK; PRIME MINISTER.

AMTMAÐUR. The office of *amtmaður*, or district governor, was established in Iceland in 1684 as part of the general reorganization of the Icelandic administrative system following the introduction of **absolutism** in 1662. As the *stiftamtmaður* (governor) lived in Copenhagen until 1770, the district governor was de facto governor of Iceland. In 1770, the administrative hierarchy was reformed again, as the country was divided into two districts instead of one. At the same time, the governor was required to live in Iceland, where he also served as district governor in the southwest district. From that time, the district governor served as a link between the bailiffs in the **counties** and the governor, collecting information from the local officials and communicating orders from the governor to the bailiffs. In 1787, the district boundaries were redrawn, and the southwest district was split into two parts—the governor serving as district governor of the south district. In 1873, the south and west districts were reunited and placed under one district governor, while the *landshöfðingi* (governor) was relieved of his duties as district governor. This arrangement was in force until the district governors' offices were abolished in 1904 with the introduction of **home rule** in Iceland.

ANIMAL HUSBANDRY. Animal husbandry was for centuries the mainstay of the Icelandic **economy**. The most important domestic animals were sheep and cattle. The former were raised for their milk, wool, and meat, and the latter were raised mostly for their milk. Horses were also vital to the peasant economy, especially for transportation over longer distances. Today, animal husbandry is still the most important element of the rural economy, but changing patterns of consumption and improvements in breeding have forced farmers to set strict quotas on their production. Thus, the number of sheep has declined drastically in recent years, from almost 900,000 heads in 1977 to around 450,000 in 2006. At the same time, there has been massive growth in the production of pork and poultry, in part because it is not restricted by quotas or subsidies. Because of increasing **population** and **urbanization**, the market for dairy products grew steadily from the early 20th century until the mid 1980s, but since then, the production has been more or less stable. *See also* AGRICULTURE.

ARASON, JÓN (1484–1550). The last **Catholic** bishop in Iceland before the **Reformation** was born in 1484 to a prosperous farmer in northern Iceland. He was ordained a priest in 1507, and after that, he rose quickly through the ranks of the church as well as the royal administration in Iceland. In 1522, he was elected bishop in the **Hólar** diocese, and he also served as a bailiff in two districts in northern Iceland. Arason is best known for his staunch opposition to the **Lutheran** Reformation in Iceland, but a Lutheran bishop governed the diocese of **Skálholt** in southern Iceland from the early 1540s. From 1548 to 1550, Arason maintained a band of armed retainers, imprisoning the bishop of Skálholt and reestablishing monasteries that the Lutherans had closed down in previous years. This led to a total rift with the **Danish** king Christian III, who sought to force all of his subjects to accept the Lutheran Church. Arason's struggle ended in 1550 when the king's men in Iceland captured him and had him and two of his illegitimate sons executed in Skálholt on 7 November 1550.

To many **nationalists** of the 19th and 20th centuries, Arason symbolized the resistance of the Icelandic nation against growing foreign authority. This is certainly an anachronistic opinion because nationalism in the modern sense of the word did not exist in the 16th century, but the victory of Lutheranism enhanced royal power in Iceland.

ARCHIVES. *See* NATIONAL AND UNIVERSITY LIBRARY OF ICELAND; NATIONAL ARCHIVES OF ICELAND (NAI).

ARI ÞORGILSSON THE "LEARNED." *See* ÞORGILSSON, ARI "THE LEARNED" (1067/8–1148).

ÁRMANN Á ALÞINGI. The first example in a string of periodicals published by Icelandic students and intellectuals in Copenhagen during the early 19th century. Baldvin Einarsson (1801–33), son of a farmer in Skagafjörður County in northern Iceland, founded and edited *Ármann á Alþingi* with the aim of providing his countrymen with practical advice on various social, **economic**, and political issues. It was constructed around a conversation among three fictional Icelanders, each of whom represented certain character traits that the editors found prevalent in Icelandic society, and a wise man living in a mountain close to Þingvellir. The journal mixed Icelandic conservatism with the ideals of the European **Enlightenment**, emphasizing both the traditional values of the Icelandic peasant economy and the possibility of social progress through **education** and a rational use of Icelandic resources. *Ármann á Alþingi* had little direct influence on Icelandic political life during the short period of its publication, but it served as an encouragement for others who followed its example. The first regular issue of *Ármann á Alþingi* was published in 1829, but the journal ceased publication with the fourth issue (1832), following the tragic death of its founder in Copenhagen in February 1833. *See also FJÖLNIR; NÝ FÉLAGSRIT.*

ARNAMAGNÆAN INSTITUTE. *See* ÁRNI MAGNÚSSON INSTITUTE FOR ICELANDIC STUDIES.

ARNARSON, INGÓLFUR (9TH AND 10TH CENTURIES). All the medieval sources on the settlement of Iceland suggest that Ingólfur was the name of the first permanent settler of Norse origins in Iceland—there is not a total accord on the name of his father, but by convention, he is called Arnarson. Ingólfur is said to have left **Norway** for Iceland around 870–74, calling his farm in the new country **Reykjavík**, or "smoke cove." According to the *Book of Settlements*, he chose this site because it was there that the posts of his high seat drifted on land, but he is supposed to have thrown them overboard when he first caught the sight of the island from his ship. Arnarson's descendants retained a high status in Icelandic society for centuries, carrying the title *allsherjargoði*, which gave them a special status in **Alþingi**. *See also* SETTLEMENT PERIOD.

ÁRNI MAGNÚSSON INSTITUTE FOR ICELANDIC STUDIES. The Stofnun Árna Magnússonar í íslenskum fræðum (Árni Magnússon Institute for Icelandic Studies) was founded in 2006 through a merger of six existing research institutions in the field of Icelandic studies. The largest of these institutions was the Árni Magnússon Institute, which was originally founded as the Handritastofnun

Íslands (Icelandic Manuscript Institute) in 1962. Its name comes from the Icelandic scholar **Árni Magnússon**, who was instrumental in collecting and transferring to Copenhagen many of the most valuable vellum and paper manuscripts in Iceland in the early 18th century. After the return of the first manuscripts from Copenhagen in 1971 (*see* MANUSCRIPTS, RETURN OF), the Árni Magnússon Institute and the Arnamagnæan Institute (now the Arnamagnæan Collection) in Copenhagen became the main depositories of these cultural treasures and centers of research in Old Norse philology and **literature**.

The other institutions forming the Árni Magnússon Institute for Icelandic Studies were the Icelandic Dictionary of the **University of Iceland**, the Sigurður Nordal Institute, the Place-Name Institute of Iceland, the Icelandic **Language** Institute, and the Icelandic Language Council. The main purpose of the institute is to preserve the various collections in its care, pursue research on the Icelandic language and medieval and early modern literature, publish scientific editions of manuscripts, and develop dictionaries on the Icelandic language, among other responsibilities. The Árni Magnússon Institute for Icelandic studies is an independent university institution, but is affiliated with the University of Iceland.

ART. Traditionally, Icelanders have considered **literature** their most important cultural genre, while painting and sculpture have received rather limited attention until fairly recently. Some of the medieval manuscripts were highly illuminated, however, especially **religious** and legal texts. Some other artistic pieces from the first centuries of Icelandic history have been preserved, such as metal objects and carving in wood or whalebone. The medieval tradition was kept alive through the centuries, mostly in religious art, but art did not play a prominent role in the Icelandic cultural life until around the turn of the 20th century. Thus, it was only in the late 19th century, when painters like Sigurður Guðmundsson (1833–74) and Þórarinn B. Þorláksson (1867–1924) returned from their studies at the Royal Academy of Art in Copenhagen, that modern visual art was really introduced to Iceland. This development was related to the general social change in the country around that time, as the development of urban society opened new possibilities for aspiring artists. In the beginning, these artists were heavily influenced by the national romanticism of their times, seeking their motives in Icelandic landscapes, folklore traditions, and the **saga** literature. This is very obvious in the art of the best-known painter of the 20th century, **Jóhannes Sveinsson Kjarval**, whose particular vision on Icelandic nature appealed strongly to the public.

During the early 20th century, some artists attempted to break with the dominating naturalist tradition in Iceland, but they met stern opposition from their more conservative colleagues and cultural authorities. Thus, it was hardly until the post–**World War II** era that modernism broke through in Icelandic art with such sculptors as Ásmundur Sveinsson (1893–1982) and Sigurjón Ólafsson (1908–82) and painters like Svavar Guðnason (1909–88) and Þorvaldur Skúlason (1906–84).

With the modernist breakthrough, Icelandic art began to closely mirror the artistic development on the European continent and America. The ties with the surrounding world have always been maintained through various personal channels; most prominent artists in Iceland have received at least part of their training abroad, and some have lived most of their lives in either Europe—for example, Erró (b. 1932), who has lived mostly in France; Sigurður Guðmundsson (b. 1942), in Holland—or the **United States**, such as Louisa Matthíasdóttir (1917–2000). The best-known young artist of Icelandic descent, Ólafur Elíasson (b. 1967), is a perfect example of this international nature of modern art, as he was born of Icelandic parents in Copenhagen but lives in Berlin and has made his name in both **Great Britain** and the United States.

ÁSGEIRSSON, ÁSGEIR (1894–1972). The second **president** of the **Republic of Iceland**, Ásgeirsson was born the son of a merchant in Mýrar County. He graduated from secondary school in **Reykjavík** in 1912 and studied theology at the **University of Iceland** from 1912 to 1915 and theology and philosophy at the universities of Copenhagen and Uppsala, Sweden, from 1916 to 1917. He taught at the Teachers College in Reykjavík from 1918 to 1927 and served as superintendent of **education** in Iceland from 1927 to 1931 and 1934 to 1938. In 1938, he became director of the Fisheries Bank of Iceland, a position he held until he was **elected** president of Iceland in 1952.

The political career of Ásgeirsson was both long and colorful. He was first elected to parliament for the **Progressive Party** (PP) in 1923, sitting in **Alþingi** continuously until 1952. In 1931, the PP appointed him minister of finance, and he served as **prime minister** from 1932 to 1934. At the end of that term, he left the PP but was reelected to Alþingi in 1934 as an independent candidate; in 1937, he joined the **Social Democratic Party**. When **Sveinn Björnsson**, the first president of Iceland and Ásgeirsson's father-in-law, died in 1952, he entered the presidential race. There he encountered staunch opposition from the two largest **political parties** in Iceland, the **Independence Party** and the PP, both of which endorsed Rev. Bjarni Jónsson, a highly regarded minister of the **Lutheran** Church in Reykjavík. After a fierce campaign, Ásgeirsson won a narrow victory in a three-way race. He was reelected president without opposition in 1956, 1960, and 1964 but stepped down at the end of his fourth term in 1968. He was generally highly regarded as president, and the controversies surrounding his first election did not affect the cordial relationship that has for the most part existed between the sitting president and the political parties in Iceland. *See also* THORODDSEN, GUNNAR (1910–83).

ÁSGRÍMSSON, HALLDÓR (1947–). The former chairman of the **Progressive Party** (PP) and **prime minister** of Iceland, he was born in Vopnafjörður in eastern Iceland on 8 September 1947. He graduated from the Cooperative College of Iceland in 1965 and received a license as a certified accountant in 1970. Ásgrímsson studied at the **Norwegian** School of **Economics** and Business Administration in Bergen, Norway, and Copenhagen Business School from 1971 to 1973 and was appointed assistant professor at the **University of Iceland** in 1973. The following year, Ásgrímsson was **elected** to parliament for the PP, where he served in various coalition governments from the early 1980s: as minister of **fisheries** from 1983 to 1991, as minister of justice and ecclesiastical affairs from 1988 to 1989, as minister of foreign affairs (*see* FOREIGN POLICY) from 1995 to 2004, and as prime minister from 2004 to 2006, replacing his longtime ally, **Davíð Oddsson**. He was elected deputy chairman of the PP in 1981 and chairman of the party in 1994, holding that position until the autumn of 2006, when he retired from politics. On 1 January 2007, Ásgrímsson became the first Icelander to serve as secretary general of the **Nordic Council** of Ministers.

Ásgrímsson was one of the most influential politicians in Iceland during his long career in parliament. He sat in **Alþingi** more or less continuously from 1974 to 2006, and of these 32 years, he served as minister for 19 years in 8 different **cabinets**.

AUÐUNS, AUÐUR (1911–99). The first **woman** in Iceland to gain a prominent position in the political establishment. Auðuns was born in **Ísafjörður**, where her father was a businessman and a politician. She graduated from **Menntaskólinn í Reykjavík** in 1929, and in 1935, she was the first woman to earn a law degree from the **University of Iceland**. She practiced law in her home town, Ísafjörður, from 1935 to 1936 and served as legal consultant in **Reykjavík** for the following years. In 1946, she was **elected** to the city council of Reykjavík for the **Independence Party** and served as council president from 1954 to 1959 and again from 1960 to 1970. From 1959 to 1960, she was the first woman to serve as mayor of Reykjavík. In 1959, Auðuns was elected to **Alþingi**, where she held a seat for Reykjavík until 1974. In 1970, she was the first woman to be appointed to a **cabinet** post in Iceland, serving as minister of justice and ecclesiastical affairs for the last months of the **Reconstruction Government**.

– B –

BALDVINSSON, JÓN (1882–1938). President of the **Icelandic Federation of Labor** (IFL) and leader of the **Social Democratic Party** (SDP). Born on 20 December 1882 to a farmer in Ísafjörður County, Baldvinsson learned the printing trade under the tutelage of editor, politician, and bailiff **Skúli Thoroddsen**, for whom he worked for eight years. From 1905 until 1918, when he became the director of the Alþýðubrauðgerðin (People's Bakery), he worked as a printer in **Reykjavík**. In March 1916, at the time of the formation of the IFL, he was chosen as its secretary, and later in the same year, he ousted Ottó N. Þorláksson, the first president of the IFL, in an **election** for the presidency of the federation. He served in this post, which automatically made him chairman of the SDP, until his death in 1938. From

1918 to 1924, Baldvinsson sat in the city council of Reykjavík for the SDP, and he entered parliament for the first time in 1921, where he held a seat until his death in 1938. In 1930, he became one of the first directors of the state-owned Fisheries Bank of Iceland. Under the leadership of Baldvinsson, the social democratic movement in Iceland took a very moderate course. He was an adamant opponent of revolutionary communism, which led to dissension in the SDP soon after **World War I**. Eventually, the radicals abandoned the party to form the **Communist Party of Iceland** in 1930. Baldvinsson and the policies he formulated had a lasting influence on the SDP, as the party was always fairly moderate compared to its Scandinavian sister parties, and it consistently remained close to the center in Icelandic politics.

BANKING. The banking system developed late in Iceland—the first savings banks were established around 1870 and the first commercial bank, the Landsbankinn [**National Bank of Iceland** (NBI)], opened in 1886—but it entered a phase of rapid expansion at the turn of the 20th century. Thus, the second bank of Iceland, the privately owned Íslandsbanki (Bank of Iceland), was established through foreign investments (mostly **Danish**) in 1903 and opened its offices in Iceland in 1904. This bank brought considerable new capital into the country at an important juncture in its **economic** history, and the bank became, in fact, a crucial player in the rapid **industrialization** of the Icelandic **fisheries** in the first two decades of the 20th century.

Early in the **Great Depression**, the Bank of Iceland endured serious difficulties, which led to its closing in 1930. The same year, two state-owned banking institutions were opened in **Reykjavík**, the Útvegsbanki Íslands [Fisheries Bank of Iceland (FBI)] and the Búnaðarbanki Íslands [Agricultural Bank of Iceland (ABI)]. From that time until the 1980s, the state owned all the leading banking institutions in Iceland.

The government not only directly owned most of the major banks and investment credit funds, but it also affected the banking industry through heavy regulation of the operation of the banks. The state exerted, for example, considerable influence on credit allocation in Iceland through various investment funds, which at one point accounted for a quarter of the total outstanding credit in Iceland. A further characteristic of the financial system was that until recently, organized markets for money, bonds, and foreign exchange were virtually nonexistent. Private companies and public bodies obtained external funds primarily through borrowing from financial institutions, giving the latter an important role in the economic development of Iceland.

The **privatization** of the banking sector started with the foundation of a new Íslandsbanki (Bank of Iceland) in 1989–90, which was formed through a merger of four small banks that had been owned by various employers' organizations and the trade unions with the state-owned FBI, which was sold to private investors. The new bank was entirely in private ownership and became the second largest bank in Iceland after the NBI. In 2006, the bank changed its name to Glitnir. This development continued with the privatization of the NBI and the ABI from 1997 to 2003. The former is operated now as a private bank under the same name as before, while the latter operates now under the name of Kaupthing Bank. The latter is now by far the largest banking institution in Iceland, with considerable operations in neighboring countries, and it is, in fact, among the 10 largest banks in the Nordic countries.

The private banks have been instrumental in the economic revolution in Iceland during the first years of the 21st century. All the three major commercial banks, NBI, Kaupthing Bank, and Glitnir, have invested heavily in Europe, primarily in **Great Britain** and Scandinavia. With large companies like **Baugur Group**, **Actavis**, and Bakkavör Group, they have broken the isolation of the Icelandic financial system, and now more than half of their revenues derive from their operations abroad. The phenomenal profits of these institutions in recent years have made financial institutions the most important sector of the Icelandic economy. *See also* CENTRAL BANKING; CURRENCY.

BAUGUR GROUP. Baugur Group is an international investment company with roots in Iceland, specializing in investments in service, retail, media, and real estate sectors in Iceland and abroad (primarily in **Great Britain** and Scandinavia). It traces its history to 1989 when **Jón Ásgeir Jóhannesson** and his father founded the discount supermarket Bónus in **Reykjavík**. Their goal was to offer the lowest prices on the Icelandic food market, and within three years, they had opened many Bónus stores in Iceland. In 1998, Bónus merged with the largest retail chain in Reykjavík, Hagkaup, to form Baugur, and since then, it has dominated the retailing market in Iceland. Bónus started its foreign investments in 1994 in the Faroe Islands, but Baugur truly entered the European scene in 2003 with the acquisition of the British toy-store chain Hamleys. Since then, it has invested heavily in Britain and Scandinavia in addition to Iceland. Companies related to Baugur Group employ over 60,000 people worldwide. Thus, the company symbolizes the revolutionary changes in the Icelandic **economy** at the turn of the 21st century, where Icelandic businessmen have become aggressive players in European investment markets. *See also* BROADCASTING.

BENEDIKTSSON, BJARNI (1908–70). One of the leading politicians of 20th-century Iceland. Benediktsson was born in **Reykjavík** on 30 April 1908 to a prominent member of the Icelandic parliament. He studied law in Reykjavík and Berlin (1926–32) and was appointed a professor of law at the **University of Iceland** in 1932 when he was only 24 years old. He resigned his professorship in 1940 to become mayor of Reykjavík, a position he held for seven years. He sat in parliament for the **Independence Party** (IP) from 1942 until his death in 1970. Selected to his first ministerial post in 1947, Benediktsson served as minister of foreign affairs and justice until 1949, minister of foreign affairs and **education** from 1949 to 1950, minister of foreign affairs and justice from 1950 to 1953, and minister of foreign affairs and education from 1953 to 1956. When the IP fell from power in 1956, he became editor of the largest newspaper in Iceland, *Morgunblaðið*, but with the formation of the **Reconstruction Government** in 1959, he resumed his former ministerial post. From 1959 to 1963, Benediktsson was minister of justice, ecclesiastical affairs, **industry**, and **health**, with the exception of the fall of 1961, when he served as **prime minister** for three months. When **Ólafur Thors**, who had served as chairman of the IP from 1934 to 1961, retired from politics in 1963, Benediktsson replaced him as prime minister. At the time of his death in 1970, Benediktsson had led the government continuously for almost seven years, which was, at the time, a record in Iceland.

Benediktsson was a forceful leader of the largest **political party** in Iceland. He served as its deputy chairman for many years and, from 1961, as its chairman. Under his leadership, the IP continued its tradition of almost absolute unity, which helped it to retain its large following in local and parliamentary elections. After **World War II**, Benediktsson was instrumental in forming the **foreign policy** of the young republic, leading the country into the western military alliance, the **North Atlantic Treaty Organization** (NATO), and close cooperation with the **United States**. His **economic** and social views followed the traditions of the IP, with a strong emphasis on free enterprise economics in theory but a support of an extensive system of welfare programs in practice.

BENEDIKTSSON, EINAR (1864–1940). Poet and entrepreneur, Benediktsson was born at Elliðavatn, a farm close to **Reykjavík**, on 31 October 1864 to **Benedikt Sveinsson**, a judge and a leading member of **Alþingi**. He graduated from secondary school in Reykjavík in 1884 and earned his law degree from the University of Copenhagen eight years later. After assisting his father for a few years, he edited the first daily newspaper in Iceland, *Dagskrá*, from 1896 to 1898. He was appointed bailiff in Rangárvellir County in 1904 but retired from this post three years later. For the next years, Benediktsson lived for the most part abroad in **Great Britain, Denmark**, and Germany. He was an untiring advocate of **economic** modernization in his country, promoting, among other things, fantastical plans for the construction of hydroelectric power plants and energy-intensive factories in Iceland. Benediktsson is, however, best known for his literary achievements, as he was a leading poet in Iceland during his lifetime. At first he was under strong influence from realism and even from socialism, but later individualism and **nationalism** became prevalent themes in his poetry. During the last years of his life, Benediktsson was a voluntary recluse on his farm on the coast of southwestern Iceland. In 1934, he was appointed professor-at-large by the **University of Iceland**, honoring his contribution to Icelandic **literature** and culture, and at his death in 1940, he was the first person to be buried in the national cemetery at **Þingvellir**.

BESSASTAÐIR. The Icelandic **presidential** residence located on Álftanes, a small headland to the south of **Reykjavík**. Bessastaðir, which was an important manor in former times, is first mentioned in the *Sturlunga Saga*, which was written in the 13th century. After the death of its owner, **Snorri Sturluson**, in 1241, the king of **Norway** took possession of Bessastaðir, and for centuries, it was the abode of the highest royal officials in Iceland. From 1805 to 1846, the only secondary school in Iceland was located there, the Latin School of Bessastaðir, but around midcentury, when Reykjavík emerged as the center of royal administration in Iceland, Bessastaðir lost all of its official functions. In 1941, when **Alþingi elected Sveinn Björnsson** *ríkisstjóri* (governor of Iceland), the owner of Bessastaðir donated the manor to the state, and since 1944, it has served as the official residence of the president of the republic. The oldest of the buildings now standing at Bessastaðir were constructed for the district governor in Iceland during the 1760s and are thus among the first stone houses to be built in Iceland. *See also* MENNTASKÓLINN Í REYKJAVÍK (MR).

BJARNHÉÐINSDÓTTIR, BRÍET (1856–1940). One of the founders and early leaders of the Icelandic **women's** movement. Bjarnhéðinsdóttir was born on 27 September 1856 to a farmer in Húnavatn County in northern Iceland. As was normal for farmers' children at the time, she enjoyed no formal schooling beyond a year in a special school for girls. The almost total lack of **educational** opportunities for women at the time alerted her to the existing gender inequalities in Iceland, against which she fought for the remainder of her life.

In 1885, during a brief stay in **Reykjavík**, Bjarnhéðinsdóttir published her first newspaper article on these issues, but it was only when she moved permanently to the town in 1887 that she established herself as the leading spokeswoman for equal rights in Iceland. From 1895 to 1919, she edited and managed a newspaper in Reykjavík, *Kvennablaðið* (*Women's Newspaper*), which was almost entirely devoted to women's issues, calling for equality of men and women in education and the workplace. In 1907, she founded the **Icelandic Society for Women's Rights**, which was affiliated with the International Women's Suffrage Alliance. In 1908, the same year women received the right to sit in local councils, Bjarnhéðinsdóttir was one of four women **elected** to the city council of Reykjavík on a special women's list. She sat on the council for 10 years.

Bjarnhéðinsdóttir was a vigorous advocate for women's rights at a time when formal equality was the main goal of the women's movement in Iceland. By modern standards, her political views were fairly moderate, but her perseverance and enthusiasm make her an example for today's feminists. *See also* WOMEN'S ALLIANCE (WA).

BJÖRGÓLFSSON, BJÖRGÓLFUR THOR (1967–). The most successful businessman in Iceland's history was born on 19 March 1967 in **Reykjavík**. After graduating from Commercial College in Reykjavík in 1987, he studied marketing at New York University, completing a B.S. in 1991. He entered the investment arena through acquiring a Russian brewery with his father, which they sold later with good profit to the Dutch giant Heineken. Björgólfsson invested his profits both in Iceland and Eastern Europe and then primarily in telecommunications and drug companies. Björgúlfsson is now based in **Great Britain**, and according to *Forbes Magazine*, in 2007, he was the 249th richest man in the world, with a net worth of US$3.5 billion.

BJÖRK. *See* GUÐMUNDSDÓTTIR, BJÖRK (1965–).

BJÖRNSSON, SVEINN (1881–1952). The first **president** of the **Republic of Iceland**. He was born in Copenhagen on 27 February 1881, the son of a prominent Icelandic journalist and publisher, who later became one of the leading politicians of his country. Björnsson graduated from **Menntaskólinn í Reykjavík** in 1900 and received a law degree from the University of Copenhagen in 1907. He practiced law in **Reykjavík** from 1907 to 1920, when he became the first Icelandic ambassador to **Denmark**. Björnsson returned to Iceland in 1924, but in 1926, he was reappointed to his former post in Copenhagen. He held this office until 1941, but as German forces occupied Denmark in 1940, he was summoned to Iceland to advise the Icelandic government on foreign affairs (*see* FOREIGN POLICY). The following year, **Alþingi elected** Björnsson *ríkisstjóri* (governor of Iceland), but this was an interim office created to substitute for the functions of the **king** during the war. When Iceland became an independent republic in 1944, Alþingi elected him Iceland's first president. Björnsson ran unopposed in 1948, but he died in 1952 when his second term was coming to an end. For the most part, Björnsson played the same role in Icelandic politics as the Danish king had before; the presidency was designed as a ceremonial office in spite of the president's extensive formal authority. As governor, he raised some controversy, however, when he bypassed Alþingi in the formation of a nonpartisan government in 1942, and he wielded considerable power behind the scenes during his time as president. *See also* WORLD WAR II.

BLACK DEATH. *See* PLAGUE.

BÓNDI. It is difficult to translate the Icelandic word *bóndi* (pl. *bændur*) into English because the meaning of the word in the Icelandic **language** has changed through time and it also has very different connotations from similar words in English. In medieval texts, the word *bóndi* could best be translated as yeoman or franklin, that is a freeholder. Thus, at first the term involved some form of landownership, although etymologically, it means simply a tiller of the earth. In modern Icelandic, the word *bóndi* has lost all of its former reference to the landowning status and includes all persons that head farming households, as long as they either rent or own enough land to sustain a substantial number of farm animals. In this meaning, the word *bóndi* can either be translated as peasant or farmer, depending on the social status of the person in question and on his or her relationship to the market. Until recently, *bændur* formed the dominant class in Iceland, both in numbers and social prestige. In the mid-19th century, censuses classified around 80 percent of Icelandic men in their 40s as *bændur*, and they played an important role in parliamentary politics until the 20th century. In recent years, the influence of the farmers' class has been declining, both in **economic** and political terms, following the thorough **industrialization** and **urbanization** of Icelandic society. Thus, in 2007, only around 3.4 percent of the Icelandic working **population** was registered in **agriculture**. *See also* LABOR BONDAGE.

BOOK OF ICELANDERS. The *Íslendingabók* (*Book of Icelanders*) is a chronicle of Icelandic history, recording the story of Icelanders from the **Settlement Period** to the beginning of the 12th century. The author of the chronicle was **Ari Þorgilsson** "the Learned," who is thought to have written the book from 1122 to 1133. The *Book of Icelanders* recounts the history of the Icelandic settlement and the formation and structure of its legal system in the early 10th century. Þorgilsson, who was a **Catholic** priest, lays great emphasis on the **conversion to Christianity** of Iceland and the development of the Roman Catholic Church. The book had a great influence on the writing of history in medieval Iceland, both because it established the chronology of the early Icelandic history and because by using the native **language** rather than Latin, Þorgilsson set the tone for later chroniclers and authors of learned **literature** in Iceland. *See also BOOK OF SETTLEMENTS*; SAGAS.

BOOK OF SETTLEMENTS. The *Landnámabók* (*Book of Settlements*) is a description of the discovery and settlement of Iceland, giving accounts of around 430 settlers and their families. Its origin is unknown because it is not preserved in its original form. It is clear, however, that the first redaction of the *Book of Settlements* dates back to the early 12th century. Today, it is preserved in five redactions, three from the Middle Ages and two from the 17th century. The internal relationship of these redactions has been disputed among scholars; some have traced two of the oldest redactions to a lost version from the early 13th century, but this theory has been challenged by other specialists. Some scholars have also doubted the historical value of the *Book of Settlements*, interpreting it as an attempt by 12th-century chieftains to legitimize their **economic** power and social authority rather than as an accurate rendering of the settlement process. Whatever the origins of the *Book of Settlements* may be or the intentions of its creators, it is at least a testimony of a remarkable interest in the history of Iceland and of a desire to preserve it in written form for posterity. *See also BOOK OF ICELANDERS*; SAGAS; SETTLEMENT PERIOD.

BROADCASTING. The Ríkisútvarpið [Icelandic State Broadcasting Service (ISBS), or RÚV in Icelandic] started radio transmissions in **Reykjavík** in 1930. The state-owned company, which had a monopoly over all broadcasting in Iceland for decades, operated only this one radio channel until 1966. In that year, the ISBS added a television channel to its operations, and soon its emissions were received throughout the country.

The ISBS has played a major role in Icelandic cultural life since its foundation. Through its financial support, the Icelandic National Symphony Orchestra was founded in 1950, and its mission is to produce noncommercial cultural programs. For this reason the company continues to be state owned in spite of repeated calls for **privatization** in recent years because many believe that the private radio and television stations will not undertake these responsibilities.

If we do not count the American broadcasting service at the military base in **Keflavík**, the state company had a monopoly on the Icelandic broadcasting market until the mid-1980s, so the ISBS did not need to cater specifically to any particular consumer group. However, because of an increasing pressure for light entertainment, the company launched a new radio channel in 1983, which devotes most of its programs to popular music and talk shows. In 1985, **Alþingi** lifted the state monopoly on broadcasting, causing revolutionary changes in this field. Today, three companies compete in the Icelandic television market, and new technology has allowed viewers to receive satellite transmissions from an increasing number of international TV channels. The radio market has undergone similar changes since the diversification in 1985. Thus, in addition to two major companies (the ISBS and the 365, a private media company owned by **Baugur Group**, which operates three television and five radio channels), a number of small radio stations are now in operation in Iceland, catering mainly to special audiences. *See also* MUSIC.

– C –

CABINET. With the **home rule** of 1904, the office of the minister of Iceland was moved from Copenhagen to **Reykjavík**. To begin with, the government of Iceland had only one minister, who was formally a member of the **Danish** cabinet. In 1913, **Alþingi** passed a law permitting the formation of a cabinet of three ministers in Iceland, and the first such government was formed in 1917. Until **World War II**, all Icelandic cabinets consisted of three ministers, but since 1939, their number has grown to 10 to 12 ministers. From 1917 to 2007, Iceland has had 36 cabinets, with the average life of 2½ years each.

As a rule, Icelandic cabinets include ministers from two or more parliamentary parties, and the ministers are usually also representatives in Alþingi. The president of the cabinet, or the **prime minister**, receives his mandate from the **president** of the republic, but governments are, in fact, normally formed through negotiations between the leaders of the different **political parties**. The role of the president in the formation of cabinets is, therefore, in normal circumstances more symbolic than active.

CATHOLICISM. When Icelanders **converted to Christianity** around the year 1000, the country came under the influence of the Roman Catholic Church. For the next 550 years, Catholicism was the dominant faith in the country, until Evangelical **Lutheranism** replaced it as the hegemonic **religious** creed in Iceland around the mid-16th century.

Although Iceland formally became a Christian country almost overnight, Catholic dogma and institutions gained acceptance only gradually in the country. The first diocese in Iceland was established at **Skálholt**, a farm in southern Iceland, during the latter half of the 11th century and the second at **Hólar** in the north at the beginning of the 12th. At the end of the 11th century, the church ensured its financial independence as Gissur Ísleifsson, bishop at Skálholt, persuaded the various chieftains in the country to allow the church to collect tithes, which were divided between the various Catholic institutions. The first monastery in Iceland was founded at the farm of Þingeyri in Húnavatn County during the early 12th century, and in the late 12th and the 13th centuries, a few other monasteries and two convents were established in the country. These institutions became centers of learning in Iceland, and they played a pivotal role in the forming of its medieval literary culture.

It is difficult to measure the influence of Catholicism on the daily life of medieval Icelanders. The old beliefs seem to have vanished fairly rapidly, however, and in the 12th century, the church had already become a relatively powerful institution in Iceland. The relations between the lay elite and the church were often tense, as the church demanded greater moral and political authority than the chieftains were ready to grant; these debates were settled for the most part in the late 13th century by the intervention of the **Norwegian king** and the archbishop in Niðarós (Trondheim), Norway.

In 1550, with the execution of **Jón Arason**, the last medieval Catholic bishop in Iceland, Catholicism was totally eradicated from the country and the state-induced Lutheran **Reformation** completed. It was only in the late 19th century that it reemerged through the missionary work of a few Catholic priests who had the primary task of serving French and Belgian fishermen working the Icelandic waters. The Catholic Church has been fairly active in Iceland for the last century, although the Catholic congregation in Iceland is very small. It ran three hospitals in Iceland for a time in the 20th century, operates a private elementary school in **Reykjavík**, and maintains a cathedral in Reykjavík. The number of Catholics in Iceland has been rising in the last decade, from 0.9 percent of the **population** in 1990 to 2.6 percent in 2007. The main reason for this is the surge in immigration in recent years, mostly from Catholic countries like Poland and the Philippines.

On 14 January 1985, Pope John Paul II declared Þorlákur Þórhallsson, bishop in Skálholt from 1178 to 1193, the guardian saint of the Icelandic nation.

CENSUSES. The first complete census of the Icelandic **population** was made in 1703, listing all inhabitants of the country by name, place of residence, age, and status. This is an invaluable source for demographic studies in Iceland and is, in fact, the oldest census of this type in the world that exists for the total population of a whole country. Two more censuses were taken in the 18th century, one in 1769 and another in 1785. The first census of the 19th century was taken in 1801, but it is only from 1835 that the administration conducted censuses on a regular basis in Iceland, at first every five years but from 1860 at the beginning of every decade. This practice continued until 1960, when other statistical information made the censuses unnecessary. The last complete census in Iceland was taken in 1981. *See also* STATISTICAL BUREAU OF ICELAND (SBI).

CENTRAL BANK OF ICELAND. *See* CENTRAL BANKING.

CENTRAL BANKING. The central **banking** function in Iceland was first established with the founding of Íslandsbanki, the Bank of Iceland, in 1904, but until then, the notes of the **Danish** National

Bank had been legal tender in Iceland (in addition to a very limited note issue of the **National Bank of Iceland** [NBI] since 1886). That **Alþingi** granted the Bank of Iceland a monopoly on note issuing—the license was for 30 years—was a remarkable decision, in light of the fact that it was a private bank under foreign ownership established at the zenith of Icelandic **nationalism**. The overriding concern at that time, however, was to provide the Icelandic **economy** with a separate money supply and, more importantly, its capital-hungry sectors with greatly increased access to capital. Opposition to the bank mounted during **World War I**, due primarily to its money-printing and relaxed lending policies, which contributed significantly to pushing **inflation** to a level far above that of other European countries. In 1921, Alþingi curtailed the bank's money-issuing rights, and its notes were to be phased out until its privilege expired in 1933, although it did not come into effect until 1939. The issue of **currency** was transferred to the NBI in 1927, which set up a separate department to perform the central banking functions in 1928. In 1957, a special management was set up for the central banking department, and three years later, ties with the NBI were fully severed. The Seðlabanki Íslands [Central Bank of Iceland (CBI)] was founded in 1961 and replaced the old department at the NBI.

The CBI is an independent state-owned institution administrated by a Board of Governors, with three members appointed by the prime minister and a seven-member supervisory board **elected** by Alþingi. In addition to its primary function of issuing bank notes and coins, CBI preserves and monitors the foreign reserves of the nation and registers the official exchange value of the *króna* once every day, which is used in public contracts. By a law of 1992, the bank was authorized to let the exchange rate of the *króna* be determined in a foreign exchange market, paving the way for exchange rate policy independent of direct government control. Thus the CBI acts as the government's bank, but it serves as its financial adviser as well. Moreover, it supervises other banking institutions and is able to influence directly their volume of lending by prescribing reserve requirements.

Since the 1980s, the CBI has gradually acquired more independence vis-à-vis the government, although it is required by law to support the economic policy of the government. According to the laws of the CBI from 2001, its primary objective is to keep the inflation rate in Iceland in check through its influence on monetary policy and its control over interest rates. The target is to keep the inflation rate below 2.5 percent, but this has proved to be difficult in the volatile Icelandic economy. This has forced the bank to keep interest rates in Iceland unusually high in order to reduce spending and thus slow down inflation. These policies have been very controversial in Iceland because they have not been particularly effective as can be seen from the fact that inflation continues to be substantially higher in Iceland than it is in neighboring countries.

CHIEFTAIN. *See GOÐI.*

CHRISTIANITY. *See* CONVERSION TO CHRISTIANITY.

CITIZENS' PARTY. Two political organizations in Iceland have carried the name Borgaraflokkur or the Citizens' Party. The first was a short-lived alliance of political groups to the right, formed before **elections** to **Alþingi** in 1923. Following its electoral success, the party dissolved, with the majority forming the **Conservative Party** the following year. Most of the people behind the Citizens' Party came together again in 1929 to form the **Independence Party** (IP).

Albert Guðmundsson, a former minister of finance for the IP, founded the second Citizens' Party in 1987. This was a response to the decision of the leadership of the IP to force him to resign his ministerial post because of alleged tax evasion. The Citizens' Party was remarkably successful in the parliamentary elections of 1987, polling 11 percent of the votes cast. After deciding to participate in a coalition government of **political parties** to the left of center from 1989 to 1991, the party disintegrated, and it ceased to exist in 1991.

COAST GUARD. Iceland has never had any military service, and it was only with the foundation of the Icelandic Coast Guard in the 1920s that Icelanders took responsibility for the defense of their territorial waters. Until then, the **Danish** navy had patrolled the sea around Iceland, but the **Act of Union** of 1918 stipulated that the Icelandic state could take over this function when it chose to do so, either on its own or in cooperation with the Danish navy. The first step toward this goal was taken in 1920 when one coast guard vessel was bought by ship owners in the **Vestmanna Islands** as a private initiative. The purpose of this ship was to guard the Icelandic **fishing limits** and to serve as a rescue vessel for the islands' fishing fleet. Five years later, the Icelandic government bought its first gunboat for the same objective, starting operations the following year. The Danish navy continued, however, to play an important role in the Icelandic waters until the outbreak of **World War II**. In 1930, the coast guard was placed under the state-run shipping company (Skipaútgerð ríkisins), but it became an independent agency with its own director in 1952.

The Icelandic Coast Guard was of crucial importance during the so-called **cod wars** of the 1950s, 1960s, and 1970s. During these episodes, its gunboats harassed the trawlers that did not respect Icelandic fishing limits. Today, the coast guard continues to police the sea around Iceland, and it also performs important rescue services inside and outside Icelandic territorial waters.

In spite of its important tasks, the fleet of the coast guard has always been small. At the height of the last cod war, it operated seven patrol boats, but they are down to three at present. The coast guard also owns one aircraft and operates three helicopters. *See also* DEFENSE.

COD WARS. The Icelandic fishing banks have attracted European fishermen for centuries, causing serious frictions over fishing rights between Icelandic authorities and the foreign "intruders." In his study of the history of these confrontations, the Icelandic historian Björn Þorsteinsson counted as many as 10 cod wars from the Middle Ages to the 1970s, in all of which British fishermen have played a prominent part. The first five of these disputes took place from 1415 to 1532, as the **Danish** monarchy sought to establish control over the government and trade in Iceland. For Icelanders, the main objective in this period was not so much to defend the Icelandic fishing banks as to prevent the foreign fishermen from establishing permanent stations in Iceland because many feared that they would unsettle the domestic social and **economic** system.

The modern cod wars have all been fought over the extension and protection of the Icelandic **fishing limits**. The primary cause for them all was the fact that new fishing techniques made it increasingly undesirable for Icelanders to allow free access to the fishing grounds around the country. The first of the modern cod wars took place at the end of the 19th century when the British government sent a small squadron to Iceland to investigate alleged encroachment upon the liberties of British trawlers around the Icelandic coast. This episode ended in 1901, when the Danish and British governments signed a treaty granting British trawlers permission to fish anywhere they desired outside the three–nautical-miles zone around the Icelandic coast.

From 1952 to 1975, the Icelandic government extended the fishing limits unilaterally from 3 to 200 nautical miles in four steps, basing their actions on the Continental Shelf Act of 1948. Various nations contested these extensions, but no government reacted as forcefully as the British. By sending a fleet to protect their trawlers from the harassment of the Icelandic **Coast Guard**, and by economic pressure, the British government tried to force Icelanders to change their position, failing on all four occasions. The last cod war ended in 1976 with a treaty between Iceland and **Great Britain**, where the latter acknowledged the 200-mile fishing limits around Iceland. *See also* FISHERIES.

COLD WAR. Until **World War II**, Iceland was fairly isolated and did not play any major role on the international scene. This changed drastically as the **United States** became more involved in European affairs because of Iceland's strategic location in the middle of the North Atlantic Ocean. All movements in air and sea between North America and Europe can be monitored from Iceland, which is crucial for controlling communications between the two continents and thus in defending the United States from a possible attack from Europe. In 1941, a few months before the United States became an official participant in the Second World War, the American military came to Iceland through a **defense** treaty with the Icelandic government. At the end of the war, the U.S. military wanted to maintain its presence in the country, but this request was turned down. As the cold war heated up, however, Iceland took a clear stand with the United States and its allies in Europe. Iceland was, for example, one of the founding members of the **North Atlantic Treaty Organization** (NATO) in 1949, and in 1951, it struck a new defense agreement with the United

States. The same year, American forces returned to Iceland, opening a military base in **Keflavík** under the auspices of NATO.

Iceland's relations to the United States were among the most divisive issues in Icelandic politics during much of the second half of the 20th century. The American base in Keflavík was viewed by many as an assault on Icelandic national sovereignty and the alliance with the United States as an undesirable departure from the neutrality policies advocated in Iceland since the country became a sovereign state in 1918. The supporters of the alliance with the United States pointed out, however, that during the cold war, neutrality was not an option, as this would only play into the hands of the nemesis of the United States, the Soviet Union.

With the end of the cold war around 1990, the attention of the United States turned away from Europe, focusing more closely on the Middle East and terrorism. As a result, the strategic importance of Iceland declined, and consequently, Washington lost interest in maintaining its military presence in Iceland. Thus, the United States withdrew most of its forces from Iceland during the 1990s, closing down the Keflavík base in 2006. *See also* REYKJAVÍK SUMMIT.

COMMONWEALTH PERIOD. The most common term for the period in Icelandic history from the foundation of **Alþingi** around the year 930 until the passing of the **Old Covenant** (1262–64) is the Commonwealth Period, or þjóðveldisöld in Icelandic; the term is sometimes translated as the "Free State Period." This was culturally a very productive period but politically a turbulent one. Thus, most of the great works of Icelandic medieval **literature** were written during the latter half of the Commonwealth Period, from the historical chronicles of the early 12th century to the family **sagas** and contemporary sagas of the 13th.

A growing struggle between various clans for political hegemony in Iceland marks the history of this period. With the foundation of Alþingi, the country was given a unified law code, but the absence of an executive branch for the whole country fueled open warfare in Iceland, primarily in the 13th century. In the beginning, the population was divided into 36 to 39 chieftaincies (*goðorð; see* GOÐI) of equal status, but later, the most powerful magnates appropriated many such chieftaincies and governed large regions by the force of their wealth and power. During the last part of the Commonwealth Period, or the **Age of the Sturlungs**, the country plunged into almost total chaos, bringing some of the leading families in Iceland toward extinction. Hence, Icelanders pledged allegiance to the **Norwegian king** and paid taxes in return for pacification of the country. The Commonwealth Period ended when Icelanders accepted a union with Norway in 1262–64. *See also GRÁGÁS; JÓNSBOK; STURLUNGA SAGA.*

COMMUNE. The traditional term for a local commune in Iceland is *hreppur.* The origin of communes is unclear, but they seem to have been founded early in the **Commonwealth Period.** From the beginning, the main function of communes was to administrate the poor relief and organize common tasks of the peasant **economy**, like collecting sheep from the mountain pastures in the fall. Originally, communes were independent entities, governed by *hreppstjórar* (overseers) and **elected** by the taxpaying peasants from their own ranks. When the monarchy grew stronger after the end of the Middle Ages, the **king** began to assume more command over the local government. Thus, bailiffs selected the overseers, for the most part, after the end of the Middle Ages. In the early 19th century, the overseers virtually became state officials, although they received no salaries from the king. At the same time, their number was reduced from three to five to one or two in each commune; the law stipulated that they should be appointed by the bailiffs and the district governors.

During the last 125 years, the system of local government has gone through radical changes, reflecting the general social and political development of the country. In 1872, new legislation established democratically elected local councils in the communes, while it separated the administrative functions of the overseer from the government of the commune. This has made the communal governments more responsive to the needs of its inhabitants, and now they play important roles in the administration of local issues, such as **education**, leisure activities, communications, power supply, and support for local businesses. Above all, however, the demographic evolution of the last century transformed the communes in Iceland. Thus, in the second half of the 20th century, some of the smallest communes had fewer inhabitants than ever before, a number of them with less than 100 inhabitants, while the **population** of the most populous commune,

Reykjavík, is now almost double that of the whole country in 1850. For this reason, the state has promoted a reduction in the number of communes in Iceland in order to strengthen their ability to deal with the various administrative tasks of modern society. The transfer of all public elementary schools from the state to the local communes in 1996 was a major reason for this development, as the smallest communes were unable to offer their inhabitants the services they require. Although this effort to consolidate the communes has met considerable opposition, as the traditional municipal divisions have a strong sentimental value in Iceland, the number of local communes has decreased drastically in recent years, dropping from a total number of municipalities of 229 in 1950 to 204 in 1990, 105 in 2002, and 79 in 2007. *See also* COUNTY.

COMMUNIST PARTY OF ICELAND (CPI). After **World War I** and the Bolshevik Revolution in Russia in 1917, there was a growing sympathy for revolutionary Marxism among Icelandic **Social Democrats**. Under the chairmanship of **Jón Baldvinsson**, the **Icelandic Federation of Labor** and the Social Democratic Party (SDP) exerted a strong opposition to these ideas. As soon as 1922, the **Social Democratic** Association in **Reykjavík** split into two factions, one of which espoused a revolutionary line, while the other remained loyal to the moderate opinions of the SDP. The two factions differed on a number of issues, most of which were typical of the rift between Social Democratic and Communist parties in Europe in the interwar period. Thus, Communists in the SDP opposed entrance into the international movement of Social Democrats, the moderate Labor and Socialist International. Domestic politics also caused dissension in the SDP, for the radical members of the SDP opposed the party's cooperation with the "bourgeois" government of the **Progressive Party**, formed during the summer of 1927. In the end, no compromise was possible between the two wings of the SDP, and in 1930, splinter groups from the SDP and other radicals formed the CPI (Kommúnistaflokkur Íslands), advocating a Marxist revolution. The party received only limited support in the beginning, just 3 percent of the votes cast in 1931, but its following increased rapidly during the **Great Depression**. Thus, the party received 7.5 percent of the votes in the parliamentary **elections** of

1933 and 8.5 percent in 1937. In the 1937 elections, the last elections in which the CPI took part under its original name, the party had its first three representatives elected to parliament. In 1938, the CPI was dissolved to form a new party with a splinter group from the SDP called the **Socialist Unity Party**. This was in accordance with the resolutions of the Communist International (Comintern) congress of 1935, which called for a united front against fascism in Iceland. *See also* OLGEIRSSON, EINAR (1902–93); VALDIMARSSON, HÉÐINN (1892–1948).

CONFEDERATION OF ICELANDIC EMPLOYERS. *See* SA-CONFEDERATION OF ICELANDIC EMPLOYERS (SA-CIE).

CONSERVATIVE PARTY (CP). A group of 20 representatives in **Alþingi** formed the CP (Íhaldsflokkur) on 24 February 1924. A strong belief in free enterprise characterized the party platform, and its objective was both to reduce and to balance the state budget. Less than a month after its foundation, the CP formed a **cabinet**, pursuing its agenda with vigor for the next three years. The government lost its majority in the parliamentary **elections** of 1927, although the CP retained its position as the largest **political party** in the country, receiving 42 percent of the votes cast. But as the electoral system favored the rural constituencies, the **Progressive Party** won more seats in parliament than the CP. In 1929, the CP coalesced with the small **Liberal Party** to form the **Independence Party** (IP). **Jón Þorláksson**, who had served as chairman of the CP from its foundation, became the first leader of the IP in 1929.

CONSTITUTION OF 1874. In 1874, the **Danish king** "gave" Iceland its first constitution, the same year the Icelandic nation commemorated the 1,000th anniversary of the settlement of Iceland. This came after a long tug-of-war between the Danish government and Icelandic representatives in **Alþingi**, as the two parties could not come to an agreement on how to arrange the union between Iceland and Denmark or how the public finances of Iceland should be arranged. The constitution of 1874 awarded Alþingi limited legislative power and full sovereignty over the Icelandic budget. The king, however, had absolute power to veto all legislation passed in the parliament — a prerogative he used frequently during the next decades—and total control over the executive branch of government in Iceland. As before, Iceland did not elect representatives to the Danish legislature, and it had, therefore, no influence on the government of the Danish state. For this reason, the constitution of 1874 did not subject Icelanders to general state taxes or require them to serve in the Danish military.

The constitution of 1874 was accepted with great reluctance in Iceland and caused fierce debates during the following decades, primarily because it confirmed the hated **Status Law** set in 1871 and did not provide for any independent executive branch under the control of Alþingi. Two major amendments corrected these shortcomings—one in 1902–4 and another in 1918–20. The first of these revisions granted Iceland **home rule**, which came into effect in 1904. The second came as a result of the **Act of Union** in 1918, which gave Iceland the status of a sovereign nation-state. Another major amendment, which was enacted in 1915, granted **women** a limited right to vote in parliamentary **elections**.

In spite of its shortcomings, the constitution of 1874 remains the basis for civil government and human rights in Iceland, and many of its provisions are still valid. It was based on a firm belief in the importance of personal liberties, freedom of expression, **religious** liberty, and democratic representation in parliament. Thus, it endorsed the principles of democracy as they were defined during the late 19th century, building upon the political traditions of Western Europe. *See also* CONSTITUTION OF 1944.

CONSTITUTION OF 1944. After total severance from **Denmark**, the **Republic of Iceland** was established on 17 June 1944. As a result, a new constitution had to be passed in order to define the functions and role of the office of **president**. The authors of the constitution opted for a weak presidency, while public authority was vested primarily in government and parliament, to which the executive branch is responsible. Except for the provisions of the presidency, the constitution of 1944 closely followed the example of earlier constitutions, building on traditions set during Danish rule. Since its introduction, **Alþingi** has made a few minor amendments to the constitution, most of which concern parliamentary **elections**, the division of the country into electoral districts, and the structure of Alþingi. The section on human rights in the constitution has also been changed to conform with the general trends in international law. *See also* CONSTITUTION OF 1874; WORLD WAR II.

CONSTITUTIVE ASSEMBLY. In 1848, **King** Frederick VII of **Denmark** renounced his absolute power in the Danish monarchy and convened a democratically **elected** constitutive assembly to write a constitution for the state. The same year, after receiving numerous petitions from Iceland, the king promised Icelanders that the constitution would not come into force in Iceland until they had deliberated on the matter in a constitutive assembly of their own. Elections for the assembly were held in the summer of 1850, but the meeting itself was held in **Reykjavík** from 4 July to 9 August the following year.

The promise of a special constitutive assembly (Þjóðfundur, or Assembly of the Nation) kindled high hopes in Iceland, and many expected that the new constitution would grant Iceland virtual autonomy in its domestic affairs. At the assembly, the great majority of the Icelandic representatives, under the leadership of the emerging leader of Icelandic **nationalism, Jón Sigurðsson**, adhered firmly to this opinion. However, according to the royal bill presented to the assembly, Iceland was to become an integral part of the new democratic Danish state; Icelanders were to elect representatives to the Danish parliament, and **Alþingi** was to serve the same purpose as other regional councils (*amtsråd* in Danish) in the monarchy. As the two sides could find no middle ground, the Danish governor of Iceland dissolved the assembly before the representatives had reached any conclusion.

As the constitutive assembly ended in an impasse, Iceland remained effectively under Danish **absolutism** until King Christian IX granted the country its own **constitution in 1874**. For Icelanders, the assembly was not without significance, however, because it forced them to consider their status in the state. Their conclusion was unequivocal; in the long run, nothing short of full sovereignty would be accepted. This set the tone for Icelandic politics for the next decades, and until the **Act of Union** of 1918, fervent nationalism dominated the Icelandic political discourse. *See also* HOME RULE; ICELANDIC NATIONALIST MOVEMENT.

CONVERSION TO CHRISTIANITY. Until the late 10th century, Icelanders practiced the old Germanic pagan **religion**, worshipping Norse deities like Odin and Thor (Óðinn and Þór in Old Norse). During the last two decades of the 10th century, an organized Christianizing effort began in Iceland. This was part of an undertaking directed from Germany to convert the Scandinavian countries to the Christian faith. Icelanders had come into earlier contact with Christianity, as some of the settlers had been converted in the British Isles before coming to Iceland. No organized Christian congregation existed in the country, however, before the end of the first millennium.

The early Christian missionaries met with only limited success, although they were able to convert some influential chieftains to their religion. But in the summer of 999 or 1000, two missionaries came to **Alþingi** with direct orders from Ólafur Tryggvason, **king** of **Norway**, to Christianize the Icelandic population. According to the *Book of Icelanders*, this split the men gathered in Alþingi into two religious camps, but after careful consideration, the leader of the non-Christian group encouraged those present to accept the Christian faith and to abandon the old religion. This was a pragmatic decision made to preserve peace in the country because many feared that a religious split would result in a civil war. Therefore, the new religious settlement took a realistic approach, allowing Icelanders to continue to practice their old religion in secret. Formally, however, from the time of the conversion, the Christian faith was to be the sole religion recognized in the country, and by the mid-11th century, it was firmly entrenched in Icelandic society. *See also* CATHOLICISM; LUTHERANISM.

COOPERATIVE MOVEMENT. The Icelandic cooperative movement has its roots in Þingey **County** in northeastern Iceland, where the first cooperative society was founded in 1882. Following the example of similar **farmers' associations** that were organized in many regions of Iceland during the 19th century, the first cooperative society was to coordinate the trade of farmers in the district with the purpose of increasing the market value of their products and lowering the prices of the goods they had to purchase. During the last decades of the 19th century, a number of such societies were founded in Iceland, especially in its northern part. One of the incentives for this development was a growing prosperity brought to this part of the country by an active trade in live sheep that were exported directly to Britain in the late 19th century. In 1902, a precursor of the Samband íslenskra samvinnufélaga (Federation of Icelandic Cooperative Societies), commonly known in Iceland by its acronym SÍS, was founded in Þingey County as three local cooperatives joined their forces. During the next decade, a number of cooperative societies in the northeast entered the federation, but this was a time of rapid expansion of the cooperative movement in general. Moreover, its influence grew drastically during **World War I**, especially because the foundation of the **Progressive Party** in 1917 gained it a powerful political ally in parliament.

In 1917, the federation moved its headquarters from **Akureyri** to **Reykjavík**, where in the next few years, it built up one of the largest commercial enterprises in Iceland. Thus, the federation acquired a dominant position in trade with farmers in Iceland, acting both as a wholesale importer for the many cooperative societies around the country and as an exporter of the goods that the farmers produced.

The prosperity of the cooperative movement continued in the years following **World War II**. Its political connections and the loyalty of its members secured the movement a strong position in a strictly regulated market. Thus, the federation moved into new spheres of operation, such as importing cars and machines and exporting fish, in addition to owning totally or a large number of shares in a bank, the largest insurance company in Iceland, a merchant shipping company, and the largest oil-distribution company in Iceland.

In the late 1980s, this **economic** giant hit hard times. Heavy debts at a time of drastic rise in interest rates caused this crisis, a problem that was heightened by the grave difficulties in **agriculture** at the time. Moreover, because of its social mission and complex structure, it was impossible for the movement to respond to these economic challenges. For this reason, the federation was more or less dissolved at the beginning of the 1990s, as it split into a number of independent holding companies. By the turn of the 21st century, the last vestiges of the cooperative movement had disappeared, and with it died the vision of creating an economic alternative to both capitalism and socialism.

COUNTY. The traditional administrative and juridical district in Iceland is the *sýsla*, or county. The term itself was first used in *Jóns-*

bók, the code of law enacted in 1281, but it was only at the close of the Middle Ages that the geographical division of the country into counties was finalized. In each county there was a *sýslumaður* (bailiff) who served as district judge, sheriff, and representative of the **king** in the county. The office of bailiff was, therefore, one of the most important administrative posts in Iceland because the bailiffs were often the only royal officials in their respective districts.

With growing centralization and **urbanization** in Iceland, the authority of the bailiffs changed. It was only, however, with a new legislation passed in 1989, which came into effect in 1992, that the legal foundation of the office was transformed with a total separation of the judicial and executive branches in the local districts. Thus, the old counties were formally abolished, although they live on in people's daily speech. With the new law, the country was divided into eight judicial districts, each served by a district court. At the same time, the function of the bailiffs was restricted to serving the executive branch; they collect taxes and head the district police.

Iceland's division into counties did not change much through the centuries, although the subdivision of the larger districts varied through time. At the time of the 1992 reform, Iceland was divided into 23 counties, which were administrated by 18 bailiffs. With the reform, the office of *bæjarfógeti* (town magistrate) was abolished, and they received the same title as the *sýslumaður* (bailiffs). At present, there are 26 bailiffs in Iceland. *See also* COMMUNE.

CURRENCY. The Icelandic monetary unit is *króna* (pl. *krónur*; the international currency code is ISK), which is divided into 100 *aurar* (sing. *eyrir*). As **Danish** currency laws applied to Iceland during the 19th century, the *króna* replaced the old *rigsbankdal* in 1873, as it did in the Danish state in general. It was related to gold, and the value was fixed at one *króna* being equal to 0.4032258 grams of fine gold. After the suspension of the gold standard in 1914, the *króna* followed the fluctuations of the Danish *krone* until 1920, when it was depreciated in order to correct the effects of high **inflation** during and after **World War I**. It was not until 1922 that banks officially acknowledged the new rate, and the Icelandic *króna* could be said to have gained independent status.

Persistent high inflation after 1960 led to a rapid depreciation of the *króna*. On 1 January 1981, a comprehensive currency reform came into effect, including the multiplication of the value of the *króna* by 100, so that 1 new *króna* became the equivalent of 100 old *krónur*. At the same time, a new set of notes and coins replaced the old one. Much lower inflation at the end of the 1980s and in the first half of the 1990s raised hopes of the currency becoming more stable than it had been for most of the postwar period. This has, at least partially, been the case, as the *króna* has held its ground to other currencies in recent years, but the exchange rate has continued to fluctuate greatly. Thus, US$1 sold for 73 ISK in January 1998. It reached 108 ISK in November 2001 but it fluctuated between 58 and 83 ISK in the period from the beginning of 2003 to the end of 2007. These fluctuations reflect the small size of the Icelandic **economy** and its vulnerability to internal and external changes. For this reason, and because of the more intense participation of Icelandic financial institutions in the international markets, many politicians and businesspeople have advocated that the *króna* be replaced by a stronger currency, particularly the euro. *See also* BANKING; CENTRAL BANKING.

– D –

DEFENSE. Through much of their history, Icelanders have not felt a great need for organized defense against foreign invasion. Because of its location as an island in the mid–North Atlantic, the country was difficult to reach for hostile forces. Moreover, the fact that the island is both fairly large and has always been sparsely populated made it almost impossible for Icelandic authorities to organize an effective military force to defend the whole country against foreign invasion. When Iceland entered the **Norwegian** monarchy in 1262–64, the first concern was not to defend the country from outside attack but to quell the civil war that had ravaged it for decades. Rather than building up royal military force to subdue the warring chieftains, the **king** chose to disarm them and their clans. This policy took centuries to implement, but gradually, Icelanders became unaccustomed to carrying arms, and therefore they have no tradition of serving in armed forces of any kind.

This meant that Icelanders did little to prepare themselves for possible invasions. The policy was, for the most part, successful, as until **World War II**, Iceland was only seriously threatened twice from the outside. This happened first in 1627, during the **Raid of the "Turks,"** and the second time during the **Icelandic Revolution** of 1809. Everything changed, however, with the Second World War and the **cold war**. At that time, revolutionary progress in transportation technology had broken the country's isolation, and the growing involvement of the **United States** in European affairs had increased Iceland's strategic importance. Thus, British forces occupied Iceland in 1940 in order to prevent the Germans from taking the country because a German occupation of Iceland would have disrupted all communications between North America and Europe. In 1941, the government of Iceland signed a defense treaty with the United States, and for the remainder of the war, American forces secured the Icelandic defenses.

In 1918, when Iceland became a sovereign state, everyone agreed that the country should stay neutral in international military conflicts, believing that this policy of neutrality would suffice as a defensive shield for the country. After World War II and the beginning of the cold war, many believed that neutrality was untenable, as the two superpowers, the United States and the Soviet Union, were locked in a global struggle that involved the whole world. The Icelandic authorities decided, therefore, first to enter the **North Atlantic Treaty Organization** (NATO) in 1949 and, second, to sign a new defense treaty with the United States in 1951. In May of the same year, U.S. forces returned, establishing a military base close to the town of **Keflavík** on the southwest coast of Iceland. From then on, Iceland was firmly in the American camp for the remainder of the cold war.

Until the end of the cold war, the base in Keflavík was very important for NATO operations in the North Atlantic. With the dissolution of the Soviet Union and a growing threat from terrorism, Washington lost interest in Iceland and the Keflavík military base. Thus, the last American soldier left Iceland in 2006, and the base was closed down. The U.S. government still guarantees Icelandic security, but it does not maintain any military presence in Iceland, and there are doubts if this is sufficient in times of global terrorism. Thus Iceland has been forced to reevaluate its defense strategies. The issue is still unsolved, but as there does not seem to be any interest in Iceland to build up a domestic armed force of any kind, it has no alternative other than to seek protection from a friendly ally.

DENMARK. The long Danish rule over Iceland began in 1380 when **Norway** became a Danish dependency following a merger of the royal houses of the two monarchies. From that time until the foundation of the **Republic of Iceland** in 1944, Iceland was tied to Denmark and its **king**.

Because of Iceland's peripheral location, the union with Denmark had little immediate influence on the Icelandic social and political system. With the **Lutheran Reformation**, which was completed in 1550, the Danish state demonstrated that it could force a drastic change against the determined opposition of its Icelandic subjects. In the 17th century, the monarchy increased its power in Iceland considerably, first with the introduction of the hated **monopoly trade** in 1602 and then with the establishment of Danish **absolutism** in Iceland in 1662. From that time until the granting of the first democratic constitution to Iceland in 1874, the Danish king totally controlled both the administrative and legislative processes, although in practice, he had to rely on the advice and information of his Icelandic officials for most of his decisions on Icelandic matters.

From the time of the **constitution of 1874** until the final severance of all ties with Denmark in 1944, various Icelandic institutions gradually took over most of the functions of the Danish king. The constitution gave **Alþingi** limited legislative power and total control over public finances in Iceland. With **home rule** in 1904, the executive power in Icelandic domestic affairs was moved from Copenhagen to **Reykjavík**, and from 1918 to 1944, the king held only a symbolic authority in Icelandic affairs.

The Icelandic population seemed to be generally content with Danish rule for most of the half millennium it lasted. One reason for this was the fact that the king usually demanded little from his Icelandic subjects; royal taxes were light, and the Danish king never required Icelanders to serve as soldiers in his army. Moreover, most officials in Iceland, except for the governor, were Icelanders, and for that reason, Icelandic was the official **language** in both church and courts. With the growing **nationalist** sentiments of the 19th century, the union with Denmark became more onerous in the eyes of many leading Icelandic politicians, and the **Constitutive Assembly** of 1851 rejected Iceland's inclusion in the emerging Danish nation-state. After that, the nationalists based their demands on claims of past injustice by the Danish government, creating widespread anti-Danish sentiment in Iceland.

The generous terms of Icelandic independence and sympathy for Icelandic nationalism in Denmark have almost totally healed all grudges toward the former mother country. Today, Iceland has strong cultural ties with Denmark, and the Danish language is still an obligatory subject in Icelandic elementary and secondary schools. Through the **Nordic Council** and numerous other formal and informal cooperative ventures, Iceland and Denmark have maintained strong links in spite of their political separation in 1944. *See also* ACT OF UNION; THE DRAFT; ICELANDIC NATIONALIST MOVEMENT; STATUS LAW.

DIRECTORATE OF FISHERIES. A government agency under the Ministry of **Fisheries** that was created in 1992 to implement laws and regulations regarding fisheries and fish processing in Iceland. The function of the directorate (Fiskistofa) is to ensure effective administration and organization of **fisheries management** and supervision of the fishing **industry** in Iceland. In this capacity, the directorate determines the annual fishing quotas for all fishing vessels in Iceland, controls the transfer of such quotas between ships, imposes penalties for illegal catches, collects information on each vessel's landings, publishes and gathers statistics on the fishing industry, and supervises monitoring onboard fishing vessels and in the various fishing ports in Iceland. Moreover, the directorate issues licenses for fishing plants and oversees their production. The directorate plays a pivotal role in the development of the Icelandic fishing industry and, consequently, in the **economy** in general. *See also* MARINE RESEARCH INSTITUTE (MRI).

DISTRICT GOVERNOR. *See AMTMAÐUR.*

THE DRAFT. The politics of the **Home Rule Period** (1904–18) were marked by the efforts of the **Danish** and Icelandic parliaments to reach an agreement on how to restructure the relationship between the two countries. Icelanders had always disputed the **Status Law** of 1871, which defined Iceland's position in the Danish monarchy, in part because the Danish parliament had passed the statute without the consent of **Alþingi**. In 1908, a committee of Danish and Icelandic parliamentary representatives wrote a draft for new legislation on the issue, which was to be discussed in the two parliaments. The **king** dissolved Alþingi in the spring of 1908 because a new parliament was to vote on the bill. In the most heated **electoral** campaigns in Icelandic history, the opponents of the Draft won a clear victory in the fall of 1908, leading to the defeat of the bill in parliament the following year.

The debates on the Draft in 1908 set the course for Icelandic politics in the following decade. First, they led to a reorganization of the Icelandic **political party** system, as new political alliances were formed on the basis of people's opinions of the Draft. Second, they helped to define the ultimate goal of Icelandic politics; that is, anything short of full sovereignty was deemed to be insufficient. In the end, the Danish parliament accepted this fact, and with the **Act of Union** in 1918, Icelandic sovereignty was fully recognized. *See also* NATIONALISM; THORODDSEN, SKÚLI (1859–1916).

– E –

ECONOMY. At the turn of the 20th century, Iceland was one of the poorest countries in Europe, with a per-capita gross domestic product (GDP) around one half of the average in Western Europe. At that time, **agriculture** was still the dominant economic sector in Iceland, as it had been from the country's settlement. Around two thirds of the Icelandic **population** earned its living from agriculture in 1901, and only 20 percent lived in villages or towns with more than 200 inhabitants. The last half of the 19th century was, however, a period of slow but perceptible change. The most obvious sign of things to come was the relative decline in agriculture, first in its share of the labor force but, from the 1880s, also in the absolute numbers of people employed in the sector. This reflected two things. First, Icelandic agriculture had reached its limit around 1880, not in terms of production, which continued to increase through much of the 20th century, but rather in the number of people it could employ. Thus, as the population continued to grow, people had to seek work elsewhere, which meant that many immigrated to America while others moved toward the burgeoning villages on the coast. Second, the **fisheries** began to take off around the turn of the 20th century, but until then, they had primarily served as a subsidiary activity to agriculture.

These tendencies continued in the years leading up to **World War I**, when the Icelandic economy modernized at a very fast pace. This happened primarily through the mechanization of the fishing industry, as motors were put into boats and trawlers were imported. The towns grew very rapidly during these years, with the capital, **Reykjavík**, leading the way. This **industrialization** revolutionized the Icelandic economic and social structures, and a new urban working class emerged at one end of the social spectrum, while the new wealth created a group of well-off capitalists at the other end. The per-capita GDP grew rapidly during these years, doubling between 1870 and 1913. With industrialization and **urbanization** came other signs of modernity in Iceland; the first bank in the country, the **National Bank of Iceland**, was founded in 1886, but a foreign-owned bank, Bank of Iceland, injected a large amount of capital into the economy after it was opened in 1904.

It was not until **World War II**, however, that Iceland began to approach its neighboring countries in wealth. In 1938, Iceland was still the poorest of the Nordic countries in terms of per-capita GDP, but in 1945, it was second only to Sweden. During the war, Iceland's location helped its inhabitants in two respects; first, as an island in the mid-Atlantic, Iceland had not suffered the devastation that laid many European societies in ruins during the war, and second, because of its strategic location, Iceland became a major military hub for the Allied forces. In the short term, British and American forces brought with them work, solving the chronic unemployment (*see* EMPLOYMENT) that had plagued the Icelandic economy since the **Great Depression**, but in the long term, they connected the country to the outside world by transforming its **transportation** infrastructures — especially the airports. The war also contributed to the continued urbanization of Iceland, as much of the military activity took place in the urban areas. Thus, in 1945, Reykjavík had become a sizable urban center, with over 60,000 inhabitants (including the suburbs), and during the war, the number of people living in towns passed the number of rural dwellers for the first time in Iceland's history.

The post–World War II period was characterized by persistent instability and growing **inflation**. The root of the problem was the fact that the economy was totally reliant upon one sector, the fisheries, which generated over 90 percent of the export revenues for Iceland from the beginning of the Second World War into the mid-1960s, falling to around 75 percent in the mid-1990s. This was problematic not only because it made the economy totally reliant on one very volatile economic sector but also because the interests of the fisheries dictated the fiscal policy of the state. Rising labor costs and fluctuations in the fish catches and prices on the international markets were met with depreciation of the **currency**, the *króna*, which led to hyperinflation. These reactions solved the short-term problems of the fisheries but rendered all long-term economic planning impossible.

The Icelandic economy entered a new phase in the 1990s, with improved relations between employers and the **trade unions**, declining inflation, and a remarkable opening of the economic system. This turnaround happened through a combination of factors. The 1990s were a period of political stability and more responsible fiscal policies. The **European Economic Area** agreement with the **European Union** (EU) was also of crucial importance, as it opened access to a huge market and integrated the Icelandic economy more tightly into the European system. Finally, extensive **privatization** schemes provided new opportunities for Icelandic investors, and this has, in combination with a strong buildup of the **energy-intensive industries**, diversified the economy and made it less susceptible to the fluctuations on the international markets for fish products.

In many respects, the history of the Icelandic economy is a remarkable success story. The economic growth in the country has been unusually strong since the mid-1990s, and today, with an average per-capita GDP at current prices of almost US$63,000 (2007), Iceland is among the richest nations in the world. In spite of this apparent success, the Icelandic economy is still the smallest of the national economies of all the member states in the Organization of Economic Cooperation and Development (OECD), with a total GDP of just over US$16 billion. It continues, therefore, to be extremely volatile, as an expansion or slowdown in one important economic sector is felt throughout the whole system. For this reason, many analysts advocate even tighter integration with Europe, maintaining that the only way of securing more stability in the future is to adopt the EU currency, the euro. *See also* BANKING; CENTRAL BANKING; ENERGY; INDUSTRY; TOURISM; TRADE, FOREIGN.

EDDIC POETRY. A term used for one of the two main categories of Old Norse poetry (the other is **skaldic poetry**). The two major genres of Eddic poetry are mythical poetry, such as *Hávamál* and *Völuspá*, and heroic poetry dealing with Old Germanic legends stemming from the time of struggles between Huns, Goths, and Germanic tribes in the fourth and fifth centuries. The former genre is specifically Nordic, serving as the best source available on Old Norse **religious** beliefs, while poems of the latter type are related to other Germanic poetry of this kind. The main source for Eddic poetry is one Icelandic manuscript, now preserved in the **Árni Magnússon Institute of Icelandic Studies** in **Reykjavík**, called *Codex Regius*, which dates from the late 13th century. The genesis of the poems preserved in this manuscript is, however, unknown. *See also* SAGAS.

EDUCATION. Until the late 19th century, primary education in Iceland was seen as the responsibility of every home, while it was the pastor's role to secure that all children in his parish were able to read at the time of their confirmation. This system seems to have worked reasonably well, as **literacy** was relatively high in Iceland in spite of the total absence of primary schools in the country until the second half of the 19th century. During the last decades of the 19th century, there was growing interest to improve public education in Iceland, and in 1880, pastors were instructed to teach the children in their parishes to read, write, and do rudimentary mathematics. The first comprehensive legislation on compulsory schooling in Iceland was passed in 1907, requiring most children of the ages 10 to 14 to attend school for a minimum of six months a year. This legislation reflected a profound transformation that took place in social and **economic** life during the late 19th and early 20th centuries because it was only with the growth of the fishing villages and towns around the coast that the foundation of elementary schools was thought to be necessary and, indeed, possible.

There is a much longer tradition of secondary education in Iceland, as its history can be traced back to the bishops' schools of **Skálholt** and **Hólar**, founded in the 11th and 12th centuries respectively. These schools were primarily **religious** seminaries, or Latin schools, preparing students to become servants of the church. At the beginning of the 19th century, the two Latin schools merged, moving permanently to **Reykjavík** from **Bessastaðir** in 1846. With the foundation of a theological college in Reykjavík in 1847, the Latin school in Reykjavík became a regular gymnasium, preparing its students for a university entrance exam. Gradually, increasing demands for professional education transformed the elite character of secondary education in Iceland, and in the 1920s, the secondary school in **Akureyri** received the right to prepare students for university studies. During the latter half of the 20th century, the secondary school system diversified greatly. Today over 30 institutions, spread around the country, have the right to offer university entrance exams, and a great majority of Icelanders now receive some form of secondary education.

The system of vocational and trade schools in Iceland has its origins in the late 19th century. A growing interest in economic progress led to the foundation of the first **agricultural** schools around 1880. In the next few decades, a number of vocational schools were founded—the Nautical School in Reykjavík in 1891, Reykjavík Trades' School in 1904, and the Commercial School of Iceland in 1904, to name a few examples. Finally, as a part of the school reform legislation of 1907, a teacher training college was founded in Reykjavík in the following year with the purpose of educating elementary school teachers.

Until the second half of the 19th century, the University of Copenhagen served as the national university of Iceland. However, with the foundation of the colleges of theology (1847), medicine (1876), and law (1908), a large part of university-level professional education moved into the country. The foundation of the **University of Iceland** in 1911 was a further step in that direction, and it has gradually developed into the largest educational institution in Iceland. In recent years, a number of colleges and smaller universities have been founded in Iceland, often on the basis of existing specialized schools (the Teacher Training College was, for example, upgraded to the Iceland University of Education in 1971; the agricultural colleges at Hvanneyri and Hólar both offer education at the university level; and the cooperative school at Bifröst in Borgarfjörður County has been transformed into a university). Moreover, in 1987, the state established a new university at Akureyri in its effort to decentralize university education in Iceland, and the private commercial college in Reykjavík changed its name to the Reykjavík University in 1998. It is currently the second largest institution of higher education in Iceland with 2,900 students (2007). Finally, the Icelandic Academy of Arts, which is a university institution for the various genres of arts, was founded in 1999.

Today, it is compulsory for all Icelandic children to attend school from the ages of 6 to 16. The primary schools are run by the **communes**, while most of the secondary schools and institutions of higher education are run by the state. All public elementary and secondary schools are free of charge, and students in public universities pay only minimal tuition fees. Private universities, such as the Reykjavík University and the Business University in Bifröst, charge their students tuition fees, but a large part of their funds come directly from the state. *See also* MENNTASKÓLINN Í REYKJAVÍK (MR).

EIRÍKSSON, JÓN (1728–87). One of the most influential Icelanders of the 18th century was born to a farmer in Skaftafell County on 31 August 1728. In 1743, he enrolled in the Latin school at **Skálholt**, where a **Danish Lutheran** minister, Ludvig Harboe, took him under his wing. Harboe was stationed in Iceland at the time on a special mission from the Danish church authorities, surveying Icelandic **religious** life and the moral conduct and **education** of the inhabitants. In 1745, when Harboe took up his position as bishop of Trondheim in **Norway**, Eiríksson went with him, never to return to Iceland. He finished secondary school in Norway, and in 1748, he enrolled in the University of Copenhagen. Soon he abandoned his plans of becoming a theologian, studying philology and philosophy, and later law, at the university. A year after earning his law degree in 1758, he accepted a teaching position in law at the prestigious Sorø Academy in Denmark—a post he held until 1771. Upon leaving his teaching position, Eiríksson moved to Copenhagen to work in the newly established Norwegian section of the Finanskollegiet (Ministry of Finance, later Rentekammeret). For the remainder of his life, he held high posts in the royal ministries in Copenhagen.

After entering the ministry, Eiríksson was a key figure in the administration of Icelandic affairs in the capital, actively supporting the efforts of reformers like **Skúli Magnússon**, who sought to diversify the Icelandic **economy**. In addition to his career as a royal official, he held various other appointments; he served as an assessor in the Danish Supreme Court from 1779 and head librarian of the royal library from 1781. In the end, a heavy workload and personal disappointments caused the deterioration of his mental health, leading to his suicide in 1787. The tremendous economic and social difficulties in Iceland following the **Laki Eruption** of 1783–84, certainly contributed to Eiríksson's despair.

Eiríksson gained respect for his remarkable energy and intelligence, on the basis of which he reached high ranks in the Danish administrative hierarchy. He remained an Icelandic patriot throughout his life, writing extensively on economic and cultural affairs. Although Eiríksson remained a loyal servant of the king to the end of his life, the **nationalist** intellectuals of the 19th and 20th centuries revered him greatly for his contributions to Icelandic social and economic development. *See also* THE ENLIGHTENMENT; INNRÉTTINGAR.

EIRÍKSSON, LEIFUR (10TH AND 11TH CENTURIES). This Norse adventurer was born around the year 970, presumably on a farm in western Iceland. He was the son of Eiríkur "the Red" Þorvaldsson, founder of the Norse settlement in **Greenland**, and he moved with his father to the new colony in 986. Around the year 1000, when he was on his way from **Norway** to Greenland, Eiríksson is said to have drifted from his course and hit an unknown land to the west of Greenland—that is, the mainland of North America. One part of this "new world" he named **Vínland**, meaning either "Vine Land" or "Meadow Land." According to legend, Eiríksson spent one winter in Vínland, returning to Greenland the following spring and bringing back a load of timber. On his way to Greenland, he is said to have rescued people from a shipwreck, a deed that earned him the nickname *heppni* (lucky). Eiríksson supposedly died around 1020.

ELDJÁRN, KRISTJÁN (1916–82). The third **president** of the Icelandic republic was born in Eyjafjörður County in northern Iceland on

6 December 1916. Eldjárn entered secondary school in **Akureyri** in 1931 and graduated five years later. After studying archaeology at the University of Copenhagen, he returned to Iceland without completing his exam in 1939 at the outbreak of **World War II**, escaping the occupation of **Denmark** by the German Nazis. Eldjárn completed a master's degree in Icelandic studies at the **University of Iceland** in 1944, and in 1957, he defended his doctoral dissertation at the University of Iceland.

In 1945, Eldjárn became an assistant at the **National Museum of Iceland**, and two years later, he was appointed director of the museum. In that capacity he served as the leading authority on all archaeological research in Iceland for over two decades. Eldjárn held this position until he entered the presidential race of 1968.

The elections of 1968 marked a watershed in Icelandic presidential politics. Eldjárn had never taken an active part in party politics, but he defeated **Gunnar Thoroddsen**, an accomplished politician with strong—but complex—ties to the political establishment. His convincing victory—receiving almost two thirds of the votes cast—demonstrated the voters' preference for a nonpartisan president. Eldjárn challenged the idea that presidents should be elderly statesmen, and the same holds true of his successor, **Vigdís Finnbogadóttir**. Eldjárn ran unopposed in 1972 and 1976 but retired at the end of his third term.

Eldjárn was a popular president, and his only controversial decision came late in his last term in 1980, when he gave his erstwhile opponent, Thoroddsen, the mandate to form a government. This decision was in clear opposition to the will of the majority of Thoroddsen's own **Independence Party**. After Eldjárn retired, the University of Iceland awarded him an honorary professorship, but his death in 1982 prevented him from pursuing his academic career.

ELECTIONS. With the foundation of modern **Alþingi** in 1843–45, democratic elections were introduced into Icelandic society for the first time. Since then, democratic processes and popular representation have become the dominant forms of political legitimation in Iceland, as the national parliament, local councils, and the **president** of the republic are all selected through popular vote. Election turnout is usually very high in Iceland (normally between 85 and 90 percent in parliamentary elections), even though no one is required by law to cast his or her ballot.

In the first Icelandic parliamentary elections held in 1844, the franchise was limited to male property holders over 25 years of age, but in 1857, it was expanded to include almost all farmers and some cottars in coastal towns. **Women** received the right to vote in a few successive steps from 1882 to 1920, and economic restrictions on the franchise were gradually lifted during the first decades of the 20th century; this development was completed in 1934, when those who had received poor relief were given the right to vote. Hence, the franchise was extended to nearly the entire adult population. In 1934, the voting age in parliamentary elections was lowered from 25 to 21 years of age and in 1967 to the age of 20. Since 1983, all Icelandic citizens who have reached the age of 18 on the day of elections and do not have a criminal record are eligible to vote.

Until the end of the 19th century, parliamentary elections in Iceland were organized on a strictly personal basis. The first formal **political parties** emerged around the turn of the 20th century, focusing first and foremost on the struggle for independence. During **World War I** and the **Great Depression**, the party system went through a radical transformation, with the foundation of parties based on social interest and political ideologies rather than opinions on relations with **Denmark**. Since then, the party system has been relatively stable, normally with four major parties competing for popular support both in parliamentary and local elections. In recent years, this stability seems to have eroded, however, in part because party loyalty, which characterized Icelandic politics for much of the 20th century, is disappearing. The introduction of a system of proportional representation in 1959 has also given small groups the opportunity to have representatives elected to parliament, and the demographic and social changes since **World War II** have transformed the socioeconomic structure of the population. Finally, the end of the **cold war** has rendered many of the dividing lines in Icelandic politics obsolete. This trend is seen in the success of the **Women's Alliance** in the 1980s and early 1990s, as its feminist agenda allowed the party to draw support from former voters of all the established political parties. *See also* CABINET; CONSTITUTION OF 1874; CONSTITUTION OF 1944; PRIME MINISTER.

EMIGRATION. *See* MIGRATION.

EMPLOYMENT. During most of the 20th century and the first years of the 21st century, the Icelandic labor market has performed remarkably well in terms of rates of employment. Participation rates have been high and unemployment modest to nonexistent in most years. Full employment has been a major macroeconomic objective for Icelandic politicians, often at the expense of low **inflation**. Earlier employment statistics are imperfect, but estimates indicate that even during the **Great Depression**, the unemployment rate did not exceed 4 percent in the most populous area in the southwest of Iceland. Moreover, apart from the recession of 1967–70, the rate was below 1 percent from the postwar period until the late 1980s. Substantial seasonal fluctuations have, however, always set their mark on the **labor market**, although the decreased importance of **agriculture** and **fisheries** has reduced these effects in recent years. This has caused significant seasonal unemployment, to which workers adjust with a high degree of regional mobility, most clearly observed in the **migration** to rural areas in the summer and urban areas in the winter.

The recession that started in 1988, caused by the deterioration in external conditions of the **economy** as well as poor fish stocks and stagnation in the **energy-intensive industries**, produced an unprecedented rise in the rate of unemployment. Unemployment went up to 5.3 percent in 1993–94 but declined again to around 2 percent in the latter half of the 1990s. From 2000 to 2006, unemployment rates remained at similar levels as they had been through most of the 20th century, fluctuating between 2.3 and 3.4 percent. This seems to be close to as low as the unemployment rates can go because an unprecedented number of people immigrated to Iceland in these years in search of work. Thus, according to official statistics, over 10 percent of people working in Iceland in 2007 were foreign citizens, which is much higher than the rate in any of the other Nordic countries. This has not had a significant impact on the unemployment rate, which remains very low (1.9 percent in 2007). *See also* INDUSTRIALIZATION.

ENERGY. Iceland is extremely rich in natural energy resources, especially in hydro- and geothermal power. For much of the country's history, these resources were not of much use, as the technology to exploit them did not exist in Iceland. Thus, the Icelandic rivers were never used to drive watermills or textile factories and were generally seen as a nuisance at best. However, with the discovery of hydro-electricity in the late 19th century, Icelanders were quick to see the potential profits that could be gained from harnessing the energy in their rivers. At the turn of the 20th century, many poets predicted, for example, that during the new century, the nation would enter the modern world, and its homes would be illuminated by electric lights and **energy-intensive industries** would bring work and prosperity to its citizens.

It took a long time, though, to realize these dreams. As it turned out, foreign investors hesitated to put their money into Icelandic projects, and politicians could not agree on where to build hydro-electric power plants. A few towns—such as Seyðisfjörður (1913) in the east—took the initiative of building small power stations serving single communities, and a few farmers bought small generators for their farms, but this did not have a major impact on the Icelandic **economy** or standards of living. In the 1920s, the first major power plant in Iceland was built by the city of **Reykjavík**, and a station in a river on the outskirt of the town—Elliðaár—was opened in 1921. In 1937, Reykjavík launched its second major power station, this time in the Sog River, about 50 kilometers east of the capital. Gradually, the energy produced in these power stations was used not only for the rapidly expanding capital but also the neighboring towns in the most populous area of the country, and thus, Iceland had finally entered the electric age.

Energy use in Iceland entered a new phase in 1969 with the opening of the power station at Búrfell on the Þjórsá River. The electricity from this station, which was by far the largest hydroelectric plant in Iceland at the time, was used to power an aluminum smelter outside of a suburb of Reykjavík, Hafnarfjörður. Since then, the owner of the power plant, the **National Power Company of Iceland**, founded in 1965, has grown into a major power company, increasing its production from 90 MW in the beginning to over 1,200 MW at the end of 2007. At present, Iceland has the highest per-capita electricity consumption in the world, almost 30,000 kilowatt-hours (2004).

The second major natural resource, geothermal power, was first used in Reykjavík in 1930, when a few houses were heated with hot water brought from the springs in Laugardalur, close to the city center. This experiment was expanded during **World War II**, when hot water was channeled from a neighboring district to Reykjavík. Since then, **Reykjavík District Heating** has grown into a major power company, providing hot water to homes in most of the capital district. Moreover, other towns have followed Reykjavík's lead by establishing their own district heating companies, and at present, around 90 percent of Icelandic homes are heated with hot water pumped from the ground.

The utilization of these Icelandic energy resources has not been without controversies because it can often cause serious **environmental** damage. Thus, around the time of **World War I**, the damming of Gullfoss, Iceland's most spectacular waterfall and one of its main **tourist** attractions, was fiercely resisted, and eventually it was averted. Similarly, around 1970, two hydroelectric projects were put on hold on environmental grounds. One plan for a dam and a reservoir in Laxárdalur Valley in northern Iceland was stopped because it would have damaged a salmon river and threatened a verdant farming district. The other, a reservoir in the Þjórsárver in the central highlands, was abandoned because it would have flooded the largest nesting area of the pink-footed goose (*Anser brachyrhynchus*) in the world. Recently, this environmentalism appears to be gaining strength, as the so-called **Kárahnjúkar** project triggered widespread demonstrations, especially in Reykjavík. Projects of this kind tend to carry with them enormous environmental sacrifices, although they also have many ecological advantages; the resources are renewable and their use does not involve any burning of fossil fuels.

ENERGY-INTENSIVE INDUSTRIES. Interest in exploiting the enormous **energy** of Icelandic rivers and geothermal areas on a grand scale first arose around 1900, but it was not until after **World War II** that the first large energy-intensive factory was built in Iceland. Financed mainly through **Marshall Aid**, the fertilizer plant (later the state fertilizer plant) at Gufunes in the vicinity of **Reykjavík** started operation in 1954. It used approximately 140 to 150 GWh of electricity a year, which was supplied by the Írafoss power plant on the Sog River east of Reykjavík. The power station was built in conjunction with the fertilizer plant and made possible through the factory's need for electricity.

Industrial policy in the 1960s concentrated on developing the energy-intensive sector. A diatomite plant at Lake Mývatn, which opened in 1968, represented the first large-scale application of geothermal energy for industrial purposes in Iceland. An aluminum smelter near a suburb of Reykjavík, Hafnarfjörður, opened formally in 1970. It was supplied with hydroelectric power from the power station at Búrfell on the Þjórsá River, which was constructed and run by the newly established, publicly owned **National Power Company of Iceland**. The construction of this factory caused acrimonious debates in the Icelandic parliament, mainly because it was owned and operated by a foreign company, Alusuisse. Many representatives protested against what they saw as a loss of **economic** sovereignty because they felt that inviting a huge multinational conglomerate into the small Icelandic market would lead to a loss of national independence. These debates continued through much of the 1970s and 1980s, pressuring Icelandic authorities to limit foreign ownership of energy-intensive industries. Thus, the second large metal factory to be built in Iceland, a ferrosilicon plant situated in Hvalfjörður to the north of Reykjavík, was in majority ownership of the Icelandic state. The factory, which opened in 1979, was later **privatized** and is now entirely owned by **Norwegian** industrial giant Elkem.

The late 1960s was a time of great urgency in the field of energy-intensive industries in Iceland. The feeling was that the country was losing out in the industrial race, as hydroelectric power would not be able to compete with atomic energy in the future. Thus, scientists at the National Energy Authority, which was established in 1967, devised fantastic plans to channel rivers from northern Iceland into the Þjórsá River, which runs to sea on the south coast. This industrial utopia met stiff resistance, however, and in 1969 and 1970, plans to flood the largest nesting area of pink-footed geese in the world and to damage a fertile **agricultural** land in a valley in the northern part of Iceland had to be put on hold because of public opposition to these projects. In spite of these setbacks, the desire to diversify the Icelandic economy and to harness the vast but underused resources of hydroelectric and geothermal energy in the country continued to motivate the promotion of energy-intensive industries in Iceland. The problem was, though, that foreign investors showed little interest in building factories in Iceland, and it was not until the mid-1990s that the expansion of energy-intensive industries took off again. In 1998, a new aluminum plant opened in Hvalfjörður, and in 2003, American aluminum giant Alcoa decided to build a large factory in the eastern fjords of Iceland.

The last project, which is to be completed in 2009, has caused a huge controversy in Iceland. It is clearly supported by a large majority of the local **population** in the east, where the power plant and the aluminum smelter are to be located. They see these projects as the only opportunity to alleviate the depressed economy of the region, although they come at a great cost. Thus, in order to build the aluminum factory, a huge power station had to be built in the highlands close to the **Kárahnjúkar** Mountains, destroying a large tract of unspoiled land. The **environmental** damage has not been disputed, but those who favor the project maintain that the sacrifice is necessary for the economic development of the area and for the benefit of Iceland in general.

Today, the energy-intensive sector uses around two thirds of all electricity consumed in Iceland. In 2007, the value of its products accounted for almost 30 percent of all Icelandic exports, doubling its share in just over a decade. Its contribution to the national income is lower than these figures imply, however, because most of the raw materials used in energy-intensive industries are imported, and the processes are capital intensive rather than labor intensive. Still, these industries have reduced the dependence on **fisheries**, led to considerable economic growth in recent years, and stabilized Icelandic foreign **currency** earnings. *See also* INDUSTRIALIZATION.

THE ENLIGHTENMENT. The Enlightenment had a strong and lasting influence on Icelandic intellectual and social life, as it did in most of Europe. The Enlightenment did not engender an organized movement in Iceland but rather a sentiment or an intellectual outlook among the elite. It was influenced by **Danish** and German thought and dominated Icelandic intellectual life from the mid- and late-18th century to the early 19th century. The central idea of the Icelandic Enlightenment, and perhaps its only coherent theme, was the belief in progress through human effort. This was an elitist ideal, as the educated few were to introduce and direct progress for the benefit of the masses, but it was also democratic in the sense that social advancement and **education** was not to be limited to the social elite but would trickle down to the working **population**. The Enlightenment in Iceland had no definite beginning, but in the works of **Eggert Ólafsson** (1726–68), a naturalist and poet, all of its basic characteristics can be traced. From 1752 to 1757, he and Bjarni Pálsson, the future surgeon general of Iceland, traveled around the country to study its nature and **economy**. His experiences later led him to write scientific descriptions of Icelandic nature and society and make exhortations to the Icelandic peasants, urging them to break out of their alleged state of lethargy. In the late 18th century, it became fashionable for educated officials to write essays on economic issues and conduct **agricultural** experiments, all in the interest of a more rational organization of Icelandic agriculture. These men, most important of whom was the first chief justice of the Icelandic **High Court**, **Magnús Stephensen** (1762–1833), were all loyal subjects of the Danish king, and many of them saw the Danish government as the most likely agent to lead Iceland out of its economic deprivation. In the first half of the 19th century, the Icelandic Enlightenment came to an end, although it has set its mark on Icelandic history ever since.

New political currents redefined public debates in Iceland, in part because of the radical changes that were taking place on the political front in Copenhagen. With the advent of **nationalism** in the 1830s, the poor state of the Icelandic economy was no longer blamed on intellectual deterioration of the Icelandic peasant class but rather on what was seen as Danish oppression and the government's ignorance and lack of interest in Icelandic affairs and national sovereignty. In spite of the new emphasis, early **nationalist** leaders, like **Jón Sigurðsson** (1811–79) and the publishers of the journal *Fjölnir*, saw themselves as heirs of the enlightened men of the 18th century. Thus, there was no clear break in Icelandic intellectual history at the end of the Enlightenment because the issues of economic and cultural progress became an integral part of 19th-century nationalistic discourse, just as they had been in the preceding century. *See also* EIRÍKSSON, JÓN (1728–87); ROYAL COMMISSIONS OF 1770 AND 1785.

ENVIRONMENTALISM. At the beginning of the 20th century, Iceland was a relatively poor and underdeveloped country. The most obvious solution to this problem seemed to be to use the unlimited power in the Icelandic rivers to establish **energy-intensive industries** to produce metals and artificial fertilizers. The first such project was the Búrfell power station and an aluminum smelter outside the town of Hafnarfjörður, completed in 1970. In the beginning, there was not much organized opposition to this policy on environmental grounds, although many objected to foreign investments in the new **industries.** This changed in the 1990s as people began to protest the serious environmental damage caused by the construction of huge hydroelectric power plants and the related buildup of heavy industries. These debates came to a head with the building of the so-called **Kárahnjúkar** power plant in eastern Iceland and the construction of an aluminum smelter in nearby Reyðarfjörður. The project was not stopped, but many believe that this will be the last large-scale project of this sort to be attempted in Iceland.

It is clear that environmentalism is increasing in Iceland as it is all over Europe. One reason for this is growing prosperity, which has reduced the need for further industrial buildup in Iceland. Second, Icelanders are well aware of the ecological problems the world is facing today, and they feel the need to respond to these issues as do all other developed nations. Finally, a growing number of Icelanders wants to preserve the natural habitat of the country while this is still possible in order to allow future generations to experience the beauty of Icelandic nature. On the other side of this debate are those who point out that Icelandic **energy** is "green" and renewable, as electricity in Iceland is produced without burning fossil fuels. Thus, it makes more ecological sense, many maintain, to use hydroelectric or geothermal power to produce energy than to produce metals like aluminum with electricity from power plants using coal or oil. It is difficult to see how a compromise can be reached on these issues, and they will certainly be at the center of political debates for years to come.

The most important environmentalist organization in Iceland is the Náttúruverndarsamtök Íslands (Icelandic Nature Conservation Association), a nongovernmental association founded in 1997 with the objective of advocating for environmentalist and nature conservation views.

EUROPEAN ECONOMIC AREA (EEA). On 2 May 1992, the member states of the **European Union** (EU) and the **European Free Trade Association** (EFTA) signed an agreement to form a common economic area called the European Economic Area. In the beginning, the agreement was seen primarily as a temporary adjustment for the EFTA countries because most of them wished to join the EU. When **Norwegian** voters rejected EU membership in a referendum in 1994, the EEA became a lasting cooperative forum for Iceland, Norway, Lichtenstein, and the EU, while Swiss voters rejected this agreement.

The EEA was approved in **Alþingi** on 12 January 1993 after a protracted debate and protests from opposition parties. This made Iceland the last of the signatories' parliaments to vote on the issue, but the agreement came into effect on 1 January 1994. The EEA was a major leap toward integration of the Icelandic **economy** into the wider European economic system. Icelanders gained virtually complete access to the EU market for their goods, services, capital, and labor on condition that they make certain financial contributions to the structural funds of the EU and accept most existing and future EU directives and regulations in the Single-Market Program. The agreement has also required legal harmonization in important areas of the economy, which has had major impact on Icelandic society. Of great importance to the Icelandic economy was a drastic reduction of EU tariffs on marine products, especially filleted fish, but the country also benefited from the removal of technical barriers, cheaper imports, and deregulation of the financial market. In addition to its economic links, the EEA agreement solidified Iceland's contacts with the EU in the fields of **education** and research. Thus, Iceland acquired full access to the educational and research programs of the EU, which has facilitated scientific cooperation and academic exchange with European universities and research institutions.

The EEA agreement sparked one of the most heated debates in the Icelandic parliament in the latter half of the 20th century, when many parliamentarians claimed that it would cause serious loss of national sovereignty. The debates around the agreement have, to a large degree, disappeared, as most people seem to agree that Iceland has benefited greatly from it. Moreover, to Icelandic "Euroskeptics," the EEA agreement provides necessary access to the EU without implying a full membership in the union. Thus, no **political party** has advocated an abrogation of the treaty, but there are lingering doubts about the agreement's future. *See also* FOREIGN POLICY.

EUROPEAN FREE TRADE ASSOCIATION (EFTA). The entry of Iceland into EFTA on 1 March 1970 marked a turning point in its international **economic** relations. Membership brought the highly protected economy closer to the European market, and duties on most industrial goods were immediately reduced by 30 percent and on raw materials and machinery by 50 percent. By 1981, all tariffs on imports from EFTA countries were virtually abolished, and Iceland obtained duty-free access to the EFTA countries for all products covered by the EFTA convention. These fundamental changes in **trade** policy have had great impact on the **industrial** sector during the last 20 years.

The role of EFTA changed drastically with the **European Economic Area** (EEA) agreement, which came into effect on 1 January 1994, and the entrance of four of the most important EFTA countries into the **European Union** (EU) in 1994. Since **Norwegian** voters rejected EU membership in a referendum, EFTA survives with four member states, Iceland, Norway, Switzerland, and Lichtenstein. As Switzerland does not take part in the EEA, EFTA's mission is unclear, although the association still exists. *See also* FOREIGN POLICY.

EUROPEAN UNION (EU). Iceland's participation in international **economic** organizations was one of the most contentious political issues of the 1960s. Membership in the European Economic Community (EEC), the precursor to the EU, was high on the agenda in the early years of the decade, but after a protracted debate, Iceland applied for membership in the **European Free Trade Association** (EFTA) instead. In 1972, Iceland negotiated a free-**trade** agreement with the EEC, taking effect on 1 April 1973, with the same general provisions as EEC's agreements with other EFTA countries. Because of disputes over Iceland's extension of its **fishing limits**, however, the EEC suspended tariff reductions for certain fish products until a satisfactory solution was established in 1976.

Economic relations with the EU have become ever more important to the Icelandic economy, as around 70 percent of Icelandic exports have been sold on that market in recent years. The expansion of the EU first to 15 member states in 1995, to 25 in 2004, and to 27 in 2007 and the formation of the **European Economic Area** (EEA) in 1994 have again raised the question of joining the EU. Concerns about the viability of the Icelandic *króna* in the Icelandic business community and a desire to replace it with the **currency** of the EU, the euro, have also fueled these debates. So far, however, membership in the EU has not enjoyed much political support in Iceland because, unlike most other countries in Europe, the political elite in Iceland tend to be rather hostile toward the idea. The main reason for this position is that the EU Common Fisheries Policy is incompatible with Icelandic national interests, but fear of losing Icelandic national sovereignty also plays a significant part in this resentment toward EU membership. *See also* FOREIGN POLICY.

– F –

FARMERS' ASSOCIATIONS. The first agricultural association in Iceland was formed in 1837, mostly by government officials. With growing interest in progress in **agriculture**, a number of regional farmers' associations were established in the 19th century to organize improvements in farming techniques and develop **education** in the field. In 1899, a federation of these farmers' associations was founded called Búnaðarfélag Íslands (Agricultural Society of Iceland). The federation grew quickly in stature, playing a vital role in the modernization of Icelandic farming in the 20th century. In 1945, a special farmers' union was established (Stéttarsamband bænda, Farmers' Union), which was to look after the **economic** interests of the farmers. As the market for agricultural products has been highly regulated, the Farmers' Union has played an important part in forming public policy for farming and setting market prices. The two associations were closely linked from the beginning, and they merged into one association called Bændasamtök Íslands (Farmers Association of Iceland) in 1995. *See also* COOPERATIVE MOVEMENT.

FEDERATION OF ICELANDIC COOPERATIVES. *See* COOPERATIVE MOVEMENT.

FILM INDUSTRY. In spite of its strong literary tradition, and although films have been very popular in Iceland since the early 20th century, the history of the Icelandic cinema industry is relatively short. The main reason for its late development is the small size of the domestic market and a lack of financial resources, which has given imported films a strong advantage over Icelandic production. There exist, however, a few early films based on Icelandic literary works, beginning with Victor Sjöström's epic film *Mountain-Eyvind and His Wife* (released in 1918), but they were for the most part foreign productions. In the 1950s and 1960s, pioneers in Icelandic filmmaking attempted to establish a domestic film industry, either through production of low-budget films or in cooperation with Scandinavian partners. Although some notable motion pictures were produced in this period, such as Arne Mattsson's *Salka Valka* (1954) based on Halldór Laxness's novel of the same name and Erik Balling's *The Girl Gógó* (1962), the conditions for independent filmmaking did not exist.

The year 1979 was a turning point for Icelandic cinema. First, in that year, the government laid the foundation for domestic film production through the creation of the Icelandic Film Fund. Second, at the same time, a new generation of cinematographers returned to Iceland after completing their studies abroad. Thus, close to 30 feature-length motion pictures were released in the 1980s, an astonishing number compared to earlier periods.

At first, this explosion in filmmaking was sustained by remarkable successes in the domestic market. Early in the decade, it was not uncommon for a film to attract an audience of more than 60,000, around a quarter of the total population. In recent years, this initial enthusiasm has subsided, making it impossible for producers to rely solely on the domestic market. The critical success of films such as Hrafn Gunnlaugsson's *When the Raven Flies* (1984), Friðrik Þór Friðriksson's *Children of Nature* (1991), and Baltasar Kormákur's *101 Reykjavík* (2000), to name just a few, opened foreign funds to Icelandic directors. This fact, in addition to the foundation of the Nordic Film and Television Fund and increased access to European cultural funds, has made producers of Icelandic films less dependent upon the domestic market than before, although, as the cost of film production rises, the life of the Icelandic motion picture industry still remains precarious at best.

Icelandic authorities support the Icelandic film industry in many ways. The Icelandic Film Center was created in 2003, which took over most of the functions of the Icelandic Film Fund. Moreover, the government has attempted to attract international filmmakers to Iceland by providing tax incentives for foreign filmmakers who shoot their films in Iceland. *See also* LITERATURE.

FINANCIAL INSTITUTIONS. *See* BANKING; CENTRAL BANKING; ICELAND STOCK EXCHANGE.

FINNBOGADÓTTIR, VIGDÍS (1930–). Fourth president of the **Republic of Iceland**. Born in **Reykjavík** on 15 April 1930, Finnbogadóttir graduated from **Menntaskólinn í Reykjavík** in 1949. She studied French literature and drama at the University of Grenoble, the Sorbonne in Paris, and the University of Copenhagen in 1949–53 and 1957–58, eventually completing a degree in English and French from the **University of Iceland** in 1968. From 1962 to 1972, she taught at two secondary schools in Reykjavík, and she was appointed director of the Reykjavík Theater Company in 1972. In 1980, she was **elected** president of Iceland in a close four-way race. She ran unopposed in 1984 and 1992 and won a landslide victory in 1988, receiving over 90 percent of the votes cast. Finnbogadóttir retired from her post as president at the end of her fourth term in 1996.

The election of Finnbogadóttir to the highest office of the Republic of Iceland was a significant victory for advocates of equal status for men and **women**. She proved to be not only a popular president but also a highly respected stateswoman both at home and abroad. During Finnbogadóttir's tenure as president, the office became more visible than before, as she traveled extensively to promote the interests of Iceland and to introduce its culture abroad. She followed closely in the footsteps of her predecessor, **Kristján Eldjárn**. In the same way, she was involved in cultural life rather than politics before becoming president, a fact that set a clear mark on her style and emphasis as president.

Since retiring from her presidential post, Finnbogadóttir has been active in various international forums, particularly the United Nations Educational, Scientific, and Cultural Organization. She was designated goodwill ambassador for the organization in 1998, and she presided over its World Commission on the Ethics of Scientific Knowledge and Technology. It is her interest in **languages** in particular that has motivated her work in this field, and since 2001, the institute for foreign languages at the University of Iceland has carried her name.

FISHERIES. While fishing and fish processing have never employed a major part of the Icelandic working **population**—now accounting for only 6 percent of the labor force—fish products have always been the most important exports from Iceland. Although their share in the Icelandic export revenues has been declining in recent decades, from around 90 percent in the 1950s to around 42 percent today (2007), fish products are still crucial for Icelandic foreign **trade**. The fishing sector is, therefore, of fundamental importance for the **economy**, and during the last century, it was the major factor for instigating the modernization of Icelandic society. The strength of the Icelandic fisheries is based on the fact that the continental shelf surrounding the island is one of the most productive fishing grounds in the world, with cod, haddock, saithe, herring, redfish, and capelin being the most important commercial species. Due to various **environmental** factors, there has always been a large annual fluctuation in the sizes of these species, especially herring, which has affected not only fisheries and their organization but the economy in general.

The main fishing grounds are in the southwest coastal waters, where demersal species (fish living near the seabed) concentrate to spawn in late winter and early spring before moving eastward and along the west coast to the sea north of Iceland. Until the late 19th century, fishing was primarily organized as a subsidiary occupation of the rural population. Most fishermen were recruited seasonally from the rural male population, who migrated toward the coastal regions in late winter during the time when most of the fishing took place—which happened to be the slack season in **agriculture**. Only a minority of households had fishing as its main source of income, in part because commercial fishing was discouraged by Icelandic social legislation. As early as the 15th century, **Alþingi** introduced legal restrictions—such as **labor bondage** and a demand for minimum property for those who wanted to establish a household outside the rural areas—that hampered the development of independent fisheries in Iceland. Authorities enforced these restrictions in one form or another until the late 19th and early 20th centuries. Furthermore, the rhythm of the fisheries varied by seasons because of the migration of cod around the coast. This made it extremely difficult for people to have fisheries as their primary means of living throughout the year. The level of technology contributed to this situation; fishing techniques remained primitive for centuries, and fishing was carried out on small rowboats with crews of two to six men using fishing lines. As boats had to return to harbor every night, fishing was confined to coastal areas that the fishermen could reach in one day. The biggest boats were 12-oar boats; hardly any decked vessels existed in Iceland until the late 19th century. The principal fish products were dried fish (stockfish) and liver oil, which, as a result of higher prices and expanding markets at home and abroad, replaced *vaðmál* (cloth) as the main export staple by the middle of the 14th century. Exports of salt cod started in the 1760s with the opening of the Spanish market and had become the dominant export article by the 1830s.

In the second half of the 19th century, the fishing sector improved substantially. Major contributing factors were better market opportunities abroad, increased accumulation of capital, improved fishing techniques, and changes in the institutional framework of the economy. The number of decked vessels increased rapidly toward the end of the century, bait became more available with the introduction of freezing techniques, and harbors and other facilities were greatly improved. At the beginning of the 20th century, mechanization of the fishing fleet revolutionized the fisheries. Motorboats and trawlers replaced decked vessels and rowboats during the first quarter of the century, changing fishing into an all-year activity and multiplying fish catches. Transformation of fishing gear also contributed to this development, with trawls on trawlers and bigger boats and the purse seine in herring fishing. Fish processing changed more slowly, however, and salt fish dominated the fish exports until the **Great Depression** and the collapse of the markets in Spain and Italy in the late 1930s. A desperate search for new marketable products led to a greater emphasis on herring fishing, but of more lasting importance was the rapid shift to the production of frozen fish for the American market.

Now, the principal export commodities are frozen fish and fish products (42 percent of all fish exports in 2007), salted and dried fish (18 percent), fresh and chilled fish (19 percent), and meal and fish oil (11 percent). A great increase in the resource base with the extension of the **fishing limits** and an enormous technological advance in both fishing and fish processing has characterized the postwar period. In 2005, the fishing fleet consisted of over 950 vessels standing at a total of 177,000 gross registered metric tons, including 65 powerful trawlers with advanced fishing gear. The most important changes in fish processing in recent years are the increase in freezing and processing of fish at sea and containerized shipping of fresh fish to European markets.

Since the early 1980s, the Icelandic government, in cooperation with the owners of the fishing vessels, has attempted to build up the fish stocks around Iceland through a strict **fisheries management** system, but the results have been mixed. Thus, the allowed catches of the most important fish species in the Icelandic waters, cod, is still only a fraction of the total catches from around the mid-20th century, and there is no indication that the situation will improve much in the near future. *See also* COD WARS; DIRECTORATE OF FISHERIES; MARINE RESEARCH INSTITUTE (MRI); TRADE, FOREIGN; WHALING.

FISHERIES MANAGEMENT. Signs of overfishing in Icelandic waters, due partly to almost open admission to the fishing grounds, were a matter of great concern in the immediate postwar period. In 1948, the passing in **Alþingi** of the Scientific Conservation of the **Fisheries** of the Continental Shelf Act provided a legal framework for fisheries management. This pioneering act gave the government authority to implement measures to prevent depletion of fish stocks. In the following decades, the most important measures regarding the preservation and management of fish stocks centered on the extension of **fishing limits**. The extension to 200 miles in 1976 brought commercial fishing around the country under Icelandic jurisdiction and, hence, laid the responsibility for conservation solely in the hands of the Icelandic government. With the closing of Icelandic waters to other nations, it has been the rapidly expanding Icelandic fishing fleet, especially after 1970, that has posed the greatest threat to the fish stocks around the Icelandic coast.

During the early 1980s, a sharp decline in cod stock led to the adoption of transferable quotas for individual vessels based on annual catches between 1981 and 1983. The aim was to limit the total catches, encourage more efficient fishing operations through transfers of fishing rights between vessels, and invite shipowners to take older vessels out of registration. Since the system's introduction, authorities have extended and reformed it in various ways. In its present form, the Fiskistofa (**Directorate of Fisheries**) allocates—at the behest of the Ministry of Fisheries—to every vessel a "quota share" in the total allowed catch of all regulated species, which now includes all the main commercial fish stocks around Iceland. In deciding the total catch allowed for each species, which covers the fishing year (1 September to 31 August), the ministry follows the recommendations of the **Marine Research Institute**. This system has halted the expansion of the fishing fleet, leading to a steady decline in the number of fishing vessels. The quota system was very unpopular in the beginning because many felt that it transferred the ownership of the resources in the sea, which should rightfully be in the hands of the entire nation, to a handful of shipowners. The quota system is, however, too entrenched now to be radically altered. *See also* COD WARS.

FISHING LIMITS. As fishing has been the major **economic** activity in Iceland for over a century, regulation of the fishing limits was one the greatest political issues in Iceland during the second half of the 20th century. In 1901, a treaty between the **Danish** government, which was in charge of Icelandic foreign affairs at the time, and **Great Britain** set the limits for the territorial waters around Iceland at three nautical miles. This was a clear retreat from earlier regulations, because until then, relatively wide but ill-defined and badly defended fishing limits had helped to protect the fishing grounds. In fact, the 1901 treaty opened the Icelandic fjords and bays to European trawlers, when they had earlier been closed to foreign fishermen. This change came at a critical juncture because new technology in fishing made it increasingly imperative for Iceland to protect its fishing grounds. As British trawlers swarmed into Icelandic waters, they hampered small Icelandic boats and threatened the breeding grounds of some of the most valuable species around the country.

After **World War II**, the Icelandic government subsidized a large-scale modernization of its fishing fleet at the same time as foreign trawlers returned to Icelandic fishing grounds following a respite imposed by the war. This situation required new regulations on fishing in order to prevent an inevitable depletion of fish stocks. The prevailing idea in Europe at the time was to prevent individual states from setting unilateral rules restricting fishing outside of the three-mile territorial waters. Rather, the theory was that regional organizations should determine such conservationist measures, allocating quotas to interested nations. The Icelandic government rejected these ideas and opted for expansion of its fishing limits. Following the example of some Latin American nations, **Alþingi** and the Icelandic government at the time set the course toward control over the entire continental area around the country. From 1952 to 1975, the government used the Scientific Conservation of the **Fisheries** of the Continental Shelf Act issued on 5 April 1948 to extend the fishing limits to 200 nautical miles. This happened in four successive steps: from 3 to 4 nautical miles in 1952, to 12 miles in 1958, to 50 miles in 1972, and to 200 miles in 1975. All these actions caused confrontations—so-called **cod wars**—between Iceland and other interested nations, especially Britain.

The objectives of the policy were twofold. First, fish is clearly a limited resource that is sensitive to overexploitation. Thus, a stringent policy of preservation based on scientific research has to be employed in order to prevent depletion of fish stocks. The expansion of the fishing limits has allowed Icelandic research institutions to formulate and enforce such policies in Icelandic waters. Second, expansion has given Icelandic fishermen a monopoly over the rich Icelandic fishing grounds. This has gradually increased their share of the catch in Icelandic waters from around 50 percent in the 1950s to almost a total monopoly of Icelandic fishing vessels at the end of the 20th century. *See also* COAST GUARD; FISHERIES MANAGEMENT.

FJÖLNIR. A periodical that became a leading organ for Icelandic **nationalism** in its formative stage. The first volume of the journal was issued in Copenhagen in 1835 and promised to contribute to the awakening of the nation from its alleged slumber. The editors were four young Icelandic intellectuals, all students at or recent graduates of the University of Copenhagen. At the time of its publication, *Fjölnir* was controversial. Its aggressive style evoked strong reaction, especially among state officials, while many simply ignored the journal. *Fjölnir* had, however, a lasting influence on the **Icelandic nationalist movement**, and it is generally regarded to have played a major part in the development of nationalist sentiment. Although many contemporaries found the journal both eccentric and uncompromising in its views on aesthetics and orthography, its emphasis on **language** and **literature** was important in projecting these issues into the core of Icelandic national identity. The last issue of *Fjölnir* was published in 1847, but by that time, all of the original editors had left the editorial group. *See also ÁRMANN Á ALÞINGI*; HALLGRÍMS-SON, JÓNAS (1807–45); *NÝ FÉLAGSRIT*; SÆMUNDSSON, TÓ-MAS (1807–41).

FOREIGN POLICY. Iceland became a sovereign state in union with **Denmark** with the **Act of Union** of 1918. To begin with, the Danish government was to take care of the Icelandic foreign service, but it was to do so at the behest of the Icelandic government. In reality, until the late 1930s, Icelanders had only a limited interest in foreign affairs. As a small nation with no experience in the international arena, Icelandic authorities were content with maintaining Iceland's status as a neutral country, even refusing to enter the League of Nations.

   World War II undermined the neutrality policies in two respects. First, during the war, Iceland cut its ties with Denmark, taking the foreign service fully into its own hands. The reason for this was the fact that the two countries were placed in opposite camps during the war, as Iceland was under the protection of the Allied countries—first **Great Britain** and then the **United States**—while Denmark was occupied by Germany. Second, Iceland's strategic position changed dramatically during the war. Until the 20th century, Iceland had been a fairly isolated periphery, which did not interest the European powers. But as the United States became a major player in the European arena, Iceland's position became crucial for controlling **transportation** routes between North America and Europe. During the war, military stations in Iceland were of great importance for the Allied forces, being used to monitor the North Atlantic, and the airports in

Reykjavík and **Keflavík** were used as fueling stations for transatlantic flights between the United States and Europe.

As the **cold war** heated up in the aftermath of the Second World War, the U.S. government wanted to prolong the presence of U.S. military forces in Iceland. This was not popular in Iceland at the time, as neutrality was still the guiding principle of Icelandic foreign policy, and Icelandic politicians were loath to sacrifice their newly acquired independence. Iceland did not become a founding member of the **United Nations** (UN) in 1945 because the government was not willing to declare war on Germany. This did not mean that Icelanders had any sympathy for the Nazi regime but rather that there was strong opposition to involving the country in any military conflicts. Gradually, Icelandic authorities began to realize that neutrality was not an option in the cold war because the two superpowers—the United States and the Soviet Union—simply divided the world between themselves into their spheres of influence. Moreover, Iceland was an important player in this struggle, as all traffic in air and on sea across the North Atlantic could be monitored from Iceland. After some hesitation, it became a strong ally of the United States, entering the **North Atlantic Treaty Organization** (NATO) in 1949 and signing a defense treaty with the United States in 1951.

Through the rest of the cold war, Iceland was a loyal ally of the United States. This was, however, a divisive issue in Iceland, as many leftist politicians and intellectuals vigorously opposed the presence of an American military force in Iceland, using **nationalistic** arguments to protest what they saw as infringement on Icelandic sovereignty. In this way, foreign policy became the central issue of Icelandic domestic politics because the Left proficiently exploited the strong nationalistic sentiments in Iceland. The Vietnam War and the widespread anti-American feelings it caused further encouraged such views. All the leading **political parties** in Iceland, except for the **Socialist Unity Party** and the **People's Alliance**, were, however, firmly behind the pro-Western leanings of the Icelandic government, supporting wholeheartedly membership in NATO and somewhat less enthusiastically the U.S. military base in Keflavík.

One of the great embarrassments of the pro-Western parties in these years was the fact that during the cold war, the most obvious adversaries of the country were not the communist regimes in

Eastern Europe but rather some of Iceland's allies in NATO—Great Britain in particular. The reason for this was Iceland's expansion of its **fishing limits** in four successive steps from 3 to 200 miles from 1952 to 1975. This resulted in repeated hostilities with Britain, called **cod wars**, and although NATO played a major role in solving these disputes in Iceland's favor, they undermined the position of NATO supporters in Iceland.

Since the end of the cold war, Iceland has been searching for its voice in the international arena. One reason for this uncertainty was the United States' desire to close down the base in Keflavík. This challenged people's opinions to the alliance with the United States because the American military presence had always been justified with reference to the Icelandic defensive needs. In an attempt to secure the base, the Icelandic government decided to join the so-called coalition of the willing, supporting the U.S. invasion of Iraq in 2003. This was, of course, an empty statement, as Iceland had no military force to offer, but it indicated a firm desire to be seen as an ally of the United States. As it turned out, this course of action did not have much influence on the U.S. government, and it unilaterally withdrew its military forces from Iceland in 2006, leaving the country without any credible defensive forces. As a result, foreign policy discourse in Iceland has changed its tone, as the relations with the United States have decreased in importance. Increasingly, Iceland's participation in European integration has become the major issue of foreign policy debates, as the recent enlargement of the **European Union** (EU) has forced Icelandic politicians to reconsider relations with Europe. In these debates, the **Independence Party** (IP), which had always been the strongest supporter of the western alliance, joined hands with the Far Left in the opposition to joining the EU, while the **Social Democratic Alliance** has promoted the idea of applying to the union.

In the future, this will certainly be the main issue of Icelandic foreign policy. Iceland is closely linked to Europe through its **economic** and cultural relations, and the **European Economic Area** agreement has integrated the country very closely into European markets. The Icelandic political elite has, however, been very reluctant to advocate full membership in the EU, regarding this as an unacceptable sacrifice of Iceland's sovereignty. The question remains if a small country will be able to defend its sovereignty without an active support of strong allies, as it did through relations with the United States during the cold war. *See also* DEFENSE; EUROPEAN FREE TRADE ASSOCIATION (EFTA); NORWAY.

– G –

GAMLI SÁTTMÁLI. *See* OLD COVENANT.

THE GENERAL PETITION. A long document published in 1795 listing various complaints against **Danish** trading practices in Iceland. The petition was drawn up and printed at the behest of a number of leading government officials in Iceland, probably under the leadership of **Magnús Stephensen** (1762–1833), who was **lawman** at the time, and Stefán Þórarinsson, district governor of the northeastern district. Using language borrowed from the revolutionary upheavals in France, the Almenna bænarskráin (General Petition) demanded the abolition of the last vestiges of the hated **monopoly trade**, pleading for free trade between Iceland and other countries. Although most Icelandic officials signed the petition, the government rejected it out of hand, reprimanding the royal servants who had given their names to the Icelandic requests.

GEYSIR. A spring of gushing hot water in Árnes County in southern Iceland, which has given its name to this natural phenomenon in many languages (the word is, for example, *geyser* in both English and French). The name comes originally from the noun *gos* or the verb *gjósa*, both of which are translated as *spurt* in English.

Geysir is a 1-meter deep (3 feet) bowl, its surface 20 meters (65 feet) in diameter. From this bowl, a pipe 1 meter in diameter descends 23 meters (75 feet) below the surface. It was probably formed by an earthquake in the late 13th century. For centuries, it spurted water as high as 70 to 80 meters (225 to 260 feet) in the air, but in the early 20th century, it more or less died down. The hot spring was revived in 1935 through alterations of its rim, but that lasted only for a few years. Strong earthquakes in June 2000 brought Geysir to life once again, but its spurts are a far cry from what they used to be in earlier times, reaching only about 10 meters in the air. Geysir and the surrounding springs remain, however, among the most renowned **tourist** attractions in Iceland.

GÍSLADÓTTIR, INGIBJÖRG SÓLRÚN (1954–). One of the most notable politicians of the Icelandic Left was born in **Reykjavík** on 31 December 1954. After completing secondary school in 1974, Gísladóttir studied history and **literature** at the **Universities of Iceland** and Copenhagen. In 1982, she was **elected** to the city council of Reykjavík for the new **Women**'s Ticket, where she served until 1988. Gísladóttir entered national politics in 1991 when she was elected to parliament for the **Women's Alliance**. In **Alþingi**, she gained respect for her independent views and her strong performance in political debates. In the local elections of 1994, she became the unifying symbol of the parties to the left of the **Independence Party** (IP) in Reykjavík, leading them to victory in elections for the city council. After the elections, Gísladóttir became mayor of Reykjavík, the second woman in the history of the city to gain that title. With this victory, she set a strong mark on Icelandic politics; not only was she instrumental in uniting the parties on the left, which have long professed their desire to build a united front without much success, but her popularity was also the main reason for their victory in the traditional stronghold of the IP. After leading the Left in two local elections in Reykjavík (1998 and 2002), beating the IP handily both times, Gísladóttir decided to enter the parliamentary race of 2003 on the ticket of the **Social Democratic Alliance** (SDA). In 2003, she was elected deputy chairwoman of the SDA, and she ousted the sitting chairman of the party, Össur Skarphéðinsson, in 2005. In May 2007, Gísladóttir, as the leader of the junior party in a coalition government of the IP and the SDA, became minister of foreign affairs. *See also* AUÐUNS, AUÐUR (1911–99).

GOÐI. The most powerful men in Iceland during the **Commonwealth Period** were the chieftains (sing. *goði*, pl. *goðar*), the group of men who held the *goðorð* (chieftaincies). Originally, around the year 930, these chieftaincies were 36 in number, but in 965, three were added to make 39 in all. Etymologically, the word *goði* is derived from *goð*, or god, which has led many to believe that they served some **religious** function before the **conversion to Christianity** in

Iceland. In fact, little is known about pre-Christian religious practices in Iceland because few reliable sources about them exist. Thus, this role of the chieftains is debated. The *goðar* were, however, certainly the most prominent leaders of the Old Icelandic society. In **Alþingi**, they carried out legislative functions, as far as laws were made in the assembly, and named people into courts, while each spring they directed local assemblies in their districts.

To begin with, all *goðar* had equal status, and each free man had the right and duty to follow a *goði* of his choice. Originally the chieftaincy was not a geographic unit but a contractual relationship between patrons and clients. During the 12th and 13th centuries, as certain individuals and families became dominant in Iceland, the chieftaincies became more or less fixed, and a few families collected most of the *goði* titles in their hands. After 1220, this led to open warfare between the most powerful chieftains in Iceland, and they scrambled for hegemony in the country. Finally, this caused political and social chaos, which ended only when the country became a part of the **Norwegian** monarchy in 1262–64. A little later, shortly after Icelanders accepted a new legal code in 1271–73, the *goðorð* were abolished. After that, Iceland was gradually divided into geographically defined **counties**, called *sýsla*, which were administered by royal officials, *sýslumenn* (bailiffs). *See also* AGE OF THE STURLUNGS.

GOÐORÐ. *See GOÐI.*

GOVERNMENT OF THE LABORING CLASSES. Stjórn hinna vinnandi stétta, or the Government of the Laboring Classes, was a coalition government of the **Progressive Party** (PP) and the **Social Democratic Party** (SDP). It was formed in late July 1934 under the leadership of **Hermann Jónasson** from the PP. This was the first government in which the SDP took part, but the party had supported the minority government of the PP from 1927 to 1931. The main objective of the government was to reduce the unemployment rates (*see* EMPLOYMENT), which had remained very high for some years because of the **Great Depression**. The coalition parties also instituted a wide range of changes through extensive legislative initiatives. The most important of these laws were those regulating the market for meat and dairy products in 1934, those founding the State Social Security Institute in 1936, and those recognizing the negotiation rights of **trade unions** in 1938.

Although the two parties mostly represented the two largest classes of working people in Iceland, that is, workers in towns and small farmers in the countryside, their programs differed on many issues. Thus, the SDP advocated nationalization of many key **industries**, especially in the fishing sector, while the PP wanted to strengthen the **cooperative movement** rather than increase the role of the state in **economic** life. During the last year of the government, the two parties were increasingly at odds over these issues, and in spite of a secure parliamentary majority, it resigned in March 1938.

GOVERNOR. *See* GOVERNOR'S PERIOD; *HIRÐSTJÓRI; LANDSHÖFÐINGI; RÍKISSTJÓRI; STIFTAMTMAÐUR.*

GOVERNOR'S PERIOD. The period from 1873 to 1904 is commonly known as the Landshöfðingjatímabilið (Governor's Period). It takes its name from the title of the governor's office, *landshöfðingi*, which was introduced in 1873. The governor took a very prominent place in Icelandic political debates at the end of the 19th century because he had a strong position in the administration of the country. The person ultimately responsible for the government of Iceland was, however, the minister of Icelandic affairs in Copenhagen—a post always held by the **Danish** minister of justice—but as he was not involved in the daily business of the country, the real executive power in Iceland was in the hands of the governor.

What characterized this period in Icelandic history is, first, a growing **economic** diversification, which appeared particularly in increasing emphasis on the **fisheries**. As a result, there was a steady **population** growth in the small fishing villages around the coast, and **Reykjavík** became the first real town in the country in this period. The main reasons for this change were population pressure in the countryside, difficult climatic conditions for **agriculture**, and technological advancement in the fishing industry. Second, a strong **nationalist** sentiment set its mark on political life during the Governor's Period. There was deep discontent in Iceland, especially concerning the status of the country in the monarchy, where a clear majority of politically active persons in Iceland demanded more independence from Denmark. During the 1880s and early 1890s, members of parliament spent a great deal of energy in a fairly futile struggle for a new constitution, and **Alþingi** attempted unsuccessfully to persuade the reactionary government in Copenhagen to transfer more of its executive authority over Icelandic affairs to Reykjavík. As the period came to a close, parliament became more conciliatory in its opinions toward the Danish government because no radical changes in the status of Iceland seemed possible. The fall of the reactionary Danish government in 1901 changed this situation completely. With more liberal politicians in power in Copenhagen, the Danish government accepted **home rule** for Iceland in 1902, and the governor's office was abolished two years later with the establishment of the Icelandic home rule government. *See also* CONSTITUTION OF 1874; HOME RULE PERIOD; STATUS LAW; *STIFTAMTMAÐUR*.

GRÁGÁS. The laws of the Icelandic commonwealth, preserved in two manuscripts dated from around the mid-13th century, are commonly named *Grágás*, meaning "gray goose." This name is a fairly late creation from the 16th century, and its origins are unclear. The two existing *Grágás* manuscripts, called *Codex Regius* and *Staðarhólsbók*, are not identical in content, but together they provide a clear picture of a legal tradition in Iceland that started with the decision in **Alþingi** in 1117 to write down the Icelandic laws. Thus, the *Grágás* law codes are more literary in style than similar codes in Scandinavia, and the extreme details of its various clauses indicate that revisions and elaborations had taken place from the time when the laws existed only in oral form. The *Grágás* laws are based, however, on Scandinavian legal traditions, where the intention is to cover all possible scenarios rather than to construct general rules that apply to various situations. In 1271–73, after Iceland entered into union with **Norway**, a law book called *Járnsíða* superseded *Grágás*, but it was written at the behest of King Magnus Håkonsson of Norway. One decade later, *Jónsbók* replaced *Járnsíða*, and it was to serve as the basis for the Icelandic legal system for centuries. *See also* COMMONWEALTH PERIOD.

GREAT BRITAIN. Relations with the British Isles go as far back as the settlement of Iceland, but they first became critical in the 15th century. English fishermen and traders began to visit Iceland around the end of the 14th century, filling a void left by a declining **trade with Norway** during the end of the medieval period. In the following decades, the English became very prominent in Iceland, often practically controlling its relations with the outer world (thus historians call the time from the early 1400s to the early 1500s the English century). For the most part, Icelanders welcomed trade with England but protested their fishing, while the **Danish** king did what he could to control Icelandic foreign trade. In the late 15th century, German merchants began to compete with the English for the Icelandic market. This often led to violent confrontations, peaking in 1532 with the killing of 15 Englishmen in Grindavík on the southwestern coast. English activities in and around Iceland declined after this as the royal grip on the trade strengthened, and English fishermen shifted their attention elsewhere.

The British began to show interest in Iceland again in the late 18th and early 19th centuries. The first example of this came in 1772 when English explorer and naturalist Sir Joseph Banks visited Iceland, setting the trend for explorations of the country in the following decades. Due to Banks's influence, Iceland received favorable treatment during the Napoleonic Wars, although the British were officially at war with Denmark. It was, however, with new fishing techniques and the liberalization of Icelandic foreign trade at the end of the 19th century that the Icelandic waters regained their former importance to the English fishing fleet. A new chapter began in British–Icelandic relations when British trawlers started to frequent Iceland around 1890. Fishing very close to the coast in the traditional grounds of the Icelandic fishermen made the trawlers very unpopular in Iceland. For this reason, Icelanders commenced a struggle to push the foreign fishing fleet away from the Icelandic coast, causing a number of so-called **cod wars** with the British in the 20th century.

Due to conflicting fishing interests, diplomatic relations between Iceland and Britain were often tense during the 20th century, however Iceland's location in the mid-Atlantic put the country in the British sphere of influence. This was clear in both world wars, as Britain took control over Icelandic foreign trade in **World War I** and occupied the country early in **World War II**. In spite of occasional confrontations, relations between the two countries remain strong, though, as evidenced by the fact that Britain is the largest importer of Icelandic products in the world. Moreover, Icelandic investors have been active in Great Britain in recent years, buying stocks in a number of British companies. For this reason, the **economic** links between the two countries remain very strong. *See also* FISHING LIMITS; FOREIGN POLICY.

GREAT DEPRESSION. The first effects of the Wall Street stock crash of 1929 and the ensuing crisis in international **trade** hit Iceland in 1930. After that, Icelanders endured an **economic** slump for almost a decade. The main causes for the depression in Iceland were a steep fall in export prices for Icelandic goods (between 40 and 50 percent between 1929 and 1933) and various restrictions on the flow of merchandise in international markets. The outbreak of the Spanish Civil War in 1936 prolonged the Great Depression in Iceland because the war closed down the most lucrative market for Icelandic goods (35 percent of Icelandic exports—mostly salt cod—went to Spain in 1926–30, compared with 2.6 percent in 1936–40). The chronic problem of unemployment ended only with **World War II**, when British and American forces stationed in Iceland provided abundant **employment** to Icelandic workers.

The Great Depression affected Icelandic society in various ways. High unemployment led to increasing political polarization in the country, with a growing radicalization of the **trade unions** and rising popularity of the **Communist Party** and later the **Socialist Unity Party**. The Depression had a lasting influence on the structure of the economy because the changes in international trade forced the country to seek new opportunities in world markets. Moreover, in these years, the state dramatically increased its participation in the economy, both by direct ownership of various businesses and through its monetary and tariff policies. In these fields, Icelanders felt the effects of the Great Depression long after the economic difficulties had ended, and it was only with the massive **privatization** initiatives around the turn of the 21st century that the Icelandic state returned fully to the free market policies that had characterized the country before the Great Depression. *See also* GOVERNMENT OF THE LABORING CLASSES; GÚTTÓSLAGURINN.

GREENLAND. In the late 10th century, as Iceland was becoming more fully settled, Norsemen expanded their settlements further to the west, exploring the island of Greenland, which is Iceland's closest neighboring country. According to Icelandic **sagas**, the first Norse settler on the island was Eiríkur Þorvaldsson, who fled Iceland in 985 or 986 after having been sentenced for killing a man. He is alleged to have given the name Greenland to his new home to attract prospective settlers from Iceland. Norse settlers inhabited two regions in Greenland, calling them the Western and Eastern Settlements, although both of them were on the southwestern coast of the island. During the first centuries of their existence, the Norse settlements in Greenland seem to have prospered; this is indicated by the ruins of a cathedral and other buildings in their center at Garðar. During the 14th and 15th centuries, contacts with Greenlanders became more sporadic, and the Norse settlements on Greenland disappeared entirely sometime between the early 15th and late 16th centuries. The reason for this is not entirely clear, but colder climate, changes in **trade** patterns, and diseas may have contributed to the fall of the settlement. *See also* EIRÍKSSON, LEIFUR (10TH AND 11TH CENTURIES); NORWAY; VÍNLAND.

GRÍMSSON, ÓLAFUR RAGNAR (1943–). Politician and a former professor of political science at the **University of Iceland**. Born on 14 May 1943 in Ísafjörður in northwest Iceland, Grímsson graduated from **Menntaskólinn í Reykjavík** in 1962. He completed a B.A. in economics and political science from the University of Manchester in 1965 and a Ph.D. in political science from the same university in 1970. The same year, he was appointed assistant professor of political science at the University of Iceland and full professor three years later. In 1978, Grímsson was **elected** to parliament for the **People's Alliance** (PA) for the first time but failed to win reelection for his third term in 1983. Although he did not sit in **Alþingi** at the time, he became chairman of Parliamentarians for Global Action, an international organization of parliamentary representatives, in 1984. From 1988 to 1991, he served as minister of finance, reentering Alþingi in 1991.

Grímsson's political career has been both colorful and controversial. He sat on the steering committee of the **Progressive Party** (PP) from 1971 to 1973 but left the PP in 1974 with a group of activists from its left wing to join the **Union of Liberals and Leftists** (ULL). He served as chairman of the steering committee of ULL in 1974–75 before he changed parties once again and joined the PA. His rise in the PA was rapid; he was elected to parliament for the party in 1978 and became chairman of its parliamentary group in 1980, chairman of its steering committee in 1983, and finally party chairman in 1987. During his tenure as chairman of the PA from 1987 to 1995, Grímsson attempted to change the emphasis of the party. This was, in part, the result of the changing scene in international politics at the conclusion of the **cold war**, but it was also a response to new currents in the socialist movement in Iceland. Some of the new policies, such as the more positive view of Icelandic membership in the **North Atlantic Treaty Organization** (NATO), were very controversial in the party, dividing it into rival wings.

In 1996, Grímsson retired from party politics to enter the race for **president** of Iceland. He was elected the fifth president of the republic in a tight race in June of that year. He ran unopposed in 2000 but was reelected with a huge majority of the votes cast in 2004. The campaign was fought in the shadow of fierce debates with the government of the **Independence Party** (IP) and the PP and then with the **prime minister**, **Davíð Oddsson**, in particular. The reason for the conflict between the president and the prime minister was the fact that a few weeks before the elections, Grímsson had vetoed a controversial media bill that had been passed in parliament. This led to a constitutional crisis because it was the first time in the history of the republic that president had exercised his constitutional power in this manner, openly challenging the authority of the government and the majority in parliament. The 2004 elections could, therefore, be interpreted as a referendum on Grímsson's political intervention, but the results were inconclusive. He was certainly reelected with an overwhelming majority of the votes cast (85 percent of the votes for a candidate), but unusually low turnout (63 percent) and many blank ballots (20 percent) indicate that there was considerable dissatisfaction with Grímsson's actions.

GRÖNDAL, BENEDIKT (1924–). This former politician and **prime minister** was born in Ísafjörður County on 7 July 1924.

Gröndal completed his secondary education in **Reykjavík** in 1943 and enrolled at Harvard University the same year. After receiving a B.A. in history from Harvard in 1946, he studied for one year at Oxford University. After completing his studies, he returned to Iceland to work for the Social Democratic newspaper *Alþýðublaðið* (the People's Newspaper), first as a journalist but later as editor-in-chief. In 1956, he was **elected** to parliament for the **Social Democratic Party** (SDP) for the first time, retaining his seat until he retired from politics in 1982. In 1974, he was elected chairman of the SDP but was ousted from this post in 1980 by **Kjartan Jóhannsson**. Gröndal served as minister of foreign affairs from 1978 to 1980 and as prime minister for a few months in 1979–80. Upon retiring from politics, he was appointed ambassador, serving in different countries from 1982 to 1991.

GUÐMUNDSDÓTTIR, BJÖRK (1965–). The best-known Icelandic musician of today and arguably the most widely known Icelander ever was born in **Reykjavík** on 21 November 1965. Björk entered the domestic **music** scene at a very early age, issuing her first solo album (the eponymous *Björk*) in 1976 at the age of 11. Björk was a member of various punk rock bands in the early 1980s but first attracted attention in 1982 for her performance in the documentary film *Rokk í Reykjavík* (Rock in Reykjavik). In 1983, she was one of the founding members of the group Kukl (Sorcery) and later of Sykurmolarnir (the Sugarcubes, 1986). The first record of the Sugarcubes, which was released in 1988, to everyone's surprise did quite well in England and later all over Europe. It was not least Björk's eclectic style and striking voice that impressed the international audiences, and in 1993, she went solo with the album *Debut*. Since then, she has released five solo records (*Post*, 1995; *Homogenic*, 1997; *Vespertine*, 2001; *Medúlla*, 2004; and *Volta*, 2007), in addition to collaborative works with people like **Danish** filmmaker Lars Von Trier and American artist Mathew Barney. Björk collaborated with Von Trier on the movie *Dancer in the Dark*, receiving the Best Actress Award at Cannes in 2000 for her role in the film, and her song from the film, "I've Seen It All," was nominated for the Academy Award for Best Song in 2001. Björk has enjoyed worldwide success and has become an icon for her avant-garde albeit relatively accessible musical style.

GUÐMUNDSSON, ALBERT (1923–94). A former professional soccer player and politician who was born in **Reykjavík** on 5 October 1923. Guðmundsson graduated from the Cooperative College in Reykjavík in 1944 and from a commercial college in Glasgow, Scotland, in 1946. From 1947 to 1954, he played professional soccer with various teams in **Great Britain**, France, and Italy. In 1956, after retiring from sports, he started a successful wholesale firm in Reykjavík. His active involvement in politics began in 1970, when he was **elected** to Reykjavík's city council for the **Independence Party** (IP). Four years later, he entered **Alþingi** as a representative for the IP, serving as minister of finance from 1983 to 1985 and minister of industries from 1985 to 1987. In 1987, the leadership of the IP forced him to resign his ministerial post because of his alleged tax evasion. In response, he quit the party to form his own political organization, the **Citizens' Party.** The new party won a resounding victory in the 1987 elections, taking 11 percent of the votes cast and sending 7 representatives to Alþingi. In 1989, Guðmundsson retired from politics and was appointed ambassador to France, a post he held until just before his death in 1994.

The political strength of Guðmundsson lay in his ability to communicate with the common man, and his populist policies earned him respect and trust among leading members of the labor movement. Thus, while he never gained full acceptance from the elite of the IP, Guðmundsson remained popular among its general voters.

GUÐMUNDSSON, VALTÝR (1860–1928). This scholar and politician was born in Húnavatn County on 11 March 1860. After graduating from secondary school in **Reykjavík** in 1883, Guðmundsson began his studies of Old Norse at the University of Copenhagen. He completed a master's degree from this university in 1887 and defended his doctoral thesis in 1889. From 1890, he taught Icelandic history and **literature** at the University of Copenhagen, becoming a full professor of Icelandic **language** and literature in 1920.

In Iceland, Guðmundsson is not primarily remembered for his distinguished academic career but for his political activities. He was elected to **Alþingi** for the first time in 1894. The following year, he caused a sensation when he suggested a novel solution to the constitutional debates between Iceland and **Denmark**. He encouraged the parliament to adopt a pragmatic approach in the **nationalist** struggle, demanding only what the Danish reactionary government would possibly accept. In his view, material progress was more important than political independence, for the time being at least. In the next few years, Guðmundsson gradually increased his support in Alþingi for his conciliatory approach, gaining the majority in parliament in 1901. Unfortunately for him, however, the same year as his proposition finally passed through Alþingi, a liberal government came to power in Copenhagen and accepted **home rule** for Iceland. This was more than Guðmundsson had demanded, and the **king** selected his political nemesis, **Hannes Hafstein**, one of the leaders of the **Home Rule Party**, to head the first Icelandic home rule government. Although Guðmundsson sat in parliament almost continuously until 1913, he did not have much influence on Icelandic politics for the remainder of his life. *See also* CONSTITUTION OF 1874; GOVERNOR'S PERIOD; STATUS LAW.

GUNNARSSON, GUNNAR (1889–1975). One of the best-known Icelandic writers of the 20th century was born in eastern Iceland on 18 May 1889. Gunnarsson enjoyed limited formal **education** in his youth because of his parents' poverty, but in 1907, he was given the opportunity to enroll in the **Danish** Folk High School at Askov. After two years of study, Gunnarsson decided to become a writer in Denmark, publishing his first book of poetry in Danish in 1911. His literary breakthrough came with the novel *Af Borgslægtens Historie* (*The Story of the Borg Family*), which came out in four volumes from 1912 to 1914. For the next decades, he established himself as the leading Icelandic author writing in Danish. All of his novels dealt with Icelandic topics and were often set in historical times. In the 1930s, Gunnarsson attracted considerable attention in Germany, as his books seemed to please Nazi authorities. Gunnarsson visited Germany a number of times during these years, even meeting Adolf Hitler in 1940. His attitudes toward the Nazi regime remained ambivalent, however, and he was never a member of any Nazi political movement nor did he express sympathy for Hitler's racist policies. But, similar to the Norwegian writer Knut Hamsun, German nationalism and antiliberalism appealed to him, and his popularity among German readers tied him to the country. In 1939, Gunnarsson returned to Iceland after over three decades in Denmark, moving into a large country house close to where he was born in Iceland's eastern part. His intention was to become a gentleman farmer, but after a few years in the countryside, he moved to **Reykjavík**, where he lived for the rest of his life. *See also* LITERATURE.

GUNNARSSON, TRYGGVI (1835–1917). One of the most influential Icelanders of his time, as a pioneer in commerce, politician, and director of the **National Bank of Iceland** (NBI). Gunnarsson was born in Þingey County in northern Iceland on 18 October 1835. As a young man, he learned carpentry from his uncle, practicing this trade for a number of years in his home region. In 1859, Gunnarsson married and started farming in his county of birth. At this time, most Icelandic **trade** was in the hands of **Danish** merchants, many of whom were extremely unpopular in Iceland. For this reason, at the end of the 1860s, a number of farmers in northern Iceland formed an association in the region with the purpose of taking trade into their own hands. Gunnarsson was one of the leaders of this group, and from 1871, he served as director of the trading company called Gránufélagið (the Grána Company).

In the next few years, Gunnarsson rose to prominence in Iceland, both as the manager of an expanding commercial enterprise and as a member of **Alþingi**. In parliament, he was a close ally of **Jón Sigurðsson** (1811–79), the leader of the **Icelandic nationalist movement**. Gunnarsson's **nationalist** fervor cooled down considerably, however, in his later years. After 1880, the prosperity of the farmers' trading company declined rapidly, both because of the general **economic** depression in the country in these years as well as declining support among farmers with a growing competition from the **cooperative movement**. Gunnarsson left the directorship of the Grána Company in 1893 to become manager of the NBI. He held this position until 1909, when his political rivals ousted him from the post.

Gunnarsson was very influential in Icelandic society during the last decades of the 19th century and the beginning of the 20th century. As director of the Grána Company, he introduced new trading practices in his district, and as the manager of NBI, his lending policies helped promote the growth of the **fishing** industry. His projects as a building contractor managing construction of the parliamentary building in **Reykjavík** on the behalf of Alþingi in 1879–81 and the first major bridge in Iceland (Ölfusá Bridge) have also secured his place in Icelandic construction history.

GÚTTÓSLAGURINN. This violent scuffle in **Reykjavík** between the police and a group of workers and radicals is one of the best-known incidents of the **Great Depression**. The riots began in early November 1932, when leftists and laborers demonstrated against a planned reduction of salaries for workers employed in a program of relief works. The **trade unions** resisted this reduction, both because the relief works were a major source of revenue for the unemployed in Reykjavík and because they feared that the proposed decrease in wages would affect the level of salaries for the working class in general. On the afternoon of 9 November, police and demonstrators clashed inside and outside the meeting hall of Reykjavík's city council, called Gúttó after the owners of the house, the Icelandic chapter of the International Organization of Good Templars, leaving between 20 and 30 persons injured. The riots ended when the city council and the government yielded to the workers' demands.

GYLFASON, VILMUNDUR (1948–83). One of the most controversial politicians in Iceland in the late 20th century. He was born on 7 August 1948 in **Reykjavík** to one of the leaders of the **Social Democratic Party** (SDP). Gylfason graduated from **Menntaskólinn í Reykjavík** in 1968, completed a B.A. in history at the University of Manchester in 1971, and an M.A. at the University of Exeter in 1973. From 1973 until his death, Gylfason taught at Menntaskólinn í Reykjavík. In 1978, he was **elected** to **Alþingi** for the SDP, and his vigorous campaign helped the party to win its largest electoral victory in its history. He served as minister of justice, ecclesiastical affairs, and **education** from 1979 to 1980. During these years, Gylfason advocated radical changes in the political and administrative systems in Iceland, calling for a clearer distinction between the legislative and executive power, with direct elections of the **prime minister**. These ideas met with limited support among professional politicians, even in his own party. For that reason, he left the SPD in 1982 to form a new political organization in the following year, the **Social Democratic Union** (SDU), which he led in the 1983 parliamentary

elections. In spite of hasty preparations, the new party gained four representatives in these elections, but after Gylfason's early death in June 1983, the SDU quickly disintegrated.

Gylfason fought for a total transformation of the Icelandic political system, which he saw as stagnant and outdated. His popularity was, however, based more on his campaign style and personal charisma than on the ideas he propounded. His energetic performance in the media, in both television and the **press**, helped him to captivate and excite people in a way that no Icelandic politician had done for a long time.

– H –

HAARDE, GEIR H. (1951–). A politician born on 8 April 1951 in **Reykjavík**. After completing a university entrance exam from **Menntaskólinn í Reykjavík** in 1971, Haarde enrolled in Brandeis University, where he graduated with a B.A. in economics in 1973. He completed two master's degrees, one in international politics from Johns Hopkins University in 1975 and another in economics from the University of Minnesota in 1977. Haarde served first as economist in the international department of the Icelandic Central Bank (1977–83) and later as an assistant to two ministers of finance (1983–87). He was first elected to **Alþingi** for the **Independence Party** (IP) in 1987, and he has maintained his seat in parliament since then. Haarde was appointed minister of finance in 1998, minister of foreign affairs in 2005, and **prime minister** on 15 June 2006. In May 2007, Haarde formed a coalition government of the IP and the **Social Democratic Alliance**, where he continues to serve as prime minister.

Haarde has served in many key positions in the IP. First, he was **elected** president of its youth organization from 1981 to 1985, chairman of its parliamentary group from 1991 to 1998, and deputy chairman of the party from 1999 to 2005. He replaced **Davíð Oddsson** as the chairman of the IP in 2005 after six years as second in command of the party. Haarde's political style is very different from his predecessor's, as Oddsson tended to be both uncompromising and abrasive, while Haarde is more flexible and less aggressive. Their main political ideals appear to be very similar, however, as both subscribe to the traditional policies of the IP, opposing Iceland's membership in the **European Union**, promoting private enterprise in the **economy**, and supporting a fairly extensive public **health** care system.

HAFSTEIN, HANNES (1861–1922). A poet and the first minister of the Icelandic **Home Rule Period**. Hafstein was born on 4 December 1861 in Eyjafjörður **County** in the north to the district governor of the North and East District of Iceland. He graduated from the secondary school in **Reykjavík** in 1880 and completed a law degree from the University of Copenhagen in 1886. After practicing law and working as secretary for the governor of Iceland in Reykjavík, he assumed the position of bailiff in **Ísafjörður** County in 1895. He sat in parliament for this county in 1900–1901, for Eyjafjörður County in 1903–15, and for the country in general from 1915–17. Hafstein became the leader of the **Home Rule Party** (HRP), which was formed as a loose federation of representatives in parliament shortly before 1900. When the **Danish** government awarded the country **home rule** in 1904, Hafstein, as the leader of the majority party in **Alþingi**, was appointed minister of Iceland. He resigned from this post in 1909 after the HRP had lost its majority in parliamentary **elections** the year before. When he stepped down, Hafstein was appointed director of the Íslandsbanki (Bank of Iceland), where he served until he resumed the ministerial post in 1912. In 1914, he was forced to resign again when the parliamentary group that stood behind him dissolved. He resumed the directorship of the Bank of Iceland, but deteriorating health forced him to retire from public life in 1917.

Hafstein first caught the attention of the Icelandic public for his poetry and later for his energetic performance as a public official, and he rose rapidly to the highest post in Icelandic politics. As a minister, he emphasized issues of social and **economic** progress, but he was ousted when advocates of fervent **nationalism** swept the parliamentary elections of 1908. It was only with the **Act of Union** that the electorate was ready to turn away from the nationalist politics that had dominated Icelandic politics since the late 19th century, but then Hafstein left the political scene. *See also* THE DRAFT; GUÐMUNDSSON, VALTÝR (1860–1928).

HAFSTEIN, JÓHANN (1915–80). This politician was born in **Akureyri** on 17 September 1915 to the bailiff of Eyjafjörður County.

After graduating from the secondary school in Akureyri in 1934, Hafstein studied law at the **University of Iceland**, completing a law degree in 1937. For a few years, he worked for the **Independence Party** (IP), first as its emissary and from 1942 to 1952 as its managing director. **Elected** to **Alþingi** for the IP in 1946, he served as one of its representatives for **Reykjavík** for over three decades. He was a member of Reykjavík's city council from 1946 to 1958, and from 1952 to 1963, he was the director of the Fisheries Bank of Iceland. Hafstein held his first ministerial post for a brief period in 1961, but from 1963 to 1970 he served as minister of justice for the IP in the **Reconstruction Government**. At the death of **Bjarni Benediktsson** in 1970, Hafstein succeeded him as chairman of the IP and as **prime minister**, but his **cabinet** had to resign after defeat in the parliamentary elections of 1971. Two years later, Hafstein resigned his position as party chairman and retired from politics in 1978.

HALLGRÍMSSON, GEIR (1925–90). Former mayor of **Reykjavík**, **prime minister**, and director of the Central Bank of Iceland. Hallgrímsson was born in Reykjavík on 16 December 1925. After completing a university entrance exam from **Menntaskólinn í Reykjavík** in 1944 and a law degree from the **University of Iceland** in 1948, he studied for a year at Harvard Law School. From 1948 to 1959, Hallgrímsson practiced law in Reykjavík. He was appointed mayor of Reykjavík for the **Independence Party** (IP) in 1959, a position he held for 13 years. **Elected** to parliament for the IP in 1970, he became party chairman in 1973. In 1974, Hallgrímsson formed a coalition government with the participation of the IP and the **Progressive Party** (PP), serving as prime minister for four years. The government lost its majority in the elections of 1978, but from 1983 to 1986, Hallgrímsson served as minister of foreign affairs in a new coalition government with the PP. He stepped down as chairman of the IP in 1983 when challenged by **Þorsteinn Pálsson**. Hallgrímsson withdrew from politics three years later. During his last years, he served as director of the Central Bank of Iceland.

A cautious politician, Hallgrímsson was highly respected as mayor of Reykjavík, and under his leadership, the IP won one of its largest electoral victories in 1974. He was not as successful, however, as a chairman of the party. The IP suffered a great electoral loss in 1978, and internal dissension plagued the party through much of the 1980s. The resignation of Hallgrímsson in 1983 did not change much in this respect, and it was only with the energetic leadership of **Davíð Oddsson** that the party regained its unity in the 1990s.

HALLGRÍMSSON, JÓNAS (1807–45). This naturalist and poet was born in Eyjafjörður County on 16 November 1807 to a country pastor. After completing a university entrance exam at the Latin School at **Bessastaðir** (1829), Hallgrímsson worked as a clerk for the royal treasurer for Iceland in **Reykjavík.** Three years later in the fall of 1832, he enrolled in the University of Copenhagen with the intention of studying law. Before completing his law degree, Hallgrímsson changed to the study of natural history at the same time as he became involved in Icelandic student politics in Copenhagen. In 1834–35, he was one of the founders of *Fjölnir*, a periodical devoted to aesthetics in **literature**, politics, and the development of Icelandic culture and society in general. From 1837 to 1842, he traveled extensively in Iceland, studying its nature and **economy.** He dedicated his last years to the publication of the results of his research but had completed none of this material at the time of his early death in 1845.

Hallgrímsson is recognized today as one of Iceland's greatest poets. His romantic poetry expresses deep affection for the Icelandic nature and history, and thus, he articulated sentiments that were of great importance to the **Icelandic nationalist movement** and continue to speak to Icelanders today. Since 1996, Hallgrímsson's birthday (16 November) is celebrated as the official day of the Icelandic **language.** *See also* SÆMUNDSSON, TÓMAS (1807–41); SIGURÐSSON, JÓN (1811–79).

HANNIBALSSON, JÓN BALDVIN (1939–). One of the most prominent politicians of the 1980s and 1990s in Iceland. Born in **Ísafjörður** on 21 February 1939 to **Hannibal Valdimarsson**, a schoolmaster, labor leader, and politician in this fishing town in northwest Iceland, Hannibalsson completed a secondary school exam from **Menntaskólinn í Reykjavík** in 1958 and an M.A. in economics from the University of Edinburgh in 1963. After studying one year at Stockholm University, Hannibalsson returned to Iceland in 1964 to become an elementary school teacher in **Reykjavík**, but from 1970 to 1979, he was a principal of the secondary school of his hometown, Ísafjörður. While serving at the secondary school in Ísafjörður, he became active in local politics, sitting on the town council for the **Social Democratic Party** (SDP). In 1979, he was hired as editor of *Alþýðublaðið*, the newspaper of the SDP.

Hannibalsson entered parliament in 1982 and was **elected** chairman of the SDP in 1984, ousting the sitting leader of the party, **Kjartan Jóhannsson**. After a short stint as minister of finance in 1987–88 in a government headed by **Þorsteinn Pálsson** of the **Independence Party** (IP), he became minister of foreign affairs in 1988. In 1991, he led the SPD into coalition government with the IP under the premiership of **Davíð Oddsson**. He kept his post as minister of foreign affairs until the IP broke relations with the SPD in 1995. As minister of foreign affairs, Hannibalsson was a passionate advocate of close cooperation with the **European Union** (EU), and he was one of the main initiators of the negotiations that led to the **European Economic Area** agreement between the EU and **European Free Trade Association** (EFTA). Hannibalsson was also noted for his resolute support of the Baltic countries when they sought independence after the fall of the Soviet Union at the beginning of the 1990s. Hannibalsson retired from politics in 1998 and became ambassador, first in Washington (1998–2002) and then in Helsinki (2002–5).

Hannibalsson was a controversial politician, even inside his own party. Under his leadership, the SDP continued its centrist course, and gradually the party severed most of its ties with the **trade unions**. During the early 1990s, there was growing friction between him and the left wing of the SDP. This friction ended when his most vocal opponents, led by the party's deputy chairwoman, **Jóhanna Sigurðardóttir**, resigned from the SDP in 1994, forming the **political party Þjóðvaki** (National Awakening) in January of the following year.

HEALTH. The Icelandic health care system developed very late, as the country was both poor and sparsely populated through much of its history. The first educated doctor in Iceland was appointed by the **Danish** king in 1760, and there were very few doctors until the late 19th century. Thus, in 1850, the country was divided into only eight medical districts, but by the turn of the 20th century, their number had grown to 42. The hospital system in Iceland was more or less nonexistent at the turn of the 20th century; the first modern hospital opened in **Reykjavík** in 1866, offering places for 14 patients, and the second in **Akureyri** in 1873. Limited access to professional doctors and inadequate knowledge of infectious diseases had serious effects in Iceland as in other European countries, which is seen in the fact that **infant mortality** rates in Iceland were among the highest in Europe until late in the 19th century.

With improved health care and rising standards of living in Iceland, the general health of the nation became radically better. Thus, the life expectancy at birth increased dramatically during the 20th century, from 60 years for **women** and 56.2 years for men in 1921 to 83.2 years and 80.2 years, respectively, in 2007. This places Iceland among the countries where people live the longest in the world, and the infant mortality rate in Iceland, 2.9 for every 1,000 children born, is actually the lowest in the world.

These statistics show that Iceland's standards of living are exceptionally high and the health care system is extensive and effective. The general rule is that every Icelander is automatically covered by public health insurance, which is financed directly by the state budget. Hospitals are, therefore, free of charge, and people pay only minimal fees when visiting state-run primary health care centers. Moreover, most drugs are subsidized by the state, and they are free for hospital patients.

The system of socialized medicine enjoys general support in Iceland, and no **political party** has shown any interest in abolishing it. The growing cost of health care has, however, put increasing pressure on the system, and it is difficult for the government to secure the necessary funds for hospitals and to pay for the rising prices of medicine. For this reason, the hospitals have had to deal with chronic deficits, and it is difficult for the system to meet the demand for various services. *See also* PLAGUE; SMALLPOX; WELFARE STATE.

HEIMASTJÓRNARTÍMINN. *See* HOME RULE PERIOD.

HEKLA. This mountain, which is the best-known volcano in Iceland, is located in Rangárvellir County in southern Iceland. Hekla rises just under 1,500 meters (4,900 feet) above sea level and has been built up through repeated eruptions on a 40-kilometer-long (25 miles) fissure; the mountain itself is about 10 kilometers (6 miles) long. Hekla is a relatively young mountain, at least in geological terms, but it has been very active throughout its short history. The first known eruption took place around 6,600 years ago, and at least 18 eruptions have been recorded since the settlement of Iceland.

During the Middle Ages, people sometimes considered Hekla to be the entrance to hell, a fable that was underlined by the havoc it repeatedly wreaked upon neighboring regions and sometimes upon large parts of the country. In 1104, scientists believe that a huge eruption in Hekla destroyed the whole community of Þjórsárdalur Valley in the region to the west of the volcano, and in 1300, 1693, and 1766, pumice and poisonous ash from the volcano caused widespread devastation. The last major eruption of Hekla took place in 1947–48, but the last four eruptions, in 1971, 1980–81, 1991, and 2000, were all relatively insignificant. The last one was notable, however, for the fact that scientists were able to foresee its beginning with great accuracy, using the knowledge of the mountain's behavior that they have accumulated in recent eruptions.

HERMANNSSON, HALLDÓR (1878–1958). Former curator of the Fiske Icelandic Collection and professor at Cornell University. Hermannsson was born on 6 January 1878 to the bailiff of Rangárvellir County. After graduating from secondary school in **Reykjavík** in 1898, he entered the University of Copenhagen to study law. During the summer of 1899, Hermannsson met Daniel Willard Fiske, the first head librarian of Cornell University and avid collector of Icelandic books, and traveled with him to Florence to assist with his Icelandic book collection. In 1905, the year after Fiske's death, Hermannsson became the first curator of the Fiske Icelandic Collection at Cornell, which Fiske had established through his will. He donated his extensive collection of Icelandic books and his remaining funds to Cornell in order to found a special Icelandic section in the library. Along with his position as a curator, Hermannsson taught Old Norse and modern Icelandic at Cornell University, and in 1924, the university promoted him to a full professorship in Scandinavian languages. Under his direction, the Fiske Icelandic Collection flourished, and it is now by far the largest collection of Icelandic books in the **United States** and one of the best Icelandic libraries outside Iceland. He founded and edited the series Islandica, which comprised a number of studies on various aspects of Icelandic history and culture. Hermannsson retired from his position at the Fiske Collection in 1948 and died in Ithaca, New York, 10 years later.

HERMANNSSON, STEINGRÍMUR (1928–). Iceland's most influential and popular politician of the 1980s was born in **Reykjavík** on 22 June 1928. Hermannsson, who is the son of **Hermann Jónasson**, former **prime minister** of Iceland and chairman of the **Progressive Party** (PP) for almost three decades, was introduced to politics at an early age. He began his career, however, as an engineer, receiving a B.S. in electrical engineering from Illinois Institute of Technology in 1951 and a master's degree from California Institute of Technology in Pasadena one year later. After serving as an engineer in Iceland and the **United States**, he was appointed director of the Icelandic Research Council in 1957.

Hermannsson was first **elected** to parliament for the PP in 1971, becoming secretary of the party in the same year and its chairman in 1979. He served as minister in a number of **cabinets** from the late 1970s through the 1980s, first as minister of justice, ecclesiastical affairs, and **agriculture** (1978–79) and later as minister of **fisheries** and communications (1980–83), prime minister (1983–87 and 1988–91), and minister of foreign affairs (1987–88). When appointed director of the Central Bank of Iceland in 1994, he retired from politics, giving up both his seat in parliament and the leadership of the PP. Hermannsson retired from the Central Bank and thus from official life in 1998.

In politics, the 1980s was, in many respects, the decade of the PP, and Hermannsson's popularity contributed greatly to the strong position of the party. He served as prime minister for most of the decade, sometimes forming coalition governments with the parties on the left and sometimes with the **Independence Party** on the right. This is a testimony to his ability to negotiate between different **political parties**. Moreover, in opinion polls, people repeatedly voted him the most popular politician in Iceland, in part because of his skill in conveying an image of flexibility and resolution that appealed to voters.

HIÐ ÍSLENSKA BÓKMENNTAFÉLAG. *See* ICELANDIC LITER
ARY SOCIETY (ILS).

HIGH COURT. Established on 11 July 1800 after the suppression of
Alþingi, the Landsyfirréttur (Icelandic High Court) met for the first
time in August 1801. The high court was the highest court in Iceland,
serving as an appeals court for cases tried by the bailiffs around the
country. It was not the highest court for Iceland, however, as its rulings could be appealed to the supreme court in Copenhagen. The high
court met in **Reykjavík**, and three justices served, one of whom was
chief justice. The high court met for the last time in December 1919,
and it was replaced by the **Supreme Court of Iceland** the following
year.

HIRÐSTJÓRI. The highest royal office in Iceland, governor, was
named *hirðstjóri* from 1270 until the mid-16th century, when the title
changed to *höfuðsmaður*. The literal meaning of the term *hirðstjóri*
is courtier, or man of the court, while *höfuðsmaður* is a military position—captain in the **Danish** navy. These names reflect the changing
nature of the royal administration in Iceland; in the beginning, the
function of the office was to lead the **king**'s men in Iceland, but
after the **Lutheran Reformation** around the mid-16th century, the
function of the office became more clearly defined than before, making it the pinnacle of the administrative system in Iceland. To begin
with, the number of *hirðstjóri* fluctuated, and they were, as a rule,
Icelandic by birth. From the 14th century, many foreigners served as
hirðstjóri, and the *höfuðsmaður* was either Danish or German. This
was against the wishes of the Icelandic elites, as they demanded that
the *hirðstjóri* or *höfuðsmaður* should be of Icelandic or **Norwegian**
descent. *See also* BESSASTAÐIR; *STIFTAMTMAÐUR*.

HÖFUÐSMAÐUR. See HIRÐSTJÓRI.

HÓLAR. A farm in Skagafjörður County in northwestern Iceland. It
became the second episcopal seat in Iceland in 1106, serving as the
residence for the bishop of northern Iceland until 1798. In 1801, **Danish** church authorities formally abolished the Hólar diocese and put
the whole country under one bishop placed in the emerging capital

of the province, **Reykjavík**. For seven centuries, Hólar was a center of **religious** and cultural life in its district. For most of this period, the bishop ran a Latin school for boys and young men at Hólar. **Jón Arason**, the last **Catholic** bishop at Hólar, founded the first printing press in Iceland there around 1530.

At the beginning of the 19th century, Hólar lost its former prestige and became a regular church farm. In the early 1880s, Skagafjörður County bought Hólar in order to turn the farm into an **agricultural** college. Similar to **Skálholt**, the other former episcopal seat in Iceland, the **Lutheran** Church has striven in recent years to restore some of the old standing of Hólar; its 18th-century church has recently been renovated and is now the residence of one of Iceland's two suffragan bishops. Moreover, the agricultural college has now been upgraded to a university specializing in such areas as aquaculture and fish biology, **tourism**, and horse breeding. *See also* THE REFORMATION.

HOME RULE. With the **constitution of 1874, Alþingi** acquired limited legislative power and full control over public expenditures in Iceland, although the executive power remained totally in the hands of the **Danish** government and officials appointed by the **king**. Moreover, the minister of Icelandic affairs sat in the Danish **cabinet**, and this ministry remained the responsibility of the Danish minister of justice. Icelanders were very dissatisfied with this arrangement, both because they felt that a Danish minister was unable to comprehend Icelandic needs and aspirations and because they preferred to have a minister who was responsible to their own parliament, Alþingi.

From 1881 to 1903, the revision of the constitution remained the central issue of political debates in Iceland. The reactionary government in Denmark rejected all demands for constitutional revision, but when parliamentary rule was introduced in Denmark in 1901, bringing the Venstre (Liberal Party) to power, the doors opened for a reorganization of the Icelandic executive branch. In 1903, the king ratified a new constitution, granting Iceland home rule. The following year, the king appointed **Hannes Hafstein**, the spokesman of the **Home Rule Party**, as the first Icelandic minister. Formally he was a member of the Danish cabinet, but as he resided in **Reykjavík**, his participation in cabinet meetings remained sporadic. Moreover, he was responsible to Alþingi but not to the Danish parliament, meaning that he did not resign when the cabinet lost its majority in the Danish parliament; however, when Hafstein proved to have lost his majority in Alþingi in 1909, he had to resign. This confirmed that the home rule government adhered to the principles of representative government and was responsible to the Icelandic parliament, not the Danish one.

Although home rule made the government more responsive to the desires of Icelanders, it did not satisfy the demands of the **nationalists**. The constitution did not revoke the **Status Law** of 1871, and it required the Icelandic minister to present all bills passed in Alþingi to the Danish cabinet. For this reason, the **Home Rule Period** was a time of intense nationalist mobilization in Iceland, reaching its peak with the debates about the so-called **Draft** in 1908. With the **Act of Union** of 1918, Iceland became a sovereign state in union with Denmark, and the Home Rule Period came to an end. *See also* GUÐ-MUNDSSON, VALTÝR (1860–1928); ICELANDIC NATIONALIST MOVEMENT.

HOME RULE PARTY (HRP). A party uniting the opponents of **Valtýr Guðmundsson** in **Alþingi** at the end of the 19th century. One of the main tenets of the HRP was a demand for **home rule** in Iceland, and with the transfer of government from Copenhagen to **Reykjavík** in 1904, **Hannes Hafstein**, spokesman of the HRP, became the first minister to reside in Iceland. The HRP lost its majority in Alþingi in 1908, and Hafstein resigned when the parliament met the following year. Like all the political groupings of its time, the HRP was more a loose federation of parliamentary representatives than an organized **political party**. From 1912, the HRP was very unstable because some of its leading members left it to form new political groups. During **World War I**, the political system in Iceland was reorganized, as issues other than attitudes toward Danish rule in Iceland began to dominate the political discourse. The **Act of Union** in 1918 granting Iceland the status of a sovereign state completed this development and rendered the prewar parties obsolete. The HRP participated in parliamentary **elections** for the last time in 1919, but its former leaders were instrumental in the formation of the **Conservative Party** in 1924. *See also* THE DRAFT; HOME RULE PERIOD.

HOME RULE PERIOD. The period from 1904 to 1918 is called the Heimastjórnartíminn (**Home Rule** Period). It opened on 1 February 1904, when the Ministry of Icelandic Affairs moved to **Reykjavík** from Copenhagen, and it ended on 1 December 1918, when Iceland became a sovereign state. Strong **economic** growth fueled by a rapid mechanization of the **fisheries** characterized the Home Rule Period. This period was also a time of fervent **nationalism**, reaching its pinnacle in 1908. In that year, voters turned against the political leadership in the country and rejected a draft of a new constitution drawn up in a committee of representatives from the Icelandic and **Danish** parliaments (usually it is called the **Draft**) because it did not declare Iceland a sovereign state. Finally, with the **Act of Union** of 1918, the Danish government gave in to Icelandic demands, accepting Icelandic sovereignty. *See also* CONSTITUTION OF 1874; HOME RULE PARTY (HRP); STATUS LAW.

HREPPUR. See COMMUNE.

– I –

ICELAND STOCK EXCHANGE. The Kauphöll Íslands [Iceland Stock Exchange (ICEX)] was founded in **Reykjavík** in 1985 by a few Icelandic **banks** and brokerage firms. The initiative came from the Central Bank of Iceland, and when the ICEX started its trading in 1986, it focused almost entirely on Icelandic government bonds. Trading in equities started in 1990, increasing rapidly through the 1990s. The extensive **privatization** schemes of the late 1990s and early 21st century boosted the ICEX because all the former state banks were listed on the exchange. In October 2006, ICEX was acquired by OMX, the company that ran the **Danish**, Finnish, and Swedish exchanges, to form the Nordic Exchange. It was Europe's sixth largest stock exchange when it was taken over by the American stock exchange giant NASDAQ in February 2008 to form NASDAQ OMX.

The phenomenal growth of the ICEX is symptomatic of the radical transformation that has taken place in Icelandic **economy** and business mentality in recent years. This growth is driven by relentless escalation of Icelandic share indexes, which rose by 550 percent from 1997 to 2006—more than double that of most of the other national indexes on the Nordic Exchange. The ICEX continues to be very small, however, in the international context, and it remains very vulnerable to fluctuations. Thus, the financial credit crisis of early 2008 hit the Icelandic stock market very hard, with almost a 50 percent fall in the main share index of the ICEX from October 2007 to March 2008. This weakness has worried foreign investors, and the upsurge of the indexes in the first years of the 21st century did not lead to much foreign investment in Iceland. See also CENTRAL BANKING.

ICELANDAIR. Icelandair is the largest airline in Iceland. It was formed in 1973 with the merger of Flugfélag Íslands (Icelandair) and Loftleiðir (Icelandic Airlines) and called Flugleiðir in Icelandic. Prior to the merger, the two airlines had waged a controlled but emotionally charged competition on the market. Icelandair, the older of the two companies (established in 1937), specialized in domestic flights in addition to serving the routes to Scandinavia and the British Isles. Icelandic Airlines were better known internationally, however, primarily for their inexpensive transatlantic flights connecting Iceland with both the **United States** and the European continent. In the long run, the small Icelandic market could not sustain these two airlines, and the competitors merged, thus uniting the domestic and international routes.

In spite of the merger, Icelandair faced great **economic** difficulties in the 1970s and 1980s, as fuel prices skyrocketed. Its survival was crucial for the Icelandic economy, however, and for a time, it enjoyed considerable financial assistance from the state. Through a major overhaul of its fleet and substantial reductions of its operating costs in the late 1980s and early 1990s, Icelandair was able to survive the crisis and become financially profitable again.

The structure of the company has drastically changed in recent years, reflecting the transformation of the Icelandic business environment and the changes in the airline industry. Thus, the company gradually grew into a giant in the Icelandic **tourist** industry, owning many of the largest hotels in Iceland, a tour bus company, a car rental service, and a travel agency, among other businesses. In 1997, the domestic flights were separated from Icelandair with the revival of

Flugfélag Íslands as a separate company owned by Icelandair. This was done, in part, as a reaction to demands from the Icelandic Competition Authorities. In 2005, the company transformed its corporate structure under the aegis of an investment company called FL Group, but currently it is one of 12 independent subsidiaries of the travel industry group Icelandair Group. *See also* TRANSPORTATION.

ICELANDIC FEDERATION OF LABOR (IFL). Representatives from various **trade unions** of unskilled workers, fishermen, and artisans formed this general organization of Icelandic labor, Alþýðusamband Íslands (usually called by its acronym, ASÍ), on 12 March 1916. The aims of the federation were to guard the interests of its members in negotiations with employers and to serve as a **political party** advocating social democratic ideals in Iceland.

In the beginning, no clear distinction was made between the IFL and the **Social Democratic Party** (SDP), thus the president of the IFL also served as chairman of the SDP. This arrangement met increasing opposition from both the Right (from members of the **Independence Party**) and the Left (from members of the **Socialist Unity Party**). From 1940 to 1942, the links between the party and the labor movement were severed, and since then, the IFL has not been aligned with any political party but focuses on **economic** and social issues of its working-class members. This change opened the IFL to people and unions of different political leanings that had been barred from the federation on political grounds, thus unifying the working class movement in one general organization.

The relations between the IFL and the **SA-Confederation of Icelandic Employers** (SA-CIE) were turbulent for much of the 20th century, as strikes were frequent and negotiations often acrimonious. In 1990, the IFL and SA-CIE made peace in order to tackle the problem of chronic **inflation** in the Þjóðarsáttarsamningar (**National Compromise Agreement**). Since then, the IFL has not called a general strike in Iceland and has worked with the SA-CIE and various governments in securing economic stability.

With the decline in union militancy, the image of the trade unions has changed considerably. Now university-educated professionals tend to represent the workers in the media, and their leaders emphasize responsibility and moderation rather than struggle and social transformation. The IFL continues, however, to play a major role in the workplace, providing various services to the Icelandic working people and defending their rights. Iceland is one of the most thoroughly unionized countries in the world, as the IFL has 108,000 members in 64 separate unions, making it the largest association in Iceland. *See also* LABOR MARKET.

ICELANDIC HISTORICAL ASSOCIATION (IHA). Sögufélag, or the IHA, was founded in 1902 for the purpose of publishing Icelandic historical sources. True to its original goal, the IHA has published the acts of the old **Alþingi**, the rulings of the **high court**, and the documents of the **royal commission of 1770–71**. In recent years, the IHA has also published a number of historical monographs and collections of essays. From the beginning, three journals have been issued under the auspices of the IHA, *Blanda* (1918–53), *Saga* (1950–), and *Ný saga* (1987–2001). The journal *Saga* (*History*), which is the main platform for academic history writing in Iceland, is issued twice a year.

ICELANDIC LITERARY SOCIETY (ILS). At the initiative of the **Danish** philologist **Rasmus Christian Rask**, Hið íslenska bókmenntafélag, or the ILS, was founded in Copenhagen in 1816. The ILS originally had one section in Copenhagen and another in Iceland, reflecting the importance of the Danish capital for Icelandic cultural life at the time. The goal of the society was to contribute to the protection and development of the Icelandic **language** and culture through the publication of educating and enlightening **literature**; thus, it combined influences from the **Enlightenment** of the 18th century and the emerging romanticism of the 19th. The incentive for this enterprise was Rask's fear for the future of the Icelandic language, but during a visit to Iceland in 1813, he predicted that it would perish in the following 100 to 200 years.

Since its foundation, publication of books and journals has been the core of ILS's activities. In 1817, in its second year, the Copenhagen section of the ILS launched a journal called *Íslenzk sagnablöð*, but a decade later, the journal *Skírnir* replaced it. This journal has been continuously published ever since. During its long history, the ILS has also published a great variety of books on such subjects as

Icelandic literature, history, **economy**, law, and popular science, emphasizing instruction aimed at the general public. In the beginning, the center of this activity was in Copenhagen, but after the death of **Jón Sigurðsson** (1811–79), who served as president of ILS's Copenhagen section from 1851 to 1879, a campaign started for the transfer of all of its operations to **Reykjavík**. It was only in 1911, however, that the two sections merged in Reykjavík.

At present, the ILS is not as dominant in its field as it was during the last century, but it is still one of the most active and prestigious publishers of academic literature and books of educational value for the general public in Iceland.

ICELANDIC NATIONALIST MOVEMENT. Icelandic **nationalism** did not engender an organized political movement until the last decades of **Danish** rule in Iceland, but from the late 1830s and the early 1840s, it became a dominant theme in Icelandic political discourse. The original demands of Icelandic nationalists were formulated by students and intellectuals in Copenhagen, soon under the leadership of philologist and archivist **Jón Sigurðsson** (1811–79). From 1845, he emerged as the most forceful spokesman of Icelandic nationalism in **Alþingi**, and he set the tone for the Icelandic demands in the **Constitutive Assembly** held in **Reykjavík** in 1851. At this meeting, Icelanders rejected all participation in the emerging Danish nation-state, calling for **home rule** and legislative power to be bestowed upon the Icelandic parliament, Alþingi.

During the 1860s, nationalist policies had clear popular support in parliamentary **elections**, and Sigurðsson remained the unquestioned leader of the nationalist movement. From 1871 to 1874, the Danish government gave Alþingi limited legislative power in Icelandic domestic affairs, although the **king** retained the full prerogative to veto all bills passed in Alþingi. This did not satisfy the nationalists, and in 1881, after a short break, their fight for sovereignty continued. Efforts to amend the **constitution of 1874** dominated parliamentary politics during the last two decades of the 19th century, ending with the establishment of home rule in 1904. The nationalist struggle reached its pinnacle in 1908, however, when the so-called **Draft** for a new constitution was rejected in parliamentary elections on the grounds that it did not fully recognize what people saw as Iceland's inalienable national rights. After the passing of the **Act of Union** in 1918, nationalism became less prevalent in Icelandic politics, as the act fulfilled most nationalist demands, but the foundation of the **Republic of Iceland** in 1944 was a logical conclusion to the nationalist struggle.

The nationalist movement was never organized in a unified association in Iceland, but nationalist sentiments remained the defining factors of Icelandic politics from the mid-19th century to the end of **World War I**. It is not surprising, therefore, that nationalism remains an important theme in Icelandic politics to this day, as the early nationalist leaders, Sigurðsson in particular, have gained near saintly status in Icelandic history. *See also FJÖLNIR.*

ICELANDIC REVOLUTION. On 25 June 1809, a British soap merchant by the name of Samuel Phelps arrested Count **Frederik Christopher Trampe**, the **Danish** governor in **Reykjavík**, and deposed him from his post. The reason for Phelps's action was Trampe's unwillingness to grant him permission to **trade** in Iceland, a measure that threatened the merchant's commercial venture in the country. Phelps's "revolution" took a drastic turn, however, when **Jörgen Jörgensen**, a Danish interpreter in his service, assumed the role of governor of Iceland. In two proclamations issued on 26 June 1809, the new ruler of Iceland proposed revolutionary changes in the administration. The country was declared free and independent under British protection. Jörgensen's intention was to establish a legislative assembly in the spirit of the old **Alþingi**, which had been abolished a few years earlier, with democratically **elected** representatives from the various districts in Iceland. To secure his popularity, the new governor lowered all taxes in Iceland, and he promised to introduce stiff price controls on grain. Jörgensen reiterated these proclamations on 11 July of the same year, when he promised to convoke a constituent assembly of elected representatives on 1 July of the following year (1810). At the same time, he declared himself protector, or virtual absolute ruler, of the island for the next year.

The revolutionary government met little resistance in Iceland. Jörgensen promised to retain all royal officials of Icelandic descent, provided that they sent him a declaration of allegiance. As the Danish government had no defensive forces in the country and communications with Copenhagen were sporadic because of the Napoleonic Wars, many officials saw no point in resisting the usurper. His rule lasted only nine weeks, however, as a British naval captain patroling Icelandic waters brought it to an end in late August 1809. In the captain's opinion, Phelps and his company had transgressed British laws because he did not consider Icelanders enemies of **Great Britain**. On 22 August 1809, Danish rule was restored in Iceland, and shortly thereafter, the revolutionaries were brought back to Britain.

The revolution did not have much influence on the course of Icelandic history, although the summer of 1809 is certainly among its most memorable periods. Jörgensen completely failed to incite Icelanders, and his revolutionary rhetoric horrified men like Sir Joseph Banks, the British naturalist and explorer who had long attempted to persuade the British government to annex Iceland. Thus, when the former authorities were back in control, Iceland returned quietly to the Danish sphere of influence, although the British government continued to control Icelandic trade throughout the Napoleonic Wars.

ICELANDIC SOCIETY FOR WOMEN'S RIGHTS (ISWR). The Kvenréttindafélag Íslands (ISWR) was founded in 1907 in **Reykjavík** at the initiative of **Bríet Bjarnhéðinsdóttir**, the early champion of **women**'s rights in Iceland. In the beginning, the main purpose of the ISWR, which was affiliated with the International Alliance of Women, was to fight for the enfranchisement of women in parliamentary **elections**. The ISWR achieved an astounding victory in 1908 when four women were elected to Reykjavík's city council from an all-female list, as the previous year's charter for the city of Reykjavík had given women the right to run for seats in the city council for the first time. For the next few years, **Alþingi** removed many of the legal barriers denying women full citizenship. In 1911, it granted women equality with men in **education** and full access to offices in the civil service, and from 1915 to 1920, they received equal suffrage in parliamentary elections. The ISWR was active in promoting all of these issues.

Until 1926, the ISWR took a prominent position in politics, offering special tickets in many local and parliamentary elections. But as the modern Icelandic party system took form, political allegiances began to split the ISWR. For this reason, the society changed its policy and became a nonpartisan organization, uniting women from all **political parties**. Since then, the ISWR has remained a strong advocate of women's rights in the workplace and the public arena, in addition to supporting various charitable organizations for women. *See also* WOMEN'S ALLIANCE (WA).

ICELANDIC STEAMSHIP COMPANY (ISC). The first Icelandic shipping company, Eimskipafélag Íslands, or the ISC, was founded in January 1914. The ISC, which was the first major public shareholding company in Iceland, was created through a well-organized campaign instigated by a group of entrepreneurs in **Reykjavík**. Their goal was free **transportation** by sea to and from Iceland from a virtual **Danish** monopoly. The effort was very successful, as the number of founding shareholders was over 13,000, around 13 percent of the Icelandic **population** at the time. In 1915, the ISC started scheduled sailings between Iceland and Europe on two new vessels, and it has remained Iceland's largest shipping company ever since. From its founding, the ISC had very strong **nationalistic** overtones. For the inhabitants of an isolated island, control over communications with the neighboring countries played a central role for national identity; at the same time, the ISC's success boosted Icelandic confidence at an important juncture in the struggle for independence.

The ISC continued to be in public ownership through most of the 20th century, securing Iceland's connection with both Europe and the **United States**. Recently, the company has—like most Icelandic businesses—gone through various changes and expansions. Thus, the majority of its stocks is now owned by two large investment funds in Iceland, and it has lost its status as the "favorite child of the nation," as the ISC was commonly called in the beginning. For a few years, the ISC merged with a number of other transportation companies, such as the airline leasing company Air Atlanta Icelandic and the British charter airlines Excel Air, to form a giant in the transportation business, but recently it decided to withdraw from this cooperation to concentrate on its core business, cargo shipping. Its current mission is now to consolidate its position as a leading transport company on the North Atlantic, connecting Iceland with both North America and Europe.

IMMIGRATION. *See* MIGRATION.

INDEPENDENCE PARTY (IP). Two different **political parties** have carried the name Sjálfstæðisflokkur, or IP, since the early 20th century. The former was established as an electoral alliance before the parliamentary **elections** of 1908, and it became a formal political party in February 1909. Although the party existed for the next 17 years, it was always marked by deep divisions, and it never developed an enduring institutional structure. In 1915, the party split into two groups; one (called the IP þversum, "crosswise" in literal translation) advocated an intransigent position in the struggle for Icelandic sovereignty, while the other (the IP langsum, or "lengthwise") was more pragmatic in its approach to these questions.

In 1923, the representatives of the former **Home Rule Party** united with the IP's parliamentary group to form the **Citizens' Party** in order to meet the challenge of the new class-based parties, the workers' **Social Democratic Party** (SDP) and the farmers' **Progressive Party** (PP). This coalition did not survive for long, as its majority founded the **Conservative Party** (CP) in 1924, while five members of its parliamentary group revived the IP. This installation of the IP ceased to exist in 1926, when one of its two remaining representatives in **Alþingi** joined the PP, while the other founded the **Liberal Party** (LP).

The second party to bear the name IP has been the largest political party in Iceland since its foundation in 1929. It was formed on 25 May of that year through a merger of the CP and the LP. The new party inherited its name from the defunct IP, but it had little more than that in common with its old namesake.

Since its foundation, the IP has incorporated diverse ideological tenets. In their original declaration, its founders aimed at full separation from **Denmark** and professed a strong belief in social and **economic** progress, and they thought that individual liberty was the best strategy to attain both goals. The party has always emphasized its support of free enterprise politics in the economic sphere, and it prefers private initiative to state enterprise in most areas of social life. In practice, the party has always been flexible on these issues. Because of its size, it spans a wide political field, both in ideological and social terms. Thus, the IP draws support from the Far Right and the Moderate Center, from towns as well as from the countryside, and even if it is often seen as probusiness, it has had a strong representation in the leadership of the **trade unions**, especially among fishermen and in the commercial workers' unions. Although the IP originally advocated strong **nationalist** views, no political party has been as resolute in its support of the American military presence in **Keflavík** and Iceland's membership in the **North Atlantic Treaty Organization**.

In its first parliamentary elections (1931), the IP captured nearly 44 percent of the popular vote. For the next four decades, its support was fairly stable, usually ranging from 37 to 42 percent. Strong popular support has made the party a major force in Icelandic politics, both on a national level and in local councils.

The 1980s was a difficult period for the IP. Due to a struggle over its leadership, the support of the party dwindled, and it seemed to be heading toward a permanent split. In 1980, **Gunnar Thoroddsen**, one of its longtime leaders and its deputy chairman at the time, broke from the IP to head a coalition government of the PP, the **People's Alliance**, and three IP representatives in parliament. In the 1987 elections, **Albert Guðmundsson**, another leading member of the party, left the IP to form his own party, which he named the Citizens' Party. As a result, the support of the IP fell to an all-time low in the polls, as it received only 27 percent of the votes cast in the 1987 parliamentary elections. The party came to the 1991 elections reunited under the leadership of **Davíð Oddsson**, the mayor of **Reykjavík**, and received just under 40 percent of the popular vote. The party formed a coalition government with the SDP in 1991, following the pattern of the **Reconstruction Government** of 1959–71. It lost some ground in the 1995 parliamentary elections, but its government retained a slim majority all the same. In order to strengthen its parliamentary majority, the leadership of the IP chose to change partners, forming a new coalition government with the PP under Oddson's leadership. These two parties governed together for three terms, but in 2007, after a shocking electoral defeat, the PP pulled out of the partnership in order to rebuild its base. In response, the IP formed a coalition government with its main rival, the **Social Democratic Alliance** (SDA). This government has overwhelming support in both parliament and the polls, as it includes parties that together polled two thirds of the votes cast in the last elections.

The IP is still the largest political party in Iceland, although its dominance is not as striking now as it was in the first half of the century. One reason for this is the challenge from the SDA, which has at times approached the IP in popularity in the polls. During the first years of the 21st century, the party also appeared to be on a downward slide, as it received only 33 percent of the votes in the 2003 elections, which was the second worst result it had had since its foundation. This may have been a temporary slump, however, created by the growing unpopularity of the longtime chairman of the IP, Oddsson, because the party—under a new leadership—bounced back in the 2007 elections. One reason for this is the popularity of the current chairman of the IP and **prime minister** of Iceland, **Geir H. Haarde.**

INDUSTRIALIZATION. Using higher rates of growth and structural changes in the **economy** as the two main albeit narrow criteria in defining industrialization, its initial phase in Iceland is dated to the turn of the 20th century. Unfortunately, national income data does not exist for the period prior to 1901 and is unreliable before 1945. The historical evidence indicates, however, that the economy entered a period of accelerated growth around 1890 based on increased exports of fish products and, to a lesser extent, **agricultural** goods. Export earnings showed an increase of 35 percent in the 1890s compared with the previous decade, and the available national income data indicate an annual growth rate of 3.9 percent from 1901 to 1914, which was well above the European average for the same period. Important contributory factors to this growth were expanding overseas markets for fish products and steadily improving terms of **trade** from 1894 to the early years of **World War I**. The growth of the **fisheries** and higher returns attracted both domestic and foreign capital and paved the way for the use of modern technology, motorboats and steam trawlers in particular.

The move from the primary into the secondary economic sector, an important criterion of industrialization, was fairly slow during the early phases of the economic transformation of Iceland. The catalyst for growth was fishing and fish processing rather than the manufacturing **industry**, making industrialization a somewhat ambiguous label for this economic change in Iceland. The share of agriculture in **employment** dropped continuously from the late 19th century, from 80 percent in 1870 to 32 percent in 1940, while the rates for fisheries, including fish processing, rose from 13 to 18 percent and for other industries from 3 to 12 percent in the same period. The proportion of the national income derived from agriculture declined from 45 percent in 1901 to 18 percent in 1940, while the fisheries dropped from 30 to 27 percent. The industrial process reversed the traditional roles of these two main sectors within the overall economic structure. The fisheries ceased to be primarily part-time employment of the rural **population** and became the main livelihood for a growing section of the urban labor force, which normally supplemented its earnings with casual farm work and construction work during slack seasons in the fisheries.

Industrialization, defined rather narrowly here, was only part of a more general and lengthy process, transforming Iceland into a modern capitalist society. Essential to this process were factors like new sources of **energy** (hydroelectric power and imported coal and oil), the development of a **transportation** system, the liberalization of foreign trade, the emergence of modern financial institutions, the creation of a free **labor market**, the shift toward freehold farming, and other changes in the institutional framework of the economy. *See also* ENERGY-INTENSIVE INDUSTRIES; URBANIZATION.

INDUSTRY. The narrow resource base and limited division of labor in the work force offered few opportunities for the development of manufacturing industries in Iceland during most of its history. In general, each household processed the materials produced on the farm or by household members, such as wool, hides, milk, meat, and fish, thus fulfilling the needs of the household for clothes and food. Some of the household production was exported, notably socks, mittens, and other knitted fabrics; wool; salted mutton; and dried and salt fish. With urbanization and growing division of labor during the second half of the 19th century, specialized artisans—carpenters, blacksmiths, stone masons, saddle makers, bakers, shoemakers—took over many of these functions. The advent of steam and electrical power after the turn of the 20th century gave rise to more diversified, modern industries, such as textile factories, creameries and dairies, and herring and fish factories. Moreover, in reaction to the **Great Depression**, light industries producing goods for the domestic market expanded rapidly under the comprehensive protection policy of the **Government of the Laboring Classes** of 1934–38.

During the 1970s, industry entered a new phase in Iceland. This happened with the emergence of **energy-intensive industries** and the reduction of various restrictions on foreign **trade** and **currency** transactions, leading to an intensified competition with imported industrial goods. This trend became more evident when Iceland entered the **European Free Trade Association** (EFTA) in 1970, but tariffs on imports from other EFTA countries were to be removed gradually over a decade. The duty-free access of Icelandic industrial products to markets in the EFTA countries has encouraged export industries, which were feeble before 1970. The experience of these changes has been, in general, positive. Thus, the share of industrial goods (excluding processed fish) in total exports increased from around 2 percent at the beginning of the 1960s to around 20 percent at the beginning of the 1970s. The rate did not change much for the next three decades, but it began to rise again during the first years of the 21st century, reaching 39 percent in 2007. This increase was, to a large degree, driven by the expansion of the energy-intensive industries, but other industries have also gained ground in recent years.

The share of industries in the gross domestic product (GDP) has, on the whole, declined in recent years, from around 16 percent at the beginning of the 1990s to around 11 percent. Moreover, industrial **employment** has, in relative terms, shrunk considerably with the consequent rise in productivity. Industries producing goods for the domestic market have not fared well in competition, in particular the manufacture of textiles, clothing, and furniture. The main reasons for this are reduced protection against foreign imports and the high exchange rate of Icelandic currency. Manufacture and export of woolen goods used to be a significant element in Icelandic **economy**, but it has been hard hit in recent years. In contrast, other export industries, such as industries related to the **fisheries** (notably the production of fishing gear and fish processing equipment) and the energy-intensive industry, have progressed considerably. *See also* INDUSTRIALIZATION.

INFANT MORTALITY. Before the mid-19th century, the infant mortality rate (IMR) in Iceland was among the highest in Europe. From the late 18th century, the time of the first reliable records, until the 1870s, between 250 and 350 of every 1,000 live-born children in Iceland died in their first year. One of the main reasons for this situation seems to be the fact that most Icelandic **women** did not, as a rule, breastfeed their children, and living conditions were usually very bad. In the latter part of the 19th century, with improved **education** of midwives and increasing knowledge of infectious diseases, the IMR declined rapidly, reaching the same levels as for the other Nordic countries at the turn of the 20th century (around 100). At present, Iceland has one of the lowest IMR recorded in the world, as only 2.9 children die of every 1,000 born. This reflects the high standards of living in Iceland and the comprehensive public **health** care system.

INFLATION. Iceland suffered higher rates of inflation than most European countries during the postwar period. Already in the 1950s, the annual rate was more than double that of the other European countries in the Organization of Economic Cooperation and Development (OECD), 9 percent compared to 4 percent. The disparity continued to grow in the following decades, culminating in an 84 percent rise in consumer prices in Iceland in 1983. In the following year, the inflation rate fell drastically, below 30 percent, but it continued to be high above what was deemed normal for countries of Western Europe. The persistent high inflation after **World War II** reflects the dependence of the **economy** on foreign **trade**, the heavy weight of fish products in total exports, and the small size of the economy.

Until the 1980s, large fluctuations in fish catches and export prices often generated swings in national income on a much larger scale than in other European countries. During periods of rising export values, salaries in the fishing industry tended to increase rapidly, a trend that was later transmitted into higher wage claims in other economic sectors. The subsequent price–wage spiral eventually led to a decline in profitability in the export industries, to which the government responded by devaluing the **currency**—which again fueled inflation. Generally, economic policy was geared toward adjusting the economy to inflation by limiting its most harmful effects rather than to fighting the causes for rising prices. This was clearly demonstrated in the relaxed fiscal and monetary policies of the 1970s and 1980s and the general indexing of wages, loans, and deposits to inflation.

This economic cycle dominated the development of prices until the end of the 1980s, when inflation dropped sharply, from 25 percent in 1988 to 1.5 percent in 1994. This drastic change was a combined result of the chronic recession that plagued Iceland from 1988 to 1996, wage agreements between the **Icelandic Federation of Labor** and the Confederation of Icelandic Employers [*see* SA-CONFEDERATION OF ICELANDIC EMPLOYERS (SA-CIE)], and a shift in government policy orientations. In recent years, the state has placed more emphasis on low inflation than high **employment**, using tight monetary and fiscal policy to fight the pressure of inflation and assigning the Central Bank the specific mission of keeping the inflationary rates below 2.5 percent on an annual basis. Although this policy has been quite successful, as inflation in Iceland has been much lower in recent years than it used to be, high inflation continues to be one of the most serious economic problems. It fluctuated wildly from 1996 to 2007, reaching as high as 6.7 percent in 2001 and falling to 2.1 percent in 2003 (0.7 percent if real estate prices are excluded). As the economy began to overheat in 2005 and 2006, inflation rates began to rise again to over 8 percent in late 2006. This development has prompted many business leaders and economists to call for a change in Icelandic currency from the weak and unstable *króna* to the stronger euro. *See also* CENTRAL BANKING.

INGÓLFUR ARNARSON. *See* ARNARSON, INGÓLFUR (9TH AND 10TH CENTURIES).

INNRÉTTINGAR. An **industrial** project contrived by a number of influential Icelanders in 1751 at the suggestion of **Skúli Magnússon**, the royal treasurer of Iceland. The original purpose was to modernize the Icelandic **economy** by introducing new industrial methods into the country and thus improve the lot of the nation. The **Danish** royal government contributed substantial sums of money to the project, which started operating small textile workshops in **Reykjavík** in the early 1750s, laying the foundation for the development of the future capital of Iceland. In the beginning, the company experimented with processing and exporting sulfur and improving fishing techniques, but from early on, it emphasized the production of woolen cloth. For various reasons, the company was never profitable, and most of its ventures were only short lived. In 1764, a Danish merchant company took over the textile workshops in Reykjavík, and in 1774, they became a royal property. The workshops were sold in 1787 and finally closed down in 1802–3; this was the end of the Innréttingar project. Seen purely as an economic investment, the Innréttingar project was a clear disaster, but it was symbolic of new economic thinking in Iceland and Copenhagen, characterized by the belief in economic and social progress through the efforts of the state. Furthermore, with it, Icelanders learned new techniques in textile production and the processing of salt cod. In this respect, the project contributed to the economic modernization in Iceland. See also EIRÍKSSON, JÓN (1728–87); THE ENLIGHTENMENT; MONOPOLY TRADE.

ÍSAFJÖRÐUR. The largest town in northwestern Iceland traces its beginning to the late 16th century, when it became a trading post for foreign merchants. After 1600 during the period of **monopoly trade**, it developed into the most important commercial center in the Western Fjords. As trading in Iceland was generally a seasonal affair that did not generate other **economic** activities, the town of Ísafjörður remained small until the mid-19th century. In 1801, only 250 inhabitants lived in the parish of Ísafjörður. In the second half of the 19th century, the town began to grow, and in 1901, it was the third largest town in Iceland, with 1,100 inhabitants. In this period of expansion, fishing on decked vessels became the foundation of the town's economy. There, the town benefited from its proximity to some of Iceland's richest fishing grounds.

The **population** of Ísafjörður and the surrounding area increased steadily until the beginning of **World War II**, approaching 3,300 inhabitants in 1940. Since then, the population has been more or less stationary. In 1996, the town merged with five other neighboring communities, with the combined population of 4,100. Fishing remains the mainstay of Ísafjörður's economy, but with improved communications, the rugged nature of this part of Iceland is also becoming a major **tourist** attraction. See also FISHERIES.

– J –

JENSEN, THOR (1863–1947). This entrepreneur and shipowner was born in Copenhagen, **Denmark**, on 3 December 1863 to a Danish carpenter. He moved to Iceland in 1878 to work as an assistant to a merchant in the northwest part of the country. From 1886 to 1901, Jensen managed general stores in Iceland, first in the towns of Borgarnes and Akranes in western Iceland and later in the town of Hafnarfjörður to the south of **Reykjavík**. In 1901, Jensen moved to Reykjavík and soon became one of the most enterprising shipowners in the capital. He was one of the founders of the first major trawler company in Iceland, Alliance, in 1905 and served as its director until 1910. In 1912, he founded the trawler company Kveldúlfur, which later became one of the largest firms in Iceland. In spite of his role in the Icelandic **industrial** revolution, Jensen always had a strong interest in **agriculture**. Thus, late in life, he retired from his trawler company to run a large farm outside of Reykjavík specializing in milk production for the growing town. This venture was not well received by his competitors, and in 1934, small farmers used their political clout to pass legislation that rendered capitalist development in agriculture more or less impossible. Jensen was one of few Danes who became fully integrated into Icelandic society. He married an Icelandic woman, and many of their children, including politician **Ólafur Thors** and diplomat Thor Thors, were prominent in Icelandic public and **economic** life.

JÓHANNESSON, JÓN ÁSGEIR (1968–). This Icelandic businessman was born on 27 January 1968 and graduated from the Commercial College of Iceland in 1989. The same year he founded a discount supermarket in **Reykjavík** with his father, Jóhannes Jónsson, called Bónus. As the managing director of the store, Jóhannesson supervised its expansion from one small outlet in Reykjavík into a retail giant in Iceland. In 1993, Jóhannesson and his associates founded the company Baugur, which was later to become **Baugur Group**, and he became its CEO in 1998. Under his leadership, Baugur began to invest heavily in Europe, primarily in **Great Britain** and Scandinavia. Among its investments are the retail companies Mosaic Fashions, which owns and operates six well-known women's fashion brands; Hamleys toy stores; tea and coffee company Whittard of Chelsea; department store chain House of Fraser; and the **Danish** department stores Magasin du Nord and Illum in Copenhagen. The company has also invested heavily in the Icelandic media, owning both a television station and newspapers.

Jóhannesson is, in many ways, symbolic of a new breed of Icelandic businessmen; at the same time, he is one of the most successful members of the contemporary Icelandic business elite. His aggressive style, both in Iceland and abroad, moved Icelandic investment companies to a new level, where all Icelandic business traditions were disregarded. This created a strong political reaction in Iceland, not least from the Right, as the leaders of the conservative **Independence Party** criticized Jóhannesson for attempting to gain a monopoly over the retail markets and the media in Iceland. Egged on by the powerful former chairman of the party **Davíð Oddsson**, the police started extensive investigations into Jóhannesson's business practices in 2002, but in spite of running the most expensive investigation in Iceland's history, Jóhannesson was only found guilty for minor accounting irregularities. *See also* BROADCASTING.

JÓHANNESSON, ÓLAFUR (1913–84). Politician and legal scholar, Jóhannesson was born in Skagafjörður County in northern Iceland to a peasant family. In 1935, after graduating from secondary school in **Akureyri**, he enrolled in the **University of Iceland**, completing a law degree in 1939. From 1939 to 1947, Jóhannesson practiced law in **Reykjavík** and worked for the Federation of the Icelandic Cooperative Societies. In 1947, he was appointed professor at the University of Iceland, where he taught at the law department until he became **prime minister** in 1971. He wrote extensively on legal issues during his university years, establishing himself as a leading authority on Icelandic constitutional law.

Jóhannesson became a professional politician fairly late in life. In 1959, he was **elected** to **Alþingi** for the **Progressive Party** (PP), where he served until his death in 1984. He was elected deputy chairman of the party in 1960 and its chairman in 1968. After the fall of the **Reconstruction Government** in the 1971 parliamentary elections, he, as the leader of the largest opposition party, was appointed to form a new coalition government. For the next 12 years, he held ministerial posts continuously, except for a brief period from late 1979 to early 1980. He served as prime minister from 1971 to 1974 and again from 1978 to 1979; as minister of justice, ecclesiastic affairs, and commerce from 1974 to 1978; and as minister of foreign affairs from 1980 to 1983. Jóhannesson was a memorable and sometimes controversial politician, and under his leadership, the PP was able to regain its status as a major force in Icelandic politics. This is a remarkable feat because the **population** of the countryside, where the party has had its traditional base of support, has shrunk steadily since **World War II.** *See also* LEFT-WING GOVERNMENT.

JÓHANNSSON, KJARTAN (1939–). Former minister of **fisheries** and **trade** and director of the **European Free Trade Association** (EFTA). Born in **Reykjavík** on 19 December 1939, Jóhannsson studied at the Royal Institute of Technology in Stockholm, completing a degree in civil engineering in 1963. In 1965, he received a master's degree in microeconomics from Illinois Institute of Technology in Chicago and a Ph.D. from the same institution in 1969. He was appointed associate professor at the **University of Iceland** in 1974. That same year, he was **elected** both deputy chairman of the **Social Democratic Party** (SDP) and a member of the town council of his hometown, Hafnarfjörður. Jóhannsson was elected to **Alþingi** in 1978 and served as minister of fisheries from 1978 to 1980 and minister of trade from 1979 to 1980. He was elected chairman of the SDP in 1980, but **Jón Baldvin Hannibalsson** defeated him in his bid for reelection in 1984. In 1989, Jóhannsson left domestic politics to become ambassador to EFTA in Geneva, and in 1994, he was appointed director of the organization, serving in that post until 2000. From 2002 to 2005, Jóhannsson was Iceland's ambassador to the **European Union** in Brussels.

JÓNASSON, HERMANN (1896–1976). One of the leading figures in Icelandic politics from the early 1930s to the end of the 1950s. Jónasson was born on 25 December 1896 to a farmer in Skagafjörður County in northwestern Iceland. After completing a law degree at the **University of Iceland** in 1924, he worked as a deputy in the office of the *bæjarfógeti* (district judge) for **Reykjavík**, and in 1928, following a reorganization of the judiciary administration in the capital, he was appointed chief of Reykjavík's police. Jónasson was **elected** to parliament for the first time in 1934 for the **Progressive Party** (PP), defeating the former chairman of the party Tryggvi Þórhallsson. That same year, Jónasson became **prime minister** in the **Government of the Laboring Classes**, which was a coalition government of the PP and the **Social Democratic Party**. For more than two decades, he remained one of the most prominent politicians in Iceland. He served as prime minister in two governments from 1934 to 1942 and again from 1956 to 1958 and as minister of **agriculture** from 1950 to 1953. Although he was de facto leader of the PP from 1934 to the early 1960s, he was only elected its chairman in 1944; he held that position until 1962. Jónasson retired from politics in 1967.

JÓNSBÓK. A written law code called "John's Book" after the **lawspeaker** Jón Einarsson, one of its authors. The code was first accepted in **Alþingi** in 1281, superseding the existing law book, *Járnsíða*. After certain amendments and revisions had been made to the original version of *Jónsbók* at the request of Icelanders, it took its final form in the early 14th century. In this form, it remained valid for around 400 years until **absolutism** was introduced in Iceland in the early 1660s. Some of its clauses, especially those dealing with **agriculture** and land use, are still in force today. The strength of *Jónsbók* lies in the fact that it was able to adapt general revisions of **Norwegian** laws written in the 1270s to Icelandic conditions. Moreover, *Jónsbók*'s durability is a testimony to the relative stagnation and conservatism of Icelandic society in the past.

Jónsbók is not preserved in an original redaction, but the code exists in numerous medieval and later manuscripts. It was one of the first secular books to be printed in Iceland (1578), which is a clear indication of its popularity and importance, and it remained one of the most widely read books in Iceland for centuries. *See also* GRÁGÁS.

JÓNSSON, ARNGRÍMUR (1568–1648). A **Lutheran** pastor and scholar. He was born to a prosperous farmer in Húnavatn County, northern Iceland, in 1568. When he was eight years old, Jónsson moved to **Hólar** to study under the influential bishop and his uncle **Guðbrandur Þorláksson**. After graduating from the diocese school at Hólar in 1585, he continued his studies in Copenhagen. In the summer of 1589, he returned to Iceland and became headmaster of the school at Hólar. He held this position for a few years, but from around 1598 until his death in 1648, he served as a rural pastor in northern Iceland. Jónsson was one of the most learned men in Iceland during his lifetime. His first work was a short essay in Latin on the nature and history of Iceland, *Brevis commentarius de Islandiae* (1593), written to correct what he saw as erroneous information on the country in contemporary foreign **literature**. In 1609, he published a book on Icelandic history in Latin called *Chrymogæa*, introducing the country and its medieval historical literature to European scholars. Jónsson formed good contacts with **Danish** colleagues of his time, writing in the spirit of European humanism.

Jónsson became important to the late-18th-century patriots like **Eggert Ólafsson** and later to **nationalists** of the 19th century for his writings on Icelandic history and culture. It was not least his emphasis on the purity of the Icelandic **language**, which he saw as the original language of Scandinavia, that connected this 17th-century intellectual to the Icelandic nationalism in the 19th and 20th centuries.

JÓNSSON, JÓNAS (1885–1968). One of the most influential politicians in Iceland in the interwar period. He was born to a poor peasant family at the farm Hrifla in Þingey County in northeast Iceland, and therefore, he was commonly referred to as Jónas from Hrifla. Jónsson's poverty prevented him from entering the **Menntaskólinn in Reykjavík**, which was required for all who wanted to pursue university studies and aspired to a career in the government bureaucracy. In 1906, he was granted support from **Alþingi** to study abroad, and he spent the next three years in **Denmark**, Germany, and England. In this period, he attended the Folk High School in Askov, Denmark; a teacher college in Copenhagen; and Ruskin College in Oxford.

Upon returning to Iceland, Jónsson received a teaching position in the new Teacher Training College in **Reykjavík**, a position he held for nine years (1909–18). During this period, he wrote a survey of Icelandic history, which was used as a primer in all elementary schools in Iceland for decades. Because of its widespread use, this book formed the historical perspective of generations of Icelanders, inculcating them with fervent patriotism. In 1918, he became the first headmaster of the Cooperative College in Reykjavík, a position he held until his retirement in 1955.

Jónsson entered politics at a time when the modern party system in Iceland was emerging. As the **nationalist** struggle was approaching its end, **economic** and social interests rather than the relationship with **Denmark** became the focus of political debates in the country.

Jónsson viewed it as his mission to further these issues, and he became one of the founders of the **Icelandic Federation of Labor** in 1916, which was, in his opinion, to be both a political organization for the working classes and a **trade union**. From 1916 to 1919, he was also the driving force behind the formation of the agrarian **Progressive Party** (PP), which under his influence became the political arm of the **cooperative movement**, although no formal ties existed between the party and the Federation of Icelandic Cooperatives.

Jónsson's political career was long and colorful. He sat in parliament from 1922 to 1949; served as chairman of the PP from 1934 to 1944; and as minister of justice, **education**, and ecclesiastical affairs from 1927 to 1932. He proved to be a vigorous and shrewd organizer, propagandist, and ideologue for the PP, using his power effectively, especially during his five-year stint as **cabinet** minister. He was an extremely prolific essayist, writing on various issues in journals and newspapers (the party organ of the PP, *Timinn*, in particular). Moreover, he maintained close personal contacts with people in all parts of the country and used this network to gather information and disseminate his ideas. Because of his fierce and often ruthless oratory, he was a controversial figure, despised by his opponents but revered by his admirers. The pinnacle of Jónsson's political career came in the late 1920s and early 1930s, but after that, he became more and more isolated in his party, and his influence waned. Although his formal authority did not last long, few 20th-century politicians had such a long-lasting influence on the course of Icelandic history.

JÖRGENSEN, JÖRGEN (1780–1841). A **Danish** adventurer known for his leading role in the **Icelandic Revolution**. Born in Copenhagen in 1780, the son of a prominent watchmaker to the Danish court, Jörgensen was apprenticed to an English collier at the age of 14, serving on British ships for over a decade. During this time, he partook in expeditions to far-off places, including South Africa and Australia. After returning to Denmark in 1806, Jörgensen became a commander on a Danish privateer. He was taken captive by a British man-of-war in early spring of 1808, but as the young commander had friends in high places in London, his captivity was fairly relaxed. Later that year, Jörgensen became acquainted with an English soap merchant by the name of Samuel Phelps, who was in desperate need of fats for his soap-boiling manufacturing. Jörgensen brought Iceland to his attention; the country was more or less isolated at the time because of the Napoleonic Wars, but it produced tallow in considerable quantities. For this reason, Phelps sent two trading expeditions to Iceland in 1809, with Jörgensen serving as an interpreter.

The second expedition arrived in Iceland in late June, but upon its arrival, the Danish governor of Iceland, Count **Frederik Christopher Trampe**, banned all commerce between his Icelandic subjects and the English merchants. As this was both in direct violation of Trampe's agreement with a British officer earlier the same month and threatened his mission, Phelps saw no other alternative but to arrest and depose the governor on 25 June. Subsequently, Jörgensen took over the governor's office and thus began one of the most bizarre episodes in Icelandic history. The new governor, or protector, as he called himself, promised revolutionary changes in the administration of Icelandic affairs, cutting all ties with Denmark, and threatened to depose all officials who refused to obey his orders. This government was only short lived, however, as a British naval officer declared Jörgensen's actions illegal on 22 August 1809. Jörgensen was brought back to England and charged with violation of his parole, as he was still formally a prisoner of war at the time of his journey to Iceland. Jörgensen, who never returned to Iceland, died in 1841 in Hobart on the island of Tasmania. *See also* GREAT BRITAIN.

JÓSEPSSON, LÚÐVÍK A. (1914–94). For many years, one of the most influential figures on the political left in Iceland. Jósepsson was born on 16 June 1914 into a fisherman's family in Neskaupsstaður, a fishing town in Suður-Múla County on the east coast of Iceland. He completed a high school exam in **Akureyri** in 1933 and taught at the elementary school in his hometown from 1934 to 1943. From 1944 to 1952, he worked for fishing companies in Neskaupsstaður, serving as director of the Community Fishing Company from 1948 to 1952.

For over half a century, Neskaupsstaður was known as a staunch socialist stronghold, and Jósepsson was instrumental in founding that legacy. He was **elected** to the town council for the newly formed **Socialist Unity Party** (SUP) in 1938 and to parliament for the same party in 1942. He sat in the town council of Neskaupsstaður for the SUP and later the **People's Alliance** (PA) until 1970 and in **Alþingi** until 1979. He served as leader of the PA's parliamentary group from 1961 to 1971 and again from 1975 to 1979 and as president of the PA from 1977 to 1980. The **fisheries** were always his main area of interest, and he served as minister of fisheries and commerce in the first two **Left-Wing Governments**, from 1956 to 1958 and from 1971 to 1974. In this capacity, he was a leading advocate of the extension of the **fishing limits**, first from 4 to 12 nautical miles and later from 12 to 50 miles. After his retirement from active politics, Jósepsson served as a member of the board of directors of the **National Bank of Iceland** for a number of years.

– K –

KÁRAHNJÚKAR. These two mountains in the eastern highlands of Iceland became a household name in the country at the end of the 1990s, when the **National Power Company of Iceland** (NPCI) introduced its plans of building a hydroelectric power station in the glacial river Jökulsá á Dal. The project was to construct a dam at the northern end of these mountains, which would create a large reservoir used for the largest power station in Iceland, now commonly known as the Kárahnjúkavirkjun (Kárahnjúkar Hydropower Station). The electricity from the station would be used to power an aluminum smelter on the coast called Fjardaál, which is owned by the American industrial giant Alcoa. The plans caused a huge uproar in Iceland, as the project would clearly cause serious **environmental** damage in the area, both because rivers have to be diverted from their natural courses and because the reservoir covers a large area of unspoiled land. In spite of the protests, **Alþingi** gave the NPCI permission to build the power station, which started operation in the fall of 2007 and is expected to be completed in 2009. This is the largest construction project in Iceland's history, costing around US$2 billion. When the station is in full operation, it will have an instilled capacity of 690 MW, generating 4,600 GWh a year and increasing the production capacity of the NPCI power stations by 40 percent. *See also* ECONOMY; ENERGY-INTENSIVE INDUSTRIES.

KATLA. One of the most active volcanoes in Iceland situated in the Mýrdalsjökull Glacier on the southern coast of the country. Katla is a large caldera, 10 kilometers (6.2 miles) in diameter and 500 to 600 meters (1,500 to 1,800 feet) deep and covered with snow. Katla has erupted around 20 times since the settlement of Iceland, and the last eruption was in 1918. As Katla is situated in a glacier, its main threat is the huge floods caused by the snow that melts when it erupts. For this reason, scientists monitor the volcano constantly in order to forewarn people living in the vicinity of the volcano about the possible eruption.

KEFLAVÍK. A small fishing port on the southwest coast of Iceland. Keflavík was an important station for seasonal fishermen in the past because of its proximity to important spawning grounds for cod. During **World War II**, Keflavík assumed a new role as a barren heath in its outskirts became the site for an airport that became a major link in transporting goods between the **United States** and Europe. At the end of the war, the U.S. government asked for a long-term lease of the airport, but the request was rejected out of hand by all **political parties**. The reason for this opposition was the **nationalistic** euphoria in the country following the foundation of the republic in 1944 and the sentiment that the presence of a foreign military force was not desired in peacetime. In 1946, the Icelandic parliament ratified a treaty with the U.S. government in which the latter promised to withdraw its forces from Iceland and to hand the control of Keflavík Airport over to the Icelandic government. At the same time, an American civilian company, the American Overseas Airlines, was entrusted with the operation of the airport at the behest of the U.S. Department of Defense, and the American military was given free access to its utilities in order to facilitate communications between the United States and its forces in Germany. Three years later, as Iceland became a founding member of the **North Atlantic Treaty Organization**, the Icelandic government reiterated its firm intention of not allowing a foreign army to be stationed in Iceland in times of peace. In 1951, as the **cold war** escalated with the emerging crisis of the Korean War, the Icelandic government struck a defense agreement with its American counterpart, allowing the U.S. military to build a base at the airport. For the first 10 years, the base was run by the U.S. Air Force, but in 1961, it was handed over to the navy.

The return of U.S. military forces in May 1951 had a great impact on the town of Keflavík. Construction on the base and services to the army provided work to the inhabitants in Keflavík and attracted people to the town. In the beginning, there were around 5,000 soldiers at the airport, and although this number declined in the 1960s to around 3,300 soldiers by 1971, the military presence continued to dominate the local **economy** in Keflavík. This is clearly reflected in the number of inhabitants in Keflavík, which rose from 3,100 to 6,300 in the 1950s. In the 1990s, as the cold war wound down, the American military began to withdraw from the Keflavík base. There were just over 3,000 soldiers at the base in 1990, while the total **population** at the base was around 5,000, but these numbers were down to 2,000 and 4,000, respectively, in 2004. In 2006, the U.S. Department of Defense decided unilaterally to close down the military base, and the last American soldier left Keflavík at the end of September the same year.

Today, Keflavík is best known for its international airport, which serves as Iceland's gateway to the world. The **fisheries** are still important for the town, but the various services required by the airport and the military base were the foundation of the town's economic prosperity in the second half of the 20th century. *See also* DEFENSE.

KINGS OF ICELAND. Iceland became a part of the **Norwegian** kingdom in 1262, when the leading members of Icelandic society accepted Norwegian rule in the country. In 1380, Iceland followed Norway into a union with **Denmark,** and from then until the foundation of the **Republic of Iceland** in 1944, Iceland was ruled by Danish kings. In the beginning, the kings did not have much effective power in Iceland, as the country was fairly distant from both Norway and Denmark, but as the royal power increased in Denmark after the **Lutheran Reformation,** their authority also grew in the provinces — including Iceland. Until the late 17th century, the Danish kings were formally **elected** by the Danish diet, but in 1660, after a disastrous war with Sweden, the king was able to establish a hereditary monarchy in Denmark. This was the beginning of the Danish **absolutism,** which was accepted in Iceland in 1662. The absolute rule was abolished in Denmark with the first constitution of the Danish state, which came into effect on 5 June 1849. In Iceland, however, the king continued to be absolute ruler until 1874 because the Danish constitution was never adopted in Iceland. With the **Act of Union**, which came into effect on 1 December 1918, Iceland was declared a sovereign state, and the country became a constitutional monarchy, with the Danish king acting as head of state. Early in **World War II**, when Germany occupied Denmark, the union between Iceland and Denmark came to an end. First, the Icelandic parliament took over the responsibilities of the king, but in 1941, it decided to elect a *ríkisstjóri* (governor of Iceland), who substituted for the king in Iceland. This was confirmed in 1944, when Iceland cut its ties with Denmark, terminating the authority of the Danish king in Iceland.

The kings were generally very highly regarded in Iceland, although the fact that they lived far away and did not visit the country until late in the 19th century made them very distant to most Icelanders. Hence, the struggle for independence was not regarded as a struggle against the king but rather against the authority of Danish politicians over Icelandic affairs. *See also* CONSTITUTION OF 1874; NATIONALISM; Appendix A.

KJARVAL, JÓHANNES SVEINSSON (1885–1972). A pioneer in Icelandic **art** and the most popular painter of 20th-century Iceland. Kjarval was born on 15 October 1885 into a poor peasant family in southeast Iceland. He came to **Reykjavík** in 1901, attending high school for a time and taking private lessons in drawing. In 1908, Kjarval opened his first exhibition in Reykjavík, and three years later, he set out on a journey to Europe to study art. Kjarval spent most of the following decade abroad, first in London, then primarily in Copenhagen. In 1914, he enrolled in the Royal Academy of Art in Copenhagen, where he studied until 1918. Four years later, he moved back to Iceland, where he gradually rose to prominence among native artists. By the mid-1930s, he was generally considered the national painter of Iceland, a position he acquired primarily for his interpretation of Icelandic nature and landscapes. For this reason, the city of Reykjavík opened an art museum in 1972 carrying Kjarval's name and celebrating his art.

KÓPAVOGUR'S MEETING. A meeting held on 28 July 1662 at Kópavogur, which is now a suburb of **Reykjavík** and the second largest town in Iceland. It was held at the request of Henrik Bjelke, the *höfuðsmaður* (governor of Iceland), who summoned all royal officials in Iceland, the two Icelandic bishops, many ministers of the **Lutheran** Church, and representatives of the farming elite to pay homage to King Frederick III of **Denmark** and accept new succession laws stipulated by the **king**. Until then, the king had, nominally at least, been **elected**, but now the rule of inheritance was fixed. The real issue was, however, royal **absolutism**, or the question of where sovereignty was placed in the state. At the Kópavogur's meeting, the 109 Icelanders present signed a declaration repealing many of the privileges that had been guaranteed in the **Old Covenant** of 1262–64 between Icelanders and **Norwegian** king Håkon VI Håkonsson. From then on, the king had de jure all legislative and executive authority in Iceland, and **Alþingi** became a mere court. During the **nationalist** struggle of the early 20th century, historians maintained that the Icelandic leaders were forced to sign the document at Kópavogur, but there is little direct evidence to prove that assertion. *See also STIFTAMTMAÐUR.*

KRISTJÁNSSON, GUÐJÓN A. (1944–). Politician born in **Ísafjörður** on 5 July 1944. Kristjánsson worked on fishing boats from 1959 to 1997, first as a deckhand but then as captain for a number of years. He was **elected** chairman of the Fishermen's Association in 1983, serving in this capacity until he was elected to parliament in 1999. Kristjánsson represented the **Independence Party** in parliament from 1999 to 2003, when he resigned from the party to join a new political movement, the **Liberal Party** (LP). He was elected to parliament for the LP in 2003 and reelected in 2007. In 2003, he was elected chairman of the LP, and his popularity in the party's stronghold in the fishing towns of the Western Fjords has been instrumental in maintaining enough electoral support for the LP to maintain the party in parliament.

KRÓNA. See CURRENCY.

– L –

LABOR BONDAGE. The labor market in preindustrial Iceland was strictly regulated by law and custom. For centuries, *vistarband* (legal restrictions) were in force to control the number of *þurrabúðarfólk* (cottagers), *húsfólk* (lodgers), and *lausafólk* (casual laborers). These restrictions were set to prevent a drain of the labor supply from **agriculture** to **fisheries** and to battle pauperism by keeping down the number of cottagers. Moreover, these rules were a form of social control, expressing a general belief in the moral benefit for young people to be raised on farms rather than in towns by the coast, and thus, they were defended as a necessary bulwark of the Icelandic social order.

The legal codes of the **Commonwealth Period** obliged dependent persons to have a fixed home on the basis of annual contracts with farmers. Initially, the law did not require people to work for the master of the house, but with time, this obligation evolved into labor service based on annual contracts. Exempted were cottagers and casual laborers, the latter on the condition that they possessed a certain minimum amount of property. Píningsdómur, a decree passed in **Alþingi** in 1490, obliged cottagers to keep livestock and have access to a plot of land in order to impede the development of an independent class of fishermen. The decree also contained an important clause prohibiting foreign merchants from maintaining stations in Iceland over the winter, reflecting the fear of foreign competition in the **labor market**. In 1783, a royal decree severely tightened the labor bondage regulations, banning altogether the class of casual laborers and allowing only lodgers and cottagers to be hired for shorter periods of time than a whole year.

Casual laborers regained their legal status in 1863 but only on the condition that they paid a considerable fee to the authorities for the permission to work on short-term contracts. At the same time, restrictions on lodgers and cottagers were relaxed to a certain degree. The growth of the nonagrarian sector and increased competition for labor after the mid-19th century upset traditional work patterns in Iceland, leading to considerable wage increases. Mounting opposition to labor bondage, increasing awareness among farmers of the **economic** disadvantages of such restrictions on personal liberty, and difficulties in enforcing the law at a time of growing **population** pressure and economic crisis in the rural areas led to its virtual abolition in 1894, followed by the ending of most legal restrictions on cottagers and lodgers in 1907.

LABOR MARKET. Among the most striking characteristics of the Icelandic labor market is its small size, as there were only around 40,000 people **economically** active in 1910 and 177,000 in 2007. The country has, however, experienced structural changes in **employment** similar to those in neighboring countries in the last century. **Agriculture**'s share in the labor force dropped from 45 percent to less than 4 percent between 1910 and 2007, while the share of manufacturing (fish processing not included) and construction doubled, from just under 9 percent to 19 percent; commerce (including hotels and restaurants) rose from 4 percent to 18 percent; and public services from 2 percent to 34 percent. **Fisheries** and fish processing have experienced a large drop in this period, from 19 percent in 1910 to 4 percent in 2007. Generally, this reflects the change from an agricultural and fishing society to an **industrialized** service society, as the share of agriculture and fisheries has fallen from around two thirds of the labor force in the early 20th century to around 8 percent in 2007, while the share of what can be broadly termed as services has risen from a quarter to over 70 percent in the same period.

Traditionally, a high rate of labor force participation has characterized the Icelandic labor market. With the unemployment rate rarely rising above 4 percent in the period since **World War II**, the participation rate has been one of the highest in the countries of the Organization of Economic Cooperation and Development, while the average workweek has been one of the longest in the Western world (47.5 hours for men and 36 hours for **women**). The rapid entry of women into the labor market has pushed the participation rate upward in recent decades, and now they constitute 46 percent of the total labor force. The participation rate for women increased from about 33 percent to 79 percent between 1960 and 2007. The participation rates for both the young and the elderly are also very high, in part because a social security pension is not collectable until the age of 67 and most private pension payments begin at the age of 70.

Iceland, along with the other Nordic countries, is among the most highly unionized in the world. Yet, this has not caused wage inflexibility; wages in Iceland seem, indeed, to be very sensitive to conditions in the labor market. The flexibility of the labor market is also demonstrated in fairly smooth geographical and occupational adjustment to employment situations—the latter feature undoubtedly related to the high level of **education**.

The most significant change of the Icelandic labor market in recent years has been the phenomenal growth of immigrant labor. In 2000, foreign citizens were around 3 percent of all employed people in Iceland, but in 2007, this number had grown to around 10 percent. This development reflects the changed relations between Iceland and the **European Union**, as the **European Economic Area** agreement has opened Iceland up to the European labor market. But it is also the result of the exceptional economic growth in Iceland in recent years, which has created a very strong demand for labor. Key economic sectors in Iceland would have collapsed if they had not had access to foreign laborers; in 2007, between 40 and 45 percent of those who were employed in the Icelandic fishing industry and construction were, for example, foreign citizens. *See also* ICELANDIC FEDERATION OF LABOR (IFL); LABOR BONDAGE; TRADE UNIONS.

LAKI ERUPTION. On 8 June 1783, an enormous volcanic eruption began in Lakagígar, a row of craters located on a fissure southwest of the **Vatnajökull** glacier. From the summer of 1783 to early 1784, 15 cubic kilometers of lava flooded to the south from the craters, covering large tracts of farmland in nearby Skaftafell County. Even worse, wind spread ash and poisonous gases (fluorine and sulphur-dioxide compounds) from the eruption site over much of northern and western Iceland, killing livestock and driving people from their homes. The gas emitted from the Laki eruption amounted to three times the total annual output from today's European industries, causing a thick sulphurous haze to spread across Western Europe and resulting in many thousands of deaths throughout 1783 and the winter of 1784. The effects of the eruption were also felt in North America, as the winter of 1783–84 was one of the coldest on record on the east coast of the **United States**.

The eruption itself ended in February 1784, but its effects crippled the Icelandic **economy** for over a year afterward. The period from 1783 to 1785, called Móðuharðindi, or Famine of the Mist—receiving its name from the haze created by the eruption—was one of the most trying periods in Icelandic history. Because cattle and sheep perished, either from consuming volcanic materials or from lack of forage in the winter, people suffered from serious food shortages during 1784 and 1785. In these two years, thousands of Icelanders died from hunger and disease, leading to a serious **population** decline in Iceland—from around 49,000 inhabitants in 1783 to just below 39,000 in 1786. In 1786, the population of Iceland reached the lowest point recorded in its demographic history, and for this reason, some contemporary commentators raised serious doubts about the viability of Icelandic society in the future.

LANDFÓGETI. The **Danish king** established the office of Royal Treasurer of Iceland, or *landfógeti,* in 1683 as a part of the reorganization of the administrative system in Iceland following the introduction of **absolutism.** The *landfógeti* was the chief financial administrator in Iceland, collecting taxes and rents of royal property. He was often entrusted with other duties, such as policing the region around **Reykjavík.** In 1806, the office of *landfógeti* and *bæjarfógeti* (town bailiff) in Reykjavík were formally united, but in 1874, these offices were separated again. The office of *landfógeti* was abolished in 1904 when Iceland obtained **home rule.** *See also* MAGNÚSSON, SKÚLI (1711–94).

LANDSHÖFÐINGI. In 1872, a royal decree changed the name of the office of governor in Iceland from *stiftamtmaður* to *landshöfðingi.* This was a part of a general reform of the Icelandic administrative system following the passing of the **Status Law** in 1871. Three men held this important office from 1873 until it was abolished in 1904: Hilmar Finsen (1873–83), Bergur Thorberg (1883–86), and **Magnús Stephensen** (1836–1917; in office 1886–1904). The last two were Icelanders by birth, and the first was a Dane of Icelandic descent.

The *landshöfðingi* was the pinnacle of the **Danish** administrative hierarchy in Iceland from 1873 to 1904, and he served directly under the minister of Icelandic affairs in Copenhagen—a post that was always held by the Danish minister of justice. His role was to execute the government policy in Iceland, advise the government on Icelandic affairs, and serve as a link between the officials beneath him in Iceland and the ministries in Copenhagen. The *landshöfðingi* represented the **king** in **Alþingi,** but he could not be dismissed by parliament. The *landshöfðingi* was a central figure in Icelandic political and social life; for this reason, the period of 1873 to 1904 is generally named after the office, *landshöfðingjatímabilið* (the **Governor's Period**).

LANDSHÖFÐINGJATÍMABILIÐ. See GOVERNOR'S PERIOD.

LANGUAGE. The Icelandic language belongs to the family of Scandinavian languages, which together form a defined subgroup of the Germanic languages. It originates in a "parent language," usually called Proto Nordic. This language was spoken in a region covering the area from central Scandinavia and **Denmark** to the vicinity of the Ejder River, which is now in North Germany close to the Danish border. On the basis of historical evidence, it seems probable that Old Icelandic, or Old Norse as it is commonly named, is primarily derived from West **Norwegian** dialects. A few loanwords of Celtic origin came into the language early on, and a number of words, mostly from Latin and Greek, were adopted after the **conversion to Christianity** around the year 1000.

Because of the isolation of the country, the Icelandic language changed only gradually through the centuries. From the 14th century, it began to become distinguishable from Norwegian, mostly because the latter changed at a much more rapid pace than Icelandic. The grammatical structure and syntax of modern Icelandic is very similar to the language of the Saga Age. Icelandic, for example, still has three genders (masculine, feminine, and neuter); four cases for nouns, adjectives, and pronouns (nominative, genitive, dative, accusative); and much more complicated verb systems than the other languages of the same linguistic group.

During the struggle for independence, linguistic conservatism became a matter of great pride for Icelandic **nationalists**. To them, this proved that modern Icelandic culture was truer to its origins than the cultures of the other Nordic countries and, consequently, that Icelanders had preserved the parent form of all the Scandinavian languages. For this reason, there was a great effort in the 19th and the early 20th centuries to "purify" the language, or to eliminate as many traces of Danish influence as possible from the Icelandic language. This effort has been fairly successful, as Icelandic is still more resistant to foreign loanwords than most European languages. The outcome of this policy of language purification is not certain, however, as it has proven to be increasingly difficult to isolate the language from the world dominance of English. Recently, some Icelandic companies have begun to operate in English, both because they are active on the international market, where English dominates, and because they employ a substantial number of people who do not speak Icelandic. This development has caused some concern, but there is little to indicate that the Icelandic language is under serious threat, as it is a fully functioning literary and cultural language and it is used at all levels of Icelandic society. *See also* ICELANDIC LITERARY SOCIETY (ILS); JÓNSSON, ARNGRÍMUR (1568–1648); LITERATURE; ÓLAFSSON, EGGERT (1726–68).

LAWMAN. An office (called *lögmaður* in Icelandic) established in 1271 shortly after Iceland entered into a union with **Norway**. The lawman presided over **Alþingi**, and its proceedings were illegal without his presence. The lawman also served as president of the courts in Alþingi, selected jurors, and directed the different functions of the assembly. There was initially only one lawman in Iceland, but from 1277 until Alþingi was abolished in 1800, they were two at a time, one for the northwestern half of the country, another for the southeastern part.

From the beginning, it was unclear who had the authority of choosing the lawmen. Formally, this was the prerogative of the **king**, or his representatives in Iceland, but until the late 17th century, Alþingi had, as a rule, a decisive influence on the nomination of a new lawman. Alþingi insisted that the lawmen were Icelandic by birth, and usually this was the case. With the introduction of **absolutism**, the **Danish** king began to nominate the lawmen without consulting Alþingi, and he continued to do so until the office was abolished at the end of the 18th century. This did not change the fact that most lawmen were Icelandic by birth, probably because most legal proceedings in Iceland were conducted in Icelandic and thus lawmen were required to speak the **language** in order to be able to conduct the job. *See also* LAW-SPEAKER.

LAW-SPEAKER. The president of **Alþingi** during the **Commonwealth Period** was called *lögsögumaður*, or law-speaker. Originally, he received this title because he had to memorize the law codes and to recite (or speak) one third of them at the meetings of Alþingi each summer. This function changed when the Icelandic law codes were written down in the early 12th century, but the law-speaker continued to direct the meetings of Alþingi, convene juries, and preside over Lögrétta, the central institution of Alþingi. In 1271, the office of law-speaker was abolished with the introduction of *Járnsíða*, a new law code of **Norwegian** origin, and replaced by the office of *lögmaður* (**lawman**).

LAXNESS, HALLDÓR (1902–98). The master of Icelandic 20th-century **literature** was born Halldór Guðjónsson on 23 April 1902. He grew up on a farm named Laxnes in Mosfellsdalur, which is a farming district north of **Reykjavík**. His first book, *Börn náttúrunnar* (*Children of Nature*, 1919) was written under the name Halldór from Laxnes, but by the time he published his second book, *Undir Helgahnúk* (*Under the Holy Mountain*, 1924), he had taken the pen name Halldór Kiljan Laxness (he dropped the middle name in 1963).

Laxness started his literary career as a very young man, as his first book came out when he was only 17 years of age. In the 1920s and 1930s, he established himself as the leading author of prose literature in Iceland, although he was a controversial figure in society. His radical views in politics and his unconventional orthography made him unpopular in conservative circles. When awarded the Nobel Prize for literature in 1955, Laxness received international recognition, and since then, he has been generally regarded as the greatest author in 20th-century Iceland.

The reason for Laxness's success was his unique ability to combine Icelandic literary traditions with cosmopolitan influences. He traveled widely throughout his long career, establishing contacts and friendship with colleagues both in Europe and the **United States**. In the early 1920s, he converted to **Catholicism**, entering a monastery in Luxemburg in 1922. With *Vefarinn mikli frá Kasmír* (*Great Weaver from Kashmir*, 1927), Laxness established himself as one of Iceland's leading authors. The same year, he left Iceland for California, where he planned to become a screenwriter in Hollywood. As it turned out, Laxness had no success in the movie business and returned from America as a committed socialist. In the 1930s, Laxness was one of the most visible advocates of communism in Iceland, even defending the Stalinist purges of 1936. He later renounced his communist convictions, criticizing his own gullibility and defense of the Soviet dictatorship.

Although Laxness had many strong **religious** and political beliefs, they never dominated his literary production. Rather, one can regard his works as a reflection of the turbulent times he experienced, while they were also deeply rooted in Icelandic history and culture.

LEFT-GREEN MOVEMENT (LGM). The Vinstrihreyfingin grænt frambod (LGM) is the party furthest to the left in Icelandic politics. It was formed in February 1999, when many former members of the **People's Alliance** (PA) did not join the **Social Democratic Alliance** in the attempt of uniting people to the left of center in one political organization. The LGM party platform is based on traditional Icelandic left-wing issues—including strong support for the welfare system (*see* WELFARE STATE), opposition to Iceland's cooperation with the United States, and doubts about **privatization**—but it also advocates radical **environmentalism**. Unlike most environmentalist parties in Europe, but in line with the PA before it, the LGM's policies are very **nationalistic** in their tenor, as the party categorically rejects all participation in the European integration process and membership in the **North Atlantic Treaty Organization**.

During its first two parliamentary **elections** in 1999 and 2003, the LGM had only limited success, polling less than 10 percent of the votes cast. Its uncompromising environmentalist position and the LGM's firm stand on various social issues have, however, increased the party's popularity in the last few years. The LGM received over 14 percent of the votes in 2007, giving the party a strong voice in **Alþingi** and consolidating its position on the far left of the Icelandic political spectrum. *See also* WOMEN'S ALLIANCE (WA).

LEFT-WING GOVERNMENT. A term used for coalition governments that united **political parties** to the left of the **Independence Party** (IP) from the 1950s to the late 1970s. The first government to be called by this name was a **cabinet** headed by **Hermann Jónasson** in 1956–58; the second was the first cabinet of **Ólafur Jóhannesson**, succeeding the **Reconstruction Government** in 1971 and resigning in 1974; and the third was the second cabinet of Jóhannesson in 1978–79. The **Progressive Party** (PP) and the **People's Alliance** (PA) participated in all three Left-Wing Governments, the **Social Democratic Party** in the first and third and the **Union of Liberals and Leftists** in the second. The three Left-Wing Governments do not have much in common beyond the fact that they all had **prime ministers** from the PP and all included ministers from the PA. There is, however, a clear continuity between the first two; both advocated strong government involvement in the **economy**, especially by actively supporting the modernization of the fishing fleet; encouraged strong **regional policies**; and vowed to close down the U.S. military base in **Keflavík**. These two governments were also instrumental in the extension of Icelandic **fishing limits**, the first extending the territorial waters to 12 miles and the second to 50 miles. Another common characteristic of all three Left-Wing Governments was their instability because none of them survived for a full four-year term.

The Left-Wing Governments hoped to formulate an alternative to the free market policies of the IP. The fact is, however, that the political parties on the left did not agree on the content of such a program, and their ambitious plans had the tendency to fuel escalating **inflation**.

LEIFS, JÓN (1899–1968). The most important and original composer in 20th-century Iceland was born on 1 May 1899 at a farm in Húnavatn County in northern Iceland. He took piano lessons in **Reykjavík** as a young man, but at that time, there were few opportunities in Iceland to study **music**. Therefore, he sailed to Germany in 1916, where he enrolled in the Leipzig Conservatory to study composing and conducting and to continue his piano lessons. Leifs graduated from the conservatory in 1921 and started his career in Germany as a composer and conductor. His music sought inspiration in Icelandic folk music, including the *tvísöngur* (two-part vocal genre) and *rímur*. Leifs enjoyed considerable success in Germany in the 1920s and 1930s, conducting orchestras in Leipzig and Hamburg. His compositions were well received, even after the Nazis came to power, because his Nordic themes appealed to German audiences and authorities. As **World War II** approached, Leifs met increasing opposition from authorities, in part because his wife was a Jew. In 1941, when the Berlin

Philharmonic performed one of his works, the audience left the hall in disgust before the orchestra finished the performance, and critics mocked the composer and his works.

Leifs managed to leave Germany with his family in 1944, reaching Iceland through Sweden the following year. After returning to Iceland, he immediately became a prominent figure in the cultural community in Reykjavík. He was, for example, instrumental in the foundation of the Icelandic Composers' Union in 1948, and he fought tirelessly for the rights and interests of Icelandic composers. His music was coolly received in Iceland, however, as people found his avant-garde style difficult to comprehend. It was, in fact, only in the 1980s—more than a decade after his death—that Leifs's works began to catch people's attention again. In recent years, his international reputation has been growing, as the Icelandic Symphonic Orchestra has performed his works on its tours abroad and recorded his music. Today, Leifs is generally recognized as Iceland's greatest composer.

LEIFUR EIRÍKSSON. *See* EIRÍKSSON, LEIFUR (10TH AND 11TH CENTURIES).

LIBERAL PARTY (LP). Two **political parties** in Iceland have carried this name. The first was formed by the few members of the first **Independence Party** (IP) who did not participate in the foundation of the **Conservative Party** (CP) in 1924. The LP was formally founded in 1926 and had one representative **elected** to parliament in 1927. The party lasted for only three years because it merged with the CP in 1929 to form the second IP.

The second LP was founded in 1998 by Sverrir Hermannsson, who had represented the IP for almost 30 years in **Alþingi** and held two **cabinet** posts on its behalf. In the beginning, the second LP was a one-issue party, as it vigorously opposed the quota system in the **fisheries**, which was very unpopular in some parts of Iceland, especially the Western Fjords. Other parts of the party's platform resembled many of the main ideals of the IP; the LP supports the free market system and opposes government intervention in the **economy**. As the quota system has faded in the Icelandic political debates, the party has gradually been drifting toward populism similar to the one espoused by many right-wing parties in Europe. Some leaders of the party have catered to those who oppose immigration (*see* MIGRA-TION) to Iceland, leading to internal friction in the party. In spite of these frictions, the LP has survived through three parliamentary elections, polling 4 percent in 1999 and 7 percent in both 2003 and 2007.

LIBRARY, NATIONAL. *See* NATIONAL AND UNIVERSITY LIBRARY OF ICELAND.

LITERACY. Little is known about literacy rates in Iceland before the 18th century, but it is often maintained that the strong literary traditions of late medieval Iceland reflect a widespread ability to read among the general public. Recent studies have demonstrated, however, that the majority of the adult **population** in Iceland was illiterate at the beginning of the 18th century—**women** and servants in particular. This situation began to change in the late 17th and early 18th centuries, when lay and **religious** authorities under the influence of Pietism began a concerted effort to ensure that everyone would learn to read. The goal was to provide the common people with the tools to study the Bible and other religious texts for themselves. This campaign was remarkably successful, given the fact that Iceland had no elementary school system at the time and literacy had become more or less common in Iceland by the end of the 18th century. Since then, literacy rates in Iceland have been among the highest in the world. *See also* EDUCATION; LITERATURE.

LITERATURE. Icelandic literature traces its beginning to the early 12th century, when Icelandic laws were written down for the first time. **Ari Þorgilsson's** *Book of Icelanders* is also from this period, but it was written sometime between 1122 and 1133. Icelandic medieval literature reached its artistic peak in the 13th century; it was during that turbulent century that some of the finest literary works of medieval Europe were written in Iceland. That was, for example, when most of the family **sagas** were composed, and **Snorri Sturluson** wrote the bulk of his works in the 1220s and 1230s. In the late medieval period, Icelandic literary tradition changed as the writing of family sagas and historical chronicles came to an end. This did not mean an end to literature in Iceland, however, because most of the extant *fornaldarsögur* (mythic-heroic sagas) stem from the 14th and 15th centuries. Moreover, a new form of poetry called *rímur* developed in the late medieval period. Influenced by **Eddic** and **skaldic poetry** in style and often using the mythical heroic legends and romances as a subject, *rímur* remained the most popular literary genre in Iceland until the 19th century.

The **Reformation** had a lasting influence on Icelandic literature. The publication of the Bible in Icelandic translation (1584) was, for example, crucial in securing the status of Icelandic as a church **language**, and much of the poetry of the 16th and 17th centuries was **religious** in character. Iceland's greatest poet of this period, **Hallgrímur Pétursson** (circa 1614–74) is best known for his hymns and other religious poetry. Furthermore, the most influential work of prose in the vernacular of the early modern period was a book of sermons written by Bishop **Jón Vídalín** and published in 1718–20.

Although printing was introduced relatively early in Iceland (around 1530), it was used mostly by the church until the late 18th century. In the last decades of the 18th century, however, there was a great expansion in the publication of secular works in the Icelandic language. To begin with, they were primarily treatises on practical issues, introducing new methods in **agriculture** and exhorting Icelanders to improve their material conditions, but with the romantic **nationalism** of the 19th century, Icelandic literature was rejuvenated. In the early 19th century, poets like Bjarni Thorarensen (1786–1841) and **Jónas Hallgrímsson** (1807–45) introduced a new voice in Icelandic poetry, and **Jón Thoroddsen's** (1818–68) *Piltur og stúlka* (*A Boy and a Girl*), published in 1850, is often regarded as the first modern Icelandic novel.

Contemporary Icelandic literature is remarkably strong and varied, considering that Icelandic is spoken by just around 300,000 people. The most notable Icelandic literary figure of the 20th century was, without doubt, **Halldór Laxness** (1902–98), who was awarded the Nobel Prize for literature in 1955. Laxness was not the only writer of his generation, of course, although he is the best known. Writers **Gunnar Gunnarsson** (1889–1975) and **Þórbergur Þórðarson** (1888–1974) were very popular in Iceland, and Gunnarsson was, indeed, one of the most widely read authors in **Denmark** and Germany in the years between the two world wars. These authors, especially

Laxness and Þórðarson, channeled new styles and ideas into the Icelandic literary scene, the first with his epic stories and the latter with his modernist essays.

The struggle between modernism and tradition was even fiercer in poetry than it was in fiction writing because the poetic styles were closely related to cultural nationalism in Iceland. In the same manner as the Icelandic language was thought to preserve an authentic culture in Iceland, the metric patterns of traditional Icelandic poetry were regarded as important markers of Icelandic national identity and culture. For the poets who came of age during a period of rapid modernization, economic depression, and world war, these traditions were increasingly seen as stultifying and outdated. New styles were needed to express the sentiments of the "atomic age," they maintained, and hence, they were called the "atomic poets." The precursor of this movement was Steinn Steinarr (1908–58), who published his most important work, *Tíminn og vatnið* (*Time and Water*), in 1948. There was always a strong nationalist streak in Icelandic modernism, however, because many of the cultural radicals were involved in the opposition to the American military base in **Keflavík**. To them, the base was a symbol of what they regarded as American imperialism in culture and politics, and it could only be combated by preserving the independence of the Icelandic nation and culture.

In recent years, novelists like Thor Vilhjálmsson (1925–), Svava Jakobsdóttir (1930–2004), Guðbergur Bergsson (1932–), Fríða Á. Sigurðardóttir (1940–), and Einar Már Guðmundsson (1954–) have all enjoyed critical success, while Arnaldur Indriðason's (1961–) murder mysteries have earned him critical acclaim in Europe and have sold extremely well both in Iceland and abroad. *See also* LITERACY; *NJÁLS SAGA*; STEPHANSSON, STEPHAN G. (1853–1927); *STURLUNGA SAGA*; ÞÓRÐARSON, STURLA (1214–84).

LIVING STANDARDS. In terms of national income, Icelanders have fared very well during the postwar period, with gross domestic products (GDP) per capita among the highest in the world in recent decades (according to the estimates of the International Monetary Fund, the per-capita GDP, at current prices, was US$63,000 in 2007, the third in the world, while the GDP based on purchasing-power-parity was US$41,700, the fifth in the world). The average annual increase has been 2.6 percent from the end of **World War II** until the late 1980s, when the **economy** entered a protracted recession caused in part by chronic hyperinflation (*see* INFLATION). A new period of growth started around the mid-1990s, with about 4 percent annual increase a year. Improved standards of living can be attributed to a combination of factors, such as expansion of the **fisheries**, exploitation of hydroelectric and geothermal **energy**, high levels of investment, adoption of high technology, and a well-**educated** labor force. Other indicators of living standards, such as average life expectancy (80.2 years for men and 83.2 for **women**), **infant mortality** (2.9 deaths per every 1,000 live births), and the number of cars (740 for every 1,000 inhabitants), telephones (over 650 lines in use for every 1,000 inhabitants and more than 1 cellular phone for every inhabitant), and doctors (3.6 for every 1,000 inhabitants), put Iceland in a very favorable light.

Postwar growth has, however, been uneven, and the great variability of output, unparalleled in the Organization of Economic Cooperation and Development countries, in combination with the consequent fluctuation in real wages has taught Icelanders not to take their everyday economic situation for granted. In addition to the uncertainty attached to the level of prosperity, one of the reasons for the high GDP per capita in Iceland has been the hard work of the **population**, which has higher participation rates and a longer working day than most European nations. In 2007, the average working week for persons working full time was 49.4 hours for men and 42.0 for women. Furthermore, the **welfare state** has not reached the same levels in Iceland as it has in the other Nordic countries. *See also* HEALTH; LABOR MARKET.

LUTHERANISM. With the **Reformation**, which was completed with the execution of the last medieval **Catholic** bishop in Iceland, **Jón Arason** in 1550, the Evangelical Lutheran Church was established as the only authorized church in Iceland. As in the other Nordic countries, the Lutheran Church was under direct control of the state, and the **Danish king** served as its supreme head. Thus, Lutheran bishops in Iceland were royal officials, although they received most of their revenues from church lands until the late 18th and early 19th centuries.

In the beginning, the Reformation did not transform the structure of church administration in Iceland, except for the suppression of **religious** houses and the severance of all ties with the pope in Rome. The two dioceses, **Skálholt** and **Hólar**, were preserved until the end of the 18th century, when they were merged and the bishop's seat moved to **Reykjavík**. In the long run, however, the Reformation strengthened royal authority in Iceland, both because the king's position as the head of the church gave him strong symbolic power in Iceland and because the confiscation of the property of the religious houses in Iceland made the king one of the largest landowners in the country.

In 1874, the first Icelandic **constitution** established for the first time religious freedom in Iceland, but Lutheranism continued to be the dominant religion in the country. In 2007, 81 percent of the **population** belonged, at least formally, to the Lutheran state church and another 5 percent to other Lutheran congregations. Moreover, although the constitution guarantees religious liberty, the fact that the Lutheran Church is a state institution gives it a considerable advantage over other religious denominations. The state pays the salaries of church employees, and the Lutheran bishop plays a strong symbolic role in many public ceremonies, serving as the spiritual head of the **Republic of Iceland**.

– M –

MAGNÚSSON, ÁRNI (1663–1730). Professor, archivist, and collector of **manuscripts**. Born on 13 November 1663, Magnússon was fostered first by his maternal grandfather and later by his uncle, both of whom were **Lutheran** pastors in Dalir County in western Iceland. He studied at the Latin school in **Skálholt** from 1680 to 1683, and in the fall of 1683, he enrolled in the University of Copenhagen. He studied theology in Copenhagen until 1685 in addition to working as an assistant to the renowned **Danish** royal antiquarian, Thomas Bartholin. After 1694, Magnússon spent over two years in Germany, and upon returning to Copenhagen in 1697, he was nominated secretary for the royal archives. He was appointed professor at the University of Copenhagen in 1701 but was dispatched as a royal emissary to Iceland the following year.

From 1702 to 1712, Magnússon and Vice **Lawman** Páll Vídalín traveled around the country, collecting information on its **economic** conditions, legal practices, and **trade**. Under their direction, the first **census** in Iceland was taken in 1703, listing all inhabitants by name, place of residence, age, and status. In this period, they also completed a description of every farm in Iceland. Magnússon was appointed librarian at the University Library in Copenhagen in 1721, effectively serving as its director. At his death in 1730, he bequeathed his manuscript collection to the University of Copenhagen in addition to establishing a special fund to provide financial support to researchers and grants for editions of manuscripts in his collection.

Magnússon is primarily remembered for his contribution to the preservation and study of Icelandic manuscripts. From an early age, he interested himself in the collection of vellum and paper manuscripts, using his connections to gather a great number of them in Iceland and transport them to Copenhagen. Although 19th- and 20th-century **nationalists** regretted that these cultural jewels had been removed from their country of origin, there is no doubt that Magnússon's work salvaged many of the Icelandic parchment manuscripts from eventual damage or destruction. *See also* ÁRNI MAGNÚSSON INSTITUTE FOR ICELANDIC STUDIES.

MAGNÚSSON, SKÚLI (1711–94). The man sometimes called the "father of **Reykjavík**" was born on 12 December 1711 to a **Lutheran** pastor in Þingey County. Magnússon studied in Copenhagen between 1732 and 1734 with the intention of becoming a clergyman. In 1734, the **king** appointed him bailiff in Skaftafell County, and he returned to Iceland the same year to take up his office. Three years later, he was promoted to the office of bailiff in Skagafjörður County, where he served for the next 12 years. In 1749, Magnússon was the first Icelander to be appointed *landfógeti*, or royal treasurer, in Iceland, an office he held for the remainder of his active life. Unlike most of his predecessors, he served his office with great zeal, furthering with vigor the **economic** development of Iceland.

After moving to **Viðey**, a small island just off Reykjavík's present-day harbor, he was instrumental in persuading the **Danish** king to establish textile workshops in Reykjavík with the intention of promoting technological innovation in the country. This venture, called

Innréttingar, was started in 1752, but it never became economically profitable, although it laid the foundation for the development of the town of Reykjavík. It was, however, Magnússon's fight against the companies monopolizing the Icelandic **trade** that has earned him the greatest praise among his countrymen. In the late 1750s, during years of high grain prices, merchants tried to increase their profits by importing rotten grain, a practice that the *landfógeti* relentlessly tried to put an end to. In 1793, then 81 years old, Magnússon retired from his office, and he died the following year.

Magnússon is rightly remembered as one of the most important persons in the history of 18th-century Iceland. With his actions as a royal official and his essays on the economy of Iceland, he was instrumental in igniting the belief in progress, which was to characterize the **nationalist** surge of the following century. *See also* MONOPOLY TRADE.

MANUSCRIPTS, RETURN OF. In the 1930s, the Icelandic parliament demanded that the **Danish** government return to Iceland the Icelandic medieval manuscripts kept in Danish research libraries, as these were deemed to be the most valuable treasures of Icelandic culture. In 1945, the government of the newly founded republic repeated the request because the return of the manuscripts was regarded as a fitting completion of the struggle for independence. Most of the manuscripts had been collected in Iceland during the 17th and 18th centuries by such men as **Árni Magnússon,** professor at the University of Copenhagen, and **Brynjólfur Sveinsson,** bishop of **Skálholt** diocese in Iceland. At his death, Magnússon bequeathed his considerable manuscript collection to the University of Copenhagen, the institution where he had served as professor and the university of Iceland at the time. The manuscripts were kept at the Royal Library in Copenhagen and the University Library in Copenhagen, where they were seen among the most valuable possessions of the institutions.

At first, the Icelandic demands were strongly opposed by Danish academics, as the return of such cultural objects is not a standard practice when former dependencies receive independence. A number of influential Danish politicians supported the Icelandic request, however, in part because they wanted to use the issue to demonstrate how the Nordic countries could solve internal conflicts in a peaceful manner. In 1961, after long and difficult negotiations, the two nations came to a conclusion about the actual division of the manuscripts: about 1,700 of them dealing with specific Icelandic topics were to be returned to Iceland in the space of 25 years, but about 900 dealing with non-Icelandic matters—including **sagas** of **Norwegian kings**—were to remain in Copenhagen. On 21 April 1971, after a decade of legal proceedings in Denmark, the Danish minister of culture returned the first two manuscripts to his Icelandic counterpart. The return of the manuscripts was completed in June 1997, and they are stored at the **Árni Magnusson Institute of Icelandic Studies** in Reykjavík. *See also* LITERATURE.

MARINE RESEARCH INSTITUTE (MRI). Founded in 1965 in **Reykjavík** to organize and develop marine research in Iceland. The Hafrannsóknarstofnunin (MRI) is a governmental institution and has been instrumental during the last decades in dictating the **fisheries** policy of the Icelandic authorities. The MRI's object is to conduct research on the marine environment around the country and consult the government on the utilization of various fish stocks in Icelandic waters. Recent reductions in catches, especially those of cod, have been enacted after warnings from the MRI, although the government has only recently dared to propose measures as drastic in this respect as the institute has advised. Since 1998, the MRI has operated the Fisheries Training Program under the **United Nations** University, training specialists from the developing world in fishing technology. *See also* DIRECTORATE OF FISHERIES; FISHERIES MANAGEMENT.

MARSHALL AID. Iceland was among the founding members of the Organization for European Economic Cooperation (later Organization for European Cooperation and Development) in 1948, set up to administer the American aid offered under the Marshall Plan. Iceland accepted the American financial aid in an agreement with the government of the **United States** on 3 July 1948, according to which it was to receive US$38.65 million, including US$29.8 million as grants and most of the rest as loans on favorable terms. The aid was largely used to facilitate U.S. imports to Iceland between 1948 and 1954, easing import restrictions, but US$7.9 million were invested in two hydroelectric power plants and a fertilizer plant. The most controversial aspect of the aid was the clause allowing the U.S. government to set aside 5, and later 10, percent of the Counterpart Fund for its free disposal in Iceland, giving it direct **economic** and political leverage in the country's internal affairs.

MENNTASKÓLINN Í REYKJAVÍK (MR). The oldest secondary school in Iceland traces its ancestry to the old Latin schools, or gymnasia, at the two bishop seats, **Skálholt** and **Hólar**. At first, these schools, founded in the 11th and 12th centuries, respectively, were meant to **educate** young men for the priesthood, and this was, in fact, one of the objectives of the Latin schools until a theological seminary was founded in **Reykjavík** in 1847. The Skálholt Latin School moved to Reykjavík in 1786, and at the beginning of the 19th century, the Hólar School merged with the Latin school in Reykjavík. From 1805 to 1846, the school was located at **Bessastaðir**, but it was moved back to Reykjavík in 1846, where a new house had been built specifically for the school in the town's center.

During the second half of the 19th century, the Latin school in Reykjavík gradually evolved into a regular secondary school, preparing its students for university studies. This development was in line with educational reforms in **Denmark**, culminating with a change in the name of the Reykjavík School to Menntaskóli in 1904. Since 1937, its formal name has been Menntaskólinn í Reykjavík, and it is commonly known by its acronym, MR.

Until the late 1920s, the MR was the only secondary school in Iceland to have the right to grant university entrance exams. As a result, almost the entire educated elite in the country had graduated from the school, providing this group with a common identity and a sense of homogeneity. In 1928, this monopoly was broken when **Jónas Jónsson**, then minister of education, granted the secondary school in **Akureyri** the same prerogative. With growing demands for university education, the number of secondary schools has rapidly increased in Iceland. At present, close to 30 such schools prepare students for university studies. *See also* UNIVERSITY OF ICELAND (UoI).

MIGRATION. From the end of the **Settlement Period** until the mid-19th century, Iceland's geographic location hampered **population** movement to and from the country. Although Iceland was in union with **Denmark** for centuries, very limited numbers of people migrated permanently between the two countries. In the latter half of the 19th century, emigration to America tempted many Icelanders to seek their fortunes abroad. The first to go were a few people who had converted to the Mormon faith, emigrating in the 1850s and 1860s to Utah in the **United States**, and a small group of people moved to Brazil in the 1860s. It was only after 1870, however, that this wave of emigration (called *vesturferðir* in Icelandic, or the "voyages to the west") really began. This was a time of revolution in **transportation**, and the efforts of a number of emigration agents, especially from Canada, provided people with the opportunity and incentive to emigrate to North America. Emigration from Iceland reached its peak in the late 1880s, with around 2,000 persons—almost 3 percent of the Icelandic population—emigrating to North America in 1887. The last wave of emigrants left the country around the turn of the century, but emigration practically ended at the beginning of **World War I**. Over 14,000 persons are known to have emigrated to America from 1870 to 1914, which is a considerable number for a country that had a population of only 78,000 in 1900.

The causes of Icelandic emigration to America were similar to those in other European countries, as it was driven by a combination of factors pulling people to the new world and pushing them from their old country. The rapidly expanding **economies** of the United States and Canada offered opportunities that did not exist in Iceland, especially during the economic difficulties of the late 19th century. Also growing overpopulation in the Icelandic countryside made it difficult for people to find **employment** in **agriculture**, forcing them either to emigrate or to move to the fishing villages around the coast. To many, the first option seemed much more appealing than the latter because of the strong prejudices in Iceland toward the **fisheries** and the people living in the villages by the coast. Another cause behind the emigration from Iceland was the fact that the climatic conditions in Iceland were unfavorable during the last decades of the 19th century and the beginning of the 20th, making it very difficult for farmers to make ends meet. Strong economic growth during the early 20th century, fueled primarily by a rapid mechanization of the fisheries, removed most of the economic reasons for emigration, and slowly the flow to America abated.

Emigration took place in a period of intense **nationalist** struggle. Hence, there was a great interest among the emigrants to retain their national identity in the new country, despite the fact that economic hardship forced many of them to leave their homeland. For this reason, they established an Icelandic "colony" on the western shores of Lake Winnipeg in Manitoba, Canada. A large group of Icelandic immigrants moved to this area, which was often called **New Iceland**, and their influence is still prominent in Winnipeg and surrounding areas. Other centers of Icelandic settlement were in North Dakota and Minnesota in the United States.

Since the end of the emigration wave to America, the balance of immigration and emigration in Iceland has usually reflected the economic situation of the country. Thus, during the economic crisis of the late 1960s, many people left Iceland in search of employment, moving to Sweden and Australia in particular. Similarly, during the economic boom after the turn of the 21st century, immigration—especially from Eastern Europe—increased dramatically in Iceland. One reason for this development is high demand for labor in Iceland, but Iceland's membership in the common European labor market through the **European Economic Area** has also helped people from the member states of the **European Union** to seek employment in Iceland. As a result, Iceland is rapidly becoming a multicultural country, with the relative number of foreign-born residents growing from around 4 percent in 1995 to over 10 percent of the population in 2007. It is still too early to predict how this change will influence Icelandic political and social life, but the idea of a homogenous nation, all speaking the same **language** and sharing common cultural heritage, does not fit the Icelandic reality anymore. *See also* LABOR MARKET.

MINISTRIES. With the establishment of **home rule** in 1904, the Ministry of Icelandic Affairs was transferred from Copenhagen to **Reykjavík**. From 1904 to 1917, the government of Iceland consisted of one ministry that was divided into three offices or departments (Office of **Education** and Justice, Office of **Economic** Affairs and **Transportation**, and Office of Finance and Revision). When the number of ministers grew to three in 1917, each minister became the head of a separate department; the **prime minister** headed the

Department of Justice and Ecclesiastical Affairs, the minister of economic affairs headed the Department of Economic Affairs and Transportation, and the finance minister headed the Department of Finances. In 1921, each of the three departments became independent ministries.

This organization remained unchanged until 1938, when **Alþingi** established a special Ministry of Foreign Affairs (*see* FOREIGN POLICY), preparing for the total secession from **Denmark**. With the growing complexity of the Icelandic administration, the number of ministries has increased steadily. At present, there are 12 separate ministries in Iceland: Office of the **Prime Minister**; Ministry of **Education**, Science and Culture; Ministry of Foreign Affairs; Ministry of **Fisheries** and **Agriculture**; Ministry of Justice and Ecclesiastical Affairs; Ministry of Social Affairs; Ministry of **Health**; Ministry of Finance; Ministry of **Communications**; Ministry of **Industries**; Ministry of Commerce; and Ministry of **Environment**. A permanent secretary heads each ministry, but individual ministers are sometimes responsible for more than one portfolio. *See also* ACT OF UNION; CABINET; REPUBLIC OF ICELAND.

MODERNIZATION GOVERNMENT. In October 1944, close to the end of **World War II**, the two parties at the opposite poles of the political spectrum, the conservative **Independence Party** (IP) and the radical **Socialist Unity Party** formed a coalition government with the participation of the **Social Democratic Party** (SDP). Each of the three parties had two ministers in the government, with **Ólafur Thors** of the IP serving as **prime minister**. The main objective of the government, which was known as Nýsköpunarstjórnin (the Modernization Government) was to secure the **economic** basis of the new republic and use the large foreign exchange reserves collected during the war to modernize Iceland's economic infrastructures. For the next two years, the government liberally spent on various projects, especially on the modernization of the fishing fleet and of the fishing industry in general. In addition to these economic measures, the government introduced extensive **educational** and social reforms, including new legislation for Icelandic primary education, a new standardized entrance exam for secondary schools, and expanded welfare legislation. In the summer of 1946, the coalition parties won a decisive victory in parliamentary **elections**, but in October of the same year, the socialist ministers resigned from the government because of their opposition to the airport agreement made between the governments of Iceland and the **United States**. In February of the following year, a coalition government of the **Progressive Party**, the IP, and the SDP replaced the Modernization Government. *See also* KEFLAVÍK.

MONOPOLY TRADE. The monopoly **trade**, which became the most hated aspect of **Danish** rule in Iceland, was formally introduced in 1602, when the Danish **king** decided to give only Danish merchants licenses to trade with Iceland and requiring all export goods from Iceland to go through specific harbors in the Danish monarchy. In the preceding century, the royal government had sold such monopoly rights over certain regions to individual Danish or German merchants, but now this system was to cover the whole country. The king wanted to increase the royal revenues from his dependency and to boost the business of the Danish merchant class. Strict monopoly regulations were in full effect in Iceland until 1786–88, when a royal edict opened the Icelandic trade to all Danish subjects. The trade restrictions were lifted further in 1816, when all subjects of the Danish king—including Icelandic merchants—could trade freely in Iceland and export Icelandic goods to the markets where they could sell them at the highest price. The last vestiges of monopoly trade policy were abolished as late as 1855, when merchants from outside of the Danish monarchy were given open access to the Icelandic market.

The monopoly trade had very adverse effects on the Icelandic **economy** because it greatly limited with whom Icelanders could trade. Its inflexibility and exclusion of all competition also stifled economic initiative because the regulations made it more or less impossible for merchants to invest their earnings in Iceland. Therefore, the profits from trade went, for the most part, out of the country. Moreover, some merchants became very unpopular for their unscrupulous trading practices; the quality of their imports was sometimes suspect and their supplies insufficient. In part, this was the result of strict price regulations on most imports to Iceland, which could lead to great losses for Danish merchants in times of scarcity. In the 19th century, Icelandic **nationalists** viewed the monopoly trade as an example of Danish oppression, but recent studies have emphasized that it was a widespread economic practice at the time in neighboring countries and, to a certain extent at least, that it served the interests of a part of the Icelandic elite. Moreover, the Icelandic market was very small, and many people believed that trade regulations were needed to secure provisions for the inhabitants. *See also* THE GENERAL PETITION; MAGNÚSSON, SKÚLI (1711–94).

MORGUNBLAÐIÐ. One of the oldest and the most influential newspapers in Iceland was founded in 1913. Although *Morgunblaðið* prides itself on being the newspaper of all Icelanders, its editorial policy has always leaned to the right in politics, and it has had strong links with the **Independence Party** (IP) from the establishment of that party in 1929. *Morgunblaðið* has, however, never had formal ties with the IP, and in recent years, it has become more independent of the party than before, while the **political parties** in Iceland have lost their influence over the **press**. At present, *Morgunblaðið* is published daily, and each issue sells over 50,000 copies—almost one copy for every six inhabitants.

MUSIC. Although some Icelandic musicians have had considerable success on the international stage in recent years, **Björk Guðmundsdóttir** in particular, Iceland does not have a very strong musical tradition. Through the centuries, **literature** overshadowed music as the cultural activity in Iceland par excellence, and Icelandic settlement patterns also hampered the development of musical culture. On a fairly large island with no towns or villages to speak of and limited communication with the outer world, people had few opportunities to meet and entertain themselves collectively or to become acquainted with European cultural fashions.

Iceland had, however, a very distinctive tradition of singing, which had its roots in the first centuries of the country's settlement. These archaic musical styles set their mark both on the traditional folk music and on the musical practices of the church. The most peculiar form of these traditional styles was the *tvísöngur* (two-part singing), which has its origins in a European medieval singing technique called *organum.* This style was practiced in Iceland until the 20th century. The only traditional musical instrument used in Iceland was the *langspil*, a primitive stringed instrument that had no other function but to serve as a background for singing. During the 19th century, European musical forms began to be introduced in Iceland. This happened in tandem with the modernization of Icelandic society and the gradual growth of the capital, **Reykjavík**. In the late 19th and early 20th centuries, a number of Icelanders studied music abroad, finding work in Iceland as music teachers, church organists, and so on. This led to the foundation of the Reykjavík Conservatory of Music in 1930 and the Philharmonic Society in Reykjavík two years later. The establishment of the Ríkisútvarpið (Icelandic State Radio) in 1930 also had a great impact on musical tastes in Iceland because radio **broadcasting** became crucial to introducing music to ordinary Icelanders who had, until then, few opportunities to listen to music performed by professional artists.

Some attempts had been made to establish a professional symphonic orchestra in Reykjavík in the years between the two world wars, but it was only in 1950—with the foundation of the Iceland Symphony Orchestra—that this dream was realized. For the first decades of its existence, the orchestra struggled, battling constant underfunding. These issues were solved in 1983, when the state, in cooperation with a few local and public bodies, including the Icelandic State Radio, agreed to secure the financial basis of the orchestra. Since then, it has established itself as one of the leading classical orchestras in the Nordic countries, with 80 musicians employed on full contracts. In addition to a professional symphony orchestra, Reykjavík also has a national opera, and many smaller chamber orchestras operate in the capital area.

Icelandic popular music became internationally known with the alternative and somewhat quirky rock band the Sugarcubes (Sykurmolarnir), which received critical acclaim for its first record, *Life's Too Good*, in 1988. The main attraction of the band was, undoubtedly, its lead singer, Björk Guðmundsdóttir, who launched her solo career in 1993 with the album *Debut*. In the following years, Björk, as she is universally known, became an international celebrity, catching people's attention with her music and eccentric behavior. Björk focused the spotlight on Icelandic pop music, and some other

Icelandic alternative bands have been able to follow in her footsteps. The best known of them is Sigur Rós, which has established a loyal fan base all over the world, and the experimental band Múm has also been hailed by critics for its imaginative music. *See also* LEIFS, JÓN (1899–1968).

– N –

NATIONAL AND UNIVERSITY LIBRARY OF ICELAND. The National Library of Iceland in **Reykjavík** was established as Stiftsbókasafn Íslands (Library of the Province of Iceland) in 1818, changing its name to Landsbókasafn Íslands in 1881. The library was opened to the public in 1848, moving to its own building in the center of Reykjavík in 1909. In 1994, with the opening of a new library building on the campus of the **University of Iceland** in Reykjavík, the Icelandic National Library merged with the university library, making it by far the largest library in Iceland. The national library is a depository for all printed material in Iceland, and a great number of private archives and manuscripts from the early modern and modern periods are stored in its manuscript section. The holdings of the National and University Library of Iceland are, therefore, of crucial importance in the study of Icelandic history and culture.

NATIONAL ARCHIVES OF ICELAND (NAI). The NAI trace their history to a proclamation made by the governor of Iceland in 1882, announcing that the archives of a few of the highest government offices in Iceland should be stored under one roof in **Reykjavík**. The NAI were formally established on 10 August 1900 under the name of Landsskjalasafn Íslands. They were given their current name, Þjóðskjalasafn Íslands, in 1915. With the **home rule** of 1904, the documents of the Icelandic Bureau in Copenhagen were moved to Iceland and stored in the NAI, and in 1928, a large number of public documents pertaining to Icelandic history were transported from Copenhagen to be placed in the NAI.

Today, the NAI are bound by law to collect and preserve public records (that are over 30 years old) from all government institutions in Iceland, including the state church, in addition to serving as a depository of private documents that are placed in their care. Moreover, the NAI oversee the management of public records in the various government agencies and supervise the preservation of documents in local archives.

NATIONAL BANK OF ICELAND (NBI). The Landsbanki Íslands (NBI) was established with an act passed in **Alþingi** in 1885 and started operations the following year. Since that time, the NBI has been the leading **banking** institution in Iceland, and at the time of its foundation, the NBI was actually the only bank in Iceland. The scale of its operations was limited in the beginning, but its activities increased considerably at the turn of the century in response to growing demand for capital from the burgeoning fishing industry. Originally, the NBI had the right to issue a limited quantity of treasury notes, but in 1904, Alþingi granted a private bank by the name Íslandsbanki (Bank of Iceland) the right to print bank notes in addition to the treasury notes of the NBI. In 1928, this permission was revoked, and the NBI received the sole right to issue currency in Iceland. For the next decades, the NBI remained a commercial bank, while it also managed the **central banking** functions of the Icelandic state; in 1961, these two functions were separated with the foundation of the Central Bank of Iceland.

Until the 1990s, the NBI was owned and operated by the Icelandic state, but it was sold to private investors in a few steps from 1997 to 2002. This **privatization** process started when the bank was changed to a holding company in 1997–98, with the state as the sole owner of the stocks. The first stocks in the bank were sold to small investors in 1998, but this process was completed at the end of 2002, when a group of large Icelandic investors bought most of the remaining shares of the state in the bank. The change in the ownership of the bank led to its rapid expansion, especially abroad. At present, the NBI is the second largest commercial bank in Iceland. It operates in 12 countries, both under its own name and through foreign subsidiaries. An increasing proportion of the bank's revenues come from its international operations, which reflects the radical change in the Icelandic **economy** in the first years of the 21st century.

NATIONAL COMPROMISE AGREEMENT. On 2 February 1990, the **Icelandic Federation of Labor** (IFL), the Union of Public Employees, and the **SA-Confederation of Icelandic Employers** signed an agreement designed to end the hyperinflation that had plagued the Icelandic **economy** for most of the 1970s and 1980s. With the agreement, the unions accepted a fairly modest rise in wages but secured a set of entitlements and benefits from both the employers and the state. This agreement marked the beginning of a new period of conciliation between employers and employees in Iceland, and since then, no general strike has taken place in the country. Moreover, the agreement opened a new era for the Icelandic economy, as **inflation** declined rapidly in the 1990s, falling to similar levels as in neighboring countries in the following two years. *See also* TRADE UNIONS.

NATIONAL MUSEUM OF ICELAND (NMI). The museum was founded in 1863 when an Icelandic farmer donated a few antiquities to Icelandic authorities in the hope that they would serve as the basis for a new collection of Icelandic antiquities. The museum was called the Forngripasafnið (Antiquarian Collection) until its name was changed to the Þjóðminjasafn Íslands (NMI) in 1911. For close to 90 years, the museum was housed in various attics in **Reykjavík**, but with the foundation of the republic in 1944, the parliament decided to construct a special building for the museum. The NMI moved to the new house, which is located on the campus of the **University of Iceland**, in 1950. The NMI serves various roles, reflecting its legal status as a national center for the preservation and management of the cultural heritage, cultural research programs, and dissemination of knowledge and information about the cultural heritage of the nation.

NATIONAL POWER COMPANY OF ICELAND (NPCI). A company established in 1965 to construct and operate the major power plants and main distribution lines in Iceland and to provide local utilities over the whole country with electricity. The Landsvirkjun (NPCI) was formed as a joint enterprise of the Icelandic state and the city of **Reykjavík** in order to provide power for the planned aluminum plant outside of the town of Hafnarfjörður close to Reykjavík. These two parties held equal shares in the NPCI until 1983, when the town of **Akureyri** became a partner. From 1983 to 2007, the state owned half of the shares in NPCI, Reykjavík 45 percent, and Akureyri 5 percent, but at the beginning of 2007, the state bought the other partners out of the company.

The first major project of the NPCI was the construction of the Búrfell Power Plant in Árnes County, which opened in 1969; since then, its activities have expanded greatly. This reflects the emphasis on **energy-intensive industry** in Iceland during the last three decades, the state having attempted to attract foreign investment to Iceland by offering inexpensive electricity. For most of the 1970s and 1980s, this strategy met with only limited success, and a severe recession in these industries in the early 1990s brought all investments to a halt. As a result, the NPCI's power plants, some of which were the largest and most complicated projects undertaken in Iceland, produced a considerable amount of surplus electricity for a number of years. Since the mid-1990s, a boom in investments, especially in aluminum smelters, has solved this problem, and the NPCI has expanded its operations greatly in recent years to meet increased demand for electricity.

In 2006, power stations owned by the NPCI generated over 7,000 GWh of electricity, which was around 76 percent of the total electricity production in Iceland. Over 70 percent of the electricity was sold to energy-intensive industries in Iceland, primarily to aluminum smelters, while the rest was sold on the general market. The production of the NPCI will increase by around 40 percent, to almost 12,000 GWh, in 2007–9, when the new **Kárahnjúkar** hydroelectric power plant in the eastern highlands will be completed. Most of its 4,600 GWh will be sold to a new aluminum factory in the eastern jjords.

During its first decades, the NPCI was generally regarded very positively in Iceland because the company was thought to herald a new age in the Icelandic **economy**. Recently, this enthusiasm seems to be declining with growing **environmentalism** in Iceland. Some even predict that the Kárahnjúkar station will be the last large-scale hydroelectric project in Iceland because the building of dams and reservoirs often causes widespread environmental damage. The NPCI has, for this reason, begun to look for new opportunities in using its expertise to construct hydroelectric power plants in other countries.

NATIONAL PRESERVATION PARTY OF ICELAND (NPPI). The NPPI, or Þjóðvarnarflokkur Íslands, was founded in 1953 to protest

U.S. military presence in **Keflavík**. Its platform focused primarily on this single issue, but it also advocated democratic socialism. The NPPI received 6 percent of the votes cast in the parliamentary **elections** of 1953, which gave it two seats in **Alþingi**. In 1956 and 1959, the party did not poll enough votes to have a representative elected to parliament, but in 1963, one of its leaders entered parliament through a cooperation with the **People's Alliance** (PA). The same year, the NPPI ceased to exist as a **political party**, and most of its support went to the PA.

NATIONALISM. The idea that Icelanders had a separate identity emerged early on in their history. There is, for example, evidence in the **saga literature** and the Old Icelandic law codes indicating that Icelanders perceived themselves as a separate **population** group from **Norwegians** as early as the **Commonwealth Period**. The same sentiment was clearly dominant in Iceland for the next centuries, in spite of the fact that the country became first a part of the Norwegian and later the **Danish** monarchy. Icelanders defended their provincial privileges, and they never abandoned the use of the Icelandic **language** in private or public life.

It was only in the early 19th century, however, that demands for political autonomy of some sort were voiced in Iceland. Spokesmen of this nationalist sentiment traced its origins to the patriotism of earlier periods, utilizing Icelandic cultural heritage to legitimate their political claims. Pride in Icelandic traditions had its roots in the writings of 18th-century patriots, such as the naturalist **Eggert Ólafsson**, but ideological currents of 19th-century Europe and contemporary developments in Denmark were the main sources of inspiration for the political agenda of the **Icelandic nationalist movement**.

During most of the 19th century and well into the 20th, nationalism remained the dominant political ideology in Iceland. Thus, opinions on Iceland's position in the Danish monarchy and the future status of the country dictated the formation of all **political parties** in Iceland until **World War I**. With the **Act of Union** in 1918, which granted Iceland full sovereignty and the status of a free state, this chapter in Icelandic political history came to an end. This did not mean the end of nationalism in Iceland, however, as the preservation of national culture and independence is still extremely important. For this reason, opposition to the **North Atlantic Treaty Organization** base in **Keflavík** was very strong during the **cold war.** Icelandic authorities have also been very hesitant about entering the **European Union** (EU) in part because of the fear that membership in the EU could compromise Icelandic sovereignty. *See also FJÖLNIR*; SÆMUNDSSON, TÓMAS (1807–41); SIGURÐS-SON, JÓN (1811–1879).

NEW ICELAND. In October 1875, a group of around 200 Icelanders settled in the Red River Valley in Manitoba on the shores of Lake Winnipeg led by government representative John Taylor. At the time, the area was only inhabited by Native American tribes, and there was enough land for the Icelandic immigrants to settle. To begin with, the Icelandic immigrants to America wanted to form a separate Icelandic community, preserving their cultural identity in the new home. For that reason, a large proportion of them moved to this area, with the town of Gimli serving as a center of the colony. To honor their country of origin, the immigrants founded a 460-square-mile independent "republic," which they called Nýja Ísland (New Iceland). In 1881, New Iceland became officially a part of the province of Manitoba, and it lost its separate legal status in 1887. The Icelandic community in New Iceland and Winnipeg preserved its cultural heritage well into the 20th century, though, publishing newspapers in Icelandic and having Icelandic congregations. Gradually, knowledge of the Icelandic **language** began to disappear, but descendants of the Icelandic immigrants still retain strong links with their country of origin. *See also* MIGRATION.

NJÁLS SAGA. The *Brennu-Njáls Saga (Saga of the Burning of Njall)*, or *Njáls Saga*, is the longest and probably best-known of the Icelandic family **sagas.** In essence, it is a tragic story of two friends, Gunnar and Njáll, living in the southern part of Iceland during the late 10th and early 11th centuries. Gunnar is a heroic figure, tall, handsome, and brave, while Njáll is renowned for his cunning and wisdom. The two men meet similar destinies, however, as both are killed by their adversaries—Gunnar by the weapons of his enemies, Njáll by fire. *Njáls Saga* is a complex story presenting a diverse set of characters in an elaborate narrative structure. It is clearly written as a literary work, although the writer was well versed in the oral traditions of his time. The saga is also interesting for its detailed description of the legal procedures at **Alþingi**. The author demonstrates a strong longing for peace and harmony in society; he is a firm believer in the importance of Christianity, but he is also a protagonist of the values of the old society that had vanished during the violent **Age of the Sturlungs**. This author is unknown, as are those of all the family sagas, but scholars have dated its composition with relative certainty to around 1275 to 1290. The great number of manuscripts of *Njáls Saga* that are preserved, from both the Middle Ages and later periods, is a clear testimony to its popularity throughout the centuries.

Njáls Saga has been translated into numerous languages, with the first English translation appearing in 1861. *See also* LITERATURE.

NORDAL, JÓHANNES (1924–). Former director of the Central Bank of Iceland (CBI) and a leading authority on Iceland's **economic** policy. Nordal, the son of the literary scholar **Sigurður Nordal**, was born in **Reykjavík** on 11 May 1924. After graduating from **Menntaskólinn í Reykjavík** in 1943, he entered the London School of Economics and Political Science, where he completed a B.S. in 1950 and a Ph.D. in 1953. He worked as economic advisor at the **National Bank of Iceland** from 1954 to 1959, when he was appointed director of the bank. At the time of the foundation of the CBI in 1961, he became one of its directors and chairman of its board of directors in 1964. He served in both of these functions until his retirement in 1993.

Nordal was one of the most influential persons in Icelandic economic life for over three decades. As director of the CBI, he played a crucial role in the formation of Icelandic monetary policy, and as chairman of numerous steering committees and governing bodies of diverse institutions and companies, such as the Icelandic Science Fund and the **National Power Company of Iceland**, he wielded a strong influence in various fields of Icelandic society during his long career. *See also* CENTRAL BANKING.

NORDAL, SIGURÐUR (1886–1974). Professor of Icelandic **literature** and one of the founders of what has been called the Icelandic School in Old Norse studies. He was born on 14 September 1886 the illegitimate son of a farm servant and a maid in northern Iceland.

Raised by his uncle, Nordal was to enjoy the privilege of secondary school **education** in **Reykjavík**, completing a university entrance exam in 1906. In the fall of the same year, he enrolled in the Department of Old Norse Studies at the University of Copenhagen. He finished a master's degree in 1912 and defended his doctoral dissertation on the **saga** of St. Olaf two years later. After studying philosophy at Oxford University for one year, Nordal returned to Iceland in 1918, becoming professor of medieval literature in the recently founded **University of Iceland** (UoI).

In this position, he established himself as a leading scholar on Old Norse literature, shaping generations of Icelandic students in this field. Throughout his career, he was a firm spokesman of a scholarly tradition called bookprose theory, which considers the Icelandic sagas as more or less pure fiction rather than historical accounts based on oral traditions. Because of his reputation as a scholar of international stature, the Icelandic government appointed him ambassador to **Denmark** in 1951. His role was primarily to negotiate a solution of a dispute between the new republic and its old mother country concerning the return of Icelandic **manuscripts** preserved in Danish research libraries. After returning to Iceland in 1957, he resumed his former post as a professor at the UoI.

For decades, Nordal was a towering figure in the field of Old Norse studies. His research shattered the old beliefs in the historical veracity of the sagas, although in later years, his approach has been criticized for ignoring their oral sources as well as their social and political message. Although modern scholars have abandoned his strict bookprose theory, Nordal's works continue to offer valuable insights into the interpretation of saga literature. In 1986, a special institute carrying his name was founded at the UoI with the purpose of promoting the teaching of Icelandic **language** and the research in Icelandic culture abroad.

NORDIC COUNCIL. The Nordic Council serves as a forum for interparliamentary and intergovernmental cooperation between the five Nordic countries (**Denmark**, Finland, Iceland, **Norway**, and Sweden) and three autonomous provinces (Åland Islands, Faeroe Islands, and Greenland). Established in 1952 and based partly on the nongovernmental Nordic Associations, the Nordic Council has served as the basis for cultural, social, and **economic** cooperation among the Nordic countries. In 1971, the Nordic Council of Ministers was established besides the Nordic Council, organizing the extensive cooperation of Nordic ministries. The Nordic Council and the Nordic Council of Ministers have furthered a strong sense of common identity among the Nordic peoples, although increasing competition for the attention of public officials and politicians since Denmark, Sweden, and Finland entered the **European Union** has put the future of the cooperation into doubt. The Nordic Council runs a cultural center in **Reykjavík** called the Nordic House and supports the Nordic Volcanic Center, which forms a part of the Institute of Earth Sciences at the **University of Iceland**. *See also* FOREIGN POLICY.

NORTH ATLANTIC TREATY ORGANIZATION (NATO). Iceland is 1 of the 12 founding member states of NATO, which was established in 1949 as the military union of the western bloc during the **cold war**. Iceland has always been an active member of NATO, although the fact that the country maintains no armed forces has limited its direct participation to nonmilitary functions. From the time of the defense agreement with the **United States** in 1951, Iceland contributed to the military operations of NATO by allowing the United States to maintain a military base in **Keflavík** on the southwest coast. In this way, the American military undertook the defense of Iceland on behalf of NATO, while the Keflavík base served as an important link in NATO's surveillance of the North Atlantic, both in air and at sea. The closing down of the Keflavík base in 2006 puts this part of the Icelandic participation in NATO's operations in doubt, though Iceland remains important to the defense strategies in the North Atlantic.

Iceland's entrance into NATO was vigorously opposed by politicians on the left, because this was regarded as a betrayal of the neutrality policy that had been a cornerstone of Icelandic **foreign policy** in the years between the two world wars. The operation of the NATO base in Keflavík was also among the most divisive issues in Icelandic politics for decades, which led many to oppose Iceland's membership in NATO. **Nationalistic** sentiments fueled these views because many perceived the U.S. military presence as a compromise of Icelandic sovereignty. Hostility toward American foreign policy, especially during the war in Vietnam, also motivated objections from the leftist parties to the base in Keflavík. Thus, the second **Left-Wing Government**, formed in 1971, vowed to revise the defense agreement with the United States, aiming at the U.S. withdrawal from Keflavík. In response, a group of Icelandic NATO supporters collected a massive number of signatures on a petition protesting the planned withdrawal. The government resigned in the summer of 1974 without fulfilling its promise.

Since that time, the question of the withdrawal of NATO forces from Iceland has gradually disappeared from the political scene, especially as the waning of the cold war helped to diffuse the issue. At present, opposition to NATO membership is no longer a cornerstone in the platform of any **political party** in Iceland, although the **Left-Green Movement** continues the traditional opposition to NATO from the left. In fact, it was the desire of the United States to scale down its operations in Iceland in response to the changed military situation in the world, which determined the fate of the Keflavík base in the end, rather than the desire of the Icelandic politicians or the public to close it down.

NORWAY. Because the first permanent settlers in Iceland were of Norwegian origin, Iceland's relations with Norway are as old as Icelandic history. From the beginning, ties between the two countries were formed and maintained through extensive personal and institutional contacts. Thus, it was in Norway that Icelanders sought the model for their first law codes, and it was through Norwegian initiative that Icelanders **converted to Christianity** around the year 1000. Moreover, when the archbishopric in Trondheim was established in 1153, the two dioceses in Iceland came under the jurisdiction of the Norwegian archbishop. It was not surprising, therefore, that the Norwegian **king** sought to augment his formal authority in Iceland during the last decades of the **Commonwealth Period**. In the early 13th century, many Icelandic chieftains had become courtiers in the service of the Norwegian king, some of them actively promoting his authority in their home country. Between 1262 and 1264, after decades of violent upheavals, Icelanders approved a treaty with the king, promising him allegiance and tributes in return for pacification of the country. In 1380, Iceland accompanied Norway into a union with **Denmark**, as the two crowns merged, although it continued to be regarded as a part of the Norwegian realm. During the last century of the Middle Ages, relations with Norway decreased in importance for Icelanders. This happened as the administrative center moved to Copenhagen in the late 14th century and as foreign **trade** with Iceland ceased to go through Norwegian harbors in the 15th century. For this reason, Iceland did not follow Norway into the Swedish monarchy in 1814, when Norway was taken from Denmark as punishment for its cooperation with France during the Napoleonic Wars. During the 19th century, Icelanders began to look to Norway for political support and **economic** contacts. Norway's status as one of the most progressive democracies in northwestern Europe and the historical ties between the two countries served as an incentive for this development.

Relations between the two countries have been extensive—and usually amicable—in recent decades. Common interests, especially concerning the **fisheries**, have often led to close cooperation, a situation that has been further enhanced through both countries' membership in such institutions as the **European Free Trade Association,** the **North Atlantic Treaty Organization,** and the **Nordic Council.** Both countries are also members of the **European Economic Area,** while they stand outside of the **European Union.**

Similar economic interests have not only stimulated economic cooperation between the two countries but have also fueled serious frictions between them. Bitter conflicts over fishing rights in the North Atlantic and the Barents Sea are recent manifestations of this antagonism, but the debates have been caused by declining fish stocks in the northern waters. The two nations have competed intensely over the limited fishing rights in these regions. *See also* ALÞINGI; OLD COVENANT.

NÝ FÉLAGSRIT. An Icelandic periodical published in Copenhagen from 1841 to 1873. Its editor and main contributor was **Jón Sigurðsson** (1811–79), the leader of the **Icelandic nationalist movement.** The journal closely reflected the views and interests of its founder, publishing primarily political essays and practical treatises on **economic** issues. The style of *Ný félagsrit* was often thought to be rather abstruse, and despite the high quality of its articles, it was never a great financial success. But because of the prestige and political importance of its editor, *Ný félagsrit* occupies a central place in the history of Icelandic journalism. *See also ÁRMANN Á ALÞINGI; FJÖLNIR; PRESS.*

– O –

ODDSSON, DAVÍÐ (1948–). One of the most prominent politicians in Iceland since the early 1980s. Oddsson was born on 17 January 1948, in **Reykjavík**. After finishing a university entrance exam from **Menntaskólinn í Reykjavík**, he studied law at the **University of Iceland**, completing his degree in 1976. He worked for the Reykjavík **Health** Insurance Fund from 1976 to 1978, serving as its director from 1978 to 1982.

Oddsson became active in politics at an early age, and in 1974, he was **elected** to Reykjavík's city council for the **Independence Party** (IP). In 1982, he led the party to an overwhelming victory in elections to the city council, regaining a majority in the council for the IP after a short interlude of left-wing control. In the same year, he became mayor of Reykjavík. Under his undisputed leadership, the IP gained a dominant position in Reykjavík's city council, and his influence in the party grew with his success in governing the capital. Oddsson took his first step toward the national leadership of the IP when he became its deputy chairman in 1989. Two years later, he defeated **Þorsteinn Pálsson**, the sitting chairman of the IP, in elections for leadership of the party. The same year, Oddsson was elected to **Alþingi** for the first time. After the elections of 1991, he was given the mandate to form a new government, as he and his party were the unquestioned victors of the elections. From 1991 to 1995, he served as **prime minister** in a coalition government of the IP and the **Social Democratic Party**, and from 1995 to 2004, he held the same office in a coalition government of the IP and the **Progressive Party** (PP).

When he stepped down from his post as prime minister in 2004, Oddsson had served continuously for 13 years, longer than any other prime minister in Iceland's history. From 2004 to 2005, Oddsson served as minister of foreign affairs in a coalition government of the IP and the PP. Oddsson retired from politics in 2005 to become one of the three directors of the Central Bank of Iceland the same year.

He has, therefore, not relinquished all of his power, as he continues to have strong influence on Iceland's **economic** policy in his capacity as the chairman of the board of governors of the Central Bank. Oddsson earned respect in his party for the effective government of Reykjavík, although his forceful political style made him controversial, at least among his adversaries. On a national level, Oddsson united the IP after a decade of internal disputes, and under his leadership, the party seems to have regained its former cohesion after serious dissension during most of the 1980s. *See also* CENTRAL BANKING; HAARDE, GEIR H. (1951–).

ÓLAFSSON, EGGERT (1726–68). Vice **lawman**, poet, and naturalist. Born to a prosperous farmer in Barðaströnd County in western Iceland, Ólafsson completed a university entry exam from **Skálholt** in 1746. He enrolled in the University of Copenhagen the same year and studied natural sciences for a few years. From 1752 to 1757, Ólafsson traveled with Bjarni Pálsson, the future surgeon general of Iceland, around the country, collecting information on its nature and society. This research led to the posthumous publication of a two-volume treatise on Iceland in 1772, which was later translated into a number of languages. Like other enlightened intellectuals of his time, Ólafsson attempted to dissipate what he saw as superstitious beliefs clouding people's understanding of Icelandic natural phenomena and hampering the **economic** development of the country. When he was appointed vice lawman in 1767, Ólafsson returned to Iceland from **Denmark** but drowned the following year at only 41 years old.

Although Ólafsson was a loyal subject of the Danish **king** and looked to him as the most likely source of economic and social progress in Iceland, he became an important inspiration for **nationalists** in the 19th century. It was primarily his fervent patriotism and emphasis on the preservation of the Icelandic **language** that earned him their respect. Ólafsson's ideas bridged the gap between the 18th-century **Enlightenment** and the romanticism of the following century. *See also FJÖLNIR*; HALLGRÍMSSON, JÓNAS (1807–45); SÆMUNDSSON, TÓMAS (1807–41).

OLD COVENANT. From 1262 to 1264, Icelanders accepted the **king** of **Norway** as their ruler, ending the **Commonwealth Period**. According to the official history of Iceland, this happened through a written treaty between the leading members of Icelandic society and the Norwegian king, which commonly is called the Gamli sáttmáli (Old Covenant). According to this treaty, Icelanders agreed to pay tribute to the king in return for protection and guarantee of a minimum amount of **trade** between the two countries.

Recently, historians have cast doubts on the authenticity of the Old Covenant, as it only exists in later copies, the earliest of which are from the 15th century. Some have argued that the existing treaty might be a forgery, "discovered" to bolster the Icelandic cause in the dealings of the Icelandic elite with the Norwegian king during the late medieval period. Fake or real, the Old Covenant was used very skillfully by **nationalist** leader **Jón Sigurðsson** (1811–79), who formulated the Icelandic demands for autonomy on its basis around the mid-19th century. According to his legal arguments, the covenant gave Icelanders collective rights in their relationship with **Denmark** because they had entered the Norwegian monarchy (through which they had come under Danish rule) through a contract but not conquest.

OLD NORSE. *See* LANGUAGE.

OLGEIRSSON, EINAR (1902–93). One of the most eloquent spokesmen of the **Communist Party of Iceland** (CPI) and the **Socialist Unity Party** (SUP) from the late 1920s until the early 1960s. He was born in **Akureyri** on 14 August 1902. After graduating from the secondary school in **Reykjavík** in 1921, Olgeirsson studied German and English at Friedrich-Wilhelm University in Berlin for three years. During his student years in Berlin, he became a committed Marxist, and upon returning to Iceland in 1924, he joined the left wing of the **Social Democratic Party**. From 1924 to 1928, he taught at the secondary school in Akureyri, but from 1928 to 1931, he served as director of the state-owned Icelandic Herring Exportation Company, working primarily on **trade** with the Soviet Union. From 1931 to 1935, he was the director of the Icelandic–Russian Trading Company.

With the foundation of the CPI in 1930, Olgeirsson became one of its most gifted agitators. He edited various communist and socialist newspapers from 1935 to 1946, and in 1937, he was **elected** to parliament as one of CPI's first three representatives. In 1939, shortly after the formation of the SUP, he became its chairman, a position he held until the party was formally dissolved in 1968. He sat in parliament for 30 years for the CPI and SUP and for the **People's Alliance** (PA) from its foundation in 1956. With the formal dissolution of the SUP and the change of the PA into a **political party** in 1968, Olgeirsson retired from political life. He left politics at the time when the Icelandic socialist movement began to distance itself from its Marxist legacy and severed its ties with the Soviet Union.

– P –

PÁLSSON, ÞORSTEINN (1947–). Minister of justice and **fisheries** and a former **prime minister**, born in Selfoss, a town in southern Iceland, on 29 October 1947. He was **educated** in **Reykjavík** and graduated with a law degree from the **University of Iceland** in 1974. From 1970 to 1975, he worked as a reporter for the largest daily in Iceland, *Morgunblaðið*, and from 1975 to 1979 as editor of the afternoon newspaper *Vísir*. In 1979, he was hired as the director of the Confederation of Icelandic Employers, a position he held until he was **elected** to parliament for the **Independence Party** (IP) in 1983.

Pálsson served his first ministerial post as minister of finance from 1985 to 1987 in a coalition government of the IP and the **Progressive Party**. He served as minister of **industries** (1987); prime minister (1987–88); and minister of justice, ecclesiastical affairs, and fisheries (1991–99). In 1999, Pálsson retired from politics and was appointed ambassador to **Great Britain** and in 2002 to **Denmark**. In 2006, he was appointed editor-in-chief of the newspaper *Fréttablaðið*.

Pálsson became involved in politics at a very young age. During his student days, he was the president of the conservative student union, and from 1975 to 1977, he sat on the steering committee of the youth organization of the IP. He was elected to the IP's central committee in 1981, and in 1983, he was elected chairman of the party. In 1991, **Davíð Oddsson** challenged and defeated him in an election for the chairmanship.

PAPAR. A name given to Irish hermits who allegedly strayed to Iceland in the seventh and eighth centuries. Irish monk and geographer Dicuil mentions in his geographical treatise *De mensura orbis terrae*, written in the early ninth century, that he had spoken with men who had visited the island of Thule around the year 795. Early Icelandic sources, such as the **Book of Settlement** and the **Book of Icelanders**, also mention the *papar*. According to these sources, the *papar* left Iceland at the beginning of the **Settlement Period** because they had no desire to live among pagans. The only traces of these first settlers of Iceland are to be found in place names, but no certain archaeological evidence of their existence has been discovered.

PARLIAMENT. *See* ALÞINGI.

PEOPLE'S ALLIANCE (PA). Alþýðubandalag, or the PA, was formed in 1956 as a political alliance of the **Socialist Unity Party** (SUP) and a group from the left wing of the **Social Democratic Party** under the leadership of **Hannibal Valdimarsson**. Originally, the PA was to be an electoral coalition only, but in 1968, it was transformed into a regular **political party**.

The basic tenets of the PA were socialism, mixed with a strong opposition to Iceland's participation in the **North Atlantic Treaty Organization** (NATO). In its last years, the socialism moderated considerably, and the party dropped all references to Marxism from its platforms. Opposition to NATO, the American base in **Keflavík**, foreign investments in Iceland, and membership in European organizations like the **European Free Trade Association** and the **European Union** (EU) made the PA one of the most **nationalistic** political parties in Iceland at the end of the 20th century.

The PA inherited most of the traditional supporters of the SUP, who came primarily from the working classes and the intelligentsia. From the late 1950s to the early 1980s, the party polled from 15 to 22 percent of the popular vote in parliamentary **elections**, putting it in third place in **Alþingi** throughout most of the period. Because of its strength in parliament, the party served in a number of coalition governments without causing any radical social change in Iceland. From the late 1980s until its dissolution in 1999, the PA suffered internal frictions, which caused a marked decline in its popular support—

down to 13 to 14 percent in the last three elections it participated in (1987, 1991, and 1995). This was, in part, the effect of a challenge from the **Women's Alliance**, but the decline was also caused by general changes in the political atmosphere in Iceland since the end of the **cold war**. In 1999, the party split, as some of its members—including its chairwoman, Margrét Frímannsdóttir—opted to join a new social democratic party, the **Social Democratic Alliance**, while another faction founded the **Left-Green Movement** (LGM). The LGM carries on many of the basic tenets of the PA, including the nationalist tendencies and the fierce opposition to Iceland's participation in international alliances such as NATO and the EU. *See also* NATIONAL PRESERVATION PARTY OF ICELAND (NPPI).

PÉTURSSON, HALLGRÍMUR (CIRCA 1614–74). Poet and clergyman Pétursson was born around 1614 at **Hólar** in Hjaltadalur, the old episcopal seat in northern Iceland, to the bellringer of the cathedral. He attended the Latin school at Hólar but did not complete his studies. After leaving school, he went abroad, most likely to Glückstadt in modern Germany and later to Copenhagen. According to legend, it was in Copenhagen that **Brynjólfur Sveinsson**, later bishop in **Skálholt**, found Pétursson working as a blacksmith in 1632. Sveinsson encouraged Pétursson to enroll in secondary school in Copenhagen, which he did, but he left without a final degree in 1637. The same year, he returned to Iceland, and in 1644, he was appointed pastor in a poor parish in southwest Iceland. Seven years later, he transferred to a more prosperous parish in western Iceland. In his last years, Pétursson suffered from leprosy, and he died in 1674.

Pétursson is commonly viewed as Iceland's greatest **religious** poet. To posterity, he is primarily known for his *Passíusálmar* (*Hymns of the Passion*), which is a set of 50 hymns describing the passion and death of Christ. *See also* LITERATURE.

PIETISM. A Lutheran **religious** movement that spread to Iceland from **Denmark** in the early 18th century. Pietism never became a popular movement in Iceland, but it had a strong influence among the clergy because of its emphasis on **education** and moral reform. From 1741 to 1745, Danish Lutheran minister Ludvig Harboe served as a special emissary from the Danish church authorities to Iceland, with the mission of examining the religious and moral state of the **population**. At his initiative, a number of reforms in the spirit of Pietism were instituted, affecting religious practices in Iceland, the administration of the church, public morality, and instruction of the young. These efforts were remarkably successful, probably because they fit the rising interest in education and social improvement that stemmed from the **Enlightenment**. Most important of these measures was, undoubtedly, the heavy emphasis on reading, as **literacy** rates in Iceland rose markedly during the latter half of the 18th century. *See also* EIRÍKSSON, JÓN (1728–87).

PÍNINGSDÓMUR. *See* LABOR BONDAGE.

PLAGUE. A serious epidemic struck Iceland in 1402–4. Although it is not entirely certain, this outbreak was most likely some form of the bubonic or pneumonic plagues that ravaged Europe during the late Middle Ages. According to existing sources, the disease spread to Iceland for the first time with a sailor who came from abroad in the fall of 1402, and by the following year, it had affected almost the whole country. No definite account of the number of deaths exists, but scholars estimate that between 30 and 60 percent of the Icelandic **population** fell victim to this epidemic. The high mortality had serious effects on the **economy**, causing a decline in property values and rising labor costs. It also affected the structure of landed wealth in Iceland, as property was concentrated in fewer hands than ever before. This particular epidemic has commonly been called the *svarti dauði* (Black Death), drawing its name from Latin (*mors nigra*).

A second plague epidemic spread to Iceland in 1494–95. Not much is known about the mortality in this attack, which has been called the Second Plague, but it seems to have been almost as severe as the Black Death of 1402–4—except in the Western Fjords, which were spared this time around. These two plague epidemics, with the **smallpox** outbreak of 1707–9, are the most severe known in Icelandic history.

POLITICAL PARTIES. The first political parties to be found in Iceland, the **Home Rule Party** and the old **Independence Party**, emerged around the turn of the 20th century, as the Icelandic democratic system was becoming fully developed. These parties were loose coalitions of parliamentary representatives rather than lasting institutions, as they had neither clear platforms nor fixed organization. In fact, both parties focused almost entirely on the relations with **Denmark**, while their members had no common agenda when it came to social or **economic** policies. During **World War I**, when the fault lines in Icelandic society were radically changing, the modern political system began to appear. The first stable party to be formed in Iceland—in 1916—was the Alþýðuflokkur [**Social Democratic Party (SDP)**], which served both as a federation of **trade unions** and a political party. Later the same year, a second party was founded, the Framsóknarflokkur [**Progressive Party (PP)**]. To begin with, this was a traditional coalition of parliamentary representatives, uniting a few farmers in **Alþingi**, but later, it practically became the political wing of the **cooperative movement**.

The formation of the SPD and the PP, both of which adhered to collectivist ideologies, forced politicians to the right of center to regroup. Their first party, established as an electoral coalition before the 1923 parliamentary **elections**, was called the Borgaraflokkur (**Citizens' Party**), but it was quickly replaced (in 1924) by the **Conservative Party (CP)**. The results of the 1923 elections, which were the first parliamentary elections where all three political movements took part, set the tone for what was to come. The Citizens' Party received over half of the votes cast, while the PP and SDP received 27 and 16 percent, respectively. In 1929, the CP merged with the small Frjálslyndi flokkurinn (**Liberal Party**), which was originally a splinter group from the Citizens' Party, to form the Sjálfstæðisflokkur [Independence Party (IP)]. The following year, the Kommúnistaflokkur Íslands [**Communist Party of Iceland (CPI)**] was founded, as the most radical wing of the SDP left their party for good. The CPI was a classic Bolshevist communist movement, which was absolutely loyal to the Soviet Union, as were most comparable parties in Europe.

Since then, the general contours of the party system in Iceland have not altered much, although parties have changed names, and new parties have come and gone. Thus, to the right, the IP has always been dominant, usually receiving between 35 and 40 percent of the votes cast. The IP's platform is a mixture of economic liberalism, promoting private initiative, and conservative **nationalism**—which now is characterized by strong opposition to membership in the **European Union**. The PP, which positioned itself at the center of the political spectrum, used to be the second largest party in Iceland, polling between 25 and 30 percent in most elections until the early 1970s. In recent years, the party's support has dwindled, in part because it has not been able establish itself fully in the urban area in the southwest. Therefore, it is now the smallest of the four traditional parties in Iceland, and it seems unlikely that it will ever be able to reclaim its former status as the main alternative to the IP. Unlike the other Nordic countries, the SDP did not manage to establish itself in Iceland as a dominating political force. The main reason for this was the fact that voters on the left have usually been split between two parties of more or less equal size, polling between 15 and 20 percent each, while those on the right were united in the IP. This points to one of the most striking anomalies of Icelandic politics, and that is the relative strength of the CPI and the parties derived from it. In 1938, the CPI, following the line from Moscow, merged with the left wing of the SDP to form the Sameiningarflokkur alþýðu—sósíalistaflokkurinn [**Socialist Unity Party** (SUP)]. The stated goal was to create a bulwark against fascism, but the SUP became, in reality, only a new incarnation of the CPI. The SUP attracted, however, much stronger electoral support than the CPI had been able to, in part because of its skillful use of nationalist rhetoric during the early phase of **World War II**.

In the period from the Second World War into the 1990s, the main changes of the party system in Iceland happened on its left fringe. One reason for this was growing disillusion with the Soviet Union, which opened opportunities for new alliances on the far left. Thus, in 1956, the SUP entered an electoral alliance with a splinter group from the SDP to form the Alþýðubandalagið [**People's Alliance** (PA)], and in 1968, this alliance was turned into an organized political party. This move was motivated by the desire to unify the left, but in the end, it changed nothing—the PA simply replaced the SUP, placing itself farthest to the left on the political spectrum.

At the end of the 1980s, it was clear that the "four party system" that had dominated Icelandic politics since the years between the two world wars was running its course. In 1983, the Kvennalistinn [**Women's Alliance** (WA)] offered candidates in parliamentary elections for the first time, expressing deep discontent with the limited opportunities the traditional parties offered to **women**. The WA had strong appeal, especially among women voters, running successfully in four parliamentary elections between 1983 and 1995. With the waning of the **cold war**, another divisive issue slowly disappeared from the political arena. One of the main reasons for the success of the SUP and later the PA had always been the staunch opposition of these parties to the American military base in **Keflavík**, which had strong resonance among the nationalistic intelligentsia. The SDP, conversely, was resolutely behind the alliance with the **United States** because it saw the Soviet Union as the main threat to western democracies. This was used skillfully by the opponents on the left to paint the SDP as unpatriotic and subservient to the "international bourgeoisie." When the hostilities between the United States and the Soviet Union ended, removing the divisions based on the cold war issues, leaders of the SDP, the PA, and the WA began to discuss forming an alliance on the left. The aim was to form a party that could challenge the hegemonic position of the IP in the Icelandic political arena. These attempts were partially successful, as people from these three parties came together in the Samfylkingin [**Social Democratic Alliance (SDA)**] in 1999. As it turned out, though, many supporters of the PA refused to join the SDA, rallying together with "independent leftists" and **environmentalists** to form a new red–green party called the Vinstrihreyfingin grænt framboð [**Left-Green Movement (LGM)**].

Since the 1930s, the Icelandic party system has been fairly constant, as it has been organized in four main parties: one large and relatively stable party on the right (the IP); one fairly large but declining party at the center, seeking most of its support in the rural areas (the PP); one social democratic party (first the SDP and later the SDA); and finally one party on the far left (the CPI, the SUP, the PA, and the LGM). Smaller parties have appeared through the years, often as splinter groups from one of the four main parties, but none of them have managed to survive for long. The most significant change in the system seems to be that the PP has lost its status to the SDA as the main opposition to the IP, as the SDA received almost 30 percent of the votes cast in the last elections, while the support of the PP fell to its all-time low of 11 percent. So far, this has not transformed Icelandic politics, and the "four party system" appears to be just as firmly entrenched now as it was through much of the 20th century. *See also* FOREIGN POLICY; NATIONAL PRESERVATION PARTY OF ICELAND (NPPI); PRIME MINISTER; SOCIAL DEMOCRATIC UNION (SDU); UNION OF LIBERALS AND LEFTISTS (ULL); ÞJÓÐVAKI.

POPULATION. Due to its natural conditions, Iceland has always been a sparsely populated country. When the first complete **census** was taken in 1703, the inhabitants tallied just over 50,000. Only scant knowledge exists of the demographic history of Iceland prior to that date, but in all likelihood, its population fluctuated somewhere between 30,000 and 70,000 from the time the country was fully settled in the 10th or 11th centuries. The 18th century was a difficult period in Iceland, when three major crises had serious effects on the demographic development of the country. As a result, the population of Iceland was at a lower level at the beginning of the 19th century than it had been a century before, just above the 47,000 mark. But since the conclusion of a famine from 1783 to 1785 caused by the **Laki eruption**, the population of Iceland has grown almost incessantly. This has happened because mortality crises, which struck the country at regular intervals in the past, have totally disappeared from the Icelandic demographic history, **infant mortality** has fallen to one of the lowest levels in the world, and improvements in public **health** care have raised the life expectancy from about 38 years for **women** and 32 for men in 1850–60 to the present levels of 83.3 and 80.2 years, respectively. This is clearly reflected in demographic development: according to the census of 1901, Iceland had 78,000 inhabitants, and in 2007, this number had grown to almost 313,000. Although population growth has abated somewhat in the last decades due to declining fertility rates, it is still one of the highest in Europe (1.4 percent per year on average in the decade from 1998 to 2007). *See also* PLAGUE; SMALLPOX; Appendix B.

PRESIDENT. The highest office of the Icelandic state, founded in 1944 with the Constitution of the **Republic of Iceland**. The principal prerogative of the president is to ratify laws passed in **Alþingi**, but according to the constitution, the legislative power is vested jointly in parliament and the president. The president does not have an absolute veto right, however, because an act he refuses to sign takes effect but is then subject to a popular referendum. So far, the president has only used this prerogative once, when **Ólafur Ragnar Grímsson** refused to sign controversial legislation on the ownership of media companies in 2004. Other constitutional duties of the president are to convene and dissolve parliament, give prospective **prime ministers** the mandate to form governments, appoint many of the highest public officials in Iceland, and give pardons to convicted felons.

The formal power of the president is extensive, but in practice, he acts almost exclusively upon the decisions of the government and Alþingi. Thus, the Icelandic president has been perceived as more of a symbolic figurehead than an independent political actor. His role is to represent the country on foreign soil and to stand above the bickering of domestic politics, although individual presidents can certainly pressure politicians through informal channels. In essence, the primary function of the office is to guarantee the democratic process in Iceland during times of crises; at the same time, the president is to serve as a unifying symbol for the nation.

The president is chosen in direct **elections** to one four-year term at a time. Any Icelandic citizen, 35 or older, who meets all the general qualifications for voting in parliamentary elections can stand as a candidate. The constitution sets no limits on how many terms each president can serve, and in cases where a sitting president runs unchallenged, no election is held. There is no vice president chosen to replace the sitting president, but in cases where the president is incapable to serve his duties (for example when he is abroad) or in case of a death in office, the president of the **supreme court**, the prime minister, and the president of Alþingi take over his duties until he returns to office or a new person is elected. It is uncommon for **political parties** to play an active role in presidential elections because there is a strong sentiment among the electorate that presidents should stand above party politics. Thus, presidential elections tend to center on personalities rather than issues, often making them fierce and emotionally charged.

So far, Iceland has had five presidents. Alþingi elected **Sveinn Björnsson** as the first president in 1944. His successor was **Ásgeir Ásgeirsson**, a successful and popular politician who defeated a candidate supported by two of the largest political parties. Ásgeirsson was first elected in 1952 and sat unchallenged for four terms. In 1968, the director of the Icelandic National Museum, **Kristján Eldjárn**, was elected president, and he was reelected without opposition in 1972 and 1976. **Vigdís Finnbogadóttir** was elected the fourth president in 1980; she was the first and only **woman** to serve this function in Iceland. In 1988, Finnbogadóttir was the first sitting president to face an opposition candidate, but she defeated her opponent handily by gaining almost 95 percent of the votes cast. Finnbogadóttir ran unopposed for her fourth term in 1992, resigning at the end of that term. Grímsson was elected the fifth president of the Republic of Iceland in June 1996. His election was a certain reversal of earlier trends, as he entered the presidential race straight from the political arena. This has, at times, caused tension between him and the government, as Grímsson has interfered more actively in politics than any of his predecessors and came to the office as a politician. *See also* CONSTITUTION OF 1944; Appendix A.

PRESS. The Icelandic press traces its history to the late 18th century when a monthly newsmagazine, *Islandske Maanedstidende (Icelandic Monthly News)*, started publication. The magazine, which was written in **Danish**, came out from 1773 to 1776 and had only limited circulation. The first newsmagazine in Icelandic was *Minnisverð tíðindi (Memorable News)*, which came out irregularly between 1796 and 1808 and was edited by the energetic publisher and **high court** judge, **Magnús Stephensen** (1762–1833). Stephensen initiated other similar ventures in the following decades, the most important of which was the monthly newsmagazine *Klausturpósturinn (The Cloister Post)* from 1818 to 1827. The first real newspaper in Iceland was *Þjóðólfur*, which came out more or less regularly twice to four times a month from 1848 to 1911. *Þjóðólfur* heralded a new era in Iceland, as increased freedom of speech and a growing interest in politics opened the road for public debates. The paper was completely independent from the Danish government and was, indeed, often very critical of Danish rule in Iceland.

For the remainder of the 19th century, a number of similar newspapers were established in Iceland, some national and others provincial. All of them were similar in form and nature, as they were issued weekly at best, and none of them could afford to employ journalists to work with the editors. The first newspaper to break this pattern was *Vísir* (*The Beginning*), which was founded in 1910 and is still published under the name of *DV*. *Vísir* was the first daily newspaper in Iceland to survive over an extended period of time, and it was also the first paper to hire a journalist to write regularly in the paper. In 1913, the second daily began its publication in **Reykjavík**, *Morgunblaðið* (*The Morning Paper*), which is still Iceland's leading newspaper.

In the aftermath of **World War I** as the modern **political parties** emerged, the whole Icelandic press was reorganized along party lines. *Vísir* and *Morgunblaðið* positioned themselves to the right of center, vigorously opposing the **Social Democratic Party** (SDP) and the centrist **Progressive Party** (PP). These parties felt the need to establish their own party organs; for the PP, it was *Tíminn* (*The Times*, founded in 1917), and for the SDP, it was *Alþýðublaðið* (*The People's Paper*, 1919). With the foundation of the **Communist Party of Iceland** in 1930, the party also established its own newspaper, *Verkalýðsblaðið* (*The Workers' Paper*); in 1936, it took the name of *Þjóðviljinn* (*The National Will*).

It was only in the 1970s that party control over the press began to break down. The first sign of this was the foundation in 1975 of a new afternoon daily, *Dagblaðið* (*The Daily*), which prided itself as being "free and independent." The new paper brought a new aggressive style into Icelandic journalism because it had no need to follow a narrow party line. Increasing financial difficulties caused by the hyperinflation (*see* INFLATION) of the 1980s in combination with decreasing party loyalties among the voters brought the papers, one after another, to their knees. First, *Dagblaðið* and *Vísir* merged in 1981, forming a new afternoon daily called *DV*. During the 1990s, *Alþýðublaðið*, *Tíminn*, and *Þjóðviljinn* all ceased publication, as they became financially insolvent.

By the turn of the 21st century, relations between the press and political parties had changed completely, as all party organs had disappeared. Moreover, *Morgunblaðið*, which had always been tightly related to the **Independence Party** even though it was not in direct ownership of the party, had become much more independent than it had been during the **cold war**. The introduction of a new genre of newspapers, which were distributed free of charge to all homes in

Reykjavík and other of the large towns in Iceland, has also revolutionized the Icelandic press. The largest newspaper in Iceland at present and a pioneer among these free newspapers, *Fréttablaðið* (*The Newspaper*), was established in 2001 by a group of Icelandic entrepreneurs. It was bought in 2003 by the largest retailer chain in Iceland, the **Baugur Group**, causing some concerns about the excessive influence of the commercial magnates in Icelandic public life. The strong financial backing of its owners has, however, allowed *Fréttablaðið* to expand, even exporting its model to Denmark. *See also ÁRMANN Á ALÞINGI; FJÖLNIR; NÝ FÉLAGSRIT.*

PRIME MINISTER. In 1917, with the enlargement of the Icelandic government from one to three ministers, the office of prime minister was established. The prime minister forms governments, usually through negotiations between the various **political parties**, and serves as their head. He receives his mandate from the **president** of the republic. Although the president is offically the head of state in Iceland, the prime minister is de facto the most influential political person in the country. Since its establishment in 1917 until—and including—the formation of **Geir H. Haarde's cabinet** on 25 May 2007, 22 persons have held the office of prime minister, presiding over 34 different cabinets. *See also* ÁSGEIRSSON, ÁSGEIR (1894–1972); ÁSGRÍMSSON, HALLDÓR (1947–); BENEDIKTSSON, BJARNI (1908–70); GRÖNDAL, BENEDIKT (1924–); HAFSTEIN, HANNES (1861–1912); HAFSTEIN, JÓHANN (1915–80); HALLGRÍMSSON, GEIR (1925–90); HERMANNSSON, STEINGRÍUR (1928–); JÓHANNESSON, ÓLAFUR (1913–84); JÓNASSON, HERMANN (1896–1976); MINISTRIES; ODDSSON, DAVÍÐ (1948–); PÁLSSON, ÞORSTEINN (1947–); THORODDSEN, GUNNAR (1910–1983); THORS, ÓLAFUR (1892–1964); ÞORLÁKSSON, JÓN (1877–1935); Appendix A.

PRIVATIZATION. Until the beginning of the 1990s, the state was an important player in the Icelandic business arena. At that time, the state owned two of the three largest commercial banks in the country, the only telephone company, a shipping company, fishmeal factories, a printing press, a fertilizer factory, and a cement factory, among other businesses. This was a legacy from the time of the

Great Depression, when the free-market policies that had guided the Icelandic government until **World War I** were abandoned and the state assumed the responsibility of providing **employment** where it was needed. The government of **Davíð Oddsson**, which came to power in 1991, decided to return to the free-market policies of the past and to privatize as many of the state companies as it could. This had been the official policy of the **Independence Party** for years, but until then, the party had not put privatization high on its agenda when it was in power.

Oddsson's government started immediately on its privatization program, selling off some of its smaller assets from 1992 to 1995. The privatization of the large and most important companies started, however, only around the turn of the 21st century, when the state sold its banks and Iceland Telecom to private investors. Most of the revenues from these sales were used to reduce public debt, bringing it down to one of the lowest rates in Europe (23.5 percent of the gross domestic product in 2006).

The privatization of recent years has not caused much controversy because most people now agree that the state should not be involved in the competitive market. The general experience from privatization has also been positive, as many of the companies—banks in particular—have expanded enormously since they came into private ownership. When it comes to basic services, however, including **health** care and **education**, where state or local authorities have traditionally been dominant, and public utilities, where competition is almost impossible, privatization and the introduction of market principles meets stiffer opposition. The same can be said of the Icelandic National **Broadcasting** Service, which is still owned by the state, although it competes with the private media on the advertisement market. *See also* BANKING; WELFARE STATE.

PROGRESSIVE PARTY (PP). Eight representatives in **Alþingi** formed the Framsóknarflokkur (PP) on 16 December 1916. In the beginning, the PP was primarily a coalition of parliamentarians, but in 1930, it was formalized as a popular movement with a fixed party structure. The PP was from the start a farmers' party, rooted in the **cooperative movement**, the **Farmers' Associations**, and the **nationalistic Youth Associations**. Moreover, the party platform has always had a populist orientation, and the PP places itself at the center of the Icelandic political spectrum.

As the Icelandic party system emerged during the 1920s, the PP established itself as the second largest party in Iceland after the **Conservative Party** and later the **Independence Party** (IP). For this reason, it formed a natural counterbalance to the IP, and through much of the 20th century, **prime ministers** came, almost exclusively, from either of these two parties. Leaders of the PP headed governments more or less continuously, from 1927 to 1942, 1950 to 1953, 1956 to 1959, 1971 to 1974, and with one short break from 1983 to 1991. The party also participated in all governments between 1971 and 2007, except for the coalition government of the IP and the **Social Democratic Party** of 1991–95.

In spite of its illustrious past, the future of the PP seems uncertain. For much of the period from the 1920s to the turn of the 21st century, the party normally polled between 17 and 25 percent of the votes cast, but in the last two **elections** (2003 and 2007), these numbers have declined to below 12 percent. The reason for this deterioration in support for the party is the fact that its traditional base is disappearing, as the majority of Icelanders have moved toward the capital area in the southwestern part of the country and the cooperative movement has collapsed. To counteract this development, the party attempted to broaden its appeal, and for decades, this policy seemed to be successful. Thus, under the leadership of **Ólafur Jóhannesson** and **Steingrímur Hermannsson**, the PP maintained its strong electoral returns, using its central position to secure its place as an unavoidable partner in almost all coalition governments. Recently, the **Social Democratic Alliance**, which was founded in 1999, has taken over the second place in the party system, and it seems unlikely that the PP will ever regain its former strength. *See also* ÁGÚSTSSON, GUÐNI (1949–); ÁSGRÍMSSON, HALLDÓR (1947–); JÓNSSON, JÓNAS (1885–1968); SIGURÐSSON, JÓN (1946–).

– R –

RAID OF THE "TURKS." In the summer of 1627, four pirate ships from the Barbary Coast in North Africa (the coast of present-day

Algeria and Morocco) arrived in Iceland, raiding villages and farms on the eastern and southern coasts. The pirates took around 400 Icelanders and Danes into captivity, selling them into slavery in North Africa. The most famous incident of the raid happened in the **Vestmanna Islands** just off the southern coast of Iceland. On these small islands, over 240 people were captured and 30 to 40 killed. Some of the captives were released a few years later after a ransom was paid, but the great majority of them never returned to Iceland. The raid struck great fear into the hearts of Icelanders, who had not experienced violent aggression of this sort before. Although the Barbary corsairs never returned, the memory of the "Turks," as the pirates were incorrectly called in Iceland, lived on for centuries.

RASK, RASMUS CHRISTIAN (1787–1832). This **Danish** linguist was born on 22 November 1787 close to the town of Odense in Denmark. As a young man, Rask learned the Icelandic **language** on his own, using published editions of **Snorri Sturluson's** *Heimskringla* as a guide. After graduating from secondary school in 1807, Rask moved to Copenhagen, where he studied linguistics at the University of Copenhagen without completing any final degree. He published his first scholarly work on the Old Icelandic language in 1811, and two years later, he had the opportunity to visit Iceland for the first and last time. Rask stayed for two years in the country, traveling extensively, both to visit historical places and to practice his linguistic skills. In fact, he mastered the Icelandic language perfectly in these years. During this long sojourn, he became convinced that the Icelandic language was rapidly disappearing, maintaining that it would almost certainly become extinct in the following century if nothing was done for its protection. Thus, in 1815–16, he founded the **Icelandic Literary Society** (ILS), which had the main purpose of preserving the Icelandic language. In 1816, after returning to Copenhagen, Rask went on a long journey that took him through Russia to India. This prevented him from working on Icelandic matters for over six years, and he was never to regain his former prestige among Icelanders—a fact that was demonstrated in 1831, the year before he died, when Icelandic students in Copenhagen ousted him from the leadership of the Copenhagen section of the ILS.

RECONSTRUCTION GOVERNMENT. One of the most stable coalition governments in Icelandic history, lasting (with a few changes of ministers) for three full terms between 1959 and 1971. The **cabinet** consisted of four ministers from the **Independence Party** (IP) and three from the **Social Democratic Party** (SDP). Ólafur Thors, chairman of the IP, formed the government after **elections** in the fall of 1959. In its platform, the new government vowed to strengthen and restructure the **economic** base of the country. In the early spring of 1960, it commenced its plan of "reconstruction" (*viðreisn*, hence the name Viðreisnarstjórn, or Reconstruction Government), proposing some radical changes in public economic policy. The **currency** was devalued by 30 percent, and multiple exchange rates were abolished. At the same time, the government liberalized foreign **trade**, introduced a 3 percent general sales tax, and made some major changes in the **welfare** system.

The first years of the Reconstruction Government were a period of economic growth due in part to favorable conditions. The dramatic increase in the herring catches during the late 1950s and early 1960s (from 50,000 tons in 1955 to 770,000 tons in 1966) was a major boost to Iceland's export revenues. This period of prosperity came to an abrupt end in 1967–68, when the **Norwegian**–Icelandic herring stock more or less disappeared from Icelandic fishing banks, leading to massive unemployment (*see* EMPLOYMENT) and a drastic fall in the value of exports. The economy recovered fairly quickly, though, as increased catches of other species and rising prices on the export markets made up for the loss. But the government did not reap the benefits of this recovery, losing its majority in the parliamentary elections of 1971 to the **political parties** at the center and to the left of the political spectrum.

The Reconstruction Government never had the support of a large majority of representatives in parliament, but it had a great impact on social life in Iceland all the same. Under its leadership, the country opened to foreign investments, with the hydroelectric power station at Búrfell and the aluminum factory in Straumsvík as the most notable cases. Finally, Iceland joined the **European Free Trade Association** in 1970 during the last term of the Reconstruction Government, linking the country more closely with the emerging European economic system. *See also* BENEDIKTSSON, BJARNI (1908–70); ENERGY-INTENSIVE INDUSTRIES.

THE REFORMATION. Until the **religious** schism between **Catholics** and **Lutherans** began in **Denmark** in the early 16th century, the Catholic faith confronted no serious religious opposition in Iceland. However, the victory of the Lutheran **king** Christian III in a competition for the Danish crown during the late 1530s forced the Icelandic church to reconsider its position. In 1539, the first Lutheran bishop, Gissur Einarsson, took over the **Skálholt** diocese, while the Catholic bishop, **Jón Arason**, held onto his office at **Hólar** in the north. During the next decade, representatives of the Danish king suppressed the Catholic faction in Iceland, overcoming staunch opposition from Arason and his supporters. On 7 November 1550, the king's representatives executed Arason at Skálholt, and since then, Lutheranism has been the dominant religious creed in Iceland.

The Reformation was a time of intense religious activity in Iceland. An Icelandic translation of the New Testament was issued in Denmark in 1540, and a translation of the Bible in its entirety was published by **Guðbrandur Þorláksson**, bishop of Hólar, in 1594. The emphasis on the use of the vernacular in the Lutheran Church and the fact that Danish did not become the **language** of the church and religious life in Iceland were certainly instrumental in preserving and developing the Icelandic language in the ensuing centuries. *See also* CONVERSION TO CHRISTIANITY.

REGIONAL POLICY. Generally, this term (*byggðastefna*) refers to policies aimed at alleviating regional inequalities and preserving habitation in rural areas and, recently, in small and remote fishing villages. In practice, this has meant adopting various regional support and development programs in order to strengthen the predominant **economic** activities outside the capital area. A coherent and well-defined long-term policy is, however, hard to discern in these programs.

Deliberate attempts to strengthen the rural economy vis-à-vis the urban economy have a long history in Iceland. During the 20th century, regional policy emerged as a response to **urbanization**, which was caused by a growing **migration** of people from the countryside to the emerging towns around the coast. Perceived as a grave and a growing social problem, the depopulation of the countryside was countered with public financial support beginning in the interwar period. Financial aid for **agriculture** was increased and farmers' access to credit facilitated in order to modernize farming, expand cultivation, and aid new settlements. Rural housing was subsidized, and schools and social services improved. The regulation of milk and meat production in the mid-1930s, which included price fixing and abolition of competition both between individual domestic producers and with foreign imports, benefitted the small farmers and sheltered the more remote rural areas against districts that were closer to the main markets.

The acceleration of migration from the rural areas to the towns during and after **World War II** and more pronounced regional imbalances in economic development have prompted various governments to make regional policy a high priority in public spending. In order to give a more effective counterweight to the urban area around **Reykjavík**, towns outside the southwest corner of Iceland were included in the regional programs. From 1944 to 1947, the big investment programs of the **Modernization Government** clearly reflected these considerations, especially regarding the renewal of the fishing fleet. In the early 1950s, regional planning started in conjunction with the Framkvæmdabanki Íslands (Development Bank of Iceland), which was established in 1953. Regional support continued in the 1960s through the annual government budget and funds designed for the purpose of correcting regional imbalances. In spite of these efforts, the primary economic sectors, agriculture and the **fisheries**, have been unable to increase their **employment** requirements significantly, and the regional policy has been largely unsuccessful. The **Left-Wing Government** of 1971–74 increased regional assistance greatly through the founding of a Framkvæmdastofnun ríkisins (State Development Institute), designing and implementing regional plans, and creating the Byggðasjóður (Regional Fund) to finance them. The authorities did not carry out the various regional plans in any consistent manner, however, and they were only loosely integrated into the general public economic policy. Regional assistance was scaled down considerably during the 1980s, partly by the replacement in 1985 of the State Development Institute and the Regional Fund with the Byggðastofnun (Institute of Regional Development), which has maintained a much lower profile than its predecessors.

It is difficult to measure the real impact of the regional policy in Iceland because in spite of concerted efforts to stem the tide, the migration to the capital area has been relentless in recent years. In 2007, around two thirds of Icelanders lived in Reykjavík and its suburbs, and large parts of the country are struggling against total desertion. One reason for this development is the fact that many of the services demanded in modern society are only offered in the only urban region of the country, and it is difficult for small communities to provide people with schools and leisure activities that are deemed necessary today. The most effective part of the regional policy seems to have been to establish **educational** institutions outside of Reykjavík, as has been seen by the example of the university in **Akureyri**. The system of **fisheries management** has also contributed to this development because many of the smaller communities have lost their quota share in recent years, leading to a lack of work in many of the traditional fishing towns around the country. Many have seen the construction of **energy-intensive** factories as the only solution to this problem because they provide considerable employment to economically depressed areas around the coast. *See also* POPULATION.

RELIGION. The Icelandic settlers who began to move to the country during the late ninth century were pagans, believing in Germanic gods like Odin and Thor. There were also some Christians among the original settlers, as they had been **converted to Christianity** in the British Isles. Not much is known about the religious practices in Iceland during the pre-Christian era, but it is clear that the chieftains, called *goði*, served some religious functions.

During the late 10th century, European church leaders began a concerted effort to convert the Scandinavians to the "true" faith. A few missionaries were sent to Iceland, who had been baptized in Germany, but it was only after **King** Ólaf Tryggvason had forced the conversion through in **Norway** that these efforts were successful. At **Alþingi**, either in 999 or 1000, the Icelandic chieftains decided to take up the new religion, claiming that it was better to preserve the peace than to hold onto their old faith. From that time, Iceland converted gradually and peacefully to Christianity. After that, the **Catholic** Church became one of the most powerful institutions in Iceland and certainly the richest. Both the church itself and the numerous convents and monasteries operated in Iceland collected immense land holdings, mostly through donations from pious Icelanders. From what is known, the church was universally accepted, and there was no known medieval heretical tradition in Iceland.

In 1550, Iceland converted to **Lutheranism**, as the last Catholic bishop of that era, **Jón Arason**, was executed. The **Reformation** came mostly from above under strong pressure from the Lutheran king in **Denmark**, although the first Lutheran influences had spread to Iceland from Germany as early as the beginning of the 1530s. From the time of the Reformation to the late 19th century, the Lutheran state church was the only allowed religious sect in Iceland, totally monopolizing Icelandic religious life.

The Lutheran Church played a very significant cultural role in Iceland, as the parish pastors had the responsibility of **educating** the young and inculcating the moral tenets of the church into their parishioners. In a sparsely populated and fairly peripheral country, the pastor was usually the only educated person in the community, and the church provided the best opportunity for people to congregate. Moreover, many of the most important stages in people's lives had to be sanctioned by the church — baptism, confirmation, marriage, and burial — granting the institution tremendous ritual power.

The religious history of Iceland from the end of the Middle Ages to the end of the 19th century — and to a certain extent to the present day — is characterized by the status of the Lutheran Church as a state institution and its monopoly on religious life in the country. This enhanced its power, as everyone was required to participate in its practices and to follow its preaching, but at the same time, it reduced the church's independence vis-à-vis the state. Nominally, the church had a very strong position through its monopoly, but it lacked the religious fire of some of the dissenting sects that never were able to take root in Iceland in the same manner as they did in the neighboring countries.

The position of religion in Iceland's contemporary life is marked very strongly by this tradition of monopoly and submission to the state. Since the Icelandic **constitution of 1874**, Icelanders have enjoyed full religious liberty, but the overwhelming majority of the **population** continues to be registered as members of the Lutheran state church. Most Icelandic children are still baptized by Lutheran pastors, and the great majority is also confirmed. But at the same time, church attendance is very low in Iceland, and religion plays no role in politics. Moral issues, like gay rights and abortion, play no significant role in the Icelandic political arena—the clear majority of the population and the politicians are in favor of granting gays full rights to marry, and while there are restrictions on abortion, in practice they are open to **women** and free of charge.

In 2007, just over 80 percent of Icelanders were registered members of the state church, while around 5 percent belonged to independent Lutheran congregations. The Roman Catholic Church was the largest non-Lutheran religious group in Iceland, with just over 2 percent of the population. *See also* PIETISM.

REPUBLIC OF ICELAND. The Republic of Iceland was founded at **Þingvellir** on 17 June 1944 with the adoption of a new **constitution**. This meant that all formal ties with the **Danish king** were severed after almost six centuries of alliance with the Danish monarchy. This event was a logical conclusion of the long struggle for independence that began with growing **nationalist** sentiments during the first half of the 19th century, and it was made possible by the rapid **economic** modernization in Iceland in the early 20th century.

The foundation of the republic was based on the **Act of Union** of 1918, which gave both partners of the union—the Danish and Icelandic parliaments—the right to demand a renegotiation of the act at the end of 1940. If they could not come to terms in a period of three years, either party had the right to revoke the act. Because of **World War II**, it proved impossible to follow this negotiation process to the letter, but **Alþingi** decided to repeal the act unilaterally anyway. A motion to abrogate the Act of Union was unanimously approved in parliament in February 1944, and a constitution for the Republic of Iceland was accepted in March of the same year. The issue was put to a referendum in May 1944, as the Act of Union required, and over 98 percent of the people who had the right to vote cast their ballot, out of which 97 percent supported the actions of Alþingi.

The method of revoking the Act of Union caused considerable bitterness in Denmark because many Danes felt that the Icelandic parliament should have waited until the end of the war rather than leaving the union during the German occupation of Denmark. Many

Icelandic intellectuals were of the same opinion, advocating restraint in the matter, but the final outcome would certainly have been the same. *See also* BJÖRNSSON, SVEINN (1881–1952); PRESIDENT; *RÍKISSTJÓRI.*

REYKJAVÍK. The capital of Iceland, located on Iceland's southwest coast. According to the *Book of Settlements*, **Ingólfur Arnarson**, who is claimed to have been Iceland's first settler, made Reykjavík his home in the late ninth century. For several centuries, Reykjavík was only a large farm surrounded with small cottages on plots parceled out from the original farmstead. From the 13th or 14th centuries, Reykjavík was the seat of a small parish church, and people living in the area supported themselves with a mixture of fishing in small open boats and **animal husbandry.** It was only in the late 18th century that a small village formed in Reykjavík after the **Danish king** assisted in the founding of small textile workshops (the **Innréttingar** project) in the emerging village and gave it special status as a chartered market town in 1786.

At the beginning of the 19th century, Reykjavík had only 300 inhabitants, but in the next few decades, the Danish government turned this small fishing village into the center of its administration in Iceland. The 19th century was also a period of **economic** growth in Reykjavík, especially in commerce and fishing. In this period, it became the first real town in the country, serving as a nucleus for an expanding government bureaucracy and emerging capitalist economy.

Reykjavík's development in the 20th century clearly reflects the economic, social, and political revolution that has transformed the country in the last hundred years. Like other modern European societies, Iceland has developed an extensive system of private and public services, including schools, financial institutions, communication networks, and hospitals. Reykjavík serves as the hub of most of this activity, and it is also an important fishing and **industrial** town. Consequently, the **population** of the capital has grown remarkably in this century, from 7,000 inhabitants in 1901 to almost 118,000 in 2007. Moreover, the second and third largest towns in Iceland, Kópavogur and Hafnarfjörður, are suburbs of Reykjavík; today around 200,000 people, 65 percent of the Icelandic population, live in the capital and the nearby towns. *See also* MAGNÚSSON, SKÚLI (1711–94); URBANIZATION.

REYKJAVÍK DISTRICT HEATING (RDH). The Hitaveita Reykjavíkur (RDH) was the pioneering power company in **Reykjavík**, providing people in the whole Reykjavík area with geothermal water to heat their houses. Planning for the heating utility started in 1926, and the first drilling for hot water took place two years later. In the early 1930s, the first houses received geothermal water from the company, and it gradually increased its operation. By 1961, the RDH served about half of Reykjavík's residents, but since 1972, it has reached more or less the whole **population** of the capital.

In 1999, RDH merged with other public utilities in Reykjavík, forming the Reykjavík Power Authority (RPA), which is owned by the town (Orkuveita Reykjavíkur). The RPA supplies most of the larger Reykjavík area with hot water, in addition to electricity and cold water. Recently, it has expanded its operations, acquiring many of the smaller public utilities in Iceland's southern and western parts. Using its size and experience, the company can offer both inexpensive **energy** and reliable service to its customers.

The RDH proved that geothermal water is an inexpensive and clean source of energy, and its example has been copied all over the country. Now, between 80 and 90 percent of Icelandic houses are heated in this way, and half of the Icelandic energy use is from geothermal power. This has had a considerable effect on the importation of fossil fuels to Iceland and reduced the emission of greenhouse gases in the country. In recent years, the company has expanded its operations into new areas, both in Iceland and abroad. Thus, the RPA is currently in the process of constructing a large-scale geothermal power plant in the vicinity of Reykjavík, which is estimated to produce 300 MW of electricity and 400 MW of thermal energy when it is completed (2009). Moreover, the RPA founded the Reykjavík Energy Invest (REI) in 2007, in order to facilitate its investment ventures abroad, using its experience in Iceland to build geothermal systems, primarily in Asia. The same year, REI planned to merge with a similar investment and development fund, Geysir Green Energy, owned by the bank Glitnir and other private investors to form the largest investment and development company in the world in the geothermal sector. This caused a great political upheaval because some objected to the participation of a public utility company in risky investments abroad, and the merger was put on hold.

REYKJAVÍK POWER AUTHORITY (RPA). *See* REYKJAVÍK DISTRICT HEATING (RDH).

REYKJAVÍK SUMMIT. A meeting held between Ronald Reagan, president of the **United States**, and Mikhail Gorbachev, leader of the Soviet Union, on 11–12 October 1986. The Soviet premier suggested Iceland as the meeting place because of its geographical location in the mid-Atlantic, right between the European continent and North America. The main item on the agenda was to discuss a ban on ballistic missiles, which Reagan had proposed earlier the same year, but it turned into a general summit on the relations between the two superpowers. As it turned out, the summit ended in a total deadlock because both leaders wanted to discuss issues other than ballistic missiles; Reagan brought up human rights in the Soviet Union and the Soviet invasion of Afghanistan, while Gorbachev insisted on linking the elimination of the Intermediate Range Nuclear Forces (INF) with the Strategic Defense Initiative of the United States. In spite of this failure, experts agree now that the **Reykjavík** Summit was crucial in preparing for the INF treaty signed between the two superpowers in Washington the following year, and thus it was an important step toward ending the **cold war**.

RÍKISSTJÓRI. When Germany occupied **Denmark** in 1940, most communications between Copenhagen and **Reykjavík** were suspended, and relations between the two capitals became more or less impossible. This created a constitutional dilemma in Iceland because the Danish **king** was also the king of Iceland. For the first year, **Alþingi** handed over the royal power to the Icelandic government, but in May 1941, it passed an act creating the office of *ríkisstjóri*, or governor of Iceland, to substitute for the king during the war. On 17 June 1941, **Sveinn Björnsson** was elected the first, and only, person to hold this office. Exactly three years later, Alþingi selected him as the first **president** of the new **Republic of Iceland**. *See also* WORLD WAR II.

ROYAL COMMISSIONS OF 1770 AND 1785. During the late 18th century, there was growing concern, both in Iceland and **Denmark**, about the **economic** well-being of Icelanders. This period was the apogee of enlightened **absolutism** in the Danish state, which developed various state-induced reforms in Danish agriculture. In the same spirit, during the 1770s and 1780s, Iceland experienced the first organized attempts to formulate a coherent state policy for the improvement of the country's economy. These efforts began with the formation of a Royal Commission in 1770, consisting of two royal officials and one merchant. The committee traveled around the country in the summer of 1770, collecting information on the economy and social practices, on the basis of which it produced detailed proposals on Icelandic economic affairs. During the next years, this led to the publication of various royal edicts, all of which had the intention of stimulating the faltering economy.

Most of these efforts came to naught, however. This was, in part, because of the great distress in the following decade caused by the **Laki eruption** in 1783–84 but also because these paternalistic measures proved to be difficult to implement. Therefore, the royal administration formed a new commission in 1785 to deal with the economic crisis in Iceland. This commission, which consisted of royal officials and directors of the royal trading company, suggested that the **monopoly trade** would be abolished, coming partly in effect with a royal act in 1787. Although the second royal commission did not directly propose any radical changes in the administration of Iceland, increased centralization of Icelandic ecclesiastical and juridical affairs around the turn of the 19th century can be traced to its deliberations.

The two royal commissions had few great or lasting effects on the development of Icelandic society, but they were a clear sign of changing opinions on this distant province among the Danish and Icelandic elites. Thus, the idea that Icelandic society was destined to poverty and stagnation retreated in the late 18th century, paving the way for the belief in progress that fueled the **nationalist** struggle in the 19th century. *See also* THE ENLIGHTENMENT; THE GENERAL PETITION; INNRÉTTINGAR.

– S –

SA-CONFEDERATION OF ICELANDIC EMPLOYERS (SA-CIE). In 1934, 82 employers founded Vinnuveitendafélag Íslands

(Society of Icelandic Employers) in **Reykjavík**, but later the name was changed to Vinnuveitendasamband Íslands [Confederation of Icelandic Employers (CIE)]. The tasks of the confederation, which was formed at the time of heightened tensions between employers and employees during the **Great Depression**, was to organize employers in their negotiations with **trade unions**, to secure tranquility in the work place by preventing strikes, and to promote the general interests of employers in Iceland. In 1999, the CIE united with the confederation of the former cooperative societies, which had earlier been organized in their own confederation (Vinnumálasambandið) to form Samtök atvinnulífsins (in English, SA-CIE). It has eight member associations representing around 2,000 businesses that employ around 50 percent of the salaried employees on the Icelandic **labor market**.

Today, the SA-CIE serves as a negotiating partner in disputes with trade unions, who represent workers in various **economic** sectors and from all parts of the country. In this capacity, the SA-CIE has had enormous influence on economic policy in recent years, as the agreements between the **Icelandic Federation of Labor** (IFL) and the CIE have often required a substantial commitment from the public authorities. The marked decrease in levels of **inflation** at the beginning of the 1990s, which since has led to more stability in the economic sphere than was present in the preceding decades, was a direct result of such cooperation between the SA-CIE, the IFL, and the government in the **National Compromise Agreement** of 1990.

SÆMUNDSSON, TÓMAS (1807–41). This pastor and romantic **nationalist** was born to a wealthy farmer in southern Iceland on 7 June 1807. He completed a university entry exam from the Latin school at **Bessastaðir** in 1827, studying theology at the University of Copenhagen from 1827 to 1832. After completing his degree in theology, Sæmundsson went on a two-year "grand tour" around Europe, visiting Germany, Bohemia, Austria, Italy, France, and Britain—and even sailing as far as Istanbul in Turkey. Such travel was unheard of in Iceland at the time, but Sæmundsson saw it as a continuation of his studies and necessary preparation for his work in Iceland. Upon returning to Copenhagen in the spring of 1834, Sæmundsson joined the editorial group of *Fjölnir*, a new literary journal founded by three

Icelandic students earlier the same year. Sæmundsson was appointed pastor at Breiðabólsstaður in Rangárvalla County in 1834, and he served this important parish until his untimely death in 1841. He was very active his whole working life in Iceland, writing extensively on politics, culture, and **religious** matters. With his writings, Sæmundsson was instrumental in introducing romantic nationalism in Iceland, but he died too early to establish himself as a political leader or to fully develop his political ideas. *See also* HALLGRÍMSSON, JÓNAS (1807–45); SIGURÐSSON, JÓN (1811–1879).

SAGAS. The Icelandic sagas form a diverse group of literary works written from the 12th to the 14th centuries. *Heilagramanna sögur* (stories of saints' lives) and *Postulasögur* (apostles' sagas) are the oldest—the earliest of them date to around the mid-12th century. Most of the *Konungasögur* (kings' sagas) are from 1190 to 1230, reaching perfection with **Snorri Sturluson**'s *Heimskringla (Orb of the World)*. *Riddarasögur* (sagas of knights) are Icelandic adaptations of European romances, from a tradition that began in the early 13th century with a Norse translation of the story of Tristran. Under the heading *Fornaldarsögur* (sagas of ancient times, often called legendary sagas or mythic-heroic sagas in English), scholars group a number of sagas based on heroic legends and adventures. Most of these sagas were written in the 14th century. It is with the *Íslendingasögur* (sagas of Icelanders), or the Icelandic family sagas, however, that the saga tradition reached its artistic pinnacle. There are between 35 and 40 family sagas preserved; the most notable of them—including *Egils Saga*, *Laxdœla Saga*, and *Njáls Saga*—rank among the finest literary works of medieval Europe. All the family sagas are anonymous (although there are strong indications that Sturluson wrote *Egils Saga*), and none of them is preserved in an original manuscript. Therefore, the dating of the sagas is unclear, but the 13th century, one of the most violent periods in Icelandic history, seems to have been the time of the most creative literary production. The saga tradition continued into the 14th century, when the stories became more fantastic than the classical sagas of the 13th century had been, but saga writing seems not to extend beyond this point.

The scene of the family sagas is, as a rule, Icelandic society in the period stretching from the time of settlement to the mid-11th century—this is sometimes called the Söguöld (Saga Age). The stories describe feuds between individuals or family clans, and the preservation of honor is usually at the center of the plot. They depict a society with no central government and relatively limited concentration of power. This was radically different from the time when the sagas were written because the 13th century was a period of a constant struggle for hegemony between a few clans and chieftains that dominated the rest of society.

The family sagas are, without a doubt, Iceland's most important contribution to Western culture and are far ahead of any medieval literature in their style, development of characters, and complex and tightly constructed plots. For a long time, scholars have debated the historical value of the family sagas. It is clear that although they may have been based on oral legends, describing events that took place centuries before they were written, the most complex sagas are, in essence, literary works. The sagas should not, therefore, be taken as accurate accounts of the history or ethics of the time they describe, and to what degree they reflect the time when they were written is also a matter of debate. The sagas do, however, give a fascinating perspective of a prestate society and will continue to be an invaluable source for the study of Old Norse social norms and processes. *See also* AGE OF THE STURLUNGS; *BOOK OF ICELANDERS*; *BOOK OF SETTLEMENTS*; LITERATURE; SETTLEMENT PERIOD; *STURLUNGA SAGA*.

SETTLEMENT PERIOD. Iceland was first settled in a period of approximately 60 years from the late 9th century to the early 10th century. The settlement started as **Norwegians**, some of them coming via Ireland, the Shetland Islands, the Orkney Islands, and the Hebrides, sought new land in the west. The exact date of the beginning of this **population** movement is unknown, but it was probably around the year 870 (the date 874 is used for official commemorations). The foundation of **Alþingi** in 930 is traditionally seen as the end of the Settlement Period, although immigration to Iceland continued on a smaller scale well beyond that year. The total number of settlers is unknown, but according to the most credible estimates, there were between 10,000 and 20,000.

The settlement of Iceland has to be seen as an integral part of Viking expansion from Scandinavia to Russia, the British Isles, France, the Mediterranean, Iceland, and **Greenland**—reaching temporarily as far west as the coast of North America. Limited **economic** resources in their countries of origins and a highly developed navigation technique were the driving forces behind this **migration**. According to the *Book of Settlements*, the main reason for the immigration to Iceland was the establishment of a unified monarchy in Norway under **King** Harald Fairhair. Whatever the reason, the settlers found the new country attractive. The island was virginal at the time, as it had never been populated before, except, perhaps, by a few stray hermits, called *papar*, coming from Ireland. For this reason, Icelandic nature was more bountiful in the Settlement Period than it was in later centuries, when human exploitation had eradicated the shrubs that had covered the lowlands, leading to extensive soil erosion.

The settlement of Iceland seems to have taken place without serious conflicts. As there was no indigenous population to suppress, the land was free to the newcomers to grab. In order to prevent fighting among themselves, the immigrants developed elaborate rules for how to take possession of land, and in the early 10th century, the settlers adopted Norwegian law codes to regulate human interaction in the country. Thus began the **Commonwealth Period**. *See also BOOK OF ICELANDERS*.

SIGFÚSSON, STEINGRÍMUR J. (1955–). The leader of the **Left-Green Movement** (LGM). Sigfússon was born on a farm in the northeastern part of Iceland in 1955. He graduated from the secondary school in **Akureyri** in 1976 and completed a B.Sc. in geology from the **University of Iceland** in 1981. Sigfússon was first **elected** to parliament for the **People's Alliance** (PA) in 1983, serving as the leader of its parliamentary group from 1987 to 1988 and as a minister for **agriculture** and **transportation** from 1988 to 1991. During the late 1990s, when the parties on the left—the **Social Democratic Party**, the **Women's Alliance** (WA), and the PA—decided to form one unified coalition of social democrats, which later was to become the **Social Democratic Alliance**, Sigfússon led a group of PA supporters who refused to join the new party. Instead, he founded the LGM, which drew most of its support from the PA and some from the WA but attracted also a number of people who had not been active in politics before. Sigfússon has served as chairman of the LGM since its foundation in 1999 and has remained one of the most noticeable politicians on the left for the last decade.

SIGURÐARDÓTTIR, JÓHANNA (1942–). One of the most prominent politicians in Iceland since the early 1990s. She was born on 4 October 1942 in **Reykjavík** as the daughter of a representative in **Alþingi** for the **Social Democratic Party** (SDP). Sigurðardóttir holds a degree from the Commercial College in Reykjavík and worked as a flight attendant from 1962 to 1971 and as an office clerk from 1971 to 1978. From 1966 to 1969, she was chairwoman for the Union of Flight Attendants, and she sat on the directing committee of the Union of Office Workers of Reykjavík from 1976 to 1983 and the SDP from 1978 to 1994. She was **elected** deputy chairwoman of the SDP in 1984 but resigned that post after a bitter dispute with the chairman, **Jón Baldvin Hannibalsson**, in 1993. In 1978, she was elected to parliament for the SDP in Reykjavík, and from 1987 to 1994, she served as minister of social affairs for the party in three different coalition governments.

Sigurðardóttir was a leading spokeswoman for the SDP's left wing during the late 1980s and early 1990s, and she fought vigorously for her policies inside and outside governments. Thus, during her period in office as minister of social affairs, she forced through a reorganization of the state-guaranteed mortgage loans for residential housing as well as public housing funds. She earned respect among voters for her resolve, although her uncompromising political style created difficulties for the coalition governments in which she participated.

In 1994, Sigurðardóttir resigned from the SDP and formed a new political organization, **Þjóðvaki** (National Awakening) the following year. In the beginning, this move evoked strong support among voters, but the new political movement failed to sustain the early enthusiasm, and in 1996, Sigurðardóttir formed a joint parliamentary group with the SDP. She was instrumental in the formation of the Samfylkingin **(Social Democratic Alliance)** in 1999 and has remained one of its most influential and popular representatives in parliament. In 2007, she became a minister of social affairs in a coalition government of the SDA and the **Independence Party**, thus reaffirming her position as a leading voice on the left in Icelandic politics.

SIGURÐSSON, JÓN (1811–79). The undisputed leader of the **Icelandic nationalist movement** from around the mid-19th century until his death in 1879. Born on 17 June 1811 to a **Lutheran** minister in northwestern Iceland, Sigurðsson studied at home with his father and later completed a university entrance exam in **Reykjavík** in 1829. In 1833, he sailed to Copenhagen to study at the University of Copenhagen. There, he emerged as a leading member of the Icelandic student community, which at the time served as an important intellectual link between the external world and Iceland. In 1841, he published the first issue of the journal *Ný félagsrit*, which served as the main organ for his views and for the Icelandic nationalist movement in general until it ceased publication in 1873. In 1845, during **Alþingi**'s first session as an **elected** assembly, Sigurðsson established himself as the most influential parliamentary politician in Iceland, a role that he was to play until the early 1870s.

Sigurðsson was, from the beginning, a spokesman for liberal-nationalist views, calling for increased autonomy from **Denmark** as well as for the development of individual liberty in Iceland. His views were moderate, and in spite of his intransigent nationalism, the Danish government looked frequently to him to represent Iceland in negotiations on Icelandic affairs; he was, for example, selected as one of five Icelandic members in the Danish **constitutive assembly** in 1848–49 and served as an agent of the government in its campaign against a serious outbreak of scab that threatened the sheep stock in Iceland during the late 1850s.

From the time Sigurðsson moved to Copenhagen to study, he returned to Iceland only for brief official visits, making the Danish capital the base for his political work and professional career. Besides his political activities, he was a distinguished scholar of Icelandic philology and a rigorous and productive editor of medieval and early modern texts and documents. Although he did not complete any university degree, he was respected in Danish academia, working for different institutions and learned societies in Copenhagen.

After his death on 7 December 1879, Sigurðsson reached almost saintly status in Iceland. He is revered for his role as a leader of the struggle for independence and as the intellectual founder of the Icelandic nationalist movement. It is clear, however, that Sigurðsson's political liberalism was often ignored by the more conservative members of Alþingi, although they generally accepted his leadership role in negotiations with the Danish government. Today, Icelanders celebrate the legacy of Sigurðsson every year on 17 June, his birthday, which has served as the official national holiday of Iceland since the foundation of the republic on that day in 1944. *See also* STATUS LAW.

SIGURÐSSON, JÓN (1946–). The former chairman of the **Progressive Party** (PP). Sigurðsson was born on 23 August 1946. He studied Icelandic **language, literature**, and history at the **University of Iceland** from 1966 to 1969 and completed a master's degree in **educational** administration from Columbia Pacific University in 1988 and a Ph.D. from the same school in 1990. In 1993, he completed an MBA from the National University in San Diego. Sigurðsson taught in various schools in Iceland from 1966 to 1975 and served as director of the Menningarsjóður (Icelandic Cultural Fund) from 1975 to 1977. From 1977 to 1978, he worked for the party organ of the PP, the newspaper *Tíminn*, and as its editor from 1978 to 1981. He was headmaster of the Cooperative Business School at Bifröst from 1981 to 1988 and served as its first rector from 1988 to 1991 after the school was upgraded to college level. From 1991 to 1996, he served as assistant professor at the same college. Between 1996 and 2003, Sigurðsson worked first for the Vinnumálasamband samvinnufélaganna (Employers' Association of the Cooperative Societies) and then as business consultant in **Reykjavík**. In 2003, he was appointed one of three governors of the Central Bank of Iceland. In 2006, when **Halldór Ásgrímsson** resigned rather unexpectedly from his post as chairman of the PP, Sigurðsson was **elected** to the post. The same year, he became minister of **industry** and commerce in **Geir H. Haarde**'s government. After the resounding electoral defeat of the PP in 2007, Sigurðsson stepped down as chairman of the party and retired from politics.

SKALDIC POETRY. One of the main categories of Old Norse poetry—the other being **Eddic poetry**. The name comes from the Old Norse word *skáld*, meaning "poet." Skaldic poetry is differentiated from Eddic poetry by the fact that its historical context and author are known. Moreover, skaldic poems are usually complex in structure and intricate in style, which is quite different from the simple meters that characterize Eddic poetry. The tradition of composing skaldic poetry is older than the settlement of Iceland, and it is commonly viewed to have come to an end around 1400, although there is no agreement on this point. Most skaldic poems are preserved as parts of prose works dating from the 12th to the 14th centuries. *See also* LITERATURE; SAGAS.

SKÁLHOLT. A farm located in Árnes County that became the first episcopal seat in Iceland. Gissur Ísleifsson, who became the second bishop of Iceland in 1082, donated Skálholt to the **Catholic** Church on the condition that it would serve as a bishop's seat for as long as Iceland remained a Christian country. From this time until the late 18th century, Skálholt was the administrative center for a diocese that covered three quarters of the country, and it was thus crucial for the development of **religious** and cultural life in Iceland. In the same period, one of the two Latin schools in Iceland was also located in Skálholt, making it one of the most important places of learning in the country.

In 1785, following a serious earthquake that left most of its buildings in ruins, a royal decree abolished the bishop's seat in Skálholt, moving it to the emerging capital of Iceland, **Reykjavík.** At the same time, the **king** sold the estate to the sitting bishop, Hannes Finnsson, who lived in Skálholt until his death in 1796. From that time, Skálholt gradually lost its prestige, but in recent years the church has attempted to revive its former glory. A new church was consecrated at Skálholt in 1963, and today it serves as cultural center and the official residence of one of Iceland's two suffragan bishops. *See also* HÓLAR; LUTHERANISM; MENNTASKÓLINN Í REYKJAVÍK (MR); THE REFORMATION.

SMALLPOX. Because of Iceland's geographic isolation and sparse **population,** smallpox never became an endemic disease in the country. Rather, Iceland suffered repeated, and sometimes extremely serious, epidemic attacks that often spread rapidly around the country. From the beginning of the 16th century to the end of the 18th, four to five such epidemics struck Iceland every century, primarily killing people born between the attacks because they lacked immunity to the smallpox virus. The epidemics varied in severity, but the worst case was the *stóra bóla* (big pox) that killed around a quarter of the Icelandic population in 1707–9. From the early 19th century, the government required inoculation of all children, leading in the end to the total eradication of smallpox in Iceland. The last time this dreaded guest visited the country (1839–40), it spread over only a limited area, and relatively few people were affected. *See also* HEALTH.

SNORRI STURLUSON. *See* STURLUSON, SNORRI (1178/9–1241).

SOCIAL DEMOCRATIC ALLIANCE (SDA). The Samfylkingin (SDA) is a social democratic party formed in 1999 by members coming from three **political parties** to the left of center in Icelandic politics—the **Social Democratic Party** (SDP), the **People's Alliance** (PA), and the **Women's Alliance** (WA). The idea behind the creation of the party was to unify people on the left in one political movement in order to establish a counterbalance to the **Independence Party** (IP) on the right. These three parties had already, with the **Progressive Party** (PP), cooperated in two local **elections** in **Reykjavík**, running the city jointly from 1994. As it turned out, a number of prominent members of the PA and the WA refused to join the SDA; some chose to join the PP, some retired from politics, and others founded a new party to the left of the SDA, the **Left-Green Movement**.

The SDA was fairly successful in its first two elections, polling 27 percent of the votes cast in 1999 and 31 percent in 2003. In the latter elections, the party was not far behind the IP, for the first time posing a serious challenge to the IP's domination in Icelandic politics. The SDA failed to repeat its success in 2007, as the party polled less than 27 percent of the votes cast. In spite of this electoral loss, the party reaffirmed its position as the second largest party in Iceland.

In its program, the SDA follows very similar policies as the social democratic parties in the other Nordic countries. It supports the idea of a comprehensive **welfare** system, while the party has not promoted the participation of the state in the **economy**. In its **foreign policy** program, the SDA follows a similar line as the SDP before it. Thus, the SDA supports participation in the **North Atlantic Treaty Organization**, although it strongly opposed the government's decision to back the invasion of Iraq in 2003. The SDA is also the only party in Iceland to advocate Iceland's application to the **European Union**. The present leader of the SDA is **Ingibjörg Sólrún Gísladóttir**, the former mayor of Reykjavík and the present minister of foreign affairs. She is the first **woman** to serve as party leader in a major political party in Iceland. *See also* UNION OF LIBERALS AND LEFTISTS (ULL); ÞJÓÐVAKI.

SOCIAL DEMOCRATIC PARTY (SDP). The Alþýðuflokkur (The People's Party), or the Social Democratic Party, was founded in March 1916, making it the first modern **political party** in Iceland. It was formed as the political wing of the **Icelandic Federation of Labor** (IFL) in order to further the interests of the working classes and advocate policies of democratic socialism in Iceland. The SDP rejected revolutionary socialism from the beginning and often stood closer to the **Independence Party** on the right than to the socialist parties on the left. In the post–**World War II** era, the SDP was an ardent supporter of Iceland's participation in such international bodies as the **North Atlantic Treaty Organization** and the **European Free Trade Association**. **Jón Baldvin Hannibalsson**, the party chairman from 1984 to 1998, was also instrumental in leading Iceland into the **European Economic Area** agreement with the **European Union** (EU), and the SDP was the first political party in Iceland to openly call for Icelandic application for membership in the EU. The traditional base for the SDP was the urban area in southwest Iceland and the fishing towns in the Western Fjords, but it never appealed to voters in the rural areas. The SDP was dissolved in 1999, when most of its leadership took part in forming the **Social Democratic Alliance**.

In the 1916 and 1919 parliamentary **elections**, the SDP polled less than 7 percent of the votes cast, but from the early 1920s until the party was dissolved, its support fluctuated between 10 and 20 percent of the popular vote. The party suffered, however, from frequent dissensions, as different factions broke away from the SDP at various points in its history. The first split came in 1930, when the left wing of the SDP formed the **Communist Party of Iceland** (CPI); eight years later, a splinter group of the SDP joined the CPI to form the **Socialist Unity Party** (SUP); in 1956, the left-wing faction of the SDP broke again away from the party, merging with the SUP to form the **People's Alli-**

ance; in 1982, the charismatic politician and former minister of justice and **education** for the SDP **Vilmundur Gylfason** left the party, founding his own **Social Democratic Union**; and finally, in 1994 the deputy chairwoman of the party, **Jóhanna Sigurðardóttir**, formed a political organization, **Þjóðvaki** (National Awakening). For this reason, the SDP never managed to gain the same dominance in Icelandic politics as the social democratic parties of the other Nordic countries.

SOCIAL DEMOCRATIC UNION (SDU). A splinter party from the **Social Democratic Party** (SDP) that formed in haste in late 1982, just before the parliamentary **elections** of 1983. The SDU was built around the charismatic politician **Vilmundur Gylfason**, who had caused great commotion in Icelandic politics in the preceding years. The SDU's platform pledged the party's support for an extensive **welfare state** in Iceland, but it also advocated radical transformation of the democratic process and a complete overhaul of the administrative structures. The SDU proposed direct elections of the **prime minister**, similar to the election of the president of the **United States**; widespread decentralization; and total separation of the legislative and executive branches of government. The party received over 7 percent of the ballots cast in 1983, which was a remarkable accomplishment considering the short time its leaders had to prepare for the electoral campaign. Later the same year, the early death of Gylfason led to a total demise of the SDU, and in 1987, it received only 0.2 percent of the votes cast. After that, the party dissolved and disappeared from the scene.

SOCIALIST UNITY PARTY (SUP). The Sameiningarflokkur alþýðu-sósíalistaflokkurinn (SUP) was formed in 1938 when the **Communist Party of Iceland** (CPI) and a group of radical social democrats under the leadership of **Héðinn Valdimarsson** merged into one **political party**. The SUP espoused a Marxist ideology and sympathized obstinately with the Soviet Union, even defending the Soviet aggression in Finland during the Winter War of 1939–40. Its support was strongest among workers and intellectuals, and some of the most prominent writers and artists in Iceland were vocal adherents of the party and its ideology. In 1956, the SUP joined hands with other groups on the left to form the **People's Alliance** (PA) and was formally dissolved in 1968 when the PA became an organized political party.

The impetus behind the formation of the SUP was both the growing radicalization of the working classes during the **Great Depression** and an instruction from Comintern, the international organization of communists, to the CPI to form a bulwark in the defense against fascism in Iceland. Rather than uniting the left, the formation of the SUP continued the split created by the establishment of the CPI, and for the next two decades the party competed fiercely with the SDP for the popular support.

In its first parliamentary **elections** (1942), the SUP became the third largest party in Iceland, receiving 16.2 percent of the votes cast. It remained a strong force in parliament for the next 16 years, but except for 1944–47, it was excluded from participation in governments because of its Marxist ideology and the suspicion of its loyalty to the Soviet Union. *See also* MODERNIZATION GOVERNMENT.

SÖGUFÉLAG. *See* ICELANDIC HISTORICAL ASSOCIATION (IHA).

STATISTICAL BUREAU OF ICELAND (SBI). Since its foundation in 1914, the Hagstofa Íslands (SBI) has been the most important institution in the collection and publication of official statistics in Iceland. With the Act on the Central Government in 1969, the SBI was made a separate **ministry**, which meant in theory that one **cabinet** member was responsible for the bureau (usually the **prime minister**), carrying the title of the minister for the SBI. In practice, however, the bureau was virtually an autonomous body that did not receive directives from the minister in question. This status was confirmed recently as the SBI lost its ministerial status and was turned into an independent public institution. The SBI is organized in three main sections: the division of social statistics, the division of **economic** statistics, and the division of resources and services. The division of social statistics collects and publishes data on **education** and culture, **employment** and living conditions, **health**, **population**, wages, and so on. The division of economic statistics deals with statistics relating to financial matters, business, **trade**, national accounts, inflation, **transport** and **tourism**, and so on. The SBI operates a comprehensive website, where most of its statistical information can be accessed online (www.statice.is).

STATUS LAW. The **Danish** parliament passed the Stöðulög (Status Law) in 1870, defining the status of Iceland in the Danish monarchy. The law, which came into effect in 1871, stipulated that Iceland was an inseparable part of the Danish realm, although the province had specific regional prerogatives. The decree also ended a long dispute about the financial separation of Denmark and Iceland, designating a considerable subsidy for the Icelandic budget. After enacting the Status Law, the Danish government reorganized the administrative structure in Iceland, creating the office of *Landshöfðingi*, or governor of Iceland.

The Status Law was immensely unpopular in Iceland, primarily because the Danish government never presented it in **Alþingi.** Thus, Icelandic **nationalists** claimed that the law violated Iceland's national rights and lacked any legitimacy. Although the majority in Alþingi, under the leadership of **Jón Sigurðsson** (1811–79), refused to accept the law, it formed the basis for relations between Denmark and Iceland until 1918, when Iceland became a sovereign state with the **Act of Union.** *See also* CONSTITUTION OF 1874; DRAFT; GOVERNOR'S PERIOD; HOME RULE.

STEFÁNSSON, ÓLAFUR (1731–1812). The first Icelander to be appointed *stiftamtmaður*, or governor of Iceland, was born on 3 May 1731 to a parish pastor in the northern part of the country. He graduated from the Latin school at **Hólar** in 1751, continuing his studies in Copenhagen. After completing a law degree in 1754, Stefánsson returned to Iceland. He rose quickly to the highest ranks in the Icelandic administrative system, serving as vice **lawman** from 1756 to 1764 and assisting his father-in-law, the district governor (**amtmaður**) from 1764 to 1766. In 1766, the **king** appointed him district governor, which was the highest administrative post in Iceland at the time. With the reorganization of the Icelandic administrative system in 1770, when authorities in Copenhagen divided the country into two districts and required the governor to live in Iceland, Stefánsson became district governor for the northeastern district. Between 1783 and 1787, he held no official post, but he resumed his career as district governor in Iceland's west district in the latter year. Three years later, he was promoted to the office of *stiftamtmaður*; he held this position until he was removed temporarily from his post in 1803 because of alleged irregularities in his administration. He retired from official life in 1806. Stefánsson was both the wealthiest and most powerful man in Iceland at the end of the 18th century. His marriage in 1761 to the only child of the district governor of Iceland, one of the country's richest landowners, secured his career in the administrative system and brought him wealth that set him apart from his contemporaries. Moreover, through marriages of his children and other family connections, his relatives dominated the government of Iceland during his time. Stefánsson's descendants, carrying the family name Stephensen, remained prominent in the Icelandic administration throughout the 19th century. *See also* STEPHENSEN, MAGNÚS (1762–1833).

STEPHANSSON, STEPHAN G. (1853–1927). A poet and leading figure among the 19th-century emigrants from Iceland to America. He was born in Skagafjörður County as Stefán Guðmundsson to poor parents on 3 October 1853. He immigrated to the **United States** with his parents in 1873, changing his name to Stephan G. Stephansson. After living in Wisconsin for a few years, he established himself as a farmer in North Dakota in 1880. Nine years later, he moved across the Canadian border to the province of Alberta, settling down in the region to the east of the Rocky Mountains. There he lived as a farmer for the remainder of his life. Stephansson was a self-**educated** man, but in North America, he became a prolific poet. All his life, he had to work hard to make ends meet, but he wrote poetry during the few spare moments he found. These poems are written in a realistic yet complex style, and they demonstrate a deep sympathy for working people and their conditions. Stephansson, or the "poet of the Rocky Mountains," as he was often called in Iceland, was well known in Iceland during his lifetime and was considered one of the finest poets to write in the Icelandic **language** around the turn of the 20th century. *See also* LITERATURE.

STEPHENSEN, MAGNÚS (1762–1833). This leader of the Icelandic **Enlightenment** was born on 27 December 1762. He was the son of **Ólafur Stefánsson,** one of the wealthiest and most powerful figures in Iceland during the latter half of the 18th century. Stephensen enrolled in the University of Copenhagen in 1781 and graduated with a law degree in 1788. While still a young student, he was dispatched to Iceland in order to investigate the **Laki eruption** of 1783–84, and two years later, he administered the first sale of the immense landholdings owned by the **Skálholt** diocese. After earning his university degree, he became vice **lawman** in Iceland's northwest district and lawman of the same district in 1789. The **king** appointed him the first chief justice of the new Icelandic **High Court** in 1800, a position he held until his death in 1833. He defended a doctoral dissertation at University of Copenhagen in 1819.

Stephensen was one of the most influential persons in Iceland during his lifetime, although he never reached his father's status in the official hierarchy. For years, he directed the only printing press in Iceland, a position that gave him a virtual monopoly over what was printed in the country. He used this situation to promote his own ideas, publishing his writings on issues ranging from legal theory to the nutritious value of seaweed. In his literary works, as well as in his office as a judge, Stephensen remained an ardent spokesman of enlightened rationalism, advocating a humane penal system, fewer strictures on foreign **trade**, and more effective methods in the administrative and juridical systems. *See also* THE GENERAL PETITION.

STEPHENSEN, MAGNÚS (1836–1917). The last *landshöfðingi*, or governor of Iceland, was born on 18 October 1836 into one of the most prominent families of the country. In 1855, after completing a university entrance exam from the Latin school in **Reykjavík**, Stephensen sailed to Copenhagen to study law. Upon finishing his university studies in 1862, he was hired as a clerk for the Bureau of Icelandic Affairs in Copenhagen, where he worked until 1870. That year, he was appointed justice of the **high court** in Reykjavík, where he served until 1886. From 1883 to 1886, he managed the office of the district governor (*amtmaður*) in the southwest district of Iceland, leading to his appointment as governor in 1886. For almost 20 years, Stephensen was the highest government official in Iceland. He occupied a central position during a crucial period in Icelandic political and **economic** history. Because of his conservative views, Stephensen was a controversial figure, but in spite of this, he was generally highly respected by his countrymen. In 1904, with the introduction of **home rule**, the governor's office was abolished, which meant that Stephensen lost his post, and he was unable to find a niche in the new administrative system. He ended his distinguished career in public service as a representative in **Alþingi**, where he served from 1903 to 1908.

STIFTAMTMAÐUR. With the introduction of **absolutism** at the beginning of the 1660s, the **Danish** government restructured the administrative system in Iceland. In line with general practice in Denmark, Iceland was made one administrative district, called *amt*, with one governor, *stiftamtmaður*, living in Copenhagen and one district governor, *amtmaður*, living in Iceland. In theory, the *stiftamtmaður* was the highest official in the Icelandic administrative hierarchy, but in reality, it was only a ceremonial post until 1770, when authorities required Governor Lauritz A. Thodal to move his residence to Iceland. This happened as a part of another reorganization of the Icelandic administration; now the country was divided into two districts—and from 1787 into three—each administered by a district governor. From that time, the *stiftamtmaður*, who also served as district governor in one of the districts, was the most important representative of the Danish government in Iceland. The office of *stiftamtmaður* was abolished in 1872–73 in conjunction with the passing of the **Status Law** and the creation of a new governor's office in Iceland, called *landshöfðingi*. *See also* STEFÁNSSON, ÓLAFUR (1731–1812); TRAMPE, COUNT FREDERIK CHRISTOPHER (1779–1832); Appendix A.

STÓRA BÓLA. See SMALLPOX.

STÓRIDÓMUR. A statute approved in **Alþingi** on 30 June 1564 and ratified by the **Danish king** the following year. *Stóridómur* (the "large" or "long judgment" in literal translation) redefined the penal code for moral offenses, especially in cases connected with adultery and sexual intercourse between persons related either through affinity or consanguinity. The ruling measured punishments on a fixed scale, ranging from small fines to capital punishment—decapitation for men, drowning for **women**. Icelandic courts enforced *Stóridómur* to the letter until the 18th century, but its last vestiges were eliminated from the Icelandic penal codes in 1870.

STURLA ÞÓRÐARSON. *See* ÞÓRÐARSON, STURLA (1214–84).

STURLUNGA SAGA. This large compilation of texts written by various authors in the 12th and 13th centuries is actually a historical chronicle dealing with the period from the early 12th century to the end of the **Commonwealth Period** in 1262–64. It belongs to a genre of Icelandic **sagas** called *samtíðarsögur* (contemporary sagas), which is comprised of a group of works written by authors who had witnessed at least some of the events they described. The *Sturlunga Saga* is, therefore, one of the main sources on the history of the last decades of the Commonwealth Period, and scholars generally believe that it gives a relatively accurate account of that turbulent era.

The centerpiece of *Sturlunga Saga* is *Íslendinga Saga*, written by **Sturla Þórðarson**, the nephew of the best-known Icelandic writer of the time, **Snorri Sturluson**. This is a combination of family history (of the Sturlung family) and a general history of Iceland in a period stretching from the late 12th to the late 13th century. The account gives a remarkably balanced picture of the period, considering that its author was deeply involved in the events he describes. The *Sturlunga Saga* provides a unique perspective on the most violent period in Icelandic history, the **Age of the Sturlungs,** while it is also a testimony of the great historical interest in Iceland present at the time it was written. *See also* LITERATURE.

STURLUSON, SNORRI (1178/9–1241). The best-known man of letters in medieval Iceland was born either in 1178 or 1179 to Sturla Þórðarson the elder at Hvammur, the man after whom the powerful Sturlung family was named. Through clever management of his financial affairs and driving ambition, Sturluson was able to amass great wealth, becoming one of the most powerful persons in Iceland around 1220–30. Although he lived in one of the most violent periods of Icelandic history, the **Age of the Sturlungs,** Sturluson was not a warrior; he based his power on keen legal erudition and a shrewd sense of how to construct political alliances. In the end, however,

Sturluson's enemies joined forces in their struggle against him and had him killed in September 1241. This was, in part, at the behest of the **Norwegian king**, Håkon Håkonsson, who wanted to punish Sturluson for allying with King Håkon's rival for the Norwegian throne, Earl Skúli.

To posterity, Sturluson is better known for his writings than for his political intrigues. In fact, he wrote some of the most superb **literature** of this culturally fertile period in Icelandic history and can truly be classified among the greatest literary figures of medieval Europe. Among his works are masterpieces like the *Prose Edda*, which is a treatise on Old Norse **skaldic poetry**, and *Heimskringla* (*Orb of the World*), the history of the kings of **Norway** to 1177. Moreover, he has also often been credited with composing one of the best-known family **sagas**, *Egil's Saga*, but this cannot be proven conclusively. *See also STURLUNGA SAGA;* ÞÓRÐARSON, STURLA (1214–84).

SUPREME COURT OF ICELAND. The Hæstiréttur Íslands (Supreme Court of Iceland) was founded by law in 1919, taking over the role of the **Danish** Supreme Court as the highest tribunal in Icelandic court cases in the following year. A two-tiered court system was established in Iceland, replacing the system of three levels that had been in use since the beginning of the 19th century. Earlier, cases could go from district courts to the **high court** in **Reykjavík** and from there to the supreme court in Copenhagen. Today, appeals proceed directly from district courts to the supreme court in Reykjavík.

Initially, five judges sat on the supreme court, but at present, the bench has nine members. They are appointed for an unlimited period of time by the **president** upon the advice of the minister of justice—which in practice means that the judges are appointed by the government. Like other public servants, supreme court judges are required to retire no later than their 70th birthday. The judges select the chief justice from among themselves for periods of two years. Cases are heard by panels of either three or five judges; in exceptional circumstances, the chief justice can decide that a case is heard by seven judges. Almost all public and private cases can be appealed to the supreme court, although certain restrictions are imposed to limit the number of petty cases that can be presented to the court. In recent years, 300–400 cases have been appealed annually to the supreme court. *See also* COUNTY.

SVARTI DAUÐI. See PLAGUE.

SVEINSSON, BENEDIKT (1826–99). A 19th-century politician and government official. Sveinsson was born in southeast Iceland on 20 January 1826 to a country pastor. He completed the secondary school exam in 1852 and sailed to Copenhagen the same year to study law. In 1859, a year after earning a law degree from the University of Copenhagen, he was appointed a judge in the Icelandic **High Court**. In 1870, he was dismissed from this post but was appointed bailiff of Þingey County in 1874. Sveinsson is best known for his political activities, but from 1881 until his death in 1899, he was the leader of a parliamentary faction seeking a revision of the Icelandic constitution (hence his policy was called revisionism—or *endurskoðun*). Sveinsson was an engaging orator and a fierce opponent of **Valtýr Guð-mundsson** and his faction in **Alþingi** because of Guðmundsson's more conciliatory attitudes toward **Danish** rule in Iceland. Although Sveinsson advocated a radical revision of Danish–Icelandic relations, his views on domestic affairs were for the most part conservative, if not reactionary. *See also* CONSTITUTION OF 1874.

SVEINSSON, BRYNJÓLFUR (1605–75). This bishop and theologian was born on 14 September 1605 to a **Lutheran** pastor in Ísafjörður County in northwestern Iceland. In 1624, after graduating from the Latin school at **Skálholt**, Sveinsson enrolled in the University of Copenhagen. He came back to Iceland in 1629 but returned to Copenhagen to resume his university studies in 1631. In 1632, Sveinsson was appointed a deputy principal of a prestigious secondary school in Roskilde, **Denmark**, and the following year, he was awarded the title *magister* from the University of Copenhagen. In 1638, Sveinsson was **elected** bishop of the diocese of Skálholt, a position he held from 1639 to 1674. Sveinsson was highly respected as a bishop, both for his great erudition and his efficient administration. He showed much interest in **literature**, both as a poet and a collector of ancient Icelandic manuscripts.

SÝSLA. See COUNTY.

– T –

THORODDSEN, GUNNAR (1910–83). A politician and legal scholar born in **Reykjavík** on 29 December 1910. Thoroddsen attended **Menntaskólinn í Reykjavík**, where he completed a university entrance exam in 1929. He received a law degree from the **University of Iceland** (UoI) in 1934, continuing his studies in **Denmark**, Germany, and **Great Britain** from 1935 to 1936. He practiced law in Reykjavík from 1936 to 1940, when he began teaching at the UoI. He was appointed professor of law at the university in 1942, resigning his professorship in 1947 in order to devote his time to a political career.

Thoroddsen entered politics at an early age. In 1934, at only 24 years of age, he was **elected** to **Alþingi** for the **Independence Party** (IP), and he represented the IP intermittently until his death in 1983 (1934–37, 1942–65, and 1971–83). He sat on Reykjavík's city council from 1938 to 1962, serving as mayor of the capital from 1947 to 1959. He became a **cabinet** member for the first time in 1959, when he was appointed minister of finance in the **Reconstruction Government**. Thoroddsen interrupted his political career in 1965, when he was appointed ambassador to Denmark. The reason for this semiretirement was his desire both to run for **president** and to pursue his academic interests. In 1968, he defended a doctoral dissertation at the UoI, but the same year, he lost to **Kristján Eldjárn** in the presidential election by a wide margin. In 1970, Thoroddsen returned to Iceland to become justice of the **Supreme Court of Iceland**, but he resigned from that post later the same year. Thoroddsen resumed his political career in the following year, when he was elected to parliament for the IP. From 1971 to 1974, Thoroddsen served as professor of law at the UoI, retiring from that post when he was appointed minister of **industry** and social affairs in 1974. In 1980, he led a small group of representatives who broke away from the IP to form a government with the **Progressive Party** and the **People's Alliance**. He served as **prime minister** from 1980 to 1983.

Thoroddsen's political career was both long and complex. He was deputy chairman of the IP from 1961 to 1965 and again from 1974 to 1981 and leader of its parliamentary group from 1973 to 1979, in addition to serving in numerous committees on behalf of the party.

In spite of his long and distinguished service for the IP, Thoroddsen's relationship with other members of the party leadership was strained throughout a large part of his career. In 1952, he broke the party ranks to support his father-in-law, the social-democrat **Ásgeir Ásgeirsson**, in Ásgeirsson's bid for the presidency. Some of his colleagues never forgave him for this move because the IP backed another candidate in the elections. His boldest defiance of party discipline came in 1980, when he formed a coalition government in open opposition to the official policy of the IP. In the spring of 1983, with the fall of his government, Thoroddsen retired from politics, and he died in September the same year.

THORODDSEN, JÓN (1819–68). This pioneer of modern Icelandic prose **literature** was born on 5 October 1819 in Barðaströnd County in western Iceland. He finished secondary school at **Bessastaðir** in 1840 and sailed to Copenhagen the following year to study law. In 1848, he interrupted his studies to join the **Danish** army in its fight against a German insurrection in the duchies of Schleswig-Holstein. After returning to Iceland in 1850, Thoroddsen was appointed bailiff in Barðaströnd County. He secured his career as a government official by completing a law degree in 1854 and served as bailiff, first in Barðaströnd County and later in Borgarfjörður County, until his death in 1868.

Thoroddsen is best known as a literary figure, especially for the novel *Piltur og stúlka* (*A Boy and a Girl*). He wrote this simple but charming love story, which is often called the first modern novel written in the Icelandic **language**, in Copenhagen during the winter of 1848–49 (it was published in Copenhagen in 1850). The story emphasizes traditional Icelandic values, warning against gluttony, indolence, and the influence of Danish language and customs on Icelandic culture. At the time of his death, Thoroddsen was working on his second novel, *Maður og kona* (*A Man and a Woman*), but he died before its completion.

THORODDSEN, SKÚLI (1859–1916). A politician, state official, and journalist who became the most prominent leader of the radical independence movement in the first decade of the 20th century. Thoroddsen was born the son of **Jón Thoroddsen**, a bailiff and a writer, on 6 January 1859. After completing a law degree from the University of Copenhagen in 1884, he became an attorney in **Reykjavík**, but later the same year, he was appointed bailiff in **Ísafjörður** County. He resigned from this post in 1895, dedicating the rest of his life to politics and journalism. In 1886, Thoroddsen was involved in the foundation of *Þjóðviljinn*, a weekly and semimonthly newspaper in the town of Ísafjörður, becoming its editor from 1887 (officially from 1892). He was **elected** to parliament in 1891, where he held a seat almost continuously until 1915. In 1908, he led the opposition to the so-called **Draft**, which was a proposal for a new act regulating the union of **Denmark** and Iceland. After the defeat of this proposal, Thoroddsen became a prominent member of the first **Independence Party**, which was formed in 1908. This was a loose federation of representatives in parliament, all of whom emphasized the fight for total independence from Denmark. In spite of his effective leadership in defeating the Draft, which led to the resignation of his nemesis **Hannes Hafstein** as minister of Iceland, Thoroddsen was unsuccessful in his bid for the post of minister. After that, he never regained his former political stature, retiring from politics in 1915. *See also* HOME RULE; POLITICAL PARTIES.

THORS, ÓLAFUR (1892–1964). Leader of the **Independence Party** (IP) and one of the most influential politicians of 20th-century Iceland. Thors was born in Borgarnes in Borgarfjörður County on 19 January 1892, the son of **Thor Jensen**, a **Danish**-born merchant. After passing a university entrance exam in **Reykjavík** in 1912, he studied law at the University of Copenhagen without completing the degree. From 1914 to 1939, he directed his father's trawler company, Kveldúlfur, but from the beginning of **World War II**, he devoted all his time to politics. Thors was first **elected** to parliament in 1926 for the **Conservative Party**, and from 1929, he represented the IP in **Alþingi**. In 1932, he served as minister of justice for a few weeks, and he was appointed minister of **economic** affairs in 1939. In the spring of 1942, he became **prime minister** for the first time, resigning later the same year.

From 1944 to 1963, Thors led four coalition governments (1944–47, 1949–50, 1953–56, and 1959–63) and sat in a fifth as minister of economic affairs (1950–53). He was an able politician and negotiator, as is reflected in the fact that he managed to form a coalition government with the **Socialist Unity Party**—the political nemesis of the IP—at the end of the war. Moreover, as chairman of the IP for almost three decades (1934–61), he effectively directed the largest **political party** through times of great political upheaval without facing any serious challenge to his leadership. *See also* MODERNIZATION GOVERNMENT; RECONSTRUCTION GOVERNMENT.

TOURISM. Tourism is one of the most important **economic** sectors in Iceland. The number of foreign visitors to the country has increased exponentially in recent decades, from around 100,000 in 1985 to 190,000 in 1995 and to 485,000 in 2007. At present, tourism provides around 13 percent of the total foreign exchange revenues and 5 percent of the gross domestic product. The expansion of tourism in Iceland has happened because of diligent efforts to promote the country abroad, especially in Europe and North America, but improved facilities and changing patterns in international tourism have also contributed to the trend. The main attraction in Iceland is its relatively untamed nature and rugged geography, but harsh climate limits the main tourist season to the fairly short period of the summer months.

TRADE, FOREIGN. Despite the distance from European markets and extreme poverty of the majority of the **population** in the past, foreign trade has always played an important role in the Icelandic **economy**. The narrow resource base and primitive division of labor called for the import of a variety of consumer and capital goods, ranging from grain, iron, and timber to manufactured goods.

Considerable foreign trade was carried out during the **Commonwealth Period**. At that time, woolen textiles (called *vaðmál* in Icelandic) and, to a lesser extent, unprocessed wool and hides were the most important export articles, while grain dominated the imports. Fish exports first became significant in the 14th century, responding to rising prices in the European markets. Changes in the location of the principal market places in Iceland reflect this increase in the relative importance of fish exports, as the centers of trade moved from **agricultural** areas in the south (Eyrar), west (Hvítárvellir), and north (Gásar) to the coastal areas close to the main fishing grounds in the southern and western parts of the country, for example the **Vestmanna Islands**, Hafnarfjörður (now a suburb of **Reykjavík**), and Hvalfjörður. Between the mid-14th century and the early 19th century, dried fish (stockfish) was Iceland's principal export article, with such agricultural products as wool, hides, tallow, and salted mutton taking second place. Grain, timber, and ironware were the main imports, although Icelanders also imported luxury articles, including fine clothes, wine, wax and tar, tobacco, and spirits in later periods. Early on, Icelanders traded mainly with **Norway**, with the Hanseatic merchants in Bergen playing the most important role, but they were pushed aside with the influx of more advanced and powerful English fishermen and traders in the early 15th century. During the late 15th century, German merchants and the **Danish king** joined hands in excluding the English from Icelandic trade, and in 1532, they were finally defeated in an armed conflict with merchants from the city of Hamburg.

Royal influence on Icelandic affairs, including foreign trade, grew rapidly during the **Reformation** era, leading to the introduction of **monopoly trade** in 1602. From then on, Icelandic trade became a special prerogative of the Danish king, who gave priority to his subjects in this regard. With the partial abolition of the monopoly system in 1787, trade practices became more flexible. The new law confined foreign trade to Danish citizens, which in practice meant that it continued to be dominated by a few Danish merchants residing in Copenhagen and channeling most trade through Denmark. With further liberalization of Icelandic trade in 1816 and the abolition of all restrictions on foreign trade in 1855, the structural impediments against free trade with the outside world were lifted. This did not lead to any revolutionary changes in Icelandic foreign trade, however, because merchants from outside the Danish realm did not show much interest in trading in Iceland. Gradually, trade was taken over by Icelandic merchants, and the control of the foreign trade in the country moved into Icelandic hands.

By 1860, Iceland ranked among the top six European countries in terms of per-capita exports, and this trend continued into the 20th century. The export of salted cod to the Mediterranean area, primarily Spain, increased significantly around 1770, making it the most important export staple in the second quarter of the 19th century. In the 1920s, this product provided up to 60 percent of all export earnings in Iceland, but frozen fish replaced salt fish in the 1940s as the principal export article. Through the 20th century, marine products were in a dominant position, accounting for as much as 90 to 95 percent of all exports in the 1950s and 1960s. This has changed rapidly in recent years, as the fish catches around Iceland have declined and the Icelandic economy has become more diversified. In 2007, fish products accounted for just over 40 percent of the Icelandic exports, while manufactured products were just under 40 percent (up from 20 percent in 1990). This reflects the growing significance of **energy-intensive industries** in the Icelandic economy, amounting to almost 30 percent of all exports from Iceland in 2007. A wide range of commodities characterizes imports because Icelanders depend heavily on the importation of finished consumer and investment goods in addition to many of the most important intermediate and raw materials.

Iceland pursued a very liberal external trade policy up to the **Great Depression** of the early 1930s, when protective tariffs were set up to encourage light domestic industry and to tackle the growing unemployment (*see* EMPLOYMENT) problem in Iceland. These protectionist policies survived longer in Iceland than in the neighboring countries, with import duties first being scaled down after 1960. Since the 1960s, Iceland has been a member of various international organizations and agreements. The country became a contracting party to the General Agreement on Tariffs and Trade in 1964 and later a member of the World Trade Organization. Iceland became a full member of the **European Free Trade Association** in 1970, followed by bilateral agreements with the **European Union**, and, most importantly, the **European Economic Area** agreement in 1994. This has obliged Iceland to open its markets to foreign competition and has had a dramatic effect on Iceland's position in the world economy. *See also* GREAT BRITAIN; MAGNÚSSON, SKÚLI (1711–94).

TRADE UNIONS. The first trade unions in Iceland emerged during the last decade of the 19th century. Fishermen were the first to organize themselves from 1894 onward in the Bárufélög, which were modeled on the temperance movement. The flurry of trade union activity around and after the turn of the century, including the foundation in 1906 of Dagsbrún, for a long time the biggest union of unskilled laborers in Iceland, culminated in the establishment of the **Icelandic Federation of Labor** (IFL) in 1916. By 1940, approximately 70 to 80 percent of the working **population** belonged to unions, largely as a consequence of the strong position the unions achieved in the early 1930s. During these years, **Alþingi** passed laws securing union members a priority to work and prohibiting employers from paying wages below those negotiated by the unions. The same trend has continued since **World War II**, and in 2004, almost 150,000 people, around 90 percent of all employed persons in Iceland, were members of trade unions. The largest labor organization is the IFL, with 108,000 registered members in 2007, covering most blue-collar workers employed in the private sector. The second largest is the Bandalag starfsmanna ríkis og bæja (BSRB; Federation of State and Municipal Employees) with 19,000 members.

In its early days the trade unions concentrated their campaign on better pay, improved working conditions, unemployment benefits, and recognition of individual unions as legitimate bargaining partners. The last demand was not fully achieved until the 1930s. Increased political mobilization among the laboring classes was also a part of its goals, so the **Social Democratic Party** (SDP) was formed as the political wing of the IFL in 1916. In the early 1940s, the labor movement severed its ties with the SDP, when radical socialists and supporters of the center-right **Independence Party** demanded equal status in the IFL.

Militancy has not been widespread in the trade unions, at least not since World War II, but strikes were frequent through much of the 20th century. A tit-for-tat relationship developed between the movement and the government, the former using strikes to maintain or raise the living standards for its members, the latter in turn resorting to devaluation of **currency** to reduce the real purchasing power of wages. In recent years, labor negotiations between the IFL and the **SA-Confederation of Icelandic Employers** have broken this stalemate, and the former has accepted a limited rise in wages in return for relatively low levels of both **inflation** and unemployment. *See also* EMPLOYMENT; GOVERNMENT OF THE LABORING CLASSES; LABOR MARKET; NATIONAL COMPROMISE AGREEMENT.

TRAMPE, COUNT FREDERIK CHRISTOPHER (1779–1832).
This **Danish governor** of Iceland was born in Denmark on 19 June
1779 into an old aristocratic family. He completed a law exam from
the University of Copenhagen in 1798 and a doctoral degree from
the University of Kiel in 1801. After pursuing a short military career,
he was appointed district governor (*amtmaður*) in Iceland's western
district in 1804. Two years later, Count Trampe became governor
(*stiftamtmaður*) of Iceland, a post he held until 1810. That year, he
moved to **Norway** to take up the post of governor in Trondheim, first
representing Denmark but after 1814—as the Danish–Norwegian
union was dissolved—the Swedish king.

Count Trampe was a governor of Iceland during a turbulent and
rather unusual period in its history. He came to Iceland at a time when
Denmark was becoming involved in the Napoleonic Wars on the side
of the French emperor. Because of the British embargo on France and
all of its allies, the relations between Iceland and the mother country
were very difficult during these years. In the summer of 1809, a British soap merchant by the name of Samuel Phelps came to Iceland to
purchase tallow for his factories, but Count Trampe refused him permission to trade in Iceland. Phelps responded by deposing Trampe,
and then Phelps's Danish interpreter, **Jörgen Jörgensen**, declared
himself governor of Iceland (this has been called the **Icelandic
Revolution**, although it received almost no support from Icelanders).
Trampe was reinstated later in the summer, and the revolution had no
lasting effects on Icelandic society or Trampe's career.

TRANSPORTATION. The location of the country and the sparse-
ness of the **population** make transportation of cargo and passengers
imperative for Iceland's **economy**. Because of the lack of most raw
materials and the relative homogeneity of the economy, Icelanders
are totally dependent upon foreign **trade**. Until the late 19th century,
however, the Icelandic transportation network was extremely primitive. Roads were almost nonexistent, making the use of vehicles all
but impossible. Since then, the modernization of the economy has
brought about a total transformation of the transportation infrastructures, establishing safe and frequent communications between
various parts of the country and with the external world. The first
major bridge to be constructed in Iceland was completed in 1891,

and Iceland's first steamship company, the Eimskipafélag Íslands (**Icelandic Steamship Company**), was founded in 1914. During the 20th century, general changes in technology revolutionized the system of communications and transportation in Iceland. In this respect, the country followed a similar track with its neighboring countries. At present, Iceland is connected with both Europe and North America by air and sea, and satellites and telecommunication cables link the country directly with the continents to the east and west. This has allowed Icelanders to participate fully in the spread of information technology, and they are among the world leaders in the use of the Internet and electronic communications of various sorts. The dramatic improvement in communications has greatly enhanced economic development in Iceland, as rapid transmission of information and materials has allowed Icelandic producers to take ample advantage of international markets for their goods. *See also* ICELANDAIR.

TURKS. *See* RAID OF THE "TURKS."

– U –

UNEMPLOYMENT. *See* EMPLOYMENT.

UNION OF LIBERALS AND LEFTISTS (ULL). The president of the **Icelandic Federation of Labor, Hannibal Valdimarsson**, who had left the **People's Alliance** (PA) in the fall of 1968, founded the Samtök frjálslyndra og vinstri manna (ULL) in 1969. The goal of the new **political party** was to promote a union of all social democrats and supporters of the **cooperative movement** in a single party, but it only added to the friction on the left of the political spectrum. The party's platform called for an end to what it called the stagnated organization of the Icelandic political system and advocated shutting down the American military base in **Keflavík**.

The ULL did quite well in the 1971 **election**, receiving 9 percent of the popular vote. Following the election, the party participated in the second **Left-Wing Government**. As the government broke up in 1974, most of the leaders of the ULL left the party, either retiring from politics or joining other parties on the left, particularly the **Social Democratic Party** (SDP) and the PA. In 1978, the party participated in elections for the last time but failed to have a candidate elected to parliament. The ULL was formally dissolved in 1979. *See also* SOCIAL DEMOCRATIC ALLIANCE (SDA).

UNITED NATIONS (UN). Iceland became a member of the UN in 1946, one year after its foundation. This was the first large international organization that the young republic joined, indicating its desire to become a full participant in the international community. Since then, Iceland has been active in most of the UN's autonomous bodies, institutions, and specialized programs, maintaining permanent representatives at the headquarters in New York and the UN offices in Geneva and Vienna. As could be expected, Iceland has always focused on ocean issues and law of the sea because the Icelandic **economy** has always been heavily dependent upon the natural resources in the ocean around the island. Recently, the government of Iceland also announced its candidacy for one of the rotating seats in the UN Security Council for the 2009–10 term. If the campaign is successful, this will raise the Icelandic profile in the UN considerably.

Iceland operates two UN programs as a part of the United Nations University (UNU). Both of these training programs are in fields related to Iceland's use of its natural resources: the UNU Geothermal Training Program was founded in 1978 and has been operating since 1979, and the UNU Fisheries Training Program started its operation in 1998. Both of these programs offer postgraduate courses in research and development in the use of geothermal power and the development of the fishing industries.

UNITED STATES OF AMERICA. Apart from a massive immigration (*see* MIGRATION) to North America in the late 19th and early 20th centuries, Iceland had relatively limited contacts with the United States until **World War II**. During the war, Iceland's strategic location became obvious, however, as the country was crucial for securing transportation between the United States and Europe. For this reason, the governments of Iceland and the United States signed a treaty in June 1941, according to which the United States assumed responsibility of defending Iceland during the war while Iceland provided land for American military installations in order to facilitate transportation of goods and people over the North Atlantic. After the war, the United States attempted to prolong its military presence in Iceland, but this was unequivocally rejected by the Icelandic government. The United States handed the **Keflavík** Airport over to Icelandic authorities in 1946, but the American military was given free access to the airport. The Keflavík Airport was operated for the next five years by an American civilian company at the behest of the U.S. government. With its entry into the **North Atlantic Treaty Organization** in 1949, Iceland firmly sided with the United States in the **cold war**. This was further accentuated by a new **defense** treaty in 1951 and the return of the American military to Iceland the same year.

World War II was a watershed in the military and diplomatic relations between the United States and Iceland. Moreover, the American army brought with it cultural influences, which were to shape tastes in Icelandic popular culture for the next decades. During the war, the United States became one of Iceland's most important trading partners: around 60 percent of Iceland's imports came from the United States in the last years of the war. From the late 1940s to the late 1980s, the United States was one of the most important markets for Icelandic fish products, especially frozen cod. In recent years, the **economic** relations between the two countries have become less important than before, as Icelandic **trade** with the United States has decreased from around one third of the Icelandic exports in the early 1970s to currently just over 10 percent.

During the cold war, Iceland played a crucial role in the surveillance of the North Atlantic. This situation gave the Icelandic government certain leverage in its dealings with the United States, and it used this position frequently to its advantage. The end of the cold war changed this situation dramatically, as Russia does not pose the same military threat to the United States as the Soviet Union did before. Therefore, the United States scaled down its military presence in Iceland during the 1990s, closing down the Keflavík base in 2006. This has cast doubt on the future of the defense treaty of 1951, and Iceland has begun to look elsewhere for military support. At the moment, it is not clear how relations between the two countries will develop, but they will probably not be as close and amicable in the future as they were in the past. *See also* FOREIGN POLICY.

UNIVERSITY OF ICELAND (UoI). The largest institution of higher learning and scientific research in Iceland, called Háskóli Íslands in Icelandic. It was formally founded on 17 June 1911 in commemoration of the centennial of the birth of Icelandic national hero **Jón Sigurðsson** (1811–79). The history of the UoI goes back to the mid-19th century to the Theological College—which later became the faculty of theology of the university—founded in **Reykjavík** in 1847. Almost three decades later, in 1876, a medical school was opened in Reykjavík and, in 1908, with the foundation of a law school in Reykjavík, the three most popular fields of university studies of the time could be pursued in Iceland. In 1911, each of these three colleges formed a separate faculty in the UoI, in addition to one new faculty, the faculty of humanities. The UoI was, from the beginning, open equally to men and **women**.

The university has grown steadily since its founding, from 45 students and 11 professors in its first year to around 10,000 students and 900 teachers, administrators, and researchers in 2007. In 2008, the UoI will grow even further as it will merge with the Iceland University of **Education** under the name of the UoI. With this change, the student numbers will grow to around 12,000 and the number of staff to around 1,100.

Presently, the UoI is divided into 11 faculties (business administration and **economics**, engineering, humanities, law, medicine, natural sciences, nursing, dentistry, pharmacy, social sciences, and theology). Each of these faculties offers advanced education in its specific fields and serves as a center of research in the country. As the great majority of the academic staff at the UoI has earned their graduate degrees abroad, the UoI has always maintained strong links with foreign universities. In recent years, it has also actively participated in student and teacher exchanges and cooperative research organized and funded by the **Nordic Council** and the **European Union**.

The UoI is a public university and receives most of its funding directly from the state. The UoI is not allowed to charge its students tuition fees, as all public education in Iceland is to be free of charge. Formally, the UoI is placed under the **Ministry** of Education, but in reality, it is fairly independent in the control of its internal affairs. Its president (rector) is elected by the staff and students, and the university has full authority over the appointment of its academic and professional staff. *See also* MENNTASKÓLINN Í REYKJAVÍK.

URBANIZATION. Until the late 19th century, Icelanders lived almost entirely in rural areas, residing on individual farmsteads spread throughout the inhabitable parts of the country. In 1901, only 16 percent of the Icelandic **population** lived in towns and villages with more than 500 inhabitants. At that time, **Reykjavík** was by far the largest town in Iceland, with approximately 6,600 inhabitants. However, a radical transformation of demographic patterns was already underway at this time, which was to revolutionize Icelandic society during the first half of the 20th century. From the mid-19th century, population pressure in the rural areas had forced a growing number of Icelanders to seek their livelihood outside the traditional **economic** spheres. As a result, small fishing villages emerged around the coast, and a considerable number of Icelanders immigrated (*see* MIGRATION) to North America. This urbanization has continued more or less continuously to the present. In 1930, more than half of the population lived in towns and villages with over 500 inhabitants; in 1960, this number had increased to around three quarters of the population, and in 2007, less than 1 in 10 Icelanders lived in rural areas or villages with less than 500 inhabitants. Today, three towns in Iceland have over 20,000 inhabitants, forming together one urban core on the southwest corner of the country: Reykjavík, Kópavogur, and Hafnarfjörður. The largest town outside of the Reykjavík area is **Akureyri** in the north, with just over 17,000 inhabitants. Reykjavík is still by far the largest city in Iceland, with 118,000 inhabitants in 2007.

The rapid decline of rural areas and the growth of towns began in spite of fierce opposition from most of the leading figures of Icelandic society. Social commentators in the late 19th and the early 20th centuries opined that this development would inevitably lead to moral degeneration of the Icelandic nation and a corruption of the national character. The demographic transformation went rather smoothly, however, as **industrialization** of the fishing industry and expansion of the service sector have provided the towns with a solid economic base. Many problems concerning population patterns are unsolved, though, because economic development seems to favor a continued concentration of the population in the capital area, threatening a total social and economic breakdown in many of the less-populated areas of the country. *See also* REGIONAL POLICY.

– V –

VALDIMARSSON, HANNIBAL (1903–91). Politician and labor leader, Valdimarsson was born into a farming family on 1 January 1903 in **Ísafjörður** County in northwest Iceland. After completing a high school exam in **Akureyri** in 1922, he studied at a **Danish** teacher college, passing a teaching exam in 1927. Upon returning to Iceland, he served as a teacher and headmaster in various elementary schools until 1931. Then he became a clerk for the cooperative branch in the town of Ísafjörður, where he worked for seven years. In 1938, he was appointed head of Ísafjörður's high school, a position he held until 1954, when he was **elected** president of the powerful **Icelandic Federation of Labor**.

At that time, Valdimarsson had been engaged in labor politics for a long time, beginning as the president of the **trade union** in Súðavík, a small village close to Ísafjörður, from 1930 to 1931. In 1932, he was elected to the same post for the union in Ísafjörður, holding that office until 1939. From 1934 to 1954, he served as president of the federation of labor in the Western Fjords district. Work for the trade unions helped him to launch a political career. He was first elected to parliament for the **Social Democratic Party** (SDP) in 1946, sitting continuously in **Alþingi** until he retired from public life in 1974. Valdimarsson was chairman of the SDP from 1952 to 1954, but in 1956, he headed a splinter group of radical members of the SDP who had resigned from the party. This group formed an electoral alliance with the **Socialist Unity Party** called the **People's Alliance** (PA). Valdimarsson served as chairman of the PA from its foundation in 1956 to 1968, when he left to form a new political organization, the **Union of Liberals and Leftists** (ULL). The party did quite well in the 1971 elections under Valdimarsson's leadership, putting him in a key position in forming a government. Valdimarsson held ministerial posts in two **Left-Wing Governments**; first he served as minister of **health** and social affairs for the PA in 1956–58 and then as minister of communications and social affairs for the ULL in 1971–73.

Valdimarsson resigned from the **cabinet** in 1973, retiring from politics the following year. Valdimarsson was a popular politician and a sincere advocate of working-class interests. His professed political mission was to unite the **political parties** on the left in one social democratic party, but in the long run, his actions only increased the confusion existing among those left of the political spectrum.

VALDIMARSSON, HÉÐINN (1892–1948). This social-democratic leader and **economist** was born on 26 May 1892 to the editor and one of the founders of the Icelandic **women**'s rights movement, **Bríet Bjarnhéðinsdóttir**. Valdimarsson graduated from the secondary school in **Reykjavík** in 1911, completing a degree in economics from the University of Copenhagen six years later. In 1917, upon returning to Iceland, he was appointed chief administrator of the Government Import Authority (GIA), a state enterprise established to organize the Icelandic import trade during **World War I**. In 1926, when the GIA was abolished, Valdimarsson became director of the State Tobacco Monopoly, but from 1928 until his death in 1948, he served as director of the Olíuverslun Íslands (Icelandic Oil Company)—the Icelandic branch of British Petroleum.

Valdimarsson became active in the **Social Democratic Party** (SDP) soon after he returned from his studies in Copenhagen, serving as president of Dagsbrún, the union of unskilled laborers in Reykjavík, for 15 years between 1922 and 1942. He sat in parliament for Reykjavík from 1927 to 1942, first for the SDP and later for the **Socialist Unity Party** (SUP). While a member of the SDP, Valdimarsson belonged to a radical faction of the party, although he did not defect with the radicals who founded the **Communist Party of Iceland** (CPI) in 1930. In 1937–38, he was among those who advocated a merger of the SDP and the CPI, forming a socialist front against fascism in Iceland. Most of his fellow social democrats disapproved of the idea, however, and in 1938, the SDP expelled him from its ranks. The same year, Valdimarsson and his supporters from the SDP established the SUP with the CPI, and he was **elected** its first chairman. Only a year later, in 1939, Valdimarsson resigned from the SUP in protest against the party's support of the Soviet invasion of Finland. This spelled the real end of Valdimarsson's political career, and he retired from politics in 1942.

VATNAJÖKULL. The largest glacier in Europe (in volume) is located in southeastern Iceland. It is around 8,300 square kilometers (3,200 square miles) in size, covering a large plateau, with valleys and mountain peaks in between. The glacier is around 420 meters (1,365 feet) thick on average, but the maximum thickness is around 1,000 meters (3,300 feet). For the most part, the glacier stands at 1,400 to 1,800 meters (4,600–6,000 feet) above sea level, but Hvannadalshnjúkur, the highest mountain peak in Iceland (2,110 meters, or 6,950 feet), is in Öræfajökull glacier, which extends to the south from Vatnajökull. Many volcanic outbreaks have taken place under Vatnajökull, and Grímsvötn, one of the largest geothermal areas in Iceland, is under the glacier. In former times, few people dared to venture out on the glacier, but today it has become both a **tourist** attraction and a field for numerous scientific expeditions. In 2007, **Alþingi** passed a law founding the Vatnajökull National Park. The park includes the whole glacier and the surrounding area. It will be one of the largest national parks in Europe, with around 15,000 square kilometers, around 10 percent of the surface of Iceland.

VESTMANNA ISLANDS. An archipelago consisting of 15 to 18 small islands, about 12 kilometers (7.5 miles) off the southern coast of Iceland. Heimaey, the largest island in the group, has been inhabited since the **Settlement Period**, and some archaeologists have contended that its habitation preceded the main Norse settlement on the Icelandic mainland. As Heimaey has an excellent natural harbor and as the islands are close to fertile fishing grounds, the Vestmanna Islands have always been one of the most important centers for Icelandic **fisheries**.

All of the Vestmanna Islands were formed through volcanic eruptions from a fissure that extends from the southern coast of Iceland into the Atlantic Ocean. In recent decades, two major eruptions have taken place in this area; in 1963, an eruption began under the sea a few kilometers south of Heimaey, forming a new island called Surtsey. A decade later, another eruption started just east of the town on Heimaey. The inhabitants, 5,300 in all, were narrowly rescued in boats and evacuated to the mainland. During the next few months, portions of the town went under lava, but a substantial part of it was saved through an effort to cool down the lava. At the end of the eruption, people returned to the Vestmanna Islands, as the harbor had been saved from the lava flow. Today, Heimaey has regained its former status as a major fishing harbor, although the town is not as large as it was before the 1973 eruption.

VÍDALÍN, JÓN (1666–1720). A **Lutheran** bishop and author of **religious** sermons. Vídalín was born to a pastor in southwestern Iceland on 21 March 1666. He studied at the **Skálholt** seminary from 1679 to 1682. For the following years, he continued his studies under private tutors, enrolling in the University of Copenhagen in 1687. After completing a degree in theology in 1689, Vídalín enlisted in the **Danish** army, where he served for two years. In 1691, Vídalín returned to Iceland to work for the bishop in Skálholt. From 1691 to 1697, he served as a pastor in Iceland, first for Skálholt Cathedral but later in the parish where he was born. In 1697, Vídalín returned to Skálholt when the bishop named him his assistant. The following year, Vídalín succeeded the bishop of Skálholt, serving the diocese until his death in 1720.

Vídalín, who lost his father at an early age, was raised in relative poverty. Through his intelligence and perseverance, he was able to reach the highest post in the Icelandic church hierarchy. His greatest gift was his oratory. This is clearly demonstrated in his book of sermons (*Vídalínspostilla*), for which he is best known. A thundering attack on human vices and the shortcomings of human society, the book is written in a forceful style and was widely read in Iceland during the 18th and 19th centuries. It was instrumental in shaping the religious ideas in Iceland of the period. *See also* LITERATURE.

VIÐEY. A small island in Kollafjörður, just off **Reykjavík**'s harbor. In the late Middle Ages, it was home to the wealthiest monastery in Iceland, founded in 1226 but abolished with the **Lutheran Reformation** in the mid-16th century. After the Reformation, the **Danish king** appropriated Viðey with the property of other **religious** houses in Iceland. This led to its decline, but the island regained some of its former glory when **Skúli Magnússon**, the royal treasurer of Iceland from 1749 to 1793, made it his home in the mid-18th century. At Magnússon's request, the royal authorities had one of the first stone houses in Iceland built on the island from 1753 to 1755, designed by a Danish architect in the style of a Danish manor house. Later in the 18th century, **Ólafur Stefánsson**, the governor of Iceland, moved to the island and, after him, his son **Magnús Stephensen** (1762–1833), chief justice of the **high court** in Reykjavík. For a short period during Stephensen's time, Viðey became a cultural center, as he operated Iceland's only printing press on the island, publishing **literature** on various subjects. In the early 20th century, Viðey played a new role because one of the first trawler companies in Iceland had its headquarters there from 1907 to 1914, but from 1913, with construction of a new harbor in Reykjavík, the fishing port of Viðey gradually declined. Today, Viðey is mostly deserted, but it remains a popular **tourist** attraction, especially since the town of Reykjavík restored the 18th-century stone house and turned it into a restaurant.

VÍNLAND. In the late 10th century, around the year 986, Viking expansion continued west from Iceland to **Greenland**, where people of Norse extraction lived at least until the early 15th century. After only a few years in the new place, the settlers of Greenland came upon a land farther to the west, that is, the North American mainland. Around the year 1000, the son of the first European settler of Greenland, a man by the name of **Leifur Eiríksson**, explored the coast of a land he named Vínland (the name means either "vine land" or "meadow land"). After spending the winter in this new place, he returned home to Greenland. In the following decades, Greenlanders made a few attempts to settle the "new world," but these ventures were all abandoned, leaving no permanent Norse settlement in present-day Canada and the **United States**.

The explorations of Vínland are described in two Icelandic **sagas**, *Grænlendinga saga* (*The Saga of Greenlanders*) and *Eiríks saga rauða* (*The Saga of Eric the Red*), both of which were composed in Iceland in the 13th century. Based on oral legends, these stories give neither a consistent account of the events nor a secure location for Vínland. Archaeologists have, however, excavated a Norse settlement on the northern tip of the Great Northern Peninsula in Newfoundland at a place called L'Anse aux Meadows, and there are clear indications from the findings there that its inhabitants had at least some contacts with regions farther south in the St. Lawrence River Valley.

– W –

WELFARE STATE. Through most of Icelandic history, the state took almost no part in supporting the poor. The family or the kin group had the responsibility to maintain all of its members, but when they were unable to do so, the local **commune** (*hreppur*) where the pauper had legal residence took over. With increased **urbanization** and a growing working class in the towns, there was mounting pressure on the state to secure minimum **health** insurance for its citizens. The first step in this direction was the foundation of state-guaranteed insurance funds for victims of **industrial** accidents in 1903, but the first comprehensive social insurance legislation was not passed until 1936. The law was passed at the behest of the **Social Democratic Party**, which demanded welfare reform when it entered the **Government of the Laboring Classes** with the **Progressive Party** in 1934. With this legislation, about half of the Icelandic **population** was covered by a state-organized health care plan, and the foundations for a general retirement and disability compensation plan were laid, as well as other welfare schemes.

The development of the Icelandic welfare state has been rapid since **World War II**. The general trend has been to expand the system into new areas of health and **educational** services, covering all Icelanders regardless of their financial means. Today, the welfare system is of similar nature to those in the other Nordic countries, and no country in the world spends as high of a percentage of its gross domestic product on public expenditures in education and health (16.4 percent in 2002–5). Low rates of unemployment (*see* EMPLOYMENT) and peculiar age structure in Iceland set their mark on the Icelandic welfare system, as high birth rates since **World War II** lower the ratio of elderly people in the total population. As in the other Nordic countries, the basic premises of the system are that the state provides all Icelanders with health care services for a minimum fee; it provides all of its citizens with pension insurance; and most of the educational institutions, from elementary school to universities, are either free of charge or demand only a fairly low registration fee. The welfare system remains among the most important issues in Icelandic politics. There is almost a complete consensus on its general principles, including the idea of a state-funded health system, but the parties disagree on how generous the system should be and to what extent people are required to pay for their education and health care.

WHALING. At the end of the 16th century, whalers from the Basque country of northern Spain and the southwest coast of France began to frequent Icelandic waters. Until then, only limited whaling had been pursued around the coast because Icelanders did not possess the techniques to hunt whales. Modern, industrialized whaling began in Iceland in the latter half of the 19th century, especially after the first **Norwegian** whaling station began operations in Iceland in 1883. From that year until a whaling moratorium in Icelandic waters came into effect in 1916, it is estimated that Norwegian whalers processed over 17,000 whales in its Icelandic factories, or over 500 whales each year on average. The whaling ban, which had originally been passed in **Alþingi** in 1913, was lifted in 1928, but whaling began in earnest after **World War II** with the foundation of the first Icelandic whaling company, Hvalur (Whale), in 1949. From 1949 to 1985, over 14,000 whales of larger species (primarily finback, sperm whale, and sei whale) were brought to land in Iceland, in addition to up to around 200 minke whales a year.

In 1982, the International Whaling Commission (IWC) suspended all commercial whaling in the world, effective from the beginning of 1986. This decision was very unpopular in Iceland because the scientific evidence to support a total ban on whaling was disputed. In spite of the general opposition to the whaling ban, a one-vote majority in Alþingi agreed to not oppose the IWC's moratorium, passing instead a resolution allowing for limited whaling for scientific purposes from 1986 to 1989. This policy was vigorously protested by such international **environmental** groups as Greenpeace, and in November 1986, members of the radical environmentalist organization Sea Shepherd sank two whaling boats in **Reykjavík**'s harbor. From the end of 1989 to 2003, the moratorium on whaling was respected in Iceland, albeit very reluctantly. Under pressure from interest groups in the **fisheries,** the government resumed the scientific whaling program in 2003, and in 2006, it allowed commercial whaling again. So far, the whaling has been limited in scope, both because they have not enjoyed universal support in Iceland and because there is an insufficient market for whale products.

Until very recently, commercial whaling enjoyed overwhelming support in Iceland because the opinions of those who opposed whale hunting were branded as unscientific and overly sentimental. Supporters of whaling have pointed out that according to most recent estimates, there are over 40,000 common minke whales in the Icelandic coastal waters and almost 26,000 fin whales, and controlled hunting would not put these species in any danger. There are, however, signs of changing attitudes in Iceland on this issue, both because whaling makes little **economic** sense and because people from the **tourist** industry have vigorously opposed it. One reason for this is the recent expansion in whale watching in Iceland, which has become a major tourist attraction all around the country. Many fear that whaling will undermine this development and thus sacrifice an important economic activity for limited gain.

WOMEN. Until the early 20th century, women in Iceland—as in all other European countries—had almost no civil rights in the public arena. The home was seen as their lawful place, and they were not allowed to take part in democratic politics or hold public offices of any kind as they began to develop in the first part of the 19th century. This does not mean that Icelandic women were powerless, though, as farmers' wives controlled some of the most important functions of their households, and widows could serve as household heads on their farms. During the late 19th century, ideas about women's rights began to emerge in Iceland, reflecting similar development in neighboring countries. In 1874, the first special school for women was founded in **Reykjavík,** and during the next decades, many such institutions were established around the country. But it was only in 1886 that women were allowed to complete examinations from the secondary school in Reykjavík or to study at the colleges of theology and medicine, and they were barred from holding public offices until 1911. The **University of Iceland,** founded in 1911, was open to women from the beginning, though.

Icelandic women received their first formal political rights as early as 1882, when farming widows were allowed to vote in local **elections**. This was a fairly insignificant step because it franchised only a tiny group of women, and they could not be elected to the local councils. This step indicated, though, that the leaders of Icelandic politics did not regard gender discrimination as inevitable or as a fact of nature. Twenty-five years later in 1907 came the first real breakthrough, as women were given equal political rights to men in local elections in the towns of Reykjavík and Hafnarfjörður, and in 1909, these rights were extended to all the local councils in the country.

Things moved much slower in parliamentary elections in spite of vigorous campaigns for women's rights by suffragettes, like **Bríet Bjarnhéðinsdóttir**, and radical representatives in **Alþingi**, including **Skúli Thoroddsen**, from the late 1880s and onward. In 1915, parliament finally gave in, passing a constitutional amendment granting women over the age of 40 the right to vote and to serve in parliament. In 1920, age restrictions for women were abolished, and all formal gender-based discrimination in politics had finally been eliminated.

In the beginning, women used their rights very actively, offering special lists both in local and parliamentary elections. They won their greatest victory in 1908, when four women were elected to the city council of Reykjavík from an all-female list. The first female representative to parliament was also elected from a similar list in 1922, but after that, women faded more or less totally from the political scene. It was only with the formation of the **Women's Alliance** (WA) in the early 1980s that this began to change because the popularity of the WA forced the traditional **political parties** to place women in secure seats on their lists, increasing the number of female representatives in parliament from 3 in 1971 (out of 60, 5 percent) to 15 in 1991 (out of 63, 24 percent). Today, Icelandic politics seem to be slowly heading toward gender equality, although there is still a long way to go. In 2007, one third of the representatives in Alþingi were women (21 out of 63), as well as 4 out of 12 members of **Geir H. Haarde**'s coalition government.

The great progress in gender equality in Icelandic politics can, without a doubt, be traced to the radical feminism of the 1970s, which culminated in a one-day general strike of Icelandic women in 1975 and in the election of **Vigdís Finnbogadóttir** as the fourth

president of Iceland in 1980. The goal was to eliminate all gender discrimination in the country and to tear down the explicit and implicit barriers to the social advancement of women. This has had considerable impact, as participation rates of women in the Icelandic **labor market** are among the highest in the world, and close to two thirds of university students are women. Women have also increasingly set their mark on Icelandic cultural life, with musician **Björk Guðmundsdóttir**, who is certainly the best-known contemporary Icelander, leading the way.

This does not mean that women have reached total equality in Iceland because although gender discrimination is illegal, the average salaries of women are persistently lower than those paid to men, and women are mostly absent from the highest echelons of the business world. This is, of course, not only an Icelandic problem, and the country has fared relatively well when compared with its neighbors. This can be seen from the fact that Iceland is in the first place on the gender-related development index calculated by the United Nation Development Program. *See also* GÍSLADÓTTIR, INGIBJÖRG SÓLRÚN (1954–); ICELANDIC SOCIETY FOR WOMEN'S RIGHTS (ISWR); SIGURÐARDÓTTIR, JÓHANNA (1942–).

WOMEN'S ALLIANCE (WA). Although Icelandic **women** received equal political rights through two constitutional amendments in 1915 and 1920, their political influence remained fairly limited for most of the 20th century. For example, from the time that the first woman was **elected** to parliament in 1922 until the early 1980s, only 12 women in all had been elected to the parliament. In the local elections of 1982, a group of women in **Reykjavík** revived the idea of presenting a separate women's list, something that had been practiced in local and parliamentary elections in Iceland from 1908 to 1926. In March 1983, following these local elections, a group of women formed a political organization they called the Kvennalistinn (WA) with the express purpose of increasing women's participation in Icelandic politics. The WA presented candidates in three districts in the parliamentary elections of 1983, receiving 7.6 percent of the votes cast in these districts, enough support to give the party three representatives in **Alþingi**. Four years later, the WA offered lists in all eight parliamentary districts, doubling its support and its number of representatives.

This support declined to around 8 percent of the votes cast in 1991, but the WA remained a force to be reckoned with. The WA presented a list for the last time in 1995, polling only around 5 percent of the popular vote, and barely got three women elected to parliament. The WA was abolished in 1999, as most of its leaders either joined the **Social Democratic Alliance** or retired from politics.

The WA had a clear impact on Icelandic politics during the 1980s and 1990s. The proportion of women sitting in parliament and local councils rose markedly from the late 1970s to the early 21st century, from around 5 percent to over 30 percent. In the beginning, this was clearly a direct result of the policy of the WA to offer only women as candidates on its lists, which later forced other **political parties** to meet the challenge and seek more gender balance on their tickets.

The WA was the first political organization since the 1930s seriously undermining the pattern of four political parties in Iceland. Their success was based primarily on the fact that their objectives found a strong resonance among the voters, particularly women. But the WA also challenged the foundation of the Icelandic political system, refusing to be placed into the traditional left–right spectrum and rejecting the practice of transforming their political movement into a traditional party institution. Unlike the other parties, the WA elected no chairperson, and it limited the time its representatives could sit in parliament to two terms in order to secure a regular renewal in its parliamentary group. *See also* BJARNHÉÐINSDÓTTIR, BRÍET (1856–1940); ICELANDIC SOCIETY FOR WOMEN'S RIGHTS (ISWR).

WORLD CHESS CHAMPIONSHIP OF 1972. On 11 July 1972, the world chess championship between the reigning champion, Boris Spassky from the Soviet Union, and the challenger, American Bobby Fischer, started in an indoor sporting arena in **Reykjavík**. This event focused world attention on Iceland because of the political implications of the match at the height of the **cold war**. Since the end of **World War II**, the chess world had been dominated by the Soviet Union, and Soviet authorities had no desire to surrender their dominance to an American challenger. The championship, which has been called the "Match of the Century," was characterized by both Fischer's erratic behavior and his brilliant games. Fischer failed to come to the opening ceremony and only showed up after being pressured by Henry Kissinger, President Richard Nixon's national security advisor. Fischer lost the first match and forfeited the second after protesting the presence of cameras inside the playing hall, and most believed that the match was over. But after Spassky had conceded to Fischer's request of playing the third game in a small backstage room, Fischer turned the championship in his favor. On 3 September, Fischer was crowned world champion, winning the championship by 12.5 points against Spassky's 8.5 in 21 matches.

In spite of the political undertones, the championship of 1972 was, first and foremost, a clash of very dissimilar personalities. Spassky may have lost his title, but he gained the respect of everyone for his sportsmanship and courteous behavior, while Fischer appeared both arrogant and unreasonable in his demands. No one doubted, however, who was the better chess player, and some predicted that Fischer would retain the title for decades.

WORLD WAR I. Although Iceland remained neutral in World War I, the war had considerable effects on Icelandic society. At its beginning, for example, **Denmark** was still Iceland's most important trading partner, as it had been from the days of the hated **monopoly trade** of the 17th and 18th centuries. This caused considerable annoyance in London, especially as the British government suspected Danish merchants of reexporting Icelandic products to Germany for high prices. In order to strengthen its **trade** embargo on Germany, the British government forced Icelanders to accept British control of their foreign trade. A special treaty between the minister of the Icelandic **home rule** and the British government was signed in London on 16 May 1916, formalizing this arrangement. The treaty stipulated that all vessels leaving Iceland for countries other than the **United States** had to pass through a British contraband control base. Furthermore, the treaty prohibited Icelanders from exporting such products as salt fish, fish oils, mutton, wool, and hides to all countries that shared borders with Germany or bordered either on the Baltic or the North Sea—including Denmark and Sweden. At the same time, the British government agreed to supply Icelanders with such staple goods as coal and salt and to purchase Icelandic products that could not be sold on the open market. To guarantee Iceland's compliance with the treaty, the British government dispatched a special envoy to Iceland, who was to serve as a consul in **Reykjavík**, overseeing all foreign trade.

During the first years of World War I, Iceland benefited considerably from rising export prices, but this trend was reversed as the war progressed. As a result of increasing German submarine warfare, it became difficult for **Great Britain** to fulfill the obligations it had agreed to earlier. Moreover, import prices in Iceland rose more rapidly than export prices, as the British government fixed the latter while the former followed general trends in international trade. For this reason, Iceland suffered a severe **economic** crisis at the end of the war. The war had, however, positive effects on the political situation because it forced Icelanders to be more independent in their **foreign policy** and lessened their economic dependency on Denmark. These factors were important in convincing Icelanders that political independence was not only feasible but also possible, a sentiment they clearly expressed in negotiations leading to the **Act of Union** in 1918. Iceland gained full sovereignty on 1 December 1918, less than a month after an armistice between Germany and the allied forces ended the war.

WORLD WAR II. In spite of Iceland's declaration of permanent neutrality in 1918, the country did not escape the effects of World War II. After the German occupation of **Denmark** in April 1940, the British government alerted its Icelandic counterpart of the danger that Iceland could also fall under German rule. A month later, on 10 May 1940, British Royal Marines landed at **Reykjavík** and declared the country occupied. The Icelandic government filed a formal complaint reiterating its neutrality, but it cooperated fully with the occupying forces from the beginning.

Because of its strategic location, Iceland became an important Allied naval and air base, playing a crucial role in the battle for the Atlantic Ocean. It also served as a station on the new air route between North America and the British Isles. In July 1941, almost half a year before the **United States** entered the war, American forces took over the military protection of Iceland according to a defense treaty made with Icelandic authorities the preceding month. The British, however, continued air and naval operations in Iceland throughout the war.

Relations between the foreign military forces and the Icelandic **population** were peaceful for the most part. In fact, the war had very positive effects on the Icelandic **economy**, as construction of military installations and the extensive services required by the soldiers ended the chronic unemployment (*see* EMPLOYMENT) that had plagued Iceland since the **Great Depression**. As a result, towns like Reykjavík grew rapidly during the war, and Icelanders were generally more prosperous than ever before at the end of World War II. The country was not untouched by the tragedies of the time, though. A number of Icelandic sailors perished at sea when German submarines and aircraft attacked Icelandic fishing vessels and cargo ships on the Atlantic Ocean between Iceland and **Great Britain**.

World War II entirely changed Iceland's position on the international scene. The German occupation of Denmark prompted the Icelandic parliament to entrust the government of Iceland with royal powers and later to replace the **king** temporarily with a special governor of Iceland (*ríkisstjóri*). From that time, Iceland had practically severed all of its ties with the Danish monarchy, a step that was finalized with the foundation of the republic in 1944. During the war, Iceland's military significance became obvious, and this fact greatly enhanced its status in such organizations as the **North Atlantic Treaty Organization** during the **cold war**. *See also* FOREIGN POLICY; KEFLAVÍK; REPUBLIC OF ICELAND.

– Y –

YOUTH ASSOCIATIONS. During the early 20th century, a number of youth associations were established in Iceland primarily following a **Norwegian** model. The aim of these associations was to cultivate patriotism in Iceland and encourage optimism and healthy lifestyles among the young. This was very much in the **nationalistic** spirit of early 20th-century Iceland, where a strong connection was made between cultivation of the country and the cultural well-being of the people. The first association was founded in the town of **Akureyri** in 1906, and the Ungmennafélag Íslands [Federation of Icelandic Youth Associations (FIYA)] was established the following year. These societies flourished in the next decades, spreading all over the country. They organized sporting events, discussion groups, and planting of trees and encouraged temperance. Today, the youth associations focus primarily on sports, although they also serve as an important platform for other cultural activities in the rural areas of the country. Since 1940, the FIYA organizes national games every third or fourth year, where representatives from the different associations in the FIYA compete in a wide variety of events. At present, over 260 associations with around 80,000 members organized in 19 regional unions form the FIYA.

– Þ–

ÞINGVELLIR. Þingvellir, or the Assembly Plains in literal translation, was the site for the general assembly called **Alþingi**, meeting annually from around 930 until its abolishment at the end of the 18th century. On rocky plains at the northern tip of Iceland's largest lake, Þingvallavatn, people from all over the country assembled for a few weeks in the summer to debate legal and political issues and to hold the highest court in the country. It was there that they made the most important decisions concerning government, including the **conversion to Christianity** around the year 1000 and an alliance with the **Norwegian king** in 1262–64.

Originally, Þingvellir was chosen for its geographic location because it is placed at a crossing where important routes connecting Iceland's northern, western, and southern parts meet. But as Þingvellir is not situated by the sea and is not well suited for **agriculture** of any sort, no permanent town formed at this center of Icelandic public life. Therefore, when a new **elected** Alþingi was established in 1843–45, it was not placed at Þingvellir but in the burgeoning capital, **Reykjavík**. This decision evoked strong controversy at the time, but it was in line with the general policy of the **Danish** government to create a definite administrative center for the country. Þingvellir has, however, retained its symbolic value, as it still holds a sacred place as a site of national memory in Iceland. During the struggle for independence, for example, representatives from all over the country frequently met at Þingvellir to formulate their demands. The sacred status of Þingvellir is also reflected in the fact that it was designated as Iceland's first national park in 1928, and it was there that Alþingi assembled on 17 June 1944 to establish the **Republic of Iceland**. Moreover, it has been the place for the most important national festivals in Iceland since the late 19th century, such as the celebration of the 1,000th anniversaries of the settlement of Iceland in 1874 and of Alþingi in 1930, the 11th centenary of the Icelandic settlement in 1974, the 50th anniversary of the Icelandic republic in 1994, and the 1,000th anniversary of the conversion to Christianity in 2000. Þingvellir National Park was declared a World Heritage Site by the **United Nations Educational**, Scientific, and Cultural Organization in 2004.

ÞJÓÐFUNDUR. *See* CONSTITUTIVE ASSEMBLY.

ÞJÓÐVAKI. A **political party** established before the 1995 parliamentary **elections**. Þjóðvaki (National Awakening) was formed around **Jóhanna Sigurðardóttir**, former minister of social affairs and deputy chairwoman of the **Social Democratic Party** (SDP). The party platform called for efforts to increase social equality and unity of all *félagshyggjufólk* ("socially minded" people) in one political movement. According to opinion polls, Þjóðvaki had considerable support in the weeks prior to the 1995 elections, but as it turned out, it received only 7 percent of the votes cast and had four representatives elected to **Alþingi**. After the elections, the party more or less dissolved, as its parliamentary group united with the SDP and took part in forming the **Social Democratic Alliance** in 1999. After that, Þjóðvaki was formally abolished.

ÞÓRARINSSON, SIGURÐUR (1912–83). Iceland's best-known geologist. He was born on 8 January 1912 to a farming family in Vopnafjörður in northeastern Iceland. He attended secondary school in **Akureyri**, enrolling in the University of Copenhagen in 1931. The following year, Þórarinsson moved to Stockholm, where he defended his doctoral dissertation in geology in 1944. In 1945, right before the end of the **World War II**, Þórarinsson returned to Iceland. First he worked as a researcher for the Icelandic Science Council, but from 1947 to 1969, he served as the director of the Icelandic Natural Museum. In 1969, he was appointed the first professor of geography and geology at the **University of Iceland**, a position he held until his retirement in 1982.

As was quite fitting for an Icelandic geologist, Þórarinsson specialized in the study of glaciers and volcanoes. He was a pioneer in using layers of volcanic ash from single eruptions, or tephra, to date archaeological findings (tephrochronology). This method has proven invaluable for Icelandic archaeologists and has been used, where it is applicable, in many other places in the world. For decades, Þórarinsson was one of the leading experts of volcanology in the world, and he paved the way for the development of the scientific study of geology in Iceland.

ÞÓRÐARSON, STURLA (1214–84). The great 13th-century historical chronicler, Þórðarson was born on 29 July 1214 into one of the leading families of the 13th century, the Sturlung family. At an early age, he became involved in the complex political intrigues of the period, something he was destined to as a member of the Sturlung family. He is remembered, however, more for his literary contributions than his political deeds. He wrote a large part of the *Sturlunga Saga* compilation, the most significant part of which is *Íslendinga Saga* (*History of Icelanders*). This is a chronicle of the period from the death of Þórðarson's grandfather and namesake until the end of the **Commonwealth Period** in 1264. A 17th-century copy of his version of the *Book of Settlements* also exists. In addition to these writings, Magnús Hákonarson, **King** of **Norway** (1263–80), hired Þórðarson to write a chronicle of his rule and his father's life. Þórðarson's historical writings give a remarkably balanced picture of the period, especially when it is considered that he was an active participant in some of the key events he describes. During his last years, Þórðarson was known as a **lawman**. He served as a **lawman** from 1277 to 1282, and he assisted with the revision of the Icelandic law codes after the country entered into union with Norway. *See also* AGE OF THE STURLUNGS; LITERATURE; STURLUSON, SNORRI (1178/9–1241).

ÞÓRÐARSON, ÞÓRBERGUR (1888–1974). One of the leading writers of 20th-century Iceland. Þórðarson was born to a farmer in southeastern Iceland on 12 March 1888 but moved to **Reykjavík** as a young man. He worked as a laborer and a fisherman for a few years and studied at the Icelandic College of Teacher Training in Reykjavík from 1909 to 1910 and the **University of Iceland** on an irregular basis (1913–19). Although he never completed a university degree, Þórðarson served as a school teacher in Reykjavík for a number of years. He published his first collection of poems in 1915, but his first major work, *Bréf til Láru* (*A Letter to Laura*), was published in Reykjavík in 1924. He was best known for his autobiographical essays, which give a satirical account of his own life. Þórðarson was, to a certain extent, a paradoxical man; he was a committed socialist but also strongly influenced by eastern spiritualism; he was thoroughly rooted in Icelandic literary tradition, a master of the Icelandic **language**, and an avid collector of folklore but was also a tireless promoter of the international language Esperanto. *See also* LITERATURE.

ÞORGILSSON, ARI "THE LEARNED" (1067/8–1148). Not much is known about the life of this first chronicler of Icelandic history. From the age of seven, Þorgilsson was fostered by Hallur Þórarinsson at the farm Haukadalur, where he studied with men like Teitur Ísleifsson, the son of the first bishop in **Skálholt**. Later, Þorgilsson is believed to have served as a priest at Staður on Snæfellsnes Peninsula, although this is not known for certain. During his lifetime, he was renowned for his learning—thus he was named *hinn fróði* ("the learned")—as is evident in the *First Grammatical Treatise* and **Snorri Sturluson**'s *Heimskringla*, where his erudition is mentioned. The *Book of Icelanders* is the only surviving work that was certainly written by Þorgilsson. There, he demonstrates knowledge of Latin historical **literature**, but he chose to write his chronicle in the Icelandic vernacular, thus setting the tone for historical writing in medieval Iceland.

ÞORLÁKSSON, GUÐBRANDUR (1541/2–1627). This influential **Lutheran** bishop and **religious** leader was born either in 1541 or 1542 to a priest in northern Iceland. He attended the Latin school at **Hólar**, completing an exam in 1559 shortly after the Lutheran **Reformation** was fully victorious in Iceland. From around 1560 to 1564, Þorláksson studied at the University of Copenhagen, returning to Iceland in 1564 to become headmaster of the Latin school at **Skálholt**.

In 1565, he became a Lutheran minister in northern Iceland. Finally, in 1571, he was consecrated bishop over Hólar diocese. He served in this post until his death in 1627.

Þorláksson was a highly learned man, well versed in mathematics and geography, in addition to his knowledge of and interest in theology. He wrote extensively on religious issues, translating and publishing a great number of hymns and religious tracts. His greatest feat, however, was having the Bible translated into Icelandic and organizing its printing at Hólar (it was published in 1584). With this momentous work, he laid the foundation for the use of Icelandic as a church **language**, contributing greatly to its preservation in spite of **Danish** rule.

ÞORLÁKSSON, JÓN (1877–1935). An engineer, politician, and businessman, Þorláksson was born on 3 March 1877 in Húnavatn County in northern Iceland into a well-off farming family. He studied to become an engineer in Copenhagen from 1897 to 1903, and in 1905, the minister of Iceland appointed him *landsverkfræðingur* (chief engineer) for the Icelandic government. In 1921, he was **elected** to parliament for **Reykjavík** on a conservative ticket, and in 1924, he was instrumental in founding the **Conservative Party** (CP). He became its first and only chairman, and under his leadership, the party received over 40 percent of the popular votes in the parliamentary elections of 1927. When the **Independence Party** (IP) was formed in 1929, he was elected its first chairman, a position he held until 1934. Þorláksson was named minister of finance in 1924 and also served as **prime minister** from 1926 to 1927. He was elected mayor of Reykjavík in 1932, and two years later, he retired from parliamentary politics.

Þorláksson was one of the founders of the modern **political party** system in Iceland. As a conservative politician but a firm believer in free enterprise, he sought to organize the opponents of both the **Social Democratic Party** and the cooperative politics of the **Progressive Party** into one united political party. Although he was not a charismatic leader, Þorláksson managed to attain that goal. Under his leadership, the CP and IP became the largest political parties in Iceland, a position that the IP has held consistently to this day.

Appendix A
Political Leaders of Iceland

KINGS OF NORWAY AND ICELAND

Håkon VI Håkonsson	1262–63
Magnus VII Håkonsson	1263–80
Eric II Magnusson	1280–99
Håkon V Magnusson	1299–1319
Magnus VII Ericsson	1319–55
Håkon VI Magnusson	1355–80

KINGS OF DENMARK AND ICELAND

Olaf II	1380–87
Margaret I	1387–1412
Erik VII of Pomerania	1412–39
Christopher III of Bavaria	1440–48
Christian I	1448–81
Hans	1481–1513
Christian II	1513–23
Frederic I	1523–33
Christian III	1534–59
Frederic II	1559–88
Christian IV	1588–1648
Frederic III	1648–70
Christian V	1670–99
Frederic IV	1699–1730
Christian VI	1730–46
Frederic V	1746–66
Christian VII	1766–1808

Frederic VI	1808–39
Christian VIII	1839–48
Frederic VII	1848–63
Christian IX	1863–1906
Frederic VIII	1906–12
Christian X	1912–44

GOVERNORS (STIFTAMTMAÐUR) OF ICELAND, 1684–1873

Ulrik Christian Gyldenløve	1684–1719
Peter Raben	1719–27
Christian Gyldencrone	1728–30
Henrik Ochsen	1730–50
Otto von Rantzau	1750–68
Christian von Proeck	1768–69
Lauritz Andreas Thodal	1770–85
Hans K. D. V. von Levetzow	1785–89
Ólafur Stefánsson	1790–1806
Frederik Christopher Trampe	1806–10
Johan C. T. von Carstenschiold	1813–19
Ehrenreich Christian Ludvig Moltke	1819–23
Peder F. Hoppe	1824–29
Lorenz A. Krieger	1829–36
Carl E. Bardenfleth	1837–41
Thorkil A. Hoppe	1841–47
Mathias H. Rosenørn	1847–49
Jørgen D. Trampe	1850–60
Þórður Jónasson (temporary appointment)	1860–65
Hilmar Finsen	1865–73

GOVERNORS (LANDSHÖFÐINGI) OF ICELAND, 1873–1904

Hilmar Finsen	1873–83
Bergur Thorberg	1883–86
Magnús Stephensen	1886–1904

PRESIDENTS OF ICELAND

Sveinn Björnsson	17 June 1944–25 January 1952
Ásgeir Ásgeirsson	1 August 1952–31 July 1968
Kristján Eldjárn	1 August 1968–31 July 1980
Vigdís Finnbogadóttir	1 August 1980–31 July 1996
Ólafur Ragnar Grímsson	1 August 1996–

MINISTERS OF ICELAND, 1904–17

Hannes Hafstein (HRP)	1 February 1904–31 March 1909
Björn Jónsson (IP)	31 March 1909–14 March 1911
Kristján Jónsson (Independent)	14 March 1911–24 July 1912
Hannes Hafstein (Union Party)	25 July 1912–21 July 1914
Sigurður Eggerz (IP)	21 July 1914–4 May 1915
Einar Arnórsson (IP)	4 May 1915–4 January 1917

PRIME MINISTERS OF ICELAND, 1917–2007

Jón Magnússon (HRP)	4 January 1917–7 March 1922
Sigurður Eggerz (IP)	7 March 1922–22 March 1924
Jón Magnússon (CP)	22 March 1924–8 July 1926
Jón Þorláksson (CP)	8 July 1926–28 August 1927
Tryggvi Þórhallsson (PP)	28 August 1927–3 June 1932
Ásgeir Ásgeirsson (PP)	3 June 1932–28 July 1934
Hermann Jónasson (PP)	29 July 1934–16 May 1942
Ólafur Thors (IP)	16 May 1942–16 December 1942
Björn Þórðarson (Independent)	16 December 1942–21 October 1944
Ólafur Thors (IP)	21 October 1944–4 February 1947
Stefán J. Stefánsson (SDP)	4 February 1947–6 December 1949
Ólafur Thors (IP)	6 December 1949–14 March 1950
Steingrímur Steinþórsson (PP)	14 March 1950–11 September 1953
Ólafur Thors (IP)	11 September 1953–24 July 1956
Hermann Jónasson (PP)	24 July 1956–23 December 1958
Emil Jónsson (SDP)	23 December 1958–20 November 1959
Ólafur Thors (IP)	20 November 1959–14 November 1963

Bjarni Benediktsson (IP)	14 November 1963–10 July 1970
Jóhann Hafstein (IP)	10 July 1970–14 July 1971
Ólafur Jóhannesson (PP)	14 July 1971–28 August 1974
Geir Hallgrímsson (IP)	28 August 1974–1 September 1978
Ólafur Jóhannesson (PP)	1 September 1978–15 October 1979
Benedikt Gröndal (SDP)	15 October 1979–8 February 1980
Gunnar Thoroddsen	8 February 1980–26 May 1983
(IP-Independent)	
Steingrímur Hermannsson (PP)	26 May 1983–8 July 1987
Þorsteinn Pálsson (IP)	8 July 1987–28 September 1988
Steingrímur Hermannsson (PP)	28 September 1988–23 April 1991
Davíð Oddsson (IP)	23 April 1991–15 September 2004
Halldór Ásgrímsson (PP)	15 September 2004–15 June 2006
Geir H. Haarde (IP)	15 June 2006–

Appendix B

Population in Iceland, 1703–1 December 2007

1703	50,358
1785	40,623
1801	47,240
1840	57,094
1850	59,157
1860	66,987
1870	69,763
1880	72,445
1890	70,927
1901	78,470
1910	85,183
1920	94,690
1930	108,861
1940	121,474
1950	143,973
1960	175,680
1970	204,578
1980	229,187
1990	255,708
2000	283,361
2007	312,872

Bibliography

CONTENTS

INTRODUCTION

As the bulk of the research on Iceland has always been published in Icelandic, a bibliography emphasizing the literature on Icelandic history, society, and culture in English can only be partial and very selective. Priority was given here to books in English, but articles of fairly general nature were also included and also a considerable number of doctoral dissertations on Icelandic subjects. The bibliography includes no entries in Icelandic and only a few monographs in German and French.

The most comprehensive English-language bibliographies on Iceland are the two editions of *Iceland* in Clio's World Bibliographic Series (compiled by John Horton in 1983 and Francis R. McBride in 1996), although they are somewhat outdated. They provide annotated references to the literature up to the mid-1990s, describing monographs and articles on Icelandic history, society, and culture in English. Another useful bibliographic source is Jóhannes Nordal and Valdimar Kristinsson, eds., *Iceland 1986: Handbook* (Reykjavík: Central Bank of

Iceland, 1987) and a more recent edition of the same book by the same publisher, *Iceland: The Republic* (1996). In addition to survey articles on various aspects of Icelandic history, culture, society, and nature, they provide a selective, classified list of books on Iceland in foreign languages (including the Scandinavian languages).

On medieval history and literature, the most comprehensive survey work is Philip Pulsiano, ed., *Medieval Scandinavia: An Encyclopedia* (New York: Garland, 1993), where Iceland is well represented. Each entry, written by a leading expert, includes comprehensive bibliographic information. The excellent *Dictionary of Literary Biography: Icelandic Writers* (Farmington Hills, MI: Gale, 2004), edited by Patrick J. Stevens, provides an in-depth analysis of 19th- and 20th-century Icelandic writers, written by experts in the field and providing comprehensive bibliographies of the authors' works in English. No comprehensive surveys in English exist for other Icelandic cultural fields, but a few short descriptions, such as the series on art and culture in Iceland, edited by Bera Nordal for the Ministry of Culture, are listed in the bibliography.

For the economy, the most accessible general information is to be found in the annual booklet *The Economy of Iceland*, published by the Central Bank of Iceland. It can be accessed electronically from the website of the bank (www.sedlabanki.is) and provides a comprehensive overview of the Icelandic economy in the preceding year. The Central Bank publishes many other reports and brochures, most of which can be accessed in electronic form from their site.

On Icelandic history, the best survey in English is, without a doubt, Gunnar Karlsson's *The History of Iceland* (Minneapolis: University of Minnesota Press, 2000)—the same book has also been published as *Iceland's 1100 Years: The History of a Marginal Society* (London: C. Hurst, 2000). This is a fairly compact but comprehensive analysis of the history of Iceland from the time of the settlement in the 9th century to the end of the 20th century. Karlsson has also written a shorter version of the book called, appropriately, *A Brief History of Iceland* (Reykjavík: Mál og menning, 2000).

All major archival resources on Icelandic history and society are to be found in Iceland, mostly in Reykjavík. The National Archives of Iceland house all public documents and many private ones, dating as far back as the 12th century. All census records are stored there, and as the Lutheran Church in Iceland is a state institution, all historical church records—including parish registers, lists of births, burials, marriages, and so on—are also kept in the National Archives. Larger towns and counties have their own local archives, collecting private and public documents pertaining to the history of the respective regions. The Árni Magnússon Institute in Reykjavík preserves most of the medieval Icelandic manuscripts, while later manuscripts and personal correspondence is stored in the manuscript section of the National and University Library of Iceland. Many Icelandic manuscripts and personal documents are also found in various archives and libraries in Copenhagen, including the Royal Library and the Danish National Archives, and many Icelandic manuscripts are also stored in Swedish, Norwegian, and British libraries.

The most complete collection of Icelandic books is to be found in the National and University Library of Iceland in Reykjavík. The library has been a depository for Icelandic books since 1886 and has more or less everything that has been printed in Icelandic since the beginning of the printing age in the 16th century. The Danish Royal Library in Copenhagen and the Fiske Collection of Cornell University in Ithaca, New York, have the most complete collections of Icelandic books outside of Iceland, while the library of the University of Manitoba, Winnipeg, has also substantial holdings.

The expansion of the Internet has revolutionized people's access to information in recent years, and this certainly applies to Iceland. All major institutions, associations, and businesses in Iceland maintain websites, providing information about themselves, their history, and their mission. In most cases, the bulk of the material is in Icelandic, except when the sites are specifically aimed at non-Icelandic readers, but the majority of the larger sites have at least some information in English. The last part of the bibliography lists some of the most important websites that have information in English, but it is far from exhaustive.

I. GENERAL

A. Bibliographies and Dictionaries

Bekker-Nielsen, Hans. *Old Norse-Icelandic Studies: A Select Bibliography.* Toronto: University of Toronto Press, 1967.

Bergsveinsson, Sveinn. *Isländisch Deutsh Wörterbuch—Íslenzk—þýzk orðabók.* Leipzig, Germany: Verlag Enzyklopadie, 1967.

Bibliography of Old Norse-Icelandic Studies. Copenhagen: Munksgaard, 1963– .

Bogason, Sigurður Örn. *Ensk-íslensk orðabók (English-Icelandic Dictionary).* Reykjavík: Ísafoldarprentsmiðja, 1976.

Boots, Gerard. *Íslenzk-frönsk orðabók (Dictionnaire Islandais-français).* Reykjavík: Isafoldarprentsmiðja, 1950.

Boots, Gerard, and Þórhallur Þorgilsson. *Frönsk-íslenzk ordabók (Dictionnaire français-islandais).* Reykjavík: Ísafoldarprentsmiðja, 1953.

Brehdal-Petersen, Fredrik E. "A Bibliography for Ethnographic Research on Iceland." *Behaviour Science Research* 1 (1979): 1–35.

Brynjólfsson, Ingvar. *Isländisch–Deutsch, Deutsch–Isländisch: Langenscheits Universal Wörterbuch.* Berlin: Langenscheit, 1964.

Cleasby, Richard, and Guðbrandur Vigfússon. *An Icelandic–English Dictionary.* 2nd ed. Supplement by W. A. Craigie. Oxford: Clarendon, 1969.

Egilsson, Sveinbjörn, and Finnur Jónsson. *Lexicon poeticum antiquae linguae septentrionalis: Ordbog over det norsk-islandske Skjaldesprog.* 2nd ed. Copenhagen: Det Kongelige nordiske oldskrift-selskab, 1966.

Einarsdóttir, Anna, Árni Einarsson, Árni Sigurjónsson, Helga Ferdinandsdóttir, Valva Árnadóttir, and Þorgerður Elín Sigurðardóttir, eds. *Books on Iceland.* Reykjavík: Mál og menning, 1999.

Ellertsson, Björn. *Íslensk-þýsk orðabók (Isländisch–Deutsch Wörterbuch).* Reykjavík: Iðunn, 1993.

Fry, Donald K. *Norse Sagas Translated into English: A Bibliography.* AMS Studies in the Middle Ages, no. 3. New York: AMS Press, 1980.

Guðjónsson, Elsa E. *Bibliography of Icelandic Historical Textiles and Costumes.* Reykjavík: National Museum of Iceland, 1977.

Hannesson, Jóhann S. *Bibliography of the Eddas: A Supplement to Islandica XIII.* Islandica, no. 37. Ithaca, NY: Cornell University Press, 1955.

———. *The Sagas of Icelanders (Íslendinga sögur): A Supplement to Islandica I and XXIV.* Islandica, no. 38. Ithaca, NY: Cornell University Press, 1957.

Hermannsson, Halldór. *A Bibliography of the Eddas.* Islandica, no. 13. Ithaca, NY: Cornell University Library, 1920.

———. *Bibliography of the Icelandic Sagas and Minor Tales.* Islandica, no. 1. Ithaca, NY: Cornell University Library, 1908.

———. *Bibliography of the Sagas of the Kings of Norway and Related Sagas and Tales.* Islandica, no. 3. Ithaca, NY: Cornell University Library, 1910.

———. *Catalogue of the Icelandic Collection Bequeathed by Williard Fiske.* Ithaca, NY: Cornell University Library, 1914.

———. *Catalogue of the Icelandic Collection Bequeathed by Williard Fiske: Additions 1913–26.* Ithaca, NY: Cornell University Library, 1927.

————. *Catalogue of the Icelandic Collection Bequeathed by Williard Fiske: Additions 1927–42.* Ithaca, NY: Cornell University Library, 1943.

————. *Icelandic Books of the Seventeenth Century.* Islandica, no. 14. Ithaca, NY: Cornell University Library, 1922.

————. *Icelandic Books of the Sixteenth Century.* Islandica, no. 9. Ithaca, NY: Cornell University Library, 1916.

————. *Old Icelandic Literature: A Bibliographic Essay.* Islandica, no. 23. Ithaca, NY: Cornell University Press, 1933.

————. *The Periodical Literature of Iceland Down to the Year 1874: An Historical Sketch.* Islandica, no. 11. Ithaca, NY: Cornell University Library, 1918.

————. *The Sagas of Icelanders (Íslendingasögur): A Supplement to Bibliography of the Icelandic Sagas and Minor Tales.* Islandica, no. 24. Ithaca, NY: Cornell University Press, 1935.

Hollander, Lee Milton. *A Bibliography of Scaldic Studies.* Copenhagen: Ejnar Munksgaard, 1958.

Hólmarsson, Sverrir, Christopher Sanders, and John Tucker. *Concise Icelandic–English Dictionary.* Reykjavík: Iðunn, 1989.

Holthausen, Ferdinand. *Vergleichendes and etymologisches Wörterbuch des Altwestnordischen.* Göttingen: Vandenhoeck and Ruprecht, 1948.

Horton, John J. *Iceland.* World Bibliographic Series, no. 37. Oxford: Clio Press, 1983.

Íslensk bókaskrá (Icelandic National Bibliography): 1974–2001. Reykjavík: Landsbókasafn Íslands, 1975–2003.

Jóhannesson, Alexander. *Isländisches etymologisches Wörterbuch.* 2 vols. Bern, Switzerland: Francke, 1951–1956.

Kalinke, Marianne E. *Bibliography of Old-Icelandic Romances.* Islandica, no. 44. Ithaca, NY: Cornell University Press, 1985.

Kvaran, Böðvar, and Einar Sigurðsson. *Íslensk tímarit í 200 ár: Skrá um íslensk blöð og tímarit frá upphafi til 1973 (200 years Icelandic Periodicals: A bibliography of Icelandic Periodicals, Newspapers, and Other Serial Publications 1773–1973).* Reykjavík: Landsbókasafn Íslands, 1991.

McBride, Francis R. *Iceland.* Rev. ed. World Bibliographic Series, no. 37. Oxford: Clio Press, 1996.

Mitchell, P. M., and Kenneth H. Ober. *Bibliography of Modern Icelandic Literature in Translation, Including Works Written by Icelanders in Other Languages.* Islandica, no. 40. Ithaca, NY: Cornell University Press, 1975.

Nordal, Jóhannes, and Valdimar Kristinsson, eds. *Iceland: The Republic.* Reykjavík: Central Bank of Iceland, 1996.

————. *Iceland 1986: Handbook.* Reykjavík: Central Bank of Iceland, 1987.

Ober, Kenneth. *Bibliography of Modern Icelandic Literature in Translation (Supplement).* Islandica, no. 47. Ithaca, NY: Cornell University Press, 1990.

Ófeigsson, Jón. *Þýzk–íslenzk orðabók (Deutsch–isländisches Wörterbuch).* 3rd ed. Reykjavík: Ísafoldarprentsmiðja, 1982.

Pulsiano, Philip, ed. *Medieval Scandinavia: An Encyclopedia.* Garland Encyclopedias of the Middle Ages, no. 1. New York: Garland, 1993.

Sigurðardóttir, Þórunn. *Manuscript Material, Correspondence, and Graphic Material in the Fiske Icelandic Collection: A Descriptive Catalogue.* Islandica, no. 48. Ithaca, NY: Cornell University Press, 1994.

Sigurðsson, Arngrímur. *Icelandic–English Dictionary.* 3rd ed. Reykjavík: Prentsmiðjan Leiftur, 1980.

Sigurmundsson, Sigurður. *Spænsk–íslensk orðabók (Diccionario espanol-islandés).* 2nd ed. Reykjavík: Gutenberg, 1995.

Sörensson, Sören. *Ensk–íslensk orðabók með alfræðilegu ívafi (English–Icelandic Dictionary).* 2nd ed. Reykjavík: Mál og menning, 1999.

Tulinius, Guðrún H., Margrét Jónsdóttir, Ragnheiður Kristinsdóttir, Sigrún Á. Eiríksdóttir, Teodoro Manrique Antón, eds. *Spænsk–íslensk orðabók (Diccionario español–islandés).* Reykjavík: Mál og menning, 2007.

Turchi, Paolo Maria. *Íslensk–ítölsk orðabók (Dizionario islandese–italiano).* Reykjavík: Iðunn, 1994.

Vries, Jan de. *Altnordisches etvmologisches Wörterbuch.* Leiden: E. J. Brill, 1962.

———. *Altnordische Literaturgeschichte.* 2nd ed. Berlin: Walter de Gruyter, 1964–67.

Zoëga, G. T. *A Concise Dictionary of Old Icelandic.* Oxford: Clarendon, 1910.

———. *Ensk–íslenzk orðabók (English–Icelandic Dictionary).* 3rd ed. Reykjavík: Sigurður Kristjánsson, 1932.

———. *Íslenzk–ensk orðabók (Icelandic–English Dictionary).* 2nd ed. Reykjavík: Sigurður Kristjánsson, 1922.

B. General Information and Interdisciplinary Studies

Biays, Pierre. *L'Islande: Que sais je?* Paris: Presses universitaires de France, 1983.

Iceland Review. (1963–). A quarterly magazine on Icelandic affairs.

News from Iceland. (1975–95). A monthly periodical with highlights from Icelandic news.

Nordal, Jóhannes, and Valdimar Kristinsson, eds. *Iceland: The Republic.* Reykjavík: Central Bank of Iceland, 1996.

———. *Iceland 1874–1974: Handbook Published by the Central Bank of Iceland on the Occasion of the Eleventh Centenary of the Settlement of Iceland.* Reykjavík: Central Bank of Iceland, 1975.

———. *Iceland 1986.* Reykjavík: Central Bank of Iceland, 1987.

Sandness, Roger K., and Charles F. Gritzner. *Iceland*. Modern World Nations Series. Philadelphia: Chelsea House, 2003.

C. Guides and Yearbooks

Höfer, Hans. *Iceland*. Singapore: APA, 1992.

Kidson, Peter. *Iceland in a Nutshell: Complete Reference Guide*. 4th ed. Reykjavík: Örn og Örlygur, 1974.

D. Statistical Abstracts

Alþingiskosningar: Elections to the Althing. Reykjavík: Statistical Bureau of Iceland, 1991– .

Hagtölur án landamæra (Statistics across Borders: Nordic Statistics on CD-Rom). Reykjavík: Statistical Bureau of Iceland, 1992– .

Icelandic Agricultural Statistics. Reykjavík: Icelandic Agricultural Information Service, 1992– .

Jónsson, Guðmundur, and Magnús S. Magnússon, eds. *Hagskinna: Sögulegar hagtölur um Ísland (Icelandic Historical Statistics)*. Reykjavík: Statistical Bureau of Iceland, 1997.

Konur og karlar (Women and Men in Iceland 1994). Reykjavík: Statistical Bureau of Iceland. 1994.

Landshagir (Statistical Yearbook of Iceland). Reykjavík: Statistical Bureau of Iceland, 1991– . Accessible on the Web page of Statistical Bureau. See www .statice.is.

Mannfjöldaskýrslur árin 1971–80 (Population and Vital Statistics 1971–1980). Reykjavík: Statistical Bureau of Iceland, 1988.

Neyslukönnun (Household Budget Survey: 1995). Reykjavík: Icelandic Statistical Bureau, 1997.

Vinnumarkaður 2002 (Labour Market Statistics). Reykjavík: Statistical Bureau of Iceland, 2003.

E. Travel and Description

Auden, W. H., and Louis MacNeice. *Letters from Iceland*. New York: Random House, 1937.

Bárðarson, Hjálmar R. *Ice and Fire: Contrasts of Icelandic Nature*. 4th ed. Reykjavík: Hjálmar R. Bárðarson, 1991.

Baring-Gould, Sabine. *Iceland: Its Scenes and Sagas*. Lost and Found series. Oxford: Signal Books, 2007 [1863].

Barth, Sabine. *Island*. Ostfildern: DuMont Reiseverlag, 2005.

Bennett, Lindsay. *Iceland*. Peterborough: Thomas Cook, 2006.

Bindloss, Joe, and Paul Harding. *Iceland*. 5th ed. Melbourne: Lonely Planet, 2004.

Bordin, Guy, Michel Breuil, Marc Moniez, Catherine Troude, and Gilles Troude. *Islande: guide de l'île aux volcans: avec les îles Féroé*. Paris: Marcus, 2006.

Boucher, Alan. *The Iceland Traveller: A Hundred Years of Adventure*. Reykjavík: Iceland Review, 1989.

Carwardine, Mark. *Iceland: Nature's Meeting Place: A Wildlife Guide*. Reykjavík: Iceland Review, 1986.

Collingwood, W. G., and Jón Stefánsson. *A Pilgrimage to the Saga-Steads of Iceland*. Ulverston, UK: W. Holmes, 1899.

Davies, Ethel. *Reykjavík*. Peterborough: Thomas Cook, 2006.

Escritt, Tony. *Iceland: The Traveller's Guide*. London: Iceland Information Centre, 1990.

Gaimard, Paul. *Voyage en Islande et au Groenland exécuté pendant les années 1835 et 1836*. 12 vols. Paris: A. Bertrand, 1838–52.

Guðmundsson, Helgi. *The Golden Circle: Þingvellir-Geysir-Gullfoss-Skálholt: A Comprehensive Guide*. Reykjavík: JPV, 2007.

Hálfdanarson, Örlygur, and Eva Hálfdanardóttir. *Iceland Road Atlas*. Reykjavík: Stöng, 2005.

Hálfdanarson, Örlygur, and Steindór Steindórsson. *The Visitor's Key to Iceland: Its Saga and Scenery*. Reykjavík: Stöng, 2005.

Harlow, Cathy. *Iceland*. Ashbourne, UK: Landmark, 2006.

Holland, Henry. *The Iceland Journal of Henry Holland 1810*. Ed. A. Wawn. London: Hakluyt Society, 1987.

Iceland. Singapore: APA, 2005.

Krakauer, Jon, and David Roberts. *Iceland: Land of the Sagas*. New York: Harry N. Abrams, 1990.

McCririck, Mary. *The Icelanders and Their Island*. Bangor, ME: Author, 1976.

Mead, Rowland. *Iceland*. London: New Holland, 2007.

Ólafsson, Eggert. *Travels in Iceland by Eggert Ólafsson and Bjarni Pálsson: Performed 1752–1757 by Order of His Danish Majesty*. 2nd ed. Reykjavík: Örn og Örlygur, 1975.

Oslund, Karen Diane. "Narrating the North: Scientific Exploration, Technological Management, and Colonial Politics in the North Atlantic Islands." Dissertation from the University of California, Los Angeles, 2000.

Stonehouse, Ann F. *Essential Iceland*. Basingstoke, England: AA, 2004.

Wawn, Andrew. "John Thomas Stanley and Iceland: The Sense and Sensibility of an Eighteenth-Century Explorer." *Scandinavian Studies* 53 (1981): 52–76.

West, John F., ed. *The Journals of the Stanley Expedition to the Faroe Islands and Iceland in 1789.* 3 vols. Tórshavn, Faroe Islands: Føroya Fróðskaparfélag, 1970–76.

II. CULTURE

A. Art and Music

Árnason, Gunnar, Halldór B. Runólfsson, and Ólafur Gíslason. *Skúlptúr/skúlptúr/skúlptúr: Íslensk samtímalis (Sculpture/sculpture/sculpture: Icelandic Contemporary Art).* Reykjavík: Kjarvalsstaðir, 1994.

The Arts in Iceland. Reykjavík: Iceland Review, 1988.

Auge, Marc. *Erró: Mythical Painter.* Paris: Lit du Vent, 1994.

Baldvinsdóttir, Inga Lára. "Icelandic Photography 1846–1946." *History of Photography* 23 (Spring 1999): 1–9.

Baldvinsdóttir, Inga Lára, and Sigurjón B. Hafsteinsson, eds. *History of Photography: Iceland.* London: Taylor and Francis, 1999.

Bergendal, Göran. *New Music in Iceland.* Reykjavík: Iceland Music Information Center, 1991.

Bløndal, Torsten et al., eds. *Northern Poles: Breakaways and Breakthroughs in Nordic Painting and Sculpture of the 1970s and 1980s.* Copenhagen: Bløndal, 1986.

Confronting Nature: Icelandic Art of the 20th century. Reykjavík: Listasafn Íslands, 2001.

Cowie, Peter. *Icelandic Films.* Reykjavík: Kvikmyndasjóður Íslands, 1995.

———. *Icelandic Films 1980–2000.* Reykjavík: Kvikmyndasjóður Íslands, 2000.

Einarsson, Sveinn. *A People's Theatre Comes of Age: A Study of the Icelandic Theatre 1860–1920.* Reykjavík: University of Iceland Press, 2006.

Eldjárn, Kristján. *Ancient Icelandic Art.* Munich, Germany: Hans Reich, 1957.

Freeman, Julian, ed. *Landscapes from a High Latitude: Icelandic Art 1909–1989.* London: Lund Humphries, 1989.

Guðnadóttir, Gréta. "An Annotated List and Survey of Violin Music by Icelandic Composers." Dissertation, Florida State University, 1995.

Hermannsson, Halldór. *Illuminated Manuscripts of the Jónsbók.* Islandica, no. 28. Ithaca, NY: Cornell University Press, 1940.

Icelandic Chamber Music. Reykjavík: Íslensk tónverkamiðstöð, 1998.

Ingólfsson, Aðalsteinn. "Iceland." In *Northern Poles: Breakaways and Breakthroughs in Nordic Painting and Sculpture of the 1970s and 1980s* (pp. 47–120).Torsten Bløndal, ed. Copenhagen: Bløndal, 1986.

Ingólfsson, Aðalsteinn. *Naive and Fantastic Art in Iceland.* Reykjavík: Iceland Review, 1989.

Ingólfsson, Aðalsteinn, and Matthías Johannessen. *Kjarval: A Painter of Iceland.* Reykjavík: Iceland Review, 1981.

Ingólfsson, Árni Heimir. "These Are the Things You Never Forget: The Written and Oral Traditions of Icelandic *Tvísöngur.*" Dissertation, Harvard University, 2003.

Ingólfsson, Guðmundur. "Photography in Iceland: Two Pioneers." In *The Frozen Image: Scandinavian Photography* (pp. 60–65). Martin Friedman, ed. New York: Abbeville Press, 1982.

Johannessen, Matthías. *Sculptor Ásmundur Sveinsson: An Edda in Shapes and Symbols.* Reykjavík: Iceland Review, 1974.

Jörundsdóttir, Auður. *11 Years—A Decade of Contemporary Art.* Reykjavík: University of Iceland Press, 2006.

Kristjánsson, Gunnar. *Churches of Iceland: Religious Art and Architecture.* Reykjavík: Iceland Review, 1988.

Kristjánsson, Jónas. *Icelandic Manuscripts: Sagas, History and Art.* Reykjavík: Hið íslenska bókmenntafélag, 1993.

Kvaran, Ólafur. "Einar Jónsson's Sculpture, Development of Form and Sphere of Meaning." Dissertation, University of Lund, 1987.

Lamm, Sigurlaug Regína. *Musik und Gemeinschaft einer Nation im Werden: Die Einführung der Kunstmusik in Island in der Zeit von ca. 1800 bis 1920.* Uppsala, Sweden: Academiae Upsaliensis, 2001.

Leifsson, Hákon. "Ancient Icelandic Heritage in Icelandic a Cappella Choral Music in the Twentieth Century." Dissertation, University of Washington, 2004.

Magnússon, Sigurður A. *Iceland Crucible: A Modern Artistic Renaissance.* Reykjavík: Vaka, 1985.

Magnússon, Þór. *A Showcase of Icelandic National Treasures.* Reykjavík: Iceland Review, 1987.

Nordal, Bera, Guðrún Ágústsdóttir, and Tryggvi Þórhallsson, eds. *Arts and Culture in Iceland: The Visual Arts.* Reykjavík: Ministry of Culture and Education, 1990.

Nordal, Bera, Sigrún Valbergsdóttir, and Guðrún Ágústsdóttir, eds. *Arts and Culture in Iceland: Theatre, Films and Ballet.* Reykjavík: Ministry of Culture and Education, 1989.

Norðfjörð, Björn Ægir. "Icelandic Cinema: Practice in a Global Context." Dissertation, University of Iowa, 2005.

Ragnarsson, Hjálmar H. *A Short History of Icelandic Music to the Beginning of the Twentieth Century.* Reykjavík: Íslensk tónverkamiðstöð, 1986.

Schram, Hrafnhildur, and Halldór Laxness. *Nína Tryggvadóttir: Serenity and Power.* Reykjavík: Iceland Review, 1982.

Sigurbjörnsson, Þorkell. *Arts and Culture in Iceland: Music*. Reykjavík: Ministry of Culture and Education, 1990.

Varnedoe, Kirk. *Northern Light: Nordic Art at the Turn of the Century*. New Haven, CT: Yale University Press, 1988.

B. Architecture, Design, and Planning

Helgason, Haraldur, Málfríður Kristjánsdóttir, and Pétur H. Ármannsson, eds. *The Nordic House: Alvar Aalto: Iceland*. Reykjavík: Nordic House, 1999.

Icelandic Architecture. Aarhus, Denmark: The School of Architecture Aarhus, 1996.

Magma: Contemporary Icelandic Design 2007. Reykjavík: Listasafn Reykjavíkur, 2007.

Valsson, Trausti. *City and Nature: An Integrated Whole*. Reykjavík: University of Iceland Press, 2000.

———. *Planning in Iceland: From the Settlement to Present Times*. Reykjavík: University of Iceland Press, 2003.

C. Language and Literature

1. Language

Árnason, Kristján. *Quantity in Historical Phonology: Iceland and Relating Cases*. Cambridge: Cambridge University Press, 1980.

———. *The Rhythms of Dróttkvætt and Other Old Icelandic Metres*. Reykjavík: Institute of Linguistics, University of Iceland, 1991.

Arnbjörnsdóttir, Birna. *North American Icelandic: The Life of a Language*. Winnipeg: University of Manitoba Press, 2006.

Barðdal, Jóhanna H. *Case in Icelandic: A Syncronic, Diacronic and Comparative Approach*. Lund, Sweden: Lund University, 2001.

Benediktsson, Hreinn. *Early Icelandic Scripts as Illustrated in Vernacular Texts from the Twelfth and Thirteenth Centuries*. Íslenzk handrit, no. 2. Reykjavík: Handritastofnun Íslands, 1965.

———, ed. *The First Grammatical Treatise*. University of Iceland Publications in Linguistics, no. 1. Reykjavík: Institute of Nordic Linguistics, 1972.

———. "Icelandic Dialectology: Methods and Results." *Lingua Islandica* 3 (1961–62): 72–112.

———. *Linguistic Studies: Historical and Comparative*. Reykjavík: Institute of Linguistics, 2002.

———. "The Vowel System of Icelandic: A Survey of its History." *Word* 15 (1959): 282–312.

Buckhurst, H. M. *Elementary Grammar of Old Icelandic.* London: Methuen, 1925.

Einarsdóttir, Auður, Guðrún Theodórsdóttir, María Garðarsdóttir, and Sigríður Þorvaldsdóttir. *Learning Icelandic.* 2nd ed. Reykjavík: Mál og menning, 2002.

Einarsson, Stefán. *Icelandic Grammar, Texts, Glossary.* 2nd ed. Baltimore, MD: Johns Hopkins University Press, 1949.

Friðjónsson, Jón G. *A Course in Modern Icelandic, 1–2: Texts, Vocabulary, Grammar, Exercises, Translations.* Reykjavík: Skák, 1978.

———. *Icelandic as a Foreign Language.* Paris: UNESCO, 1984.

———. *Phonetics of Modern Icelandic.* Reykjavík: Skák, 1984.

Gordon, E. V. *An Introduction to Old Norse.* 2nd ed. Oxford: Oxford University Press, 1957.

Groenke, Ulrich. "On Standard, Substandard, and Slang in Icelandic." *Scandinavian Studies* 38 (1966): 217–30.

Guðmundsson, Helgi. *The Pronominal Dual in Icelandic.* Reykjavík: Institute of Nordic Linguistics, 1972.

Halldórsson, Halldór. "Icelandic Purism and Its History." *Word* 30 (1979): 76–86.

———. *Old Icelandic Heiti in Modern Icelandic.* University of Iceland Publications in Linguistics, no. 3. Reykjavík: Institute of Nordic Linuistics, 1975.

Hermannsson, Halldór. *Modern Icelandic: An Essay.* Islandica, no. 12. Ithaca, NY: Cornell University Library, 1919.

Heusler, Andreas. *Altisländisches Elementarbuch.* 7th ed. Heidelberg, Germany: C. Winter, 1967.

Hróarsdóttir, Þorbjörg. *Verb Phrase Syntax in the History of Icelandic.* Tromsø, Norway: University in Tromsø, 1999.

———. *Word Order Change in Icelandic: From OV to VO.* Amsterdam: Benjamins, 2000.

Jónsdóttir, Margrét. "Linguistics in Iceland before 1800: An Overview." In *Studies in the Development of Linguistics in Denmark, Finland, Iceland, Norway, and Sweden* (pp. 102–22). Carol Henriksen, ed. Oslo: Novus, 1996.

Jónsson, Jón Hilmar. *Das Partizip Perfekt der schwachen ja-Verben: Die Flexionsentwicklung im Isländischen.* Monographien zur Sprachwissenschaft, no. 6. Heidelberg, Germany: Carl Winter, 1976.

Karlsson, Stefán. *The Icelandic Language.* London: Viking Society for Northern Research, 2004.

Kress, Bruno. *Isländische Grammatik.* Leipzig, Germany: Verlag Enzyklopädie, 1982.

Kristinsson, Ari P. *The Pronounciation of Modern Icelandic: A Brief Course for Foreign Students.* 3rd ed. Revkjavik: Institute of Linguistics, University of Iceland, 1988.

Kvaran, Guðrún. "Icelandic Personal Names in Past and Present." *Onoma* 37 (2002): 293–300.

Maling, Joan, and Annie Zaenen, eds. *Modern Icelandic Syntax*. Syntax and Semantics, no. 24. San Diego: Academic Press, 1990.

Oresnik, Janez. *Studies to the Phonology and Morphology of Modern Icelandic*. Hamburg, Germany: Buske, 1985.

Ottósson, Kjartan G. *The Icelandic Middle Voice: The Morphological and Phonological Development*. Lund, Sweden: University of Lund, Department of Scandinavian Languages, 1992.

Pálsson, Gísli. "Language and Society: The Ethnolinguistics of Icelanders." In E. Paul Durrenberger and Gísli Pálsson, eds., *The Anthropology of Iceland* (pp. 121–39). Iowa City: University of Iowa Press, 1989.

Pétursson, Magnús. *Isländisch: Eine Übersicht über die moderne isländische Sprache mit einem kurzen Abriss der Geschichte and Literatur Islands*. Hamburg, Germany: Buske, 1978.

———. *Manuel d'islandais*. Paris: Éditions Klincksieck, 1996.

Rask, Rasmus Christian. *A Short Practical and Easy Method of Learning the Old Norsk Tongue or Icelandic Language*. London: Franz Thimm, 1868.

Sigurðsson, Halldór Ármann. *Verbal Syntax and Case in Icelandic: In a Comparative GB Approach*. Lund, Sweden: University of Lund, Department of Scandinavian Languages, 1989.

Sigurjónsdóttir, Sigríður. "Binding in Icelandic: Evidence from Language Acquisition." Dissertation, University of California Los Angeles, 1992.

Thomson, Colin D. *Íslensk Beygingafræði (Isländische Formenlehre; Icelandic Inflections)*. Hamburg, Germany: Buske, 1987.

Þráinsson, Höskuldur. *On Complementation in Icelandic*. Outstanding Dissertations in Linguistics, no. 23. New York: Garland, 1979.

———. *The Syntax of Icelandic*. Cambridge Syntax Guides. Cambridge: Cambridge University Press, 2007.

2. Literature

Anderson, Sarah M., and Karen Swenson, eds. *Cold Counsel: Women in Old Norse Literature and Mythology: A Collection of Essays*. New York: Garland, 2002.

Andersson, Theodore M. *The Icelandic Family Saga: An Analytic Reading*. Harvard Studies in Comparative Literature, no. 28. Cambridge, MA: Harvard University Press, 1967.

———. *The Problem of Icelandic Saga Origins: A Historical Survey*. Yale Germanic Studies, no. 1. New Haven, CT: Yale University Press, 1964.

Andersson, Theodore M., and W. I. Miller, eds. *Law and Literature in Medieval*

Iceland: Ljósvetninga Saga and Valla-Ljóts Saga. Stanford, CA: Stanford University Press, 1989.

Baetke, Walter. *Die Isländersaga.* Wege der Forschung, no. 15. Darmstadt, Germany: Wissenschaftliche Buchgesellschaft, 1974.

———. *Über die Einstehung der Isländersagas.* Berlin: Akademie Verlag, 1956.

Beck, Richard. *History of Icelandic Poets 1800–1940.* Islandica, no. 34. Ithaca, NY: Cornell University Press, 1950.

———. *Icelandic Poems and Stories: Translations from Modern Icelandic Literature.* Princeton, NJ: Princeton University Press, 1943.

———. *Jón Þorláksson: Icelandic Translator of Pope and Milton.* Studia Islandica, no. 16. Reykjavík: Bókaútgáfa Menningarsjóðs, 1957.

Benediktsson, Einar. *Harp of the North: Poems.* Charlottesville: University of Virginia Press, 1955.

Benediktsson, Jakob. *Arngrímur Jónsson and His Works.* Biblioteca Arnemagnæana, no. 12. Copenhagen: Arnemagneana Institute, 1957.

Benedikz, Eirikur, ed. *An Anthology of Icelandic Poetry.* Reykjavík: Icelandic Ministry of Education, 1969.

Bjarnason, Loftur. *An Anthology of Modern Icelandic Literature 1800–1950.* 2 vols. Berkeley: University Extension, University of California, 1961.

Boucher, Alan, ed. *Icelandic Poems of Today: From Twenty-Five Modern Icelandic Poets.* Reykjavík: Iceland Review, 1971.

Boyer, Régis, trans. *Contes populaires d'Islande.* Reykjavík: Almenna bókafélagið, 2004.

———, ed. and trans. *L'Edda poétique.* Paris: Fayard, 1996.

———. *L'Islande médiévale.* Paris: Belles lettres, 2001.

———. *La poésie scaldique.* Paris: Éditions du Porte-Glaive, 1990.

———, trans. *La saga des Sturlungar.* Paris: Les Belles Lettres, 2005.

———, trans. *Sagas islandaises.* Bibliothèque de la Pléiade. Paris: Gallimard, 1987.

———. *Les sagas islandaises.* Paris: Payot, 1978.

Bragason, Úlfar. "On the Poetics of Sturlunga." Dissertation, University of California, Berkeley, 1986.

Carleton, Peter. "Tradition and Innovation in Twentieth-Century Icelandic Poetry." Dissertation, University of California, 1967.

Ciklamini, Marlene. *Snorri Sturluson.* Boston: Twayne, 1978.

Clover, Carol J. *The Medieval Saga.* Ithaca, NY: Cornell University Press, 1982.

Clover, Carol J., and John Lindow. *Old Norse-Icelandic Literature: A Critical Guide.* Islandica, no. 45. Ithaca, NY: Cornell University Press, 1985.

Clunies Ross, Margaret, ed. *Old Icelandic Literature and Society.* Cambridge: Cambridge University Press, 2000.

————. *Old Norse Myths, Literature and Society.* Odense, Denmark: Odense University Press, 2003.

————. *Skáldskaparmál: Snorri Sturluson's Ars Poetica and Medieval Theories of Language.* Odense, Denmark: Odense University Press, 1987.

Cook, Robert, trans. *Njals Saga.* London: Penguin, 2001.

Craigie, W. A. *The Art of Poetry in Iceland.* Oxford: Clarendon, 1937.

————. *The Icelandic Sagas.* Cambridge: Cambridge University Press, 1913.

Driscoll, Matthew James. *The Unwashed Children of Eve: The Production, Dissemination and Reception of Popular Literature in Post-Reformation Iceland.* Enfield Lock, England: Hisarlik Press, 1997.

Dronke, Ursula, ed. and trans. *The Poetic Edda.* 2 vols. Oxford: Oxford University Press, 1969–97.

————, ed. *Speculum norroenum: Norse Studies in Memory of Gabriel Turville-Petre.* Odense, Denmark: Odense University Press, 1981.

Einarsson, Stefán. *A History of Icelandic Literature.* Baltimore, MD: Johns Hopkins University Press, 1957.

————. *History of Icelandic Prose Writers 1800–1940.* Islandica, nos. 32–33. Ithaca, NY: Cornell University Press, 1948.

Faulkes, Anthony, trans. *Snorri Sturluson: Edda.* London: Dent, 1987.

Frank, Roberta. *Old Norse Court Poetry: The Dróttkvætt Stanza.* Islandica, no. 42. Ithaca, NY: Cornell University Press, 1978.

Gade, Kari Ellen. *The Structure of Old Norse Dróttkvætt Poetry.* Islandica, no. 49. Ithaca, NY: Cornell University Press, 1995.

Glauser, Jürg. *Isländische Märchensagas. Studien zur Prosaliteratur im spätmittelalterlichen Island.* Basel, Switzerland: Helbing and Lichtenhahn, 1983.

Glauser, Jürg, and Gert Kreutzer, eds. *Isländische Märchensagas.* Trans. Jürg Glauser, Gert Kreutzer, and Herbert Wäckerlin. Darmstadt, Germany: Wissenschaftliche Buchgesellschaft, 1998.

Gunnarsdóttir, Margrét. "Theorizing Character: The Icelandic Family Saga." Dissertation, University of Georgia, 1991.

Gunnarsson, Gunnar. *The Black Cliffs.* Trans. Cecil Wood. Madison: University of Wisconsin Press, 1967.

————. *Frères jurés: roman.* Ed. and trans. Régis Boyer. Paris: Fayard, 2000.

————. *The Good Shepherd.* Trans. Kenneth C. Kaufmann. Indianapolis: Bobbs-Merrill, 1940.

————. *Guest the One-Eyed.* Trans. W. Worster. London: Gyldendal, 1920.

————. *The Night and the Dream.* Trans. Evelyn Ramsden. London: Jarrolds, 1938.

————. *Seven Days Darkness.* Trans. Roberts Tarpley. New York: Macmillan, 1930.

————. *Ships in the Sky.* Trans. Evelyn Ramsden. London: Jarrolds, 1938.

————. *The Sworn Brothers.* Trans. C. Field. London: Gyldendal, 1920.

Hafstað, Baldur. *Die Egils Saga and ihr Verhaltnis zu anderen Werken nordischen Mittelalters.* Reykjavík: Research Institute, University College of Education, 1995.

Hallberg, Peter. *Halldór Laxness.* New York: Twayne, 1971.

————. *The Icelandic Saga.* Trans. Paul Schach. Lincoln: University of Nebraska Press, 1962.

————. *Old Icelandic Poetry: Eddic Lay and Skaldic Verse.* Trans. Paul Schach and Sonja Lindgrenson. Lincoln: University of Nebraska Press, 1975.

Hallmundsson, Hallberg, ed. *An Anthology of Scandinavian Literature: From the Viking Period to the Twentieth Century.* New York: Collier, 1965.

Helgason, Jón, ed. *Manuscripta Islandica.* Copenhagen: Munksgaard, 1954– .

Helgason, Jón Karl. *The Rewriting of Njáls Saga: Translation, Ideology, and Icelandic Sagas.* Clevedon, UK: Multilingual Matters, 1999.

Hermannsson, Halldór. *Icelandic: Authors of Today.* Islandica, no. 6. Ithaca, NY: Cornell University Library, 1913.

————. *Old Icelandic Literature.* Islandica, no. 23. Ithaca, NY: Cornell University Library, 1933.

————, ed. *The Saga of Þorgils and Hafl–i.* Islandica, no. 31. Ithaca, NY: Cornell University Press, 1945.

————, ed. *The Vinland Sagas.* Islandica, no. 30. Ithaca, NY: Cornell University Press, 1944.

Hollander, Lee Milton. *Old Norse Poems: The Most Important Non-Skaldic Verse not Included in the Poetic Edda.* New York: Columbia University Press, 1936.

————, trans. *The Poetic Edda.* 2nd ed. Austin: University of Texas Press, 1986.

————, trans. *The Saga of the Jómsvíkings.* Austin: University of Texas Press, 1989.

————, trans. *The Sagas of Kormák.* Princeton, NJ: Princeton University Press, 1949.

————, trans. *The Skalds: A Selection of Their Poems.* Ann Arbor: University of Michigan Press, 1968.

Hreinsson, Viðar, ed. *The Complete Sagas of Icelanders: Including 49 tales.* 5 vols. Reykjavík: Leifur Eiríksson, 1997.

————, ed. *The Sagas of Icelanders: A Selection.* London: Penguin, 2000.

————. "Western Icelandic literature, 1870–1900." *Scandinavian Canadian Studies* (1993): 1–14.

Jakobsdóttir, Svava. *The Lodger and Other Stories.* Reykjavík: University of Iceland Press, 2001.

Kalinke, Marianne E. *The Book of Reykjahólar: The Last of the Great Medieval Legendaries.* Toronto: University of Toronto Press, 1996.

————. *Bridal-Quest Romance in Medieval Iceland.* Islandica, no. 46. Ithaca, NY: Cornell University Press, 1990.

Keel, Aldo. *Innovation und Restauration: Der Romancier Halldór Laxness seit dem Zweiten Weltkrieg.* Basel, Switzerland: Helbing and Lichtenhahn, 1981.

Ker, W. P. *Epic and Romance.* New York: Dover, 1957.

Kirby, Ian J. *Bible Translations in Old Norse.* Geneva: Librairie Droz, 1986.

Koht, Halvdan. *The Old Norse Sagas.* London: George Allen and Unwin, 1931.

Kötz, Günter. *Das Problem Dichter und Gesellschaft im Werke von Halldór Kiljan Laxness: Ein Beitrag zur modernen isländischen Literatur.* Giessen, Germany: W. Schmitz, 1966.

Kress, Helga. "'You Will Find It All Rather Monotonous': On Literary Tradition and the Feminine Experience in Laxdæla Saga." F. E. Andersen and J. Weinstock, eds., *The Nordic Mind: Current Trends in Scandinavian Literary Criticism* (pp. 181–96) Lanham, MD: University Press of America, 1986.

Kristjánsson, Gunnar. *Religiöse Gestalten und christliche Motive im Romanwerk "Heimsljós" von Halldór Laxness.* Bochum, Germany, 1991.

Kristjánsson, Jónas. *Eddas and Sagas: Iceland's Medieval Literature.* 3rd ed. Reykjavík: Icelandic Literary Society, 1997.

————. *Iceland and Its Manuscripts.* Reykjavík: Stofnun Árna Magnússonar, 1989.

Larrington, Carolyne, trans. *The Poetic Edda.* Oxford: Oxford University Press, 1996.

Laxness, Halldór. *The Atomstation.* Sag Harbor, NY: Second Chance, 1982.

————. *La cloche d'Islande: Roman.* Paris: Flammarion, 1991.

————. *The Fish Can Sing.* New York: Thomas Y. Crowell, 1967.

————. *The Happy Warriors.* London: Methuen, 1958.

————. *Independent People.* New York: Knopf, 1946.

————. *Salka Valka.* New York: Houghton, 1936.

————. *Under the Glacier.* Reykjavík: Vaka-Helgafell, 1990.

————. *World Light.* Madison: University of Wisconsin Press, 1969.

Liestøl, Knut. *The Origin of the Icelandic Family Sagas.* Cambridge, MA: Harvard University Press, 1930.

Lindow, John. *Handbook of Norse Mythology.* Santa Barbara, CA: ABC-Clio, 2001.

Lindow, John, Lars Lönnroth, and Gert Wolfgang Weber. *Structure and Meaning in Old Norse Literature: New Approaches to Textual Analysis and Literary Criticism.* Odense, Denmark: Odense University Press, 1986.

Littérature d'Islande. Paris: Europe, 1983.

Lönnroth, Lars. *Njáls Saga: A Critical Introduction.* Berkeley: University of California Press, 1976.

Loth, Agnete, ed. *Late Medieval Icelandic Romances*. Editiones Arnamagnæanæ, Series B, 20–24. 5 vols. Copenhagen, 1962–65.

Magnússon, Magnús, and Hermann Pálsson, trans. *Laxdæla Saga*. London: Penguin, 1975.

Magnússon, Sigurður A., ed. *Icelandic Writing Today*. Reykjavík: Ministry of Education, 1982.

———. *The Postwar Poetry of Iceland*. Iowa City: University of Iowa Press, 1982.

———. "The World of Halldór Laxness." *World Literature Today* 66 (1992): 457–63.

McTurk, Rory, ed. *A Companion to Old Norse-Icelandic Literature and Culture*. Oxford: Blackwell, 2005.

McTurk, Rory, and Andrew Wawn, eds. *Úr Dölum til Dala: Guðbrandur Vigfússon Centenary Essays*. Leeds, England: Leeds Studies in English, 1989.

Meulengracht-Sørensen, Preben. *The Unmanly Man: Concepts of Sexual Defamation in Early Northern Society*. Odense, Denmark: Odense University Press, 1983.

Modern Nordic Plays: Iceland. Oslo: Universitetsforlaget, 1973.

Neijmann, Daisy, ed. *A History of Icelandic Literature*. Lincoln: University of Nebraska Press, 2006.

Nordal, Guðrún. *Ethics and Action in Thirteenth-Century Iceland*. Odense, Denmark: Odense University Press, 1998.

———. *Tools of Literacy: The Role of Skaldic Verse in Icelandic Textual Culture of the Twelfth and Thirteenth Centuries*. Toronto: University of Toronto Press, 2001.

Nordal, Sigurður. *The Historical Element in the Icelandic Family Sagas*. Glasgow: Jackson, 1957.

———. *Hrafnkels saga Freysgoða*. Cardiff: University of Wales Press, 1958.

Ober, Kenneth H. *Bibliography of Modern Icelandic Literature in Translation 1981–1992*. Scandinavica, supplement. Norwich, UK: Norvik Press, 1997.

———. "Modern Icelandic Literature Abroad since 1970." *Scandinavica* 27 (1988): 167–73.

O'Donoghue, Heather. *Old Norse-Icelandic Literature: A Short Introduction*. Oxford: Blackwell, 2004.

Ólafsson, Örn. "Le mouvement littéraire de la gauche islandaise dans l'entre-deux-guerres." Dissertation, University of Lyon, 1984.

Ólason, Vésteinn. *Dialogues with the Viking Age: Narration and Representation in the Sagas of the Icelanders*. Reykjavík: Mál og menning, 1998.

———. *The Traditional Ballads of Iceland: Historical Studies*. Reykjavík: Stofnun Arna Magnússonar, 1982.

Óskarsdóttir, Svanhildur. "Universal History in Fourteenth-Century Iceland: Studies in AM 764 4to." Dissertation, University of London, 2000.

Pálsson, Hermann, trans. *Hrafnkel's Saga and Other Icelandic Stories*. London: Penguin, 1976.

———. *Oral Tradition and Saga Writing*. Vienna: Fassbaender, 1999.

———. "Studies in Early Icelandic History and Literature." Dissertation, Edinburgh University, 1980.

Pálsson, Hermann, and Paul Edwards, trans. *Eyrbyggja Saga*. London: Penguin, 1989.

Pétursson, Ásgeir, and Steingrímur J. Þorsteinsson, eds. *Seven Icelandic Short Stories*. 2nd ed. New York: American Scandinavian Foundation, 1961.

Pétursson, Hallgrímur. *Hymns of the Passion: Meditations on the Passion of Christ*. Trans. Arthur Charles Gook. Reykjavík: Hallgrímskirkja, 1966.

Pétursson, Sigurður. "Iceland." In Minna Skafte Jensen, ed., *A History of Nordic Neo-Latin Literature* (pp. 96–128). Odense, Denmark: Odense University Press, 1995.

Poole, Russel G., ed. *Skaldsagas: Text, Vocation and Desire in the Icelandic Sagas of Poets*. Berlin: Gruyter, 2000.

———. *Viking Poems on War and Peace: A Study in Skaldic Narrative*. Toronto Medieval Texts and Translations, no. 8. Toronto: University of Toronto Press, 1991.

Ringler, Dick. *Bard of Iceland: Jónas Hallgrímsson, Poet and Scientist*. Madison: University of Wisconsin Press, 2002.

Schach, Paul. *Icelandic Sagas*. Twayne World Authors Series, no. 717. Boston: Twayne, 1984.

Schier, Kurt, ed. *Märchen aus Island*. 2nd ed. Cologne, Germany: Diederichs, 1987.

———. *Sagaliteratur*. Stuttgart, Germany: J. B. Metzler, 1970.

Schottmann, Hans. *Die isländische Mariendichtung: Untersuchungen zur volkssprachigen Mariendichtung des Mittelalters*. Munich, Germany: Fink, 1973.

Scudder, Bernard, trans. *Egil's Saga*. Introduction by Svanhildur Óskarsdóttir. London: Penguin, 2004.

———, trans. *The Saga of Grettir the Strong*. Introduction by Örnólfur Thórsson. London: Penguin, 2005.

See, Klaus von. *Edda, Saga, Skaldendichtung: Aufsätze zur skandinavischen Literatur des Mittelalters*. Skandinavistische Arbeiten, no. 6. Heidelberg, Germany: Winter, 1981.

———. *Skaldendichtung: Eine Einführung*. Munich, Germany: Artemis, 1980.

Sigurðsson, Gísli. *Gaelic Influence in Iceland: Historical and Literary Contacts: A Survey of Research*. 2nd ed. Reykjavík: University of Iceland Press, 2000.

———. *The Medieval Icelandic Saga and Oral Tradition: A Discourse on Method*. Cambridge, MA: Milman Parry Collection, 2004.

Sigurðsson, Gísli, and Vésteinn Ólason, eds. *The Manuscripts of Iceland.* Reykjavík: Stofnun Árna Magnússonar á Íslandi, 2004.

Sigurjónsson, Árni, Bera Nordal, and Guðrún Ágústsdóttir, eds. *Arts and Culture in Iceland: Literature.* Reykjavík: Ministry of Culture and Education, 1989.

Stephansson, Stephan G. *Selected Translations from Andvökur.* Edmonton, AB: Stephan G. Stephansson Homestead Restoration Committee, 1982.

Stevens, Patrick J., ed. *Dictionary of Literary Biography: Icelandic Writers,* vol. 293. Farmington Hills, MI: Gale, 2004.

Sturluson, Snorri. *L'Edda: Récits de mythologie nordique.* Trans. François Xavier Dillmann. Paris: Gallimard, 1991.

————. *Heimskringla: History of the Kings of Norway.* Trans., with introduction and notes by Lee M. Hollander. Austin: University of Texas Press, 1964.

Sveinsson, Einar Ólafur. *Dating the Icelandic Sagas: An Essay in Method.* Viking Society for Northern Research. Text series, no. 3. London: Viking Society, 1958.

————. *Njáls Saga: A Literary Masterpiece.* Ed. and trans. Paul Schach, with an introduction by E. O. G. Turville-Petre. Lincoln: University of Nebraska Press, 1971.

————. *Studies in the Manuscript Tradition of Njálssaga.* Studia Islandica, no. 13. Reykjavík: Leiftur, 1953.

Swenson, Karen. *Performing Definitions: Two Genres of Insult in Old Norse Literature.* Columbia, SC: Camden House, 1991.

Thompson, Lawrence S., ed. *Eddukvæði: Norse Mythology: The Elder Edda in Prose Translation.* Trans. Guðbrandur Vigfússon and F. York Powell. Hamden, CT: Archon, 1974.

Tucker, John, ed. *Sagas of the Icelanders: A Book of Essays.* New York: Garland, 1989.

Tulinius, Torfi H. *The Matter of the North: The Rise of Literary Fiction in Thirteenth-Century Iceland.* Odense, Denmark: Odense University Press, 2002.

Turville-Petre, G. *Nine Norse Studies.* Viking Society for Northern Research. Text series, no. 5. London: Viking Society, 1972.

————. *Origins of Icelandic Literature.* Oxford: Oxford University Press, 1953.

————. *Scaldic Poetry.* Oxford: Oxford University Press, 1978.

Wawn, Andrew, ed. *Northern Antiquity: The Post-Medieval Reception of Edda and Saga.* Enfield Lock, England: Hisarlik Press, 1994.

Whaley, Diana. *Heimskringla: An Introduction.* Viking Society for Northern Research. Text series, no. 8. London: Viking Society, 1991.

Wolf, Kirsten. *An Annotated Bibliography of North American Doctoral Dissertations on Old Norse-Icelandic Studies.* Islandica, no. 50. Ithaca, NY: Cornell University Press, 1998.

———, ed. *The Old Norse-Icelandic Legend of Saint Barbara*. Toronto: Pontifical Institute of Mediaeval Studies, 2000.

Young, Jean I., ed. and trans. *The Prose Edda of Snorri Sturluson: Tales from Norse Mythology*. Introduction by Sigurður Nordal. Berkeley: University of California Press, 1964.

Þórðarson, Þórbergur. *In Search for My Beloved*. New York: Twayne, 1967.

Þorgilsson, Ari. *The Book of the Icelanders*. Ed. and trans., with an introductory essay and notes by Halldór Hermannsson. Islandica, no. 20. Ithaca, NY: Cornell University Library, 1930.

III. ECONOMY

Agnarsson, Sveinn, and Guðmundur Jónsson. "Explaining Economic Growth: Growth Accounting and Labour Productivity in Iceland, 1870–1945." In Guðmundur Jónsson, ed., *Nordic Historical National Accounts* (pp. 215–32). Reykjavík: Institute of History, University of Iceland, 2003.

Annual Report. Reykjavík: Central Bank of Iceland, 1997– .

Árnason, Ragnar. "Efficient Harvesting of Fish Stocks: The Case of the Icelandic Demersal Fisheries." Dissertation, University of British Columbia, 1984.

———. *The Icelandic Fisheries: Evolution and Management of a Fishing Industry*. Oxford: Fishing News, 1995.

Árnason, R., and Tryggvi B. Davíðsson, eds. *Essays on Statistical and Modelling Methodology for Fisheries Management*. Reykjavík: University of Iceland, 1996.

Árnason, R., and Hannes H. Gissurarson, eds. *Individual Transferable Quotas in Theory and Practice*. Reykjavík: University of Iceland, 1999.

Árnason, R., William E. Schrank, and Rögnvaldur Hannesson, eds. *The Cost of Fisheries Management*. Aldershot, England: Ashgate, 2003.

Ásgeirsdóttir, Tinna Laufey. "Health, Lifestyle, and Labor-Market Outcomes: The Case of Iceland." Dissertation, University of Miami, 2006.

Baldvinsdóttir, Herdís Dröfn. "Networks of Financial Power in Iceland: The Labour Movement Paradox." Dissertation, Lancaster University, 1998.

Bjarnason, Arnar. *Export or Die: The Icelandic Fishing Industry: The Nature and Behaviour of Its Export Sector*. Reykjavík: University of Iceland, Fisheries Research Institute, 1996.

Blöndal, Gísli. "The Development of Public Expenditure in Relation to National Income in Iceland." Dissertation, London School of Economics, 1965.

Blöndal, Sveinbjörn. "Export Supply Shocks, Credit, and Macroeconomic Policy in a Small Open Economy: Iceland 1960–1980." Dissertation, Cambridge University, 1986.

The Currency of Iceland: Issues and Features of Icelandic Notes and Coins. 2nd ed. Reykjavík: Numismatic Collection of the Central Bank of Iceland and the National Museum of Iceland, 2002.

Economic Indicators. Reykjavík: Central Bank of Iceland, 2001– .

The Economy of Iceland. Reykjavík: Central Bank of Iceland, 1987– .

Eggertsson, Þráinn. "No Experiments, Monumental Disasters: Why It Took a Thousand Years to Develop a Specialized Fishing Industry in Iceland." *Journal of Economic Behavior and Organization* 30, no. 1 (1996): 1–23.

————. "Sources of Risk: Institutions for Survival, and a Game against Nature in Premodern Iceland." *Explorations in Economic History* 35 (1998): 1–30.

Einarsson, Tór. "A Supply Shock Model of a Small Open Economy Incorporating Rational Expectations, and Its Application to Iceland in the 1970s." Dissertation, University of Essex, 1984.

Energy Resources and Dams in Iceland. Reykjavík: Icelandic National Committee on Large Dams, 1989.

Financial Stability. Reykjavík: Central Bank of Iceland, 2005– .

Guðmundsson, Már. "Exchange Rate Regime and Central Bank Independence in a Small Volatile Economy: The Case of Iceland." In H. M. Scobie, ed., *The European Single Market Monetary and Fiscal Policy Harmonization* (pp. 129–43). London: Chapman and Hall, 1994.

Guðmundsson, Már, Tryggvi Þór Herbertsson, and Gylfi Zoëga, eds. *Macroeconomic Policy: Iceland in an Era of Global Integration.* Reykjavík: University of Iceland Press, 2000.

Gunnarsson, Guðmundur Örn. *The Economic Growth in Iceland 1910–1980: A Productivity Study.* Studia Oeconomica Uppsaliensia, no. 17. Uppsala, Sweden: Almquist and Wiksell, 1990.

Gunnarsson, Gunnar Águst. "Industrial Policy in Iceland 1944–1974. Political Conflicts and Sectoral Interests." Dissertation, University of London, 1989.

Haraldsson, Gunnar. "Effects of Imperfections in the Icelandic Fisheries Management System." Dissertation, University of Toulouse, 2006.

Herbertsson, Tryggvi Þór. *Why Icelanders Do Not Retire Early.* Stockholm: Pensionsforum, 2001.

Herbertsson, Tryggvi Þ., and Gylfi Zoëga. *A Microstate with Scale Economies: The Case of Iceland.* Working Paper, no. 1. Reykjavik: University of Iceland, Institute of International Studies, Center for Small State Studies, 2003.

Icelandic Fisheries in Figures 2006. Reykjavík: Ministry of Fisheries, 2007.

Jónsson, Sigfús. *The Development of the Icelandic Fishing Industry 1900–1940.* Reykjavík: Economic Development Institute, 1981.

Magnússon, Gylfi. "Internal and External Migration in Iceland 1960–94: A Structural Model, Government Policies and Welfare Implications." Dissertation, Yale University, 1997.

Mer, Jacques. *L'Islande: Une ouverture obligée mais prudente.* Paris: Documentation française, 1994.

Möller, Alda, ed. *Fifty Years of Fisheries Research in Iceland.* Reykjavík: Icelandic Fisheries Laboratories, 1985.

Monetary Bulletin. Reykjavík: Central Bank of Iceland, 1999– .

OECD Economic Surveys: Iceland: 2006. Paris: OECD, 2006.

Pálsson, Gísli, and Guðrún Pétursdóttir, eds. *Social Implications of Quota Systems in Fisheries: Proceedings of a Seminar Held in the Vestman Islands in May 1996.* Copenhagen: Nordic Council of Ministers, 1997.

Stefánsson, Sigurður B. "Inflation and Economic Policy in a Small Open Economy: Iceland in the Postwar Period." Dissertation, University of Essex, 1981.

Trade Policy Review: Iceland. Geneva: World Trade Organization, 2000.

IV. HISTORY

A. General

Björnsson, Árni. *High Days and Holidays in Iceland.* Reykjavík: Mál og menning, 1995.

Hitzler, Egon. *Sel. Untersuchungen zur Geschichte des isländischen Sennwesens seit der Landnahmezeit.* Oslo: Universitetsforlaget, 1979.

Ísberg, Jón Ó. *Milestones in Icelandic History.* Reykjavík: Iceland Review, 1996.

Karlsson, Gunnar. *A Brief History of Iceland.* Reykjavík: Mál og menning, 2000.

———. *The History of Iceland.* Minneapolis: University of Minnesota Press, 2000.

Lacy, Terry G. *Ring of Seasons: Iceland, Its Culture and History.* Reykjavík: University of Iceland Press, 1998.

Magnússon, Magnús. *Iceland Saga.* London: Bodley Head, 1987.

Rosenblad, Esbjörn, and R. Sigurðardóttir-Rosenblad. *Iceland from Past to Present.* Reykjavík: Mál og menning, 1993.

Tomasson, Richard. *Iceland: The First New Society.* Minneapolis: University of Minnesota Press, 1980.

Þórarinsson, Sigurður. *The Thousand Years Struggle against Ice and Fire.* Reykjavík: Museum of Natural History, 1956.

Þorsteinsson, Björn. *Thingvellir: Iceland's National Shrine*. Reykjavík: Örn og Örlygur, 1987.

B. Archaeology and Prehistory

Archaeologica Islandica. 1– (1998–).

Einarsson, Bjarni F. *The Settlement of Iceland, a Critical Approach: Granastaðir and the Ecological Heritage*. Reykjavík: Hið íslenska bókmenntafélag, 1995.

Friðriksson, Adolf. *Sagas and Popular Antiquarianism in Icelandic Archaeology*. Aldershot, England: Avebury, 1994.

Hermanns-Auðardóttir, Margrét. *The Early Settlement of Iceland: Research Based on Excavations of a Merovingian and Viking Farm Site at Herjólfsdalur in the Westman Islands, Iceland*. Umeå, Sweden: Umeå University, 1989.

Kristjánsdóttir, Steinunn. *The Awakening of Christianity in Iceland: Discovery of a Timber Church and Graveyard at Þórarinsstaðir in Seyðisfjörður*. Gothenburg, Sweden: University of Gothenburg, 2004.

Nordahl, Elsa. *Reykjavík from the Archaeological Point of View*. Uppsala, Sweden: Societas Archeologica Upsaliensis, 1988.

Sigurðardóttir, Kristín Huld. "Viking Iron Relics from Iceland with a Special Emphasis on Provenience Studies." Dissertation, University College London, 1999.

Sveinbjarnardóttir, Guðrún. *Farm Abandonment in Medieval and Postmedieval Iceland: An Interdisciplinary Study*. Oxford: Oxbow Books, 1992.

Þórarinsson, Sigurður. "Tephrochronology and Medieval Iceland." In Rainer Beger, ed., *Scientific Methods in Medieval Archeology* (pp. 295–328). Berkeley: University of California Press, 1970.

C. Settlement and Commonwealth Period

Aðalsteinsson, Jón Hnefill. *Under the Cloak: The Acceptance of Christianity in Iceland with Particular Reference to the Religious Attitudes Prevailing at the Time*. Studia Ethnologica Uppsaliensia, no. 4. Stockholm: Almquist and Wiksell, 1978.

Bagge, Sverre. *Society and Politics in Snorri Sturluson's Heimskringla*. Berkeley: University of California Press, 1991.

Bergþórsson, Páll. *The Wineland Millennium: Saga and Evidence*. Reykjavík: Mál og menning, 2000.

Byock, Jesse L. *Feud in the Icelandic Saga*. Berkeley: University of California Press, 1982.

———. *Medieval Iceland: Society, Sagas, and Power*. Berkeley: University of California Press, 1988.

————. *Viking Age Iceland*. London: Penguin, 2001.

Cormack, Margaret Jean. *The Saints in Iceland: Their Veneration from the Conversion to 1400*. Subsidia hagiographia, no. 78. Brussels: Société des Bollandistes, 1994.

Dillmann, François-Xavier. *Les magiciens dans l'Islande ancienne*. Uppsala, Sweden: Kungl, Gustav Adolfs Akademien för svensk folkkultur, 2006.

Durrenberger, E. Paul, and Gísli Pálsson. "The Importance of Friendship in the Absence of State, According to the Icelandic Sagas." In Sandra Bell and Simon Coleman, eds., *The Anthropology of Friendship* (pp. 59–77). Oxford: Berg, 1999.

Faulkner, Anthony, and Richard Perkins, eds. *Viking Revaluations: Viking Society Centenary Symposium 14–15 May 1992*. London: University College, 1993.

Foote, Peter, and David M. Wilson. *The Viking Achievement: The Society and Culture of Early Medieval Scandinavia*. London: Sidgwick and Jackson, 1970.

Gelsinger, Bruce E. *Icelandic Enterprise: Commerce and Economy in the Middle Ages*. Columbia: University of South Carolina Press, 1981.

Hastrup, Kirsten. *Culture and History in Medieval Iceland: An Anthropological Analysis of Structure and Change*. Oxford: Clarendon, 1985.

Hermannsson, Halldór. *The Problem of Wineland*. Islandica, no. 26. Ithaca, NY: Cornell University Press, 1936.

Jakobsson, Sverrir. "Defining a Nation: Popular and Public Identity in the Middle Ages." *Scandinavian Journal of History* 24 (1999): 191–201.

Jochens, Jenny M. "Late and Peaceful: Iceland's Conversion through Arbitration in 1000." *Speculum* 74, no. 3 (1999): 621–55.

————. *Old Norse Images of Women*. Philadelphia: University of Pennsylvania Press, 1996.

————. *Women in Old Norse Society*. Ithaca, NY: Cornell University Press, 1995.

Jóhannesson, Jón. *Íslendinga Saga: A History of the Old Icelandic Commonwealth*. Winnipeg: University of Manitoba Press, 1974.

Karlsson, Gunnar. "Goðar and Höfðingjar in Medieval Iceland." *Saga Book of the Viking Society of Northern Research* 19 (1977): 358–70.

Kuhn, Hans. *Das alte Island*. Jena, Germany: Diederichs, 1971.

Miller, William Ian. *Bloodtaking and Peacemaking: Feud, Law, and Society in Saga Iceland*. Chicago: University of Chicago Press, 1990.

————. *Humiliation and Other Essays on Honor, Social Discomfort, and Violence*. Ithaca, NY: Cornell University Press, 1993.

Morris, Katherine. *Sorceress or Witch? The Image of Gender in Medieval Iceland and Northern Europe*. Lanham, MD: University Press of America, 1991.

Njarðvík, Njörður P. *Birth of a Nation: The Story of the Icelandic Commonwealth.* 2nd ed. Reykjavík: Iceland Review, 1985.

Nordal, Sigurður. *Icelandic Culture.* Trans. Vilhjálmur Bjarnar. Ithaca, NY: Cornell University Press, 1990.

Pálsson, Gísli, ed. *From Sagas to Society: Comparative Approaches to Early Iceland.* Endfield Lock, England: Hisarlik Press, 1992.

Pálsson, Hermann, and Paul Edwards, trans. *Book of Settlements: Landnámabók.* University of Manitoba Icelandic Studies, no. 1. Winnipeg: University of Manitoba Press, 1972.

Rafnsson, Sveinbjörn. "The Atlantic Islands." In Peter Sawyer, ed., *The Oxford Illustrated History of the Vikings* (pp. 110–33). Oxford: Oxford University Press, 2001.

Sigurðsson, Jón Viðar. *Chieftains and Power in the Icelandic Commonwealth.* Odense, Denmark: Odense University Press, 1999.

Sölvason, Birgir T. R. "Ordered Anarchy, State, and Rent-Seeking: The Icelandic Commonwealth, 930–1262." Dissertation, George Mason University, 1991.

Storek, Martha H. "Women in the Time of the Icelandic Family Saga." Dissertation, Bryn Mawr College, 1946.

Sveinsson, Einar Ólafur. *The Age of the Sturlungs: Icelandic Civilization in the Thirteenth Century.* Islandica, no. 36. Ithaca, NY: Cornell University Press, 1953.

Vésteinsson, Orri. *The Christianization of Iceland: Priests, Power, and Social Change 1000–1300.* Oxford: Oxford University Press, 2000.

Wawn, Andrew, and Þórunn Sigurðardóttir, eds. *Approaches to Vínland.* Reykjavík: Sigurður Nordal Institute, 2001.

Þorgilsson, Ari. *Íslendingabok (The Book of Icelanders).* Trans., with an introductory essay by Halldór Hermannsson. Islandica, no. 20. Ithaca, NY: Cornell University Library, 1930.

Þorláksson, Helgi, ed. *Church Centres: Church Centres in Iceland from the 11th to the 13th Century and Their Parallels in Other Countries.* Reykholt, Iceland: Snorrastofa, 2005.

———. "Enterprizing Explorers in the North Atlantic." In Anna Agnarsdóttir, ed., *Voyages and Exploration in the North Atlantic from the Middle Ages to the XVIIth Century: Papers Presented at the 19th International Congress of Historical Sciences, Oslo 2000* (pp. 13–28). Reykjavík: University of Iceland, 2001.

D. Late Medieval and Early Modern Period

Bjarnar, Vilhjálmur. "The Laki Eruption and the Famine of the Mist." In C. F. Bayersmith and E. J. Fries, eds., *Scandinavian Studies: Essays Presented to Henry Goddard Leach* (pp. 410–21). Seattle: University of Washington Press, 1965.

Boulhosa, Patricia Pires. *Icelanders and the Kings of Norway: Mediaeval Sagas and Legal Texts.* Leiden, Netherlands: Brill, 2005.

Gunnarsson, Gísli. *Fertility and Nuptiality in Iceland's Demographic History.* Meddelande från Ekonomisk-historiska institutionen, Lunds Universitet, no. 12. Lund, Sweden: Ekonomisk-historiska institutionen, 1980.

———. *Monopoly Trade and Economic Stagnation: Studies in the Foreign Trade of Iceland 1602–1787.* Lund, Sweden: Ekonomisk-historiska föreningen, 1983.

———. *The Sex Ratio, the Infant Mortality and the Adjoining Societal Response in Pre-transitional Iceland.* Meddelande från Ekonomisk-historiska institutionen, Lunds Universilet, no. 32. Lund, Sweden: Ekonomisk-historiska institutionen, 1983.

Gustafsson, Harald. *Political Integration in the Old Regime: Central Power and Local Society in the Eighteenth-Century Nordic States.* Lund, Sweden: Studentliteratur, 1994.

Guttormsson, Loftur. "The Development of Popular Religious Literacy in the Seventeenth and Eighteenth Centuries." *Scandinavian Journal of History* 15, no. 1 (1990): 15–35.

———. "Pietism and the Definition of Childhood: Evidence from Eighteenth-Century Iceland." *History of Education* 20 (1991): 27–35.

Hastrup, Kirsten. *Nature and Policy in Iceland 1400–1800: An Anthropology of History and Mentality.* Oxford: Clarendon, 1990.

Hreinsson, Einar. "'Noblesse de Robe' in a Classless Society: The Making of an Icelandic Elite in the Age of Absolutism." *Scandinavian Journal of History* 30, nos. 3–4 (2005): 225–37.

Júlíusson, Árni D. "Peasant Unrest in Iceland." In Kimmo Katajala, ed., *Northern Revolts: Medieval and Early Modern Peasant Unrest in the Nordic Countries* (pp. 118–48). Helsinki: Finnish Literature Society, 2004.

Karlsson, Gunnar. "Plague without Rats: The Case of Fifteenth-Century Iceland." *Journal of Medieval History* 22, no. 3 (1996): 263–84.

Lárusson, Björn. *The Old Icelandic Land Registers.* Lund, Sweden: Gleerup, 1967.

Magnússon, Jón. *Histoire de mes souffrances.* Trans. Einar Már Jónsson. Classiques du nord. Lumières, no. 5. Paris: Belles lettres, 2004.

Steingrímsson, Jón. *A Very Present Help in Trouble: The Autobiography of the Fire-Priest.* Trans. Michael Fell. American University Studies: Theology and Religion, vol. 215. New York: Peter Lang, 2002.

Vasey, D. E. "Population Regulation, Ecology, and Political Economy in Preindustrial Iceland." *American Ethnologist* 23, no. 2 (1996): 366–92.

Wawn, Andrew. *The Anglo Man: Þorleifur Repp, Philology and Nineteenth-Century Britain.* Studia Islandica, no. 49. Reykjavík: Menningarsjóður, 1991.

E. 19th Century

Agnarsdóttir, Anna. "The Challenge of War on Maritime Trade in the North Atlantic: The Case of the British Trade to Iceland during the Napoleonic Wars." In Olaf Uwe Janzen, ed., *Merchant Organization and Maritime Trade in the North Atlantic 1660–1815* (pp. 221–58). St. John's, NF: International Martime Economic History Association, 1998.

———. "Great Britain and Iceland 1800–1820." Dissertation, London School of Economics, 1989.

———. "Iceland 1800–1850: New Beginnings." In Max Engmann and Åke Sandström, eds., *Det nya Norden efter Napoleon* (pp. 79–118). Stockholm: Almqvist and Wiksell, 2004.

Bakewell, Sarah. *The English Dane: From King of Iceland to Tasmanian Convict.* London: Chatto and Windus, 2005.

Bjarnason, Halldór. "The Foreign Trade of Iceland, 1870–1914: An Analysis of Trade Statistics and a Survey of Its Implicatons for the Icelandic Economy." Dissertation, University of Glasgow, 2001.

Garðarsdóttir, Ólöf. "The Implications of Illegitimacy in Late-Nineteenth-Century Iceland: The Relationship between Infant Mortality and the Household Position of Mothers Giving Birth to Illegitimate Children." *Continuity and Change* 15, no. 3 (2000): 435–61.

———. *Saving the Child: Regional, Cultural and Social Aspects of the Infant Mortality Decline in Iceland, 1770–1920.* Umeå, Sweden: Umeå University, 2002.

Gunnlaugsson, Gísli Agúst. "'Everyone's Been Good to Me, Especially the Dogs': Foster-Children and Young Paupers in Nineteenth-Century Southern Iceland." *Journal of Social History* 27, no. 2 (1993): 341–58.

———. *Family and Household in Iceland 1801–1930: Studies in the Relationship between Demographic and Socio-Economic Development, Social Legislation and Family and Household Structures.* Uppsala, Sweden: Acta Universitatis Upsaliensis, 1988.

Hálfdanarson, Guðmundur. "Defining the Modern Citizen: Debates on Civil and Political Elements of Citizenship in Nineteenth-Century Iceland." *Scandinavian Journal of History* 24 (1999): 103–16.

———. "Iceland: A Peaceful Secession?" *Scandinavian Journal of History* 25, nos. 1–2 (2000): 87–100.

———. "Language, Identity and Political Integration." In Harald Gustafsson and Hanne Sanders, eds., *Vid gränsen: Integration och identiteter i det förindustiella Norden* (pp. 230–47). Lund, Sweden: Centrum för Danmarksstudier, Lunds University, and Makadam, 2006.

———. "Old Provinces, Modern Nations: Political Responses to State-Integration in Late Nineteenth and Early Twentieth-Century Iceland and Brittany." Dissertation, Cornell University, 1991.

————. "Social Distinctions and National Unity: On Politics of Nationalism in Nineteenth-Century Iceland." *History of European Ideas* 21 (November 1995): 763–79.

Jónsson, Guðmundur. "Changes in Food Consumption in Iceland 1770–1940." *Scandinavian Economic History Review* 46, no. 1 (1998): 24–41.

————. "Institutional Change in Icelandic Agriculture 1780–1940." *Scandinavian Journal of History* 41 (1993): 101–28.

Karlsson, Gunnar. "The Emergence of Nationalism in Iceland." In Sven Tägil, ed., *Ethnicity and Nation Building in the Nordic World* (pp. 32–62). London: Hurst, 1995.

Kjartansson, Helgi Skúli. "Icelandic Emigration." In P. C. Emmer and M. Morner, eds., *European Expansion and Migration: Essays on the Intercontinental Migration from Africa, Asia, and Europe* (pp. 105–19). New York: St. Martin's, 1992.

Kristinsson, Júníus. *Vesturfaraskrá 1870–1914: A Record of Emigrants from Iceland to America 1870–1914.* Reykjavík: Institute of History, University of Iceland, 1983.

Magnússon, Sigurður G. "The Continuity of Everyday Life: Popular Culture in Iceland 1850–1940." Dissertation, Carnegie-Mellon University, 1993.

————. "From Children's Point of View: Childhood in Nineteenth-Century Iceland." *Journal of Social History* 29, no. 2 (1996): 295–323.

Magnússon, Sigurður G., and Davíð Ólafsson. "Barefoot Historians: Education in Iceland in the Modern Period." In K.-J. Lorenzen-Schmidt and B. Poulsen, eds., *Writing Peasants: Studies on Peasant Literacy in Early Modern Northern Europe* (pp. 175–209). Kerteminde, Denmark: Landbohistorisk Selskab, 2002.

Óskarsdóttir, Þórkatla. "Ideas of Nationality in Icelandic Poetry 1830–1874." Dissertation, University of Edinburgh, 1982.

Sigurðsson, Ingi. "The Historical Works of Jón Espólín and His Contemporaries." Dissertation, University of Edinburgh, 1972.

Sprod, Dan. *The Usurper: Jörgen Jörgensen and His Turbulent Life in Iceland and Van Diemen's Land 1780–1841.* Sandy Bay, Australia: Blubber Head Press, 2001.

Þór, Jónas. *Icelanders in North America: The First Settlers.* Winnipeg: University of Manitoba Press, 2002.

F. 20th and 21st Centuries

Bittner, Donald F. *The Lion and the White Falcon: Britain and Iceland in the World War II Era.* Hamden, CT: Archon, 1983.

Corgan, Michael T. "Franklin D. Roosevelt and the American Occupation of Iceland." *Naval War College Review* 45, no. 4 (1992): 34–54.

———. *Iceland and Its Alliances: Security for a Small State.* Scandinavian Studies, vol. 8. Lewiston, IL: Edwin Mellen, 2002.

———. "Icelandic Security Policy: 1979–1986." Dissertation, Boston University, 1991.

Friðriksson, Þorleifur. "Economic Assistance from the Nordic Social Demographic Parties to Icelandic Social Democracy, 1918–1939: Internationalism or Manipulation?" *Scandinavian Journal of History* 13, nos. 2–3 (1988): 141–65.

Garðarsdóttir, Ólöf. "Working Children in Urban Iceland 1930–1990: Ideology of Work, Work-Schools and Gender Relations in Modern Iceland." In Ning de Coninck-Smith, Bengt Sandin, and Ellen Schrumpf, eds., *Industrious Children: Work and Childhood in the Nordic Countries 1850–1990* (pp. 160–85). Odense, Denmark: Odense University Press, 1997.

German-Icelandic Fisheries History: Aspects of the Development since 1945. Bremerhaven, Germany: Deutsches Schiffahrtsmuseum, 2003.

Gíslason, Gylfi Þ. *The Challenge of Being an Icelander.* 2nd ed. Reykjavík: Almenna bókafélagið, 1990.

Gröndal, Benedikt. *Iceland: From Neutrality to NATO Membership.* Oslo: Universitetsforlaget, 1971.

Gunnlaugsson, Gísli Agúst. "The Historiography on Iceland in the Second World War." In J. Rohwer and H. Müller, eds., *Neue Forschungen zum Zweiten Weltkrieg: Literaturberichte und Bibliographien aus 67 Ländern* (pp. 210–14). Koblenz: Bernard and Graefe, 1990.

Gunnlaugsson, Gísli Ágúst, and Loftur Guttormsson. "Household Structure and Urbanization in Three Icelandic Fishing Districts, 1880–1930." *Journal of Family History* 18, no. 4 (1993): 315–40.

Guttormsson, Loftur. "The Breakthrough of Social History in Icelandic Historiography." In Frank Meyer and Jan Eivind Myhre, eds., *Nordic Historiography in the 20th century* (pp. 265–79). Oslo: University of Oslo, 2000.

Hákonardóttir, Inga Huld. "Philanthropy, Politics, Religion and Women in Iceland before the Modern Social Welfare System, 1895–1935." In Pirjo Markkola, ed., *Gender and Vocation: Women, Religion, and Social Change in the Nordic Countries, 1830–1940* (pp. 177–210). Studia historica, no. 64. Helsinki: SKS, 2000.

Hálfdanarson, Guðmundur. "Severing the Ties: Iceland's Journey from a Union with Denmark to a Nation-State." *Scandinavian Journal of History* 31, no. 3 (2006): 237–54.

———. "Þingvellir: An Icelandic 'Lieu de Mémoire.'" *History and Memory* 12 (2000): 4–29.

Harðarson, Sólrún B. Jensdóttir. *Anglo–Icelandic Relations during the First World War.* New York: Garland, 1986.

Hart, Jeffrey A. *The Anglo–Icelandic Cod War of 1972–1973: A Case Study of a Fishery Dispute.* Research Series, no. 29. Berkeley: University of California Press, Institute of International Studies, 1976.

Hermannsson, Birgir. *Understanding Nationalism: Studies in Icelandic Nationalism.* Stockholm Studies in Politics, no. 110. Stockholm: Stockholm University, 2005.

Hunt, John Joseph. "The U.S. Occupation of Iceland 1941–1945." Dissertation, Georgetown University, 1966.

Ingimundarson, Valur. "Buttressing the West in the North: The Atlantic Alliance, Economic Warfare and the Soviet Challenge in Iceland, 1956–1959." *International History Review* 21 (1999): 80–103.

———. "Immunizing against the American Other: Racism, Nationalism, and Gender in U.S.–Icelandic Military Relations during the Cold War." *Journal of Cold War Studies*, 6, no. 4 (2004): 65–88.

———. "Die politischen und kulturellen Beziehungen zwischen der SED und der Isländischen Sozialistischen Partei." In Jan Hecker-Stampehl, ed., *Nordeuropa und die beiden deutschen Staaten 1949–1989: Aspekte einer Beziehungsgeschichte im Zeichen des Kalten Krieges* (pp. 75–90). Leipzig, Germany: Kirchhof and Franke, 2007.

———. "Post–Cold War Historiography in Iceland." In Thorsten B. Olesen, ed., *The Cold War and the Nordic Countries: Historiography at a Crossroads* (pp. 83–96). Odense: University Press of Southern Denmark, 2004.

———. "The Role of NATO and the U.S. Military Base in Icelandic Domestic Politics." In Gustav Schmidt, ed., *A History of NATO: The First Fifty Years* (pp. 285–302). Vol. 2. New York: Palgrave, 2001.

Jóhannesson, Guðni T. "To the Edge of Nowhere? U.S. Icelandic Defence Relations during and after the Cold War." *Naval War College Review* 57, nos. 3–4 (2004): 114–37.

———. *Troubled Waters: Cod War, Fishing Disputes, and Britain's Fight for the Freedom of the High Seas, 1948–1964.* Studia Atlantica, no. 11. Reykjavík: North Atlantic Fisheries History Association, 2007.

Jónsson, Guðmundur. "Icelandic Economic History: A Historiographical Survey of the Last Century." *Scandinavian Economic History Review* 50, no. 3 (2002): 44–56.

———. "The Icelandic Welfare State in the Twentieth Century." *Scandinavian Journal of History* 26, no. 3 (2001): 249–67.

———. "The State and the Icelandic Economy, 1870–1930." Dissertation, London School of Economics and Political Science, 1991.

———. "The Transformation of the Icelandic Economy: Industrialisation and Economic Growth, 1870–1950." In Sakari Heikkinen and Jan Luiten van

Zanden, eds., *Exploring Economic Growth: Essays in Measurement and Analysis: A Festschrift for Riitta Hjerppe on Her 60th Birthday* (pp. 131–66). Amsterdam: Academic, 2004.

Jónsson, Hannes. *Friends in Conflict: The Anglo–Icelandic Cod Wars and the Law of the Sea*. Hamden, CT: Archon Books, 1982.

Kristjánsdóttir, Ragnheiður. "Communists and the National Question in Scotland and Iceland, c. 1930 to c. 1940." *Historical Journal* 45, no. 3 (2002): 601–18.

Magnússon, Magnús S. *Iceland in Transition: Labour and Socio-Economic Change before 1940*. Skrifter utgivna av Ekonomisk-historiska föreningen i Lund, no. 45. Lund, Sweden: Lunds Ekonomisk-historiska foreningen, 1985.

Matthíasdóttir, Sigríður. "The Renovation of Native Pasts: A Comparison between Aspects of Icelandic and Czech Nationalist Ideology." *Slavonic and East European Review* 78, no. 4 (2000): 688–709.

Schuler, Martin. *Búsetuþrkóun á Íslandi 1880–1990 (Settlement History of Iceland 1880–1990)*. Reykjavík: Statistical Bureau of Iceland, 1994.

Sigurðsson, Ingi. "The Professionalization of Icelandic Historical Writing." In Frank Meyer and Jan Eivind Myhre, eds., *Nordic Historiography in the 20th century* (pp. 149–63). Oslo: University of Oslo, 2000.

Valdimarsdóttir, Laufey. *A Brief History of the Woman Suffrage Movement in Iceland*. London: International Alliance of Women for Suffrage and Equal Citizenship, 1929.

Welch, Andrew. *The Royal Navy in the Cod Wars: Britain and Iceland in Conflict 1958–61, 1972–73, 1975–76*. Liskeard, Cornwall: Maritime Books, 2006.

Whitehead, Þór. *The Ally Who Came in from the Cold: A Survey of Icelandic Foreign Policy 1946–1956*. Reykjavík: Center for International Studies, University of Iceland Press, 1998.

———. "Iceland and the Second World War 1939–45." Dissertation, Oxford University, 1978.

Þór, Jón Þ. *British Trawlers in Icelandic Waters: History of British Steam Trawling off Iceland 1889–1916 and the Anglo–Icelandic Fisheries Dispute 1896–1897*. Reykjavík: Fjölvi, 1992.

V. LAW

Aðalsteinsson, Ragnar, and Stefán Már Stefánsson. "Incorporation and Implementation of Human Rights in Iceland." In Martin Scheinin, ed., *International Human Rights Norms in the Nordic and Baltic Countries* (pp. 169–202). The Hague: Matinus Nijhoff, 1996.

Arnardóttir, Oddný Mjöll, Davíð Þór Björgvinsson, and Viðar Már Matthías-son. "The Icelandic Health Sector Database." *European Journal of Health Law* 3 (1999): 307–62.

Árnason, Ágúst Þór. "The History of the Icelandic Constitution and Some Economic Issues." In Lise Lyck, ed., *Constitutional and Economic Space of the Small Nordic Jurisdictions: The Aaaland Islands, the Faroe Islands, Greenland, Iceland* (pp. 48–72). Stockholm: NordREFO, 1997.

Benediktsson, Jakob, ed. *Skarðsbók, Jónsbók and Other Laws and Precepts: Ms. no. 350-fol. in the Arna-Magnæean Collection in the University Library of Copenhagen.* Corpus codicum islandicorum medii aevi, no. 16. Copenhagen: E. Munksgaard, 1943.

Dennis, Andrew, Peter Foote, and Richard Perkins, trans. *Laws of Early Iceland: Grágás 1.* University of Manitoba Icelandic Studies, no. 3. Winnipeg: Univeristy of Manitoba Press, 1980.

Fisheries Jurisdiction in Iceland. Reykjavík: Ministry of Foreign Affairs, 1972.

Gauksdóttir, Guðrún. "Iceland." In Robert Blackburn and Jorg Polakiewicz, eds., *Fundamental Rights in Europe: the ECHR and Its Member States, 1950–2000* (pp. 399–422). Oxford: Oxford University Press, 2001.

Hermannsson, Halldór. *The Ancient Laws for Norway and Iceland.* Islandica, no. 4. Ithaca, NY: Cornell University Library, 1911.

Jónsson, Hannes, ed. *The Evolving Limit of Coastal Jurisdiction.* Reykjavík: Government of Iceland, 1974.

Líndal, Sigurður. "Labour Legislation and Industrial Relationship in Iceland." *Journal of Comparative Labour Law and Industrial Relations* (1995): 112–32.

———. "Law and Legislation in the Icelandic Commonwealth." *Scandinavian Studies in Law* 37 (1993): 53–92.

Pencak, William. *The Conflict of Law and Justice in the Icelandic Sagas.* Amsterdam: Rodopi, 1995.

See, Klaus von. *Altordische Rechtswörter: Philologische Studien zur Recht-sauffassung und Rechtsgesinn und der Germanen.* Tübingen, Germany: Niemeyer, 1964.

Smearman, Claire Ann. "At the Crossroads: Domestic Violence and Legal Reform in Iceland." *Úlfljótur* 49, nos. 3–4 (1996): 275–377.

Stefánsson, Stefán Már. *The EEA Agreement and Its Adoption into Icelandic Law.* Oslo: Universitetsforlaget, 1997.

Torfason, Hjörtur. "The Supreme Court of Iceland: History, Structure and Functions: An Overview." In Pál Solt, János Sanathy, and Tibor Zinner, eds., *The History of the Supreme Courts of Europe and the Development of Human Rights* (pp. 214–20). Budapest: Blende SP, 1999.

Þórðarson, Gunnlaugur. *Les eaux territoriales d'Island en ce qui concerne la pêche.* Reykjavík: Hlaðbúð, 1958.

VI. POLITICS AND GOVERNMENT

A. Domestic

Davis, Morris. *Iceland Extends Its Fisheries Limits: A Political Analysis.* Oslo: Universitetsforlaget, 1963.

Grímsson, Ólafur Ragnar. *The Icelandic Multilevel Coalition System.* Reykjavík: University of Iceland, 1977.

Harðarson, Ólafur Þ. "The Icelandic Electoral System 1844–1999." In Bernard Grofman and Arend Lijphart, eds., *The Evolution of Electoral and Party Systems in the Nordic Countries* (pp. 101–66). New York: Agathon Press, 2002.

———. *Parties and Voters in Iceland: A Study of the 1983 and 1987 Althingi Elections.* Reykjavík: Social Science Research Institute, University of Iceland, 1995.

Kristinsson, Gunnar Helgi. *Farmers' Parties: A Study in Electoral Adaptation.* Reykjavík: Social Science Research Institute, University of Iceland, 1991.

Kristjánsson, Svanur. "Conflict and Consensus in Icelandic Politics 1916–1944." Dissertation, University of Illinois, 1977.

———. *Corporatism in Iceland?* Reykjavík: Social Science Research Institute, University of Iceland, 1979.

Kristmundsson, Ómar H. *Reinventing Government in Iceland: A Case Study of Public Management Reform.* Reykjavík: University of Iceland Press, 2003.

Magnússon, Þorsteinn. "The Icelandic Althingi and Its Standing Committees." Dissertation, University of Exeter, 1987.

Óskarsdóttir, Stefanía. "The Use of Incomes Policies: The Case of Iceland 1969–1994." Dissertation, Purdue University, 1995.

Styrkársdóttir, Auður. *From Feminism to Class Politics: The Rise and Decline of Women's Politics in Reykjavík, 1908–1922.* Research Report, no. 6. Umeå, Sweden: Umeå University, Department of Political Science, 1998.

Þórhallsson, Baldur, ed. *Iceland and European Integration: On the Edge.* New York: Routledge, 2004.

———. "Iceland's Involvement in Global Affairs since the Mid-1990s: What Features Determine the Size of a State." *Stjórnmál og stjórnsýsla* 2, no. 2 (2006): 197–223.

B. Foreign Relations

Bernharðsdóttir, Ásthildur E., and Lina Svedin. *Small-State Crisis Management: The Icelandic Way.* Crisis Management Europe Research Program, no. 25. Stockholm: Crisis Management Europe Research Program, 2004.

Fairlamb, John Robin. "The Evolution of Icelandic Defense Decision Making 1944–1981." Dissertation, University of South Carolina, 1981.

Goodeve, E. A. "Iceland and the European Union: An In-Depth Analysis of One of Iceland's Most Controversial Debates." *Scandinavian Studies* 77, no. 1 (2005): 85–104.

Gunnarsson, Gunnar. *The Kefavik Base: Plans and Projects.* Occasional Papers, no. 3. Reykjavík: Icelandic Commission on Security and International Affairs, 1986.

Ívarsson, Jóhann Viðar. *Science, Sanctions and Cetaceans: Iceland and the Whaling Issue.* University of Iceland's Center for International Studies. Publication, no. 7. Reykjavík: Center for International Studies, University of Iceland, 1994.

Jónsson, Albert. *Iceland, NATO and the Keflavík Base.* Reykjavík: Icelandic Commission on Security and International Affairs, 1989.

Nuechterlein, Donald E. *Iceland: Reluctant Ally.* 2nd ed. Westport, CT: Greenwood Press, 1975.

VII. SCIENCE AND NATURE

A. General

Acta Naturalia Islandica. Reykjavík: Icelandic Institute of Natural History, 1946–92.

Baldursson, Snorri, Helgi Torfason, and Hörður Kristinsson. *Natural Conditions and the Conservation Value of Natural Phenomena North of the Glacier Vatnajökull: Summary.* Reykjavík: Icelandic Institute of Natural History, 2003.

Iceland: National Report to UNCED. Reykjavík: Ministry for the Environment, 1992.

Review of National Science, Technology and Innovation Policy, Iceland. 2 vols. Paris: Organization of Economic Cooopration and Development, Committee for Scientific and Technological Policy, 1992.

B. Botany

Feilberg, Jon, and Benny Génsbøl. *Plants and Animals of Iceland.* Reykjavík: Mál og menning, 2003.

Kristinsson, Hörður. *A Guide to the Flowering Plants and Ferns of Iceland.* 2nd ed. Reykjavík: Mál og menning, 1998.

Löve, Áskell. *Flora of Iceland.* Reyjavík: Almenna bókafélagið, 1983.

Ostenfeld, C. A., and J. Gröntved. *The Flora of Iceland and the Faeroes.* Copenhagen: Levin and Munksgaard, 1934.

Wolseley, Pat. *A Field Key to the Flowering Plants of Iceland.* Sandwick, Shetland: Thule Press, 1979.

C. Geography

Ahlmann, Hans W., and Sigurður Þórarinsson. *Vatnajökull: Scientific Results of the Swedish-Icelandic Investigations 1936–40.* Stockholm: Geographiske annaler, 1943.

Friðriksson, Sturla. *Surtsey: Ecosystems Formed.* Reykjavík: Varði, 2005.

Gísladóttir, Guðrún. *Geographical Analysis of Natural and Cultural Landscape: Methodological Study in Southwestern Iceland.* Stockholm: Stockholm University, 1993.

Icelandic Geographic 1– (2002–).

Malmström, Vincent H. *A Regional Geography of Iceland.* Washington, DC: National Academy of Sciences, National Research Council, 1958.

Ólafsdóttir, Rannveig. *Land Degradation and Climate in Iceland: A Spatial and Temporal Assessment.* Lund, Sweden: Lund University, 2002.

Preusser, Hubertus. *The Landscapes of Iceland: Types and Regions.* The Hague: W. Junk, 1976.

Roberts, Brian B. *Iceland.* London: Geographic Handbook Series, 1942.

Þorsteinsson, Björn. *Thingvellir: Iceland's National Shrine.* Reykjavík: Örn og Örlygur, 1987.

D. Geology and Environment

Annels, Alwyn Ernest. "The Geology of Hornafjörður Region, Southwest Iceland." Dissertation, Imperial College, London, 1967.

Áskelsson, Jóhannes. *A Contribution to the Geology of Kerlingafjöll.* Reykjavík: Náttúrufræðistofnun Íslands, 1946.

Áskelsson, Jóhannes, G. Böðvarsson, T. Einarsson, G. Kjartansson, and Sigurður Þórarinsson. *On the Geology and Geophysics of Iceland: A Guide to Excursion.* No. A2. Reykjavík: Museum of Natural History, 1960.

Barth, Thomas F. W. *Volcanic Geology: Hot Springs and Geysers of Iceland.* Washington, DC: Carnegie Institution of Washington, 1950.

Björnsson, Helgi. *Hydrology of Ice Caps in Volcanic Regions.* Societas scientiarium Islandica, no. 45. Reykjavík: Societas scientiarium Islandica, 1988.

Caseldine, C., Andrew Russell, Jórunn Harðardóttir, and Óskar Knudsen, eds. *Iceland: Modern Processes and Past Environments.* Developments in Quaternary Science, no. 5. Amsterdam: Elsevier, 2005.

Einarsson, Þorleifur. *Geology of Iceland: Rocks and Landscape.* Reykjavík: Mál og menning, 1994.

Friðriksson, Sturla. *Surtsey: Evolution of Life on a Volcanic Island.* London: Butterworth, 1975.

Guðmundsson, Ari Trausti. *Living Earth: Outline of the Geology of Iceland.* Reykjavík: Mál og menning, 2007.

Hjartarson, Árni. "Skagafjörður Unconformity: North Iceland and Its Geological History." Dissertation, University of Copenhagen, 2003.

Hróarsson, Björn, and Sigurður S. Jónsson. *Geysers and Hot Springs in Iceland.* Reykjavík: Mál og menning, 1992.

Hug-Fleck, Christof. *Islands Geologie.* Kiel, Germany: Conrad Stein Verlag, 1988.

Jacoby, W., A. Björnsson, and D. Möller, eds. *Iceland: Evolution, Active Tectonics, and Structure.* Journal of Geophysics, no. 47. Berlin: Springer, 1980.

Jóhannesson, Björn. *The Soils of Iceland.* Reykjavík: University Research Institute, 1960.

Maizels, Judith, and Chris Caseldine, eds. *Environmental Change in Iceland: Past and Present.* Dordrecht, Netherlands: Kluwer Academic, 1991.

Pálsson, Sveinn. *Draft of a Physical, Geographical, and Historical Description of Icelandic Ice Mountains on the Basis of a Journey to the Most Prominent of Them in 1792–1794 with Four Maps and Eight Perspective Drawings.* Reykjavík: Icelandic Literary Society, 2004.

Steingrímsson, Jón. *Fires of the Earth: The Laki Eruption 1783–1784.* Reykjavík: Nordic Volcanological Institute, 1998.

Thordarson, Thorvaldur, and Ármann Höskuldsson. *Iceland.* Classic Geology in Europe, no. 3. Harpenden, UK: Terra, 2002.

Thordarson, Thorvaldur, and Stephen Self. "Atmospheric and Environmental Effects of the 1783–1784 Laki Eruption: A Review and Reassessment." *Journal of Geophysical Research-Atmospheres* 108, no. D1 (8 January 2003): Art. No. 4011.

Þórarinsson, Sigurður. *Hekla: A Notorious Volcano.* Reykjavík: Almenna bókafélagið, 1970.

Þórarinsson, S., Þ. Einarsson, and G. Kjartansson. "On the Geology and Geomorphology of Iceland." *Geografiska annaler* 41 (1959): 135–69.

E. Meteorology and Climate

Gunnarsson, Gisli. *A Study of Causal Relations in Climate and History with Emphasis on the Icelandic Experience.* Meddelande fran Ekonomiskhistoriska institutionen, no. 17. Lund, Sweden: Lund University, 1980.

Jónsson, Trausti, and Hilmar Garðarsson. "Early Instrumental Meteorological Observations in Iceland." *Climatic Change* 48, no. 1 (2001): 169–87.

Ogilvie, Astrid E. J. "Climate and Society in Iceland from the Medieval Period to the Late Eighteenth Century." Dissertation, University of East Anglia, 1981.

————. "The Climate of Iceland, 1701–1784." *Jökull* 36 (1986): 57–73.

Ogilvie, Astrid E. J., and Trausti Jónsson, eds. *The Iceberg in the Mist: Northern Research in Pursuit of a 'Little Ice Age.'* Dodrecht, Netherlands: Kluwer, 2001.

————. "'Little Ice Age' Research: A Perspective from Iceland." *Climatic Change* 48, no. 1 (2001): 9–52.

Second Status Report for Iceland: Pursuant to the United Nations Framework Convention on Climate Change. Reykjavík: Ministry for the Environment, 1997.

F. Zoology and Ornithology

Bárðarson, Hjálmar R. *Birds of Iceland.* Reykjavík: Hjálmar R. Bárðarson, 1986.

Breuil, Michel. *Les oiseaux d'Islande: Ecologie et biogéographie.* Paris: Lechavlier, Chabaud, 1989.

Einarsson, Þorsteinn. *Guide to the Birds of Iceland.* Reykjavík: Örn og Örlygur, 1991.

Feilberg, Jon, and Benny Génsbøl. *Plants and Animals of Iceland.* Reykjavík: Mál og menning, 2003.

Hersteinsson, Páll. "The Behavioural Ecology of Arctic Foxes (Alopx Lagopus) in Iceland." Dissertation, University of Dundee, 1984.

Hilmarsson, Jóhann Óli. *Icelandic Bird Guide.* Reykjavík: Iðunn, 2000.

Nielsen, Ólafur Karl. "Population Ecology of the Gyrfalcon in Iceland with Comparative Notes on the Merlin and the Raven." Dissertation, Cornell University, 1986.

Sæmundsson, Bjarni. *Synopsis of the Fishes of Iceland.* Reykjavík: Vísindafélag Íslendinga, 1927.

The Zoology of Iceland. Nos. 1– . Copenhagen: Munksgaard,1937– .

VIII. SOCIETY

A. Anthropology

Björnsdottir, Inga Dóra. "Nationalism, Gender and the Contemporary Icelandic Women's Movement." Dissertation, University of California, Santa Barbara, 1992.

Björnsson, Árni. *Icelandic Feasts and Holidays: Celebrations, Past and Present.* Reykjavík: Iceland Review, 1980.

Bredahl-Petersen, Frederik E. "Family Organization in Rural Iceland." Dissertation, University of Edinburgh, 1973.

Durrenberger, E. Paul. *The Dynamics of Medieval Iceland: Political Economy and Literature.* Iowa City: University of Iowa Press, 1992.

———. *Icelandic Essays: Explorations in the Anthropology of Modern Life.* Iowa City: Rudi, 1995.

Durrenberger, E. Paul, and Gísli Pálsson, eds. *The Anthropology of Iceland.* Iowa City: University of Iowa Press, 1989.

———. *Images of Contemporary Iceland: Everyday Lives and Global Contexts.* Iowa City: University of Iowa Press, 1996.

Harðardóttir, Kristín E., and Gísli Pálsson. "Icelandic biobanks." In Örn D. Jónsson and Edward H. Huijbens, eds., *Technology in Society, Society in Technology* (pp. 305–21). Reykjavík: University of Iceland Press, 2005.

Hastrup, Kirsten. *Culture and History in Medieval Iceland: An Anthropological Analysis of Structure and Change.* Oxford: Oxford University Press, 1985.

———. *Island of Anthropology: Studies in Past and Present Iceland.* Odense, Denmark: Odense University Press, 1990.

———. *Nature and Policy in Iceland 1400–1800: An Anthropological Analysis of History and Mentality.* Oxford: Oxford University Press, 1990.

———. *A Place Apart: An Anthropological Study of the Icelandic World.* Oxford Studies in Social and Cultural Anthropology. New York: Oxford University Press, 1998.

Helgason, Agnar. "The Ancestry and Genetic History of the Icelanders: An Analysis of mtDNA Sequences, Y Chromosome Haplotypes and Genealogies." Dissertation, University of Oxford, 2001.

Helgason, Agnar, Sigrún Sigurðardóttir, Jayne Nicholson, Bryan Skyes, Emmeline W. Hill, Daniel G. Bradley, Vidar Bosnes, Jeffery R. Gulcher, Ryk Ward, and Kári Stefánsson. "Estimating Scandinavian and Gaelic Ancestry in the Male Settlers of Iceland." *American Journal of Human Genetics* 67 (2000): 697–717.

Ingimundarson, Jón Haukur. "Of Sagas and Sheep: Toward a Historical Anthropology of Social Change and Production for Market, Subsistence and Tribute in Early Iceland (10th to the 13th century)." Dissertation, University of Arizona, 1994.

Koester, David C. "Historical Consciousness in Iceland." Dissertation, University of Chicago, 1990.

———. "Icelandic Confirmation Ritual in Cultural-Historical Perspective." *Scandinavian Studies* 76, no. 4 (1995): 476–515.

Kristmundsdóttir, Sigríður Dúna. *Doing and Becoming: Women's Movements and Women's Personhood in Iceland 1870–1990.* Reykjavík: Institute of Social Research, University of Iceland, 1997.

Magnússon, Finnur. *The Hidden Class: Culture and Class in a Maritime Setting, Iceland 1880–1942.* North Atlantic Monographs, no. 1. Århus, Denmark: Århus University Press, 1990.

Pálsson, Gísli. "The Birth of the Aquarium: The Political Ecology of Icelandic Fishing." In Tim S. Gray, ed., *The Politics of Fishing* (pp. 209–27). London: Macmillan, 1998.

———. *Coastal Economies, Cultural Accounts: Human Ecology and Icelandic Discourse*. Manchester: Manchester University Press, 1991.

———, ed. *From Sagas to Society: Comparative Approaches to Early Iceland*. Enfield Lock, UK: Hisarlik, 1992.

———. "The Life of Family Trees and the Book of Icelanders." *Medical Anthropology* 21, nos. 3–4 (2002): 337–67.

———. *The Textual Life of Savants: Ethnography, Iceland and the Linguistic Turn*. Basel, Switzerland: Harwood, 1995.

Pálsson, Gísli, Agnar Helgason, and Gunnar Óðinsson. "Property, Knowledge, and Agency: The Objectification of Icelandic Fishing." In Alf Hornborg and Gísli Pálsson, eds., *Negotiating Nature: Culture, Power and Environmental Argument* (pp. 153–77). Lund Studies in Human Ecology, no. 2. Lund, Sweden: Lund University Press, 2000.

Rich, George W. "Core Values, Organizational Preferences, and Children's Games in Akureyri, Iceland." Dissertation, University of California, Davis, 1976.

Skaptadóttir, Unnur Dís. "Fishermen's Wives and Fish Processors: Continuity and Change in Women's Position in Icelandic Fishing Villages 1870–1990." Dissertation, City University of New York, 1995.

———. "Mobilities and Cultural Difference: Immigrants' Experiences in Iceland." In Valur Ingimundarson, Kristín Loftsdóttir, and Irma Erlingsdóttir, eds., *Topographies of Globalization: Politics, Culture, Language* (pp. 133–48). Reykjavík: University of Iceland, 2004.

Turner, Victor. "An Anthropological Approach to the Icelandic Saga." In T. O. Beidelman, ed., *The Translation of Culture: Essays to E. E. Evans-Prithchard* (pp. 349–74). London: Tavistock, 1971.

Þórarinsdóttir, Hallfríður. "The Policy of Purism in Icelandic Natioanalism." Dissertation, New School for Social Research, New York, 1999.

B. Education

Education Policy Analysis: Focus on Higher Education 2005–2006. Paris: Organisation for Economic Cooperation and Development, 2006.

Gubjörnsdóttir, Guðný. "Cognitive Development, Gender Class and Education: A Longitudinal Study of Icelandic Early and Late Cognitive Developers." Dissertation, University of Leeds, 1987.

Guðmundsson, Reynir. "Media Education in the City of Reykjavík, Iceland." Dissertation, Boston University, 1984.

Gunnarsson, Þorsteinn V. "Controlling Curriculum Knowledge: A Documentary Study of the Icelandic Social Science Project (SSCP), 1974–1984."

Dissertation, Ohio University, 1990.

Hansen, Börkur. "School Leadership in Iceland." In Lejf Moos, Stephen Carney, Olof Johansson, and Jill Mehlbye, eds., *Skoleledelse i Norden: En kortlægning af skoleledernes arbejdsvilkår, rammebetingelser og opgaver* (pp. 171–96). Copenhagen: Nordic Council of Ministers, 2000.

———. "Secondary School Reorganization in Iceland: A Policy Analysis." Dissertation, University of Alberta, 1987.

Hanson, George. "Icelandic Education: Tradition and Modernization in a Cultural Perspective." Dissertation, Loyola University of Chicago, 1979.

Hilmarsson, Eiríkur. "The Role of Education in the Icelandic Labor Market." Dissertation, University of Wisconsin, 1989.

Ingvarsdóttir, Hafdís. "The Heart of the Matter: The Nature, Use and Formation of Teachers' Subjective Theories in Secondary Schools in Iceland." Dissertation, University of Reading, 2003.

Jóhannesson, Ingólfur Á. "The Formation of Educational Reform as a Social Field in Iceland and the Social Strategies of Educationists 1966–1991." Dissertation, University of Wisconsin, 1991.

———. "Professionalization of Progress and Expertise among Teacher Educators in Iceland: A Bourdieuean Interpretation." *Teaching and Teacher Education* 9, no. 3 (1993): 269–81.

Jósepsson, Bragi S. "Education in Iceland: Its Rise and Growth with Respect to Social, Political and Economic Determinants." Dissertation, George Peabody College for Teachers, 1968.

———, ed. *Current Laws on Compulsory Education and School System in Iceland.* Reykjavík: Icelandic College of Education, 1986.

Óskarsdóttir. Gerður G. *Education in Iceland.* Reykjavík: Ministry of Education, 1991.

———. *The Forgotten Half: Comparison of Dropouts and Graduates in Their Early Work Experience: The Icelandic Case.* Reykjavík: Social Science Research Institute, University of Iceland, 1995.

Pálsson, Hreinn. "Educational Saga: Doing Philosophy with Children in Iceland." Dissertation, Michigan State University, 1987.

Proppé, Ólafur Jóhann. "A Dialectical Perspective on Evaluation as Evolution: A Critical View of Assessment in Icelandic Schools." Dissertation, University of Illinois, 1982.

Sigurðsson, Jón. "Keeping Abreast of the Times: A Report of a Transformation of an Icelandic College in the Context of Educational Administration and of Instructional Methodology." Dissertation, Columbia Pacific University, 1990.

Suppanz, Hannes. *Adapting the Icelandic Education System to a Changing Environment.* Economics Department Working Papers, no. 516. Paris: Organization for Economic Cooperation and Development, 2006.

Trial, George T. *History of Education in Iceland.* Cambridge: Heffer, 1945.

C. Environment and Society

Árnason, Þorvarður. *Views of Nature and Environmental Concerns in Iceland.* Linköping, Sweden: University of Linköping, 2005.

Brydon, Ann. "The Predicament of Nature: Keiko the Whale and the Cultural Politics of Whaling in Iceland." *Anthropological Quarterly* 79, no. 2 (2006): 225–60.

Jónsson, Örn D., ed. *Whales and Ethics.* Reykjavík: University of Iceland, Fisheries Research Institute, 1992.

OECD Environmental Performance Reviews: Iceland. Paris: Organization for Economic Cooperation and Development, 2001.

Welfare for the Future: Iceland's National Strategy for Sustainable Development 2002–2020. Reykjavík: Ministry of the Environment, 2002.

D. Health

Ásgeirsdóttir, Tinna Laufey. "Health, Lifestyle, and Labor-Market Outcomes: The Case of Iceland." Dissertation, University of Miami, 2006.

Ásmundsson, Gylfi, and Hildigunnur Ólafsdóttir. *Alcohol Problems in Iceland 1930–1980: A Study of Medical and Social Problems in Relation to the Development of Alcohol Consumption.* Reykjavík: University Hospital, 1988.

Björnsdóttir, Kristín, "Private Lives in Public Places: A Study in the Ideological Foundation of Nursing in Iceland." Dissertation, Columbia University, 1992.

Gunnarsdóttir, Anna Lilja. "Performance Management in Health Care in Iceland." Dissertation, University of Southern California, Los Angeles, 2000.

Halldórsson, Matthías Eggert. *Health Care Systems in Transition: Iceland.* Ed. Vaida Bankauskaite. Health Care Systems in Transition, vol. 5, no. 4. Copenhagen: World Health Organization, 2003.

Hannesdóttir, Helga. *Studies on Child and Adolescent Mental Health in Iceland.* Turku, Finland: University of Turku, 2002.

Helgason, Lárus. *Psychiatric Services and Mental Illness in Iceland: Incidence Study (1966–1967) with 6–7 Year Follow-up.* Acta psychiatrica Scandinavica, supplement 268. Copenhagen: Munksgaard, 1977.

Helgason, Tómas. *Epidemiology of Mental Disorders in Iceland: A Psychiatric and Demographic Investigation of 5,395 Icelanders.* Copenhagen: Munksgaard, 1964.

Jensson, Ólafur. *Studies on Four Hereditary Blood Disorders in Iceland.* Reykjavík: Landsspítalinn, 1978.

Jónsson, Vilmundur. *Health in Iceland.* Reykjavík: n.p., 1940.

Magnússon, Hallgrímur. *Mental Health of Octogenarians in Iceland: An Epidemiological Study.* Copenhagen: Munksgaard, 1989.

Ólafsdóttir, Hildigunnur. *Alcoholics Anonymous in Iceland: From Marginality to Mainstream Culture.* Reykjavík: University of Iceland Press, 2000.

Samúelsson, Siguður. *Tuberculosis in Iceland: Epidemiological Studies.* Washington, DC: U.S. Public Health Service, 1950.

Sigurgeirsdóttir, Sigurbjörg. *Health Policy and Hospital Mergers: How the Impossible Became Possible.* Reykjavík: University of Iceland Press, 2006.

E. Migration and Urbanization

Jónsdóttir, Salvör, and Nanna Hermannsson. *Iceland: Reykjavík.* Scandinavian Atlas of Historical Towns, no. 6. Reykjavík: Árbæjarsafn and Odense University Press, 1988.

Reynarsson, Bjarni. "Residential Mobility, Life Cycle Stages, Housing and the Changing Social Patterns in Reykjavík 1974 to 1976." Dissertation, University of Illinois, 1980.

F. Religion

Aðalsteinsson, Jón Hnefill. *Under the Cloak: The Acceptance of Christianity in Iceland with Particular Reference to the Religious Attitudes Prevailing at the Time.* Studia Ethnologica Uppsaliensia, no. 4. Uppsala, Sweden: Uppsala University, 1978.

Björnsson, Björn. *The Lutheran Doctrine of Marriage in Modern Icelandic Society.* Oslo: Universitetsforlaget, 1971.

Bradshaw, Robert. *The Catholic Church Returns to Iceland (Mid-19th Century).* Privately printed, 1991.

Jónasson, Haukur Ingi. "In a Land of Living God: The Healing Imagination and the Icelandic Heritage." Dissertation, Columbia University, 2005.

Jónsson, Örn Bárður. "Disciplining a Nation Parish Renewal within the Evangelical Lutheran Church of Iceland." Dissertation, Fuller Theological Seminary, 1996.

Kirby, Ian J. *Biblical Quotations in Old Icelandic–Norwegian Religious Literature.* 2 vols. Reykjavík: Stofnun Árna Magnússonar, 1976–80.

Swator, William H., and Loftur R. Gissurarson. *Icelandic Spiritualism: Mediumship and Modernity in Iceland.* New Brunswick, NJ: Transaction, 1997.

Woods, Fred E. *Fire on Ice: The Story of Icelandic Latter-Day Saints at Home and Abroad.* Provo, UT: Religious Studies Center, Brigham Young University, 2005.

Þórðarson, Sigurður Árni. "Liminality in Icelandic Religious Tradition." Dissertation, Vanderbilt University, 1988.

Þórðarson, Steinþór B. "A Study of Factors Related to the Numerical Growth of the Seventh-Day Adventist Church in Iceland From 1950 to 1980." Dissertation, Andrew University, 1985.

G. Sociology and Social Policy

Bernburg, Jón Gunnar, and Þórólfur Þórlindsson. "Violent Values, Conduct Norms, and Youth Aggression: A Multilevel Study in Iceland." *Sociological Quarterly* 46, no. 3 (2005): 457–78.

Bjarnason, Dóra S. *New voices from Iceland: Disability and Young Adulthood.* New York: Nova Science, 2004.

Björnsson, Sigurjón, and Wolfgang Edelstein. *Exploration in Social Inquiry: Stratification, Dynamics and Individual Development in Iceland.* Berlin: Max Planck Institute, 1977.

Einarsdóttir, Þorgerður. *Culture, Custom and Caring: Men's and Women's Possibilities to Parental Leave.* Reykjavík: Centre for Gender Equality, University of Iceland, 2004.

Einarsson, Ingimar. *Patterns of Societal Development in Iceland.* Uppsala, Sweden: Uppsala University, 1987.

Eydal, Guðný Björk. *Family Policy in Iceland 1944–1984.* Gothenburg, Sweden: Department of Sociology, Gothenburg University, 2005.

Gíslason, Ingólfur V. *Enter the Bourgeoisie: Aspects of the Formation and Organization of Icelandic Employers 1894–1934.* Lund, Sweden: Lund University, 1990.

Gunnlaugsson, Helgi. "The Social Reality of Crime in Iceland: Criminal Punishment in a Land with Little Crime." Dissertation, University of Missouri, 1992.

Gunnlaugsson, Helgi, and John F. Galliher. *Wayward Icelanders: Punishment, Boundary Maintenance, and the Creation of Crime.* Madison: University of Wisconsin Press, 2000.

Hrafnsdóttir, Steinunn. *The Mosaic of Gender: The Working Environment of Icelandic Social Service Managers.* Reykjavík : University of Iceland Press, 2004.

Kristinsdóttir, Guðrún. *Child Welfare and Professionalization.* Umeå Social Work Studies, no. 15. Umeå, Sweden: Umeå University, 1991.

Ólafsson, Stefán. *The Making of the Icelandic Welfare State: A Scandinavian Comparison.* Reykjavík: Social Science Research Institute, University of Iceland, 1989.

———. "Modernization and Social Stratification in Iceland." Dissertation, Oxford University, 1982.

Pétursson, Pétur. *Church and Social Change: A Study of the Secularization Process in Iceland 1830–1930.* Lund, Sweden: Plus Ultra, 1983.

Rúdólfsdóttir, Annadís Gréta. "The Construction of Femininity in Iceland." Dissertation, London School of Economics and Political Science, 1997.

Tomasson, R. *Iceland: The First New Society.* Minneapolis: University of Minnesota Press, 1980.

Valgeirsson, Gunnar. "Sport in Iceland: A Case Study of the Voluntary Sport Movement." Dissertation, Bowling Green State University, 1991.

Þórlindsson, Þórólfur. "Social Organization, Role-Taking, Elaborated Language, and Moral Judgment in an Icelandic Setting." Dissertation, University of Iowa, 1977.

IX. SELECTED WEBSITES

Alþingi, Icelandic parliament. www.althingi.is. General information on the parliament, the representatives in parliament in the past and the present, parliamentary debates, and all existing laws in Iceland.

Árni Magnússon Institute for Icelandic Studies. www.arnastofnun.is.

Center for Icelandic Art. www.cia.is. Platform for Icelandic plastic arts and artists.

Central Bank of Iceland. www.sedlabanki.is. Numerous online publications in English of the Icelandic economy.

City of Reykjavík. www.rvk.is. Official website.

Culture in Iceland. www.culture.is. A website maintained by the Icelandic government, with information on Icelandic culture, cultural events, and education.

Financial Supervisory Authority of Iceland. www.fme.is. Information on the rules regulating the Icelandic financial market.

Forn Íslandskort. kort.bok.hi.is. Antique maps of Iceland, preserved in the Icelandic National Library, Reykjavík.

Government Offices of Iceland. www.government.is. The official site of the Icelandic government, providing links to all ministries.

Iceland Naturally. www.icelandnaturally.com. A joint site maintained by a number of Icelandic tourist services and businesses, with a wealth of information for foreign tourists.

Icelandic Film Centre. www.icelandicfilmcentre.is. English website.

Icelandic Foreign Service. www.iceland.org. Official site, with links to all of Iceland's diplomatic missions.

Icelandic Meteorological Office, English version. andvari.vedur.is/English. Provides weather forecasts, weather news, historical meteorological data, earthquake information, and so on.

Icelandic Nature Conservation Association. www.inca.is. English site of the association, which is the main environmentalist organization in Iceland.

Icelandic Statistical Bureau. www.statice.is. The English site of the bureau, providing vast statistical information on Iceland, Icelandic society, demography, the economy, politics, and so on.

Icelandic Tourist Board. www.visiticeland.com.

Jónas Hallgrímsson: Selected Poetry and Prose. www.library.wisc.edu/etext/ Jonas. Translations of Jónas Hallgrímsson's poetry by Prof. D. Ringler, University of Wisconsin.

Ministry for Foreign Affairs. iceland.is. Official gateway to Iceland.

National Archives of Iceland. www.archives.is.

National Catalogue of Icelandic Libraries. www.gegnir.is. Includes all major libraries in Iceland.

National Gallery of Iceland, Reykjavík. www.listasafn.is.

National Land Survey of Iceland. www.lmi.is/english. In English.

National Library of Iceland. www.bok.hi.is.

National Museum of Iceland, Reykjavík. www.natmus.is.

Nordic Exchange. omxnordicexchange.com. Including the Icelandic Stock Exchange.

Responsible Fisheries. www.fisheries.is. Information Centre of the Icelandic Ministry of Fisheries in Reykjavík.

Reykjavík. www.visitreykjavik.is. Official tourist website.

Sagnanet, Icelandic Medieval Literature. sagnanet.is. Images of books and manuscripts published before 1901.

Timarit. www.timarit.is. This site, which is operated by the National Library of Iceland, provides access to most Icelandic periodicals and newspapers until the 1920s (and some until the turn of the 21st century) in facsimile.

Tónlist. www.tonlist.is. A portal offering Icelandic music for sale.

Trade Council of Iceland. www.icetrade.is. The Trade Council is formed to facilitate Icelandic exports, but the site also provides useful information about the Icelandic economy.

Travels in 19th Century Iceland. www.edjackson.ca/19thcenturyiceland. Sources, maps, and images.

University of Iceland. www.hi.is.

Útlendingastofnun (Directorate for Immigration). www.utl.is/english.

About the Author

Guðmundur Hálfdanarson (B.A., University of Iceland and Lund's University, Sweden; Cand.Mag., University of Iceland; M.A. and Ph.D., Cornell University) is professor of history in the Department of History at the University of Iceland. He is an expert on European social history, specializing in theories and practices of nationalism. His doctoral dissertation, "Old Provinces, Modern Nations: Political Responses to State-Integration in Late Nineteenth and Early Twentieth-Century Iceland and Brittany," is a comparative study of two European regions in a period of state formation. His most recent books are *Íslenska þjóðríkið: Uppruni og endimörk* (2001) and *Racial Discrimination and Ethnicity in European History* (2003; editor). He is also one of three coauthors (with Henrik Jensen and Lennart Berntson) of *Europa 1800–2000* (2003), coeditor (with Ann Katherine Isaacs) of *Nations and Nationalities in Historical Perspective* (2001), and coeditor (with Ann Katherine Isaacs and Steven Ellis) of *Citizenship in Historical Perspective* (2006). Since 2005, he has served as cocoordinator of CLIOHRES .net, a large European research network of excellence funded by the Sixth Framework Program of the European Union.

NOV 17 2010

LaVergne, TN USA
20 August 2010
194088LV00006B/112/P